Bar Breaker Vol. I

Introduction
Torts
Community Property
Evidence
Criminal Law & Procedure

by Jeff Adachi, Esq.

Bar Breaker, Vol. I-II
by Jeff Adachi, Esq.

ISBN 1-882278-04-6

Published by: Survival Series Publishing Company
Post Office Box 77313
San Francisco, CA 94107
(415) 979-6785 tel., (415) 586-8870 fax
www.survival-series.com

Author:	Jeff Adachi, Esq.
Legal Editors:	Rudy Hirota, Esq.
	Brian Chu, Esq.
	Kristin Carter, Esq.
	Alisa Kim, Esq.
Technical Editor:	Susan Kalra, Esq.
Cover Design:	Hiroki Asai
Cover Graphics:	Romeo Carambas, RCC Designs
	Oshiro Design and Illustration
Word Processing:	Kathy Asada, Esq.
	Marian Sata
Special Thanks:	Mutsuko Adachi

Permission to reprint questions: California State Bar, Committee of Bar Examiners

Other books by the Survival Series Publishing Co.:
Bar Exam Survival Kit
Bar Cards
Complete Bar Cards
Law School Survival Kit
Legal Limericks
MBE Survival Kit
Bar/Bri California Essay Exam Workbook (not for retail sale)

For more information, visit www.survival-series.com

Bar Breaker

Master Table of Contents

Volume I

Volume II

BAR BREAKER

MASTER EXAM EVALUATORS

BARBREAKER

introduction

I. INTRODUCTION

"A total commitment is paramount to reaching the ultimate in performance."

> ---- Tom Flores
> NFL Coach

Welcome to the *Bar Breaker*. This book is designed to provide you with the strategies and techniques necessary to succeed on the essay section of the California bar examination.

The first part of this book focuses exclusively on giving you a system of problem solving. We begin by defining the challenge which awaits you on the essay section of the examination. You will learn what the bar examiners expect of you, how the bar examination differs from law school examinations, who will be grading your examination and how your exam will be graded. We will introduce you to the *Ten Strategies of Effective Exam Writing* and then will give you a system of problem solving, known as the *Six Steps of Exam Writing*. These essential steps of problem solving should be applied to any essay question that confronts you on the examination.

In the second part of this book we demonstrate the application of the *Six Steps of Exam Writing* to over one hundred past bar exam questions spanning each of the tested subject areas. There are specifically tailored writing approaches for each subject area. For example, the chapter on Community Property features a specific approach on how to solve California Community Property essay questions. Each approach is followed by a self-study section containing ten essay questions per bar subject. In the self-study section, you will take actual bar examinations and receive specific feedback on your writing progress through the application of special writing techniques.

Keep in mind that this book contains much more than a series of bar questions and model answers. This book stands apart from others because it shows you how to solve questions using a consistent system of problem solving.

Most exam writing books contain model answers written by different individuals employing different writing methods. Because a consistent system is not followed, it is difficult to tell whether you are on the right track. In addition, the mere act of reading a model examination only tells you what issues you should have analyzed, not necessarily what is wrong with your examination. Without meaningful feedback, practice examinations are a valueless exercise.

The unique problem solving approach and writing techniques contained in this book let you know where you stand from examination to examination. Each examination exercise is loaded with valuable feedback and provides you with the information you need to know to chart your progress. We give you common pitfalls and errors that students made and give you actual examples of poor exam answers.

Most importantly, these exercises make learning fun. No one ever said that preparing for the bar exam has to be a painful and arduous task. In this way, this book gives you the tools necessary to realize your greatest potential on the Essay Section of the California bar examination.

Perhaps equally important, you will improve the problem solving skills that you will use throughout your legal career. As you use the information and strategies in this book to solve bar exam questions, you will find that your understanding of the law as well as your ability to solve problems will expand dramatically.

So without further ado, let's get down to basics and talk about what the essay section of the California bar examination is really about.

II. DEFINING THE CHALLENGE

"Accept the challenges, so that you may feel the exhilaration of victory."

---- General George S. Patton

Before discussing how to solve bar exam essay questions, you must fully understand the challenge that lies before you. It is critical that you know the rules of the bar exam essay section and how bar exam problems may differ from the type of examinations you have experienced in law school.

A. WHAT THE BAR EXAMINERS EXPECT OF YOU

Let's take a moment and read the instructions which appear on the face of the essay examination booklet:

Your answer should demonstrate your ability to analyze the facts in the question, to tell the difference between material facts and immaterial facts, and to discern the points of law and fact upon which the case turns. Your answer should show that you know and understand the pertinent principles and theories of law, their qualifications and limitations, and their relationships to each other.

Your answer should evidence your ability to apply the law to the given facts and to reason in a logical, lawyer-like manner from the premises you adopt to a sound conclusion. Do not merely show that you remember legal principles. Instead, try to demonstrate your proficiency in using and applying them.

If your answer contains only a statement of your conclusions, you will receive little credit. State fully the reasons that support your conclusions, and discuss all points thoroughly.

Your answer should be complete, but you should not volunteer information or discuss legal doctrines which are not pertinent to the solution of the problem.

Unless a question expressly asks you to use California law, you should answer accordingly to legal theories and principles of general application.

After carefully reading these instructions, you might ask yourself what exactly the Bar Examiners expect of you. Stated simply, the Examiners want to see a well reasoned and organized objective analysis that identifies the issues raised by the fact pattern, states the relevant law and exceptions, and applies the law to the fact pattern in reaching a conclusion.

In a nutshell, you need a system which accomplishes the following:

(1)   Tells the difference between material facts and immaterial facts;

(2)   Discerns the points of law upon which the case turns;

(3) Shows that you know and understand the law;

(4) Evidences your ability to apply the law to the given facts;

(5) Demonstrates your ability to analyze the facts and reason in a lawyer-like manner;

(6) Reaches a sound conclusion.

Perhaps the most important sentence in the instructions is that you should "state fully the reasons that support your conclusions, and discuss all points thoroughly." The Bar Examiners are concerned with your ability to use common sense to solve problems by applying the facts to the law. The true essence of your answer is in the application, and that is what you receive most credit for.

In meeting this challenge, you must have a system which produces consistent results regardless of the subject area. While each bar subject differs in substance, the process of problem solving remains the same. This is where the *Six Steps of Exam Writing* comes in. The *Six Steps of Exam Writing* give you an organized "system" by which to solve problems.

B. HOW THE BAR EXAM DIFFERS FROM LAW SCHOOL EXAMINATIONS

"Creative minds have always been known to survive any kind of bad training."
---- Anna Freud (1896-1982)

Of course you have successfully taken essay examinations before. Does the bar examination differ from law school examinations?

The answer is that bar examination questions do differ substantially from those in the typical law school exam, and you must therefore become accustomed to taming a very different kind of animal.

It bears noting that "different" does not necessarily mean "more difficult." In fact, you will find that bar examination questions are in many instances easier than that you learned how bar exam questions are different, and to a certain extent, why they are different.

First, the scope of law you must know is usually greater on the bar exam than the typical law school exam. In law school, your instructor is largely concerned with your ability to analyze a legal problem using the law you have learned in class. On the bar exam, you are responsible for all the law in a given area, and therefore the scope of legal knowledge is generally broader. For example, in Contracts your professor may have skipped over third party beneficiaries or remedies but on the bar exam, you will be held responsible for those areas irrespective of whether you learned them in law school or not. A good outline like those contained in the *Law Charts* of the book, *Bar Exam Survival Kit* provides you with all the areas within a particular topic you need to know to pass the bar exam.

The Bar Examiners will not reveal which subject areas are tested prior to the examination. In law school, you know what subject you will be tested on. On the bar exam however, the problems are not so designated. You will be expected to: first, determine the area of law being tested, and second, apply the pertinent law. Thus, in solving an exam problem, the first question you must answer is: "What area of law is being tested? Contracts? Professional Responsibility?" And so on.

In addition, cross-over type questions have become increasingly more popular with the Bar Examiners. A cross-over question is one which involves multiple bar subjects. For example, one problem might simultaneously test contracts, real property and remedies. The facts and interrogatories will usually contain hints as to what subject areas are at issue. In this book, you will learn how to tackle cross-over questions and how to identify a multistate essay problem.

Law school professors tend to give students only general interrogatories at the conclusion of the fact pattern. The "interrogatory" at the end of the fact pattern directs the student to the issue or issues upon which to focus. For example, a law school torts exam may have had the following interrogatory, "Please discuss the liability of all parties and all causes of actions and defenses which can be raised by each." Basically, your professor is telling you to talk about everything raised by the fact patter involving the law of torts.

By contrast, on the bar exam, you are given specific interrogatories and are told

By contrast, on the bar exam, you are given specific interrogatories and are told what issues the Bar Examiners want you to address. The reason for this is two-fold. For one, the Bar Examiners want to test your specific knowledge of the law. The second reason is a practical one. Can you imagine how difficult it would be to grade thousands of examinations if the examinee received no instructions as to the order in which the parties and claims should be analyzed? The use of specific interrogatories avoids a nightmare for the exam grader by requiring the examinee to follow the order in which the interrogatories are presented.

Specific interrogatories provide the examinee with a substantial advantage. Rather than being presented with a vague interrogatory, it is much easier to identify the issue when you are told, "Does a federal court sitting in State Y have personal jurisdiction over the defendant?" While you must determine what sub-issues are presented, you are at least given the general issue.

The next difference between bar examinations and law school exams is that bar examinations do not require long discussions of public policy, legislative history and other dissertations of the law which law school professors expect. While you should fully discuss each issue, lengthy policy discussions are generally unnecessary.

Although there are many differences between law school exams and the bar exam, some similarities exist. In most law school examinations, the conclusion reached is irrelevant. The same is true of the bar exam essay problem; the grader wants to see how you got to that conclusion, and will grade you based on your reasoning process. As the instructions state, "If your answer contains only a statement of your conclusions, you will receive little credit . . . " Heed that warning and remember that a conclusion, standing alone, is given little weight.

C. MEET THE BAR EXAM GRADER

> *"Know thy enemy and know yourself; in a hundred battles you will never be in peril. When you are ignorant of the enemy but know yourself, your chances of winning or losing are equal. If ignorant both of your enemy and of yourself, you are certain in every battle to be in peril."*
>
> ---- Sun Tzu, *The Art of War* (500 B.C.)

A major difference between law school exams and the bar exam is <u>who</u> will be grading your exam. Unlike a law school professor, a paid academician who may vigorously enjoy the chore of grading exam papers, the bar exam grader may not be so inclined.

Most bar graders are full-time attorneys who have agreed to grade bar exams for the State Bar. For this difficult task they are paid a set amount of compensation for each examination graded, and must grade the examinations by a deadline.

The bar grader will receive large batches of exams, sometimes numbering over a thousand. Each grader grades the same examination; in other words, a different grader will grade each one of your essay answers.

Like most lawyers, the bar grader is probably working fifty to sixty hours each week in his or her regular employment. If the bar grader is married and has a family, his or her time will be even more restricted. Add to this the burden of reading and grading hundreds of exams, and you begin to understand the circumstances under which your exam will be graded.

The challenge before you is to make the bar grader's job as easy as possible. Is an illegible essay answer likely to infuriate or at least frustrate the grader? Will the grader be offended by poor organization and complete chaos in analysis? Conversely, will the grader respond positively to a well-organized, easy-to-read answer? Do bees buzz?

Once you understand the dynamics behind the grading process, you begin to see why it is important that your answer be well organized. Instead of invoking the wrath of the bar grader, your goal is to engender the grader's sympathies, and to present the grader with every reason to give you a passing grade. You want the grader to hear violins in the background as you intertwine the facts and the law into a beautiful and awe-inspiring answer to end all answers.

In all probability, the grader will spend between ten to fifteen minutes reading your answer. Even fifteen minutes is not a lot of time to spend reading something that took you an hour to conjure up. Take one of your examinations and read it for fifteen minutes and see how much mileage you can rack up. If you are like most people, you will read the first few pages more carefully. Further, what you read first will influence your opinion of the entire answer.

The moral of this story is that the first few pages of your examination answer are critical. It's like meeting someone for the first time and making a bad impression: it is extremely difficult to overcome that initial judgment, and so the best remedy is to make a good impression from the very beginning.

Just as we focus on the conclusion of a story or a movie, or the punch line of a joke, the bar grader will also take the time to see how your exam story ends, and to see whether you finished the examination. Therefore, it is also important that you end your answer on a strong note.

This is not to say that you should not write a strong analysis throughout; just remember that the first two pages and the last page of your analysis are critical to your exam success, and are likely to be the pages upon which the grader focuses the most.

The overall point here is to remember **for whom** you are writing.

Remember that your examination will be one of thousands. After grading thousands of bar exams, and interviewing bar graders, I can attest to the mundane nature of the grading process. Make no mistake, grading an essay examination is a subjective process and is affected by factors such as when your examination is graded, the quality of the exam read before and after your examination and other factors beyond your control. Instead of worrying about things out of your control, do everything you can to insure that your exam answer will be easy on the bar grader's mind and eyes.

D.   HOW YOUR EXAMINATION WILL BE GRADED

"You have to . . . learn the rules of the game. And then you have to play it better than anyone else."

---- Dianne Feinstein (1933 -   )

Before taking any test, it is important to know how your response will be evaluated by the grader.

What does the bar grader expect to see when grading your examination? What

8

can you do to impress the grader by meeting those expectations so that you receive a passing grade? This section addresses these questions, and the remaining sections explain how to accomplish these tasks, using the *Ten Strategies of Successful Bar Exam Writing* and the *Six Steps of Exam Taking.*

You will receive a numerical score from 0-100 for each of the six essay questions on the California Bar Examination. Thus, the total possible numerical score on the essay portion of the bar exam is 600. On the performance examination, the total possible score is 400, or 200 points for each performance exam. On the multi-state, the total raw score is 200, or one point for each question answered correctly. In turn, each of the respective scores for the essay, performance and multi-state sections of the bar examination are scaled according to difficulty. In other words, the raw scores are converted to a 0-2000 point system according to how difficult a particular problem is, and from that number, it is determined whether a particular applicant "passed" the examination.

Applicants receiving a total scaled score of 1,460 or greater pass the examination, while those who score 1,390 or below fail. Of the applicants who score between 1,390 and 1,460, their essay and performance examinations will be re-read and re-scored by different graders. These scores are then averaged with the original scores, and applicants who have new scores of 1,440 or above pass the examinations. Applicants who score below 1,412 fail the examination. Of those remaining applicants who have scores between 1,412 and 1,440, their entire examination is reviewed and re-read by a member of the Board of Reappraisers who determines whether the applicant has demonstrated adequate skills to qualify as a lawyer.

The essay examination accounts for 39% of your total score, the performance examination is 26% and the multi-state exam is 35%. As you can see, the essay questions are the most heavily weighed of the three sections of the bar examination.

While it is impossible to say what exact score will result in a passing grade on any individual essay problem given the scaled system noted above, generally a 75 score is "clearly passing" while a 65 score is "clearly not passing." A 70 score, as you might guess, sits on the pass-fail fence, and may or may not be considered passing depending on how that particular question is scaled.

The bar graders award numerical scores in gradations of five. That is, the bar graders must grade in five-point jumps. This grading method eliminates the close-but-no-cigar grade because the grader cannot avoid awarding a no-pass score by giving a compromise score. Thus, the grader is forced to give you a score that falls on one side of the fence or the other.

The objective of this book is to show you how to write a clearly passing answer to avoid being caught in the "Twilight Zone" of a 70 answer. You do not want your fate to be decided by an exam grader's whim or fancy.

Now, let us consider what the bar grader expects to see in your paper. To do this, assume that you are a bar grader who has already successfully passed the bar examination the year before and are getting ready to exact a certain amount of satisfaction by judging bar exams. Also, assume those things which we already learned about the bar grader:

(1)   The bar grader is a human being, subject to the same human frailties which affect us all;

(2)   The bar grader has only a few minutes to grade your examination;

(3)   The bar grader has probably worked a full eight-to-twelve-hour day before sitting down to read your examination;

(4)   Your examination is one of the thousand or so examinations the grader must grade;

(5)   The bar grader wants to be fair.

What thoughts (other than, when will this be over?!?) go through your mind as you are reading the exam before you? Interestingly enough the things all bar graders expect to see are universally the same.

Here are the questions that will go through your mind as you grade the examination:

(1)   Does this person (the applicant) really know what's going on here?

(2)   **Does the applicant understand the relevant principles of law?**

(3)   **Did the applicant identify the pertinent issues?**

(4)   **Did the applicant exhibit sound legal reasoning and analysis?**

(5)   **Does the applicant have a good command of the facts?**

(6)   **Does the applicant have common sense and good judgment?**

(7)   **Can the applicant write in a lawyer-like fashion?**

(8)   **Is the applicant a good problem solver?**

(9)   **Can the applicant distinguish between trivial and important facts and issues?**

(10)   **Does the applicant deserve to pass?**

Let's take a moment to study each of the bar grader's criteria:

(1)   **Does this person (the applicant) really know what's going on here?**

The bar grader wants to know whether you really have a handle on problem solving, and whether you are able to execute the tasks necessary to solve the essay problem. The essay exam tests your ability to quickly respond to a new factual situation by testing your legal reasoning skills. The essay examination gives you the perfect opportunity to showcase these abilities, or to demonstrate your lack thereof.

(2)   **Does the applicant understand the relevant principles of law?**

In order to pass the essay section of the bar exam, you must know and understand the law and demonstrate that knowledge by stating the applicable rules. Thus, you must know the law like the back of your hand.

The bar grader wants to see that you know and understand the relevant principles of law. Never assume the bar grader knows the law. Write as if the bar grader is a layperson entirely unfamiliar with the law. You should fully state each and every legal principle applied in your analysis.

On the other hand, mere regurgitation of the applicable rules alone will not result in a passing score. The bar grader will grade you primarily on your ability to apply the legal principles to the fact pattern and in this way reach a sound conclusion. The statement of just legal principles, is insufficient.

(3) Did the applicant identify the pertinent issues?

The bar grader wants to see whether you are able to read a fact pattern and determine what issues are presented. In other words, the bar grader will keep a running tab of what issues you identified and what issues you failed to identify.

Therefore it is imperative that you identify each and every issue on the bar grader's list. Missing even one major issue or a group of minor issues may result in a failing score. In order to insure that you identify all issues, you must utilize a comprehensive systematic approach to problem solving.

(4) Did the applicant exhibit sound legal reasoning and analysis?

The bar grader wants to see how you think and whether you really understand the legal principles at issue. The true test of understanding is in the application of a legal principle to an actual problem. A superficial analysis is indicative of a sloppy problem solver who really does not understand the problem or the law which applies. You must impress the bar grader with comprehensive analysis of the legal issues involved. You should include a discussion of both sides of the argument where appropriate and an explanation of why a particular position is either sound or unsound. The ultimate conclusion reached is generally irrelevant, for it is your reasoning, not the conclusion, with which the grader is concerned.

(5) Does the applicant have a good command of the facts?

The bar grader will pay great attention to whether you recognize the relevant facts and your use of those facts to solve the problem. Put a different way, the bar grader wants to know whether you are the type of person who takes the time to understand the problem before trying to solve it.

(6) Does the applicant have common sense and good judgment?

In evaluating your application of the facts to the law, the bar grader will judge your ability to use common sense to solve problems. A lawyer's most valued resource is good judgment and common sense. After all, a client's fate may very well rest on these two essential commodities.

(7) Can the applicant write in a lawyer-like fashion?

The bar grader wants to see if you are able to write like a lawyer. This does not mean that you must write like Justice Cardozo, but this does mean that you must write professionally, using proper grammar and diction. Most bar graders will unconsciously penalize you for poor writing ability, and this fact alone can result in a failing score.

(8) Is the applicant a good problem solver?

The bar grader is interested in whether you are an effective problem solver. In this regard, a confused or disorganized analysis indicates poor problem solving skills, as does lack of confidence and other factors which bear negatively on problem solving. Your exam answer should clearly communicate to the bar grader that you are a systematic and careful problem solver. Your exam should demonstrate to the grader that you can handle the responsibilities of a member of the bar.

(9) Can the applicant distinguish between trivial and important facts and issues?

A lawyer's ability to judge between the important and unimportant is essential. On the bar exam, all issues are not created equally. In any given essay problem, you will find major and minor issues as well as non-issues embedded in the fact pattern. The bar grader will determine not only whether you identified the relevant issues, but also whether you were able to distinguish between major and minor ones. Applicants who over-analyze minor issues while failing to adequately discuss major issues will be penalized by the bar grader.

(10) Does the applicant deserve to pass?

This may seem like a totally subjective question, but it is probably the most prevalent thought in the grader's mind as he or she grades your exam. The grader is, after all, an attorney, and feels the responsibility of insuring that an incompetent attorney not be unleashed upon the public. By handing you a passing score, the grader is saying, "Yes, I think this person should be licensed to practice law." In order to secure the grader's vote of confidence, you must impress upon the grader that you are deserving of a license to practice law --- that you take the responsibility of being a lawyer seriously and will use your best talents and abilities to solve the legal problems of your clients.

The grader will also be cognizant of any moral issues that are raised by the fact pattern. In recent years, more attention has been focused on an attorney's moral and professional responsibility to the bar and to the public. In this regard, the essay portion of the bar exam has included the subject area of professional responsibility. The graders have also been instructed to consider moral fitness in grading the essay examination. It follows that an unethical solution to a legal problem should be avoided, or at least pointed out to be unethical. The grader will therefore be concerned with your ability to "do the right thing" when the facts present an ethical dilemma.

A final note on how to use the above information. After taking each examination in this book, assume the persona of the bar grader by reviewing the bar grader's five characteristics listed above. Read through your own examination and ask yourself each of the ten questions above. Better yet, switch exam papers with a fellow applicant and grade each other's examination.

This exercise will assist you in becoming more aware of what the bar grader will be looking for in your exam answer. If you can answer each of these ten questions floating around in the bar grader's conscious (or sub-conscious) with a resounding "YES!!!!" you will be well on your way to writing a winning exam answer.

E.   CHAPTER SUMMARY

The following summarizes what we have learned in this section.

- THE BAR EXAM IS DIFFERENT FROM LAW SCHOOL EXAMINATIONS IN THE FOLLOWING WAYS:

(1)   The Bar Examiners test you on specified areas of law which may or may not mirror what you learned in law school.

(2)   You will not be told beforehand which subjects will appear on the essay portion of the bar exam.

(3)   You may be simultaneously tested in more than one subject area in a single bar exam essay question, i.e., the "cross-over" question.

(4)   On the bar exam you will be given specific interrogatories, telling you what general issues the Bar Examiners want you to analyze, and the order in which to analyze the issues.

- WHEN WRITING FOR THE BAR EXAM, REMEMBER <u>WHO</u> YOU ARE WRITING FOR:

(1)   Make the bar grader's job as easy as possible.

(2)   Give the grader every reason to award you a passing score.

(3)   The bar grader will tend to pay more attention to the first few pages and conclusion of your answer.

(4)   Never forget <u>who</u> you are writing for.

- AVOID THE TWILIGHT ZONE OF A 65-70 EXAMINATION

- WHEN WRITING THE ANSWER PUT YOURSELF IN THE GRADER'S SHOES

III. THE TEN STRATEGIES OF SUCCESSFUL BAR EXAM WRITING

In this book, you will learn numerous exam writing techniques and strategies. *The Ten Strategies of Successful Bar Exam Writing* make it easier for the grader to read and score your exam answer. Think of these strategies as you would "proper exam manners or etiquette," like not putting your elbows on the table while eating.

A. USE HEADINGS

Headings are simply short words and phrases which tell the grader what issue is being analyzed. It is like properly introducing oneself before engaging in conversation with a stranger.

For example, you should always state the parties involved in the cause of action you are analyzing, e.g., <u>People v. Evita</u> or <u>Elvis v. Madonna</u>. Stating the parties will help you organize your answer and will let the grader know which parties' claims you are addressing.

Headings may also be used to identify the cause of action or defense you are analyzing. For example, in analyzing an intentional torts problem, your headings might read "Battery" or "False Imprisonment." In discussing the defenses to those torts, your headings might read "Consent" or "Defense of Others." Again, these headings serve the same purpose of notifying the grader of what issue you are addressing. In analyzing a negligence problem, your headings might read, "Duty," "Standard of Care," "Breach," "Causation," and "Damages." These headings immediately notify the grader that you are discussing these particular torts and have correctly identified the relevant issues. Moreover, they serve to keep you focused on the issue at hand.

Here is an example demonstrating the use of headings in a torts problem involving issues of battery, assault and negligence:

I. <u>Phantom v. Oprah</u>

    A. <u>Intentional Torts</u>
       1. Battery
          Defenses to Battery
       2. Assault
          Defenses to Assault

    B. <u>Negligence</u>
       1. Duty

2. Standard of Care
3. Breach of Standard of Care
4. Causation
   a. Actual or legal cause
   b. Proximate cause
5. Damages
6. Defenses to Negligence
   a. Contributory/comparative negligence
   b. Last Clear Chance Doctrine
   c. Assumption of the Risk

Here is a second example, involving a contracts legal formation issue:

<u>Mork v. Mindy</u>

<u>Letter of January 5th</u>

  <u>Invitation for an Offer</u>
  <u>Offer</u>
  <u>Termination of the Offer</u>
  <u>Acceptance</u>
  <u>Consideration</u>

  Headings may also be used to denote particular discussions of issues and rules. For example, if you are discussing the doctrine of res ipsa loquitur in a negligence action, your answer might include a heading to the same effect. If discussing the doctrine of collateral estoppel in a civil procedure problem, you might use a heading naming that principle.

  Headings will also assist you in compartmentalizing or separating your discussion of each issue. If you have problems keeping your discussion of individual issues from overlapping, headings will force you to separate your discussion of each issue from another. For example, in discussing the elements of an offer, you might include three headings, e.g., (1) intent to contract; (2) terms of the offer; (3) communicated to the offeree, to avoid confusing your discussion of each issue.

  Of course, like anything else in life, headings may be abused. It is quite unnecessary and perhaps even annoying to have a heading for each and every thought that crosses your mind. Used effectively and sparingly, headings can improve your exam score considerably.

B.   WRITE LEGIBLY

Imagine a huge stack of exams, blue book upon blue book. Now imagine having to read each of those examinations. Now add to this scenario the fact that a few hundred of those examinations are completely unreadable! Sound like a nightmare? You bet.

Nothing offends a bar grader's good graces and patience more than horrendous handwriting. If you have ever had the experience of attempting to read someone else's chicken scratch, you will concur with the age-old caveat: THOU SHALT WRITE LEGIBLY. If penmanship is not one of your areas of expertise, then you should consider typing your exam.

One question which almost always arises is: "Should I skip lines in the exam booklet?" If writing on every other line makes your exam answer more presentable or readable, then by all means skip lines. The bar grader will not penalize you for writing on every other line.

C.   USE PROPER GRAMMAR

You are expected to use correct grammar and syntax in writing bar exam answers. There is absolutely no room for sentence fragments, parallel structure problems, misspellings, slang or colloquialisms and other grammatical errors. You are expected to communicate your reasoning in a clear, concise and grammatically correct fashion, and will be penalized for failing to do so.

If grammar is not one of your strong suits, then seek outside tutoring or buy a book on basic grammar and essay writing, because poor grammar could mean the difference between passing and not passing the bar exam.

D. USE SIMPLE LANGUAGE AND SIMPLE VOCABULARY

"The language of truth is unadorned and always simple."

---- Marcellinus Ammianus (4th Cent. A.D.)

The Bar Examiners are not conducting a spelling bee or a vocabulary test. Clarity of expression is everything. Use simple sentences to illustrate whatever point you are making.

Further, do not write paragraphs that run on forever. Generally, each paragraph should not contain more than four to seven sentences. If you are writing more than seven sentences per paragraph, chances are that you are either repeating yourself or not compartmentalizing each component of your analysis. Economy of words is always the rule.

One note about citations. Case citations are not required. I'll say it one more time. You need not cite cases in your answer. However, if you employ citations make sure that the cited cases support your argument. Mistakes in citation will be penalized. Occasionally, a fact pattern on an essay examination raises certain issues which naturally focuses discussion on one or two leading cases. This is particularly true of constitutional law and community property. For example, in order to value the community interest in a spouse's business, you will have to know the Van Camp and Pereira formulas. Similarly, with Constitutional Law, you may wish to be familiar with major decisions, such as Roe v. Wade. Of course, you may discuss the principles involved in those cases without actually referring to the case names, because as a general rule you need not cite case names on the bar examination.

By taking the practice exams in this book and studying the model answers, you will learn those cases which you need to know to pass the bar exam.

If you are unable to remember the name of a case, do not panic. If you remember the principle for which the case stands, merely say, "In a recent case, the U.S. Supreme Court held . . . ." Whatever you do, play it conservatively. If you are not sure of what a case stands for, or whether a given case applies, do not cite it. For an attorney, misciting a case is almost as bad as making up a case citation to support your argument.

E. WRITE PROFESSIONALLY

Do not try to write like a comedian or an Oscar-winning scriptwriter. While the bar grader may possess a sense of humor, your exam answer must not. A bar exam answer is not a place for pretentious contentions (e.g., "The plaintiff is a lying scuzz-bucket!"), jovial remarks (e.g., "Assuming that D does not stand for Dummy, . . ."), or arrogant proclamations (e.g., "Obviously the law is in error and anyone who cannot see the same has the mind of a gnat!"). The exam answer should not be a piece of creative writing. Bar examination writing requires a largely objective and logical, point by point, well-organized analysis of a legal problem.

Avoid personalizing your views by refraining from the use of the first person. Always write in the third person and state your arguments using the named party who makes such an argument, i.e., "Plaintiff argues . . ." or "Defendant maintains . . ." Thus, "I think that the plaintiff has proven a case for intentional infliction of emotional distress," becomes "Plaintiff has proven a case for intentional infliction of emotional distress."

Never use contractions or abbreviations in your exam answer. As I have previously emphasized, legal writing is formal writing and should be devoid of slang words, cliches, and other informal language.

Always remember that the instructions in the essay section clearly direct you to write in a "lawyer-like manner." If you think you have problems writing in a lawyer-like fashion, adopt the writing style contained in this book.

F. KNOW WHAT YOU ARE GOING TO WRITE BEFORE WRITING IT

Good exam writing rarely results from writing what comes to mind. It is imperative that you know what you are trying to say before writing it so that you do not miss important issues.

Before writing out your examination answer, outline. Outlines should include: the discussion of numerous issues, the facts of the case, the issues presented, the rules of law, your application and conclusions. Do not become carried away with creating the perfect outline to an exam answer. The bar graders will not give any credit for writing an outline.

In this book, you will learn how to outline your exam answer and more importantly, how to use your outline to write a winning exam answer. Initially, outlining might seem to be a waste of time, but as you learn how to effectively use it your outline will actually save you time.

G. ARGUE BOTH SIDES OF AN ISSUE WHERE APPROPRIATE

Just as there are two sides to every story, there are usually two or more arguments that can be made in analyzing a legal issue. When do you argue both sides of an issue? The answer is: whenever appropriate. Some issues require you to argue both sides. You must determine whether an issue warrants arguments on both sides.

In answering a bar exam question, you should discuss all arguments which can reasonably be made. This means discussing both sides when the facts so require. In discussing both sides, reach a conclusion one way or the other. Do not be wishy-washy unless the issue is truly one that is incapable of resolution. Also, each argument should be explored and articulated. Generally, the more effective argument should be framed first, followed by the less effective argument.

If the fact pattern practically hands you an issue or element on a silver platter, then an extensive discussion of that issue is not required. A comprehensive analysis of a minor issue is a waste of time and energy. Thus, it is important for you to resist the temptation to say all you know about a particular subject when such a discussion is not required. On the other hand, do not ignore minor issues, because even minor issues still need to be addressed.

Beware of creating non-issues. A non-issue is an issue which is not raised by the fact pattern and need not be discussed in relation to solving the problem.

The key to arguing both sides is putting yourself in the shoes of the party making the argument. As a lawyer, you will be required to understand your opponent's arguments and contentions, whether it be the point of view of the plaintiff, defendant, prosecution, defense, appellant or appellee, judge or juror. A good lawyer considers and studies all possible perspectives that may have some bearing upon the issue. A good problem solver is one who has the ability to understand and anticipate the concerns of all interested parties.

The Bar Examiners want to know whether you are able to distinguish among major, minor and trivial issues presented by the facts. An important component of problem solving is being able to tell what's important and what's not. The ability to distinguish between major and minor issues is important from the perspective of time. Because your examination time is limited to one hour you must determine how much time to allocate to each issue. If there are three issues and fifteen minutes you must apportion your time by determining how much discussion each issue warrants.

In this book, you will learn how to distinguish between major and minor issues by taking examinations and making judgment calls as to how much discussion a particular issue requires. As you write out your answers to the problems in this book, carefully compare the amount of time, energy and exam booklet space spent analyzing a particular issue with that of the model answer. In this way, you will know whether you are weighing the importance of the issues correctly.

H.   USE COMMON SENSE

In solving bar exam problems, use common sense. All too often, in the flurry of rules, law and logic, common sense is left standing outside the door. You may begin to feel like a robot, processing a fact pattern. Remember that the Bar Examiners are testing your ability to use common sense to solve problems, similar to the types of problems and cases you will later face in your career. Application is not a mere recitation of the relevant facts in response to an issue; the essential link is how you think the law should be applied given a particular situation. Once again, the Bar Examiners are interested in testing you on how you think, not your ability to regurgitate the law and facts.

I.   MANAGE YOUR TIME

On the bar exam you must learn how to solve problems quickly and efficiently because the Bar Examiners expect you to finish the examination. Unlike law school examinations, some of which are incapable of being completed in the allotted time, the Bar Examiners carefully evaluate the proposed problem to insure that it can be completed in an hour's time. An incomplete answer means an incomplete grade, and failing to complete the examination will result in a loss of points. Thus, reaching the finish line is extremely important. By using the *Six Steps of Exam Taking*, you should be able to complete any essay examination within the time constraints given.

The only cure for lack of speed is practice. Be absolutely aware of the time constraints imposed on you. You are well advised to time yourself during each practice examination to monitor your speed in completing the problems.

However, in beginning your preparation for the bar examination, do not focus exclusively on time concerns. You must first learn how to solve bar exam questions before worrying about time. Speed will come with practice. Initially, take whatever time is necessary to thoroughly analyze and solve a problem. As you take more and more practice examinations, concern yourself with the element of time.

As you begin taking practice examinations, you will find it necessary to allocate your available time to each of the six exam taking steps which follow. In the one hour you have to solve an essay problem, you might apportion 10-15 minutes to read and visualize the problem, 10 minutes to decide what issues are presented and to outline an answer, and the remaining 35-40 minutes to write out your answer.

The classic bar examination horror story is that of the applicant who writes a beautiful, textbook answer to the first essay question. The answer is worthy of entrance to the Hornbook Hall of Fame and publication in the nation's top law review, but because of the time constraints, the applicant never even reaches the second or third essay examination and sadly fails. You do not want to star in this story.

J.   DO NOT PANIC

> *"No passion so effectually robs the mind of all its powers of acting and reasoning as fear."*
> ---- Edmund Burke (1729-1797)

From time to time, in writing examinations, you may experience writer's block or, even worse, your mind may go blank. This is not unusual, and happens to the best legal minds. The lesson to learn is not to panic.

When experiencing writer's block, close your eyes for a moment and take a deep breath. Clear your mind and then set upon the problem before you.

K.   CONCLUSION

This potpourri of exam writing tips may seem overwhelming. Rather than attempting to master these skills overnight, take each strategy one at a time, and master it before moving on to the next. For example, if the first tip on your list is "neatness," then spend a week or two writing meticulous exam answers and improving your handwriting. After your handwriting is satisfactory, then tackle the use of headings. As your skills as a problem solver increase, you will be surprised at the speed with which you are able to incorporate these concepts into your exam writing repertoire.

L.   CHAPTER SUMMARY

Follow these ten strategies of exam writing in every essay examination you take:

(1)   USE HEADINGS: State the parties and use headings to focus the grader on the issues you have analyzed. Headings will also help you compartmentalize your discussion of each issue.

(2)   WRITE LEGIBLY: Write neatly and legibly or learn how to type. Skip lines if it makes your exam answer more presentable.

(3)   USE PROPER GRAMMAR: Grammatical errors will cost you dearly.

(4)   USE SIMPLE LANGUAGE AND SIMPLE VOCABULARY: Economy of words and simplicity are always the rule. Your analysis should be clear, concise and to the point.

(5)   WRITE PROFESSIONALLY: Avoid slang, cliches and other informal language and write in a "lawyer-like" manner.

(6)   KNOW WHAT YOU ARE GOING TO WRITE BEFORE WRITING IT: Outline your answer.

(7)   ARGUE BOTH SIDES OF AN ISSUE WHERE APPROPRIATE: When presented with a major issue, argue both sides. Distinguish

between major and minor issues when writing your exam answer. Do not create issues where none exist.

(8) USE COMMON SENSE: Your exam answer should show sound reasoning, good judgment and an abundance of common sense.

(9) MANAGE YOUR TIME: Avoid being caught in a time warp. Always keep the finish line in mind and complete the examination.

(10) DO NOT FREAK OUT: Keep your cool even during the most trying moments on the bar exam.

Now we're ready for the *Six Steps of Exam Taking*!

IV. THE SIX STEPS OF EXAM TAKING

The task before you on the bar examination is indeed monstrous. First, you must master fifteen subject areas and be ready to solve problems which contain a multitude of issues in any subject area. With each new fact pattern you have one hour to: figure out what areas of law and issues are presented, organize and write an answer which discusses each issue by applying the relevant facts, and reach a conclusion.

You must have a system to accomplish these tasks, a method to the madness. Only by using the *Six Steps of Exam Taking* will you slay the essay exam dragon:

(1) READ THE QUESTION

(2) VISUALIZE THE FACT PATTERN

(3) DETERMINE WHAT QUESTIONS ARE PRESENTED AND OUTLINE THE ANSWER

(4) MAKE A SNAP DECISION ABOUT HOW MUCH TIME YOU WILL SPEND ANALYZING EACH ISSUE

(5) APPLY YOUR PROBLEM SOLVING APPROACH TO THE FACTS

AND WRITE OUT YOUR ANSWER, FOLLOWING THE TEN
STRATEGIES OF SUCCESSFUL EXAM WRITING

(6)   REACH A CONCLUSION, SMILE AND MOVE ON!

The above steps are the most efficient method to solve an essay question on the
bar exam and will also give you a consistent strategy to follow. This system of
problem solving is applicable to any problem that appears on the bar exam, regardless
of subject area. While these steps are quite simple and straightforward, it is often the
obvious which eludes the examinee under exam pressures. It is important that you
master these steps in the weeks to come. Now, let's review each step carefully.

A.   READING THE QUESTION

"You can observe a lot just by watching."

---- Yogi Berra (1925 -   )

1.   How to Read a Bar Exam Question

You must read a bar exam question as if your life and happiness (and of course
your ticket to practice law) depends on it. Misreading a fact pattern can produce fatal
results on the bar exam, since even the smallest error can take the analysis far off
course. Not reading the question carefully enough is one of the major sources of
exam failure. While we all know how to read, careless reading under exam pressures
often results in missed issues, incorrectly stated or analyzed parties and a later
misstatement of facts in the exam answer. In short, learning how to read a bar
question is critical.

Each essay examination question consists of two parts: a fact pattern and
specific interrogatories. The fact pattern consists of a factual situation to which you
apply the law. The interrogatories tell you what issues to focus upon or solve.

There are different theories on how to read a bar exam question. Some
authorities suggest that the student read the interrogatories first to get a grasp of what
is being tested. Others maintain that the examinee should begin at the top and read
straight down to the interrogatories. The point here is to select a method that works

for you and follow it. If you find that reading the interrogatories first helps you, then do so. If you are more comfortable reading the question from top to bottom, then by all means do that. Once you have determined just how you will read a bar question, follow that same procedure on <u>every</u> bar exam question you read.

Whether you read the question backwards or forwards, you must learn how to read a bar question. Read the bar question slowly.

The objective in reading the exam the first time is to simply understand the facts. Do not attempt to analyze the facts. Read the exam once for content. Once you have familiarized yourself with the facts, then read the fact pattern again with an eye towards analyzing what issues are presented. Only when you feel you have a strong understanding of the facts should you attempt to solve the problem.

The reason for reading the exam strictly for content first is that there is a tendency to begin analyzing the problem before understanding it. Think of a person who begins to render advice without listening to or knowing all the facts. Such a person is likely to give faulty advice.

2.   What to Read For in a Bar Exam Question

When **READING** a bar exam question, you must look for certain things. You must constantly make judgment calls about what appears in the fact pattern. Is this fact relevant? Is it a red herring, i.e., an irrelevant factor thrown in to distract you? To what area of law is this fact relevant?

Generally, the Bar Examiners do not include large clusters of irrelevant facts that are sometimes found in law school examinations. The reason is that "red herrings" make the examination more difficult to grade. The Bar Examiners prefer clean, to-the-point essay examinations rather than tricky and deceptive fact patterns that hide the true issues. In fact, the Bar Examiners generally will tell you through the interrogatories what issues they want you to discuss.

However, irrelevant facts occasionally do appear in bar questions. Therefore you must read through and determine which facts are relevant. One of a lawyer's most important skills is being able to distinguish between a fact of major significance and a fact which goes only to a trivial issue.

Even if all the facts of a given problem are relevant, some facts will be pertinent to solving one issue, while other facts will be relevant to solving another issue. Thus, you must determine which facts are applicable to solving which issues.

Once you have the issues firmly implanted in your mind, you should then re-read the hypothetical in order to determine which facts you will use to solve those issues. Because each fact pattern is different, there is no litmus test by which you can determine whether a particular fact is relevant or irrelevant.

3. How Many Times Should You Read a Bar Exam Question?

The simple answer is: As many times as necessary. When taking practice examinations, if you need to read the exam question fifty times in order to understand it, then read it fifty times. Speed will come with time.

Even the most seasoned exam taker will find it necessary to read the fact pattern exam more than once. After years of taking bar questions, I must still read a fact pattern at least three times before attempting to solve it. As suggested above, read the question once purely for content, to familiarize yourself with the parties and the events which unfold. Then read the question at least one more time, while asking yourself which facts are relevant to solving the problem.

4. How Much Time Should You Spend Reading the Question?

How much time you should take to read the question depends on how much time you need to obtain a firm grasp of the facts. On the bar exam, the length of fact patterns will vary from problem to problem. Sometimes bar questions come in the form of lengthy fact patterns filling almost an entire page, while other questions barely fill half a page. Obviously, a longer fact pattern will take longer to read than a shorter fact pattern.

However, as a general rule, because you must complete your essay answer within one hour, you should spend 10-15 minutes reading and visualizing the question. Reserve at least 10 minutes to outline the question before writing, leaving no less than 35 minutes to write the examination answer.

Do not be intimidated by the length of the fact pattern. Just as you cannot judge a book by its cover, you cannot judge a bar question by its length. The Bar Examiners know that it will take anyone a longer time to read a lengthier fact pattern, therefore more time is allotted by the Examiners for this purpose. A lengthier fact pattern may also mean that the issues presented are not very complicated, since you will need more time to read the question.

Regardless of the length, you will have sufficient time to read the fact pattern three to four times. The Bar Examiners take great pains to insure that their examination is a fair one, and "fair" means that it is capable of being completed in an hour's time. What this means is that the Examiners have factored in the time it will take the examinee to read the question.

Once you are comfortable with reading and comprehending a bar exam question, set a particular time limit and stick to it. Time limitations without discipline are meaningless. A key to problem solving is the ability to move on to the next task, especially where time is a concern. By the time you are sitting for the actual bar exam, you should have a mental alarm clock that tells you when to stop reading the question. Thus, even in taking practice examinations, once you have decided how much time you will devote to reading the problem, stop reading and move on.

5.   Summary of Reading Strategy

Devise a system of reading bar questions and follow the same procedure on each and every bar question. One possible strategy might be as follows:

- READ THE FACT PATTERN ONCE PURELY FOR CONTENT
- READ THE INTERROGATORIES
- DETERMINE WHAT GENERAL AREA OF LAW IS BEING TESTED
- READ THE FACT PATTERN AGAIN TO DETERMINE WHAT ISSUES ARE RAISED
- READ THE FACTS AGAIN TO DETERMINE WHAT FACTS ARE RELEVANT TO SOLVING WHICH ISSUES AND TO THROW OUT IRRELEVANT FACTS
- SET STRICT TIME LIMITATIONS AND STICK TO THEM, I.E., COMPLETE THE ABOVE TASKS IN 10 MINUTES

B.   VISUALIZING THE FACT PATTERN

"Vision is the art of seeing things invisible."

---- Jonathan Swift (1667-1745)

1. Fact Visualization and Why It Is Important

Visualizing the fact pattern, often overlooked by most examinees, is one of the most valuable and critical steps in the problem solving process. The old saying goes, "A picture is worth a thousand words." This is because we think based on images, not words. When you think about what you did today, what comes into your mind? Are they words, such as "I went to my bar review course this morning?" or do you have an image of yourself, sitting in your bar review class, scrupulously taking notes?

The bar question represents a real life legal problem, and the Bar Examiners want to see whether you are able to apply common sense and legal principles to solving that problem. In real life, you will not be dealing with one dimensional characters with first names only; you will be dealing with real clients. You will conduct an investigation of the facts, visit the scene of the incident and thoroughly familiarize yourself with all the facts. Similarly, in solving a bar exam problem, you must see the problem occur right in front of you, in your mind's eye. To do this, you must learn how to visualize the fact pattern.

A torts problem will necessarily involve people committing private wrongs upon other people; a community property problem will raise the question of which spouse gets what upon dissolution, divorce or death. In order to solve the problem, you must see each character come to life. Imagine that each character introduced into the fact pattern is an actual living, breathing person, who is doing the things stated in the problem.

The Bar Examiners typically use nondescript names such as "Mrs. Jones" or "Mr. Smith" in writing bar exam questions. When visualizing the fact pattern, it helps immensely to think of real life characters. If you have difficulty visualizing the fact pattern, then borrow a friend or acquaintance's face to help you bring the characters to life. If you cannot think of a friend's face, think of a celebrity or cartoon character. Not only will fact visualization make it easier for you to remember and relate to a fact pattern, but it will make the bar examination process more fun.

Do not use visualization as a poetic license to add facts to the fact pattern. Remember that legal problem solving is <u>not</u> the same as creative writing; a lawyer is strictly limited to the facts before him or her. Do not add facts to make the bar question more interesting or easier to remember.

After you have mastered visualization, you should not spend more than five minutes on this task. As with reading bar questions, speed will come with time. If you are not used to visualizing the facts, initially take your time.

Once you master Steps One and Two, you will find that you are able to do both simultaneously, that is, while reading the facts you will be able to visualize them. However, until you become proficient at visualization, treat it as a separate problem solving task.

2. Summary of Visualization Strategy

After reading the fact pattern, take the time to VISUALIZE the fact pattern: see it happen in your mind's eye.

- ASSIGN A FACE TO EACH CHARACTER
- AS YOU READ EACH SENTENCE, PAUSE A MOMENT AND FORM A MENTAL PICTURE OF WHAT IS STATED IN THE SENTENCE
- SEE IT OCCUR AS EACH FACT IS UNRAVELED BEFORE YOU
- SET A TIME LIMIT IN WHICH TO VISUALIZE THE PROBLEM AND FOLLOW IT

After you have followed the reading strategies in Step One, and have visualized the fact pattern, you will have a strong understanding of the facts underlying the problem and can move on to the next step.

C. DETERMINING WHAT QUESTIONS ARE PRESENTED AND OUTLINING THE ANSWER

As previously mentioned, the Bar Examiners provide you with interrogatories that tell you what issues to analyze and the order in which to address them. However, these interrogatories will only raise the general issues they want you to discuss. Therefore you must still determine what precise issues of law are presented. How do you know what specific issues are presented by a particular fact pattern? How do you ask the right questions?

1. How to Determine What Questions Are Presented by the Exam Problem

A wise person once said: "There are two ways to ask the right question. You can ask the right question, or you can ask every question."

Unless you are Oliver Wendell Holmes reincarnated or a legal whiz, chances are that you will not always ask the right question when solving a problem. What do you do? Apply the problem solving approach presented in this book.

A problem solving approach is a checklist of the questions or issues you must ask when confronted with a particular legal problem. Because the law is constant, you apply the same law to different fact patterns.

For example, in answering an intentional torts problem, what is the first question you ALWAYS ask? Which intentional torts: Battery, Assault, False Imprisonment, Intentional Infliction of Emotional Distress, Trespass to Land, Trespass to Chattels, Conversion. If you conclude that a battery might have occurred, you must determine if all of the elements of a battery exist. First, is there an affirmative act? Did the defendant act voluntarily, or is there evidence of coercion, duress or involuntary action? Second, is the intent requirement met? Did the defendant intend to make contact with the plaintiff, and was the defendant substantially certain contact would occur? Third, is there actual contact between the defendant and plaintiff, or something closely connected to the plaintiff's person? Finally, is the contact which occurred harmful or offensive to the reasonable person?

The concept behind the problem solving approach is simple. Law is a general rule that is applied to specific situations. The law is comprised of a series of tests which must be met in order for the law to apply. In a similar fashion a doctor who is operating on a patient follows a general procedure. The patient might first be anesthetized. Then the doctor checks the patient's readings, and so on. The procedure is the same in every operation. Like a medical procedure, the law is applied step by step, point by point.

An essay writing approach to each subject area on the bar exam is included in this book. The writing approaches in this book were specifically designed to answer each and every question that could possibly confront you on the California bar examination. Thus, in order to identify the issues presented by the problem, you need only apply the writing approaches suggested in this book.

Note that each writing approach begins with a discussion of the "big picture." You must have a grasp of the big picture because in determining what specific issues are raised by a bar question, you always begin with the general issues. For example, in a torts problem, the big picture is:

(1)   WHAT CAUSES OF ACTION EXIST AND ARE THE ELEMENTS OF TORTS MET?

(2)   DO ANY DEFENSES APPLY?

(3)   DO ANY GENERAL CONSIDERATIONS APPLY?

In order to determine what specific issues must be analyzed, you ask these three simple questions whenever confronted with a torts problem. Each and every issue which can possibly be tested in the area of torts will fall within one of these three general areas. These questions will allow you to quickly eliminate non-issues.

Before taking the examinations in this book, study the approaches carefully, and make sure that you understand how to apply them. You may develop your own wiring formula but the approaches in this book will serves as excellent models of problems. You will also find 15 model approaches, called *Law Charts*, in the book, *Bar Exam Survival Kit*.

2. Why you Must Outline Your Answer

We have already discussed why it is important to outline your answer before writing the answer in Part III. Let's quickly recap these reasons:

(1)   Outlining acts as a road map.
(2)   It helps you keep on course.
(3)   It makes writing the examination a simple task because you know where

you are going.

(4)   It organizes your thoughts.

A good outline, like a good map, shows you exactly how to get where you are going. The outline also helps you to keep on course by drawing you back to the correct path if you start discussing non-issues or going off on tangents. If you get lost in your analysis, you can quickly refer to your outline to find your way.

Also, it is much easier to write an examination when you know what to write. We have all had the experience of trying to write something without knowing just what to say. Outlining your answer avoids this painful situation by plotting out exactly what to write and the order in which to write it. Perhaps most importantly, outlining organizes your thoughts on paper <u>before</u> you begin writing. It is much more difficult to attempt to organize your thoughts while writing your answer.

3.   How to Outline Your Answer

In Part III we discussed the need to know what you are writing before you write it. Now ask yourself, "How do I outline and what do I include in the outline?"

Your outline should mirror the writing approach you are following. For example, in a problem involving intentional torts, defenses and general considerations, your writing approach dictates the organization of your outline and the headings used:

(1) WHAT CAUSES OF ACTION EXIST AND ARE THE ELEMENTS OF THE TORT MET?

Intentional Torts
  Battery
  Assault
  False Imprisonment

(2) DO ANY DEFENSES APPLY?

Defenses
  Consent
  Necessity

(3) DO ANY GENERAL CONSIDERATIONS APPLY?

Vicarious Liability
  Respondeat-superior

Begin by asking the "big picture" questions and then run through your checklist of sub-issues to determine which issues are raised by the fact pattern. As you can see in the above example, by applying your problem solving approach and identifying the pertinent issues you have already created a map of your analysis. From this outline, you already know that you will first discuss the intentional tort of battery, followed by a discussion of assault and false imprisonment. You will then turn to the defenses and discuss the privileges of consent and necessity. Finally, you will discuss the doctrine of respondeat-superior. Of course, you may wish to add more detail to this bare-bones outline, such as some of the facts to be analyzed or the exceptions to the rule, but the principle of outlining is illustrated.

Throughout this book you will find numerous examples of outlining. Different ways to outline an answer and the most effective outlining strategies are shown. The key is to find a method of outlining that works for you, and to use that method consistently to achieve a winning bar exam answer.

35

4.   Summary of Outlining Strategies:

- STUDY THE INTERROGATORIES, DETERMINE WHAT AREAS OF LAW ARE BEING TESTED AND GLEAN THE GENERAL ISSUES YOU MUST ANALYZE

- APPLY YOUR PROBLEM SOLVING APPROACH TO DETERMINE WHAT SPECIFIC ISSUES YOU MUST ANALYZE

- APPLY THE OUTLINING STRATEGIES YOU WILL LEARN IN THIS BOOK

D.   MAKE A SNAP DECISION ABOUT HOW MUCH TIME TO SPEND ANALYZING EACH ISSUE

"If you're there before it's over, you're on time."

---- James ("Jimmy") Walker (1881-1946)

I have already emphasized that you have one hour to spend on each essay question. Because each bar question is designed to be solved in an hour, time is always of the essence.

1.   How to Decide How Much Time to Spend on Each Issue

The question addressed in this section is how to most effectively use the remaining time, after you have read, visualized and outlined your answer. The final task is to write out your exam answer. However, before writing out your answer you must quickly decide how to allocate your time among the issues.

If you follow the time limits suggested in this book, you will divide the one hour time period as follows:

READING THE QUESTION: 10 MINUTES
VISUALIZING THE FACT PATTERN: 5 MINUTES
OUTLINING THE ANSWER: 10 MINUTES
WRITING THE ANSWER: 35 MINUTES

36

Assuming that the first three steps of exam taking will consume 25 to 30 minutes, you will be left with 30 to 35 minutes to write out your answer. Since you will know what issues you must analyze and how much time remains, you need only divide the number of issues by the time remaining to obtain an estimate of how much time you should spend discussing a particular issue.

Remember that it is a **snap** decision. Under no circumstances should you spend five or ten minutes of your valuable time to figure out how much time to spend analyzing each issue. To do so would be self-defeating and a tragic waste of time and energy. Here is an illustration of this principle:

(1) WHAT CAUSES OF ACTION EXIST AND ARE THE ELEMENTS MET?
<u>Intentional Torts</u>
    Battery (2.5 minutes)
    Assault (2.5 minutes)
    False Imprisonment (5 minutes)

(2) DO ANY DEFENSES APPLY?
<u>Defenses</u>
    Consent (5 minutes)
    Necessity (5 minutes)

(3) DO ANY GENERAL CONSIDERATIONS APPLY?
<u>Vicarious Liability</u>
    Respondeat-superior (15 minutes)

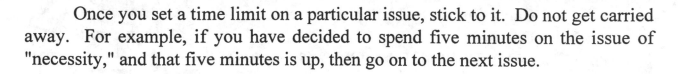

Once you set a time limit on a particular issue, stick to it. Do not get carried away. For example, if you have decided to spend five minutes on the issue of "necessity," and that five minutes is up, then go on to the next issue.

2. How to Use Time As Your Ally

The one hour time limit in which you must complete your answer is a factor that you can use in your favor, if you know how. Remember what was said earlier about how the Bar Examiners draft the bar questions. Because the Examiners strive to be fair, they will always give you an examination that is capable of being solved in one hour's time.

This fact is significant because you can determine whether your analysis is correct by comparing the issues to be analyzed with the available time. In other words you can judge the accuracy of your answer by comparing the available time limits with the issues you must discuss.

For example, using the outline noted above, assume that you misanalyzed the problem and mistakenly included a negligence analysis in your outline:

(1) WHAT CAUSES OF ACTION EXIST AND ARE THE ELEMENTS MET?
     <u>Intentional Torts</u>
          Battery (2.5 minutes)
          Assault (2.5 minutes)
          False Imprisonment (5 minutes)
(2) DO ANY DEFENSES APPLY?
     <u>Defenses</u>
          Consent (5 minutes)
          Necessity (5 minutes)

(1) WHAT CAUSES OF ACTION EXIST AND ARE THE ELEMENTS MET?
     <u>Negligence</u> (15 minutes)
          Duty
          Standard of care
          Breach
          Causation: actual and proximate cause
          Damages
(2) DO ANY DEFENSES APPLY? (5 minutes)
          Contributory/comparative negligence
          Assumption of the Risk

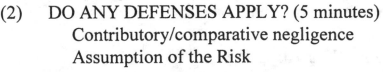

(3) DO ANY GENERAL CONSIDERATIONS APPLY?
     <u>Vicarious Liability</u>
          Respondeat-superior (15 minutes)

From these time estimates, you can see that this problem is incapable of being solved in an hour if you allow 25-30 minutes to read, visualize and outline the answer before writing it. This should tell you that something is wrong with your analysis. Here the element of time tells you that your analysis is off because the Bar Examiners will not give you a problem that will require 55 minutes to write.

This technique is especially helpful on "sucker" questions. "Sucker" questions are ones that draw in the examinee and appear to include major issues deserving of extensive discussion. The "sucker" question, in the form of an interrogatory, usually appears right before a major issue. The examinee then spends an inordinate amount of time addressing what he or she believes to be a major issue, and then runs out of time when he or she really gets to the major issue. Do not be fooled by "sucker" questions --- they are like a wolf in sheep's clothing.

In this book, we have included and identified a number of "sucker" questions to help to distinguish between a real and imagined major issue.

3. What to Do If You Run Out of Time

If you do run out of time in analyzing an issue or bar question, then move on. Remember that you must stick to your time constraints or suffer the consequences of not completing your exam answer.

Exceeding your time limits will result in a snowballing effect, with you under the snowball. For example, if you take an extra ten minutes to solve the first two essay questions, you will have only 40 minutes time to complete the final essay question in the exam session. Your failure to stick to time limitations on the first two questions adversely affects the score you receive on the third essay answer. Remember that each essay is weighed equally. Three scores of 75, 75 and 60 results in an overall average of 70. Doing well on two examinations therefore does not justify running out of time on the third examination.

After reading and visualizing the question, determining what questions are presented, outlining your answer and making a snap decision as to how much time to spend on each issue, you are now ready to write out your answer!

4. Summary of Time Allocation Strategies

- SPEND BETWEEN 10-15 MINUTES READING THE QUESTION
- SPEND 10 MINUTES OUTLINING YOUR ANSWER
- SPEND 30-35 MINUTES WRITING OUT YOUR ANSWER
- DIVIDE YOUR AVAILABLE TIME TO WRITE YOUR ANSWER AMONG THE ISSUES YOU MUST ADDRESS, DEPENDING UPON THE IMPORTANCE OF EACH ISSUE
- USE TIME AS YOUR ALLY: QUICKLY CHECK THE TIME PARAMETERS YOU HAVE SET TO DETERMINE WHETHER YOU MAY HAVE MISANALYZED THE PROBLEM
- IF YOU RUN OUT OF TIME, MOVE ON!

Following these time allocation strategies will allow you to complete the essay section of the bar examination in the time provided by the Examiners. In fact, when you perfect these strategies, you may find you have time to spare!

I suggest that when you first begin taking practice examinations, do not concern yourself with time. Instead focus your efforts on writing a "clearly passing" answer, even if it takes you five hours. It is worthless to write an awful examination in an hour. Speed will come with practice!

E. APPLY THE PROBLEM SOLVING APPROACH TO THE FACTS AND WRITE OUT YOUR ANSWER

Once you have outlined, writing out the answer is easy. As we have already seen, your outline should include the general headings that you will use in your analysis, and a list of the issues. In writing out your answer, just follow the course laid out in your outline.

What information should you include in your answer? How should you organize your discussion of each issue? What is the most efficient way to write an exam answer? These questions and others are addressed in this section.

1. How to Write Your Exam Answer

The Bar Examiners expect to see a well-reasoned analysis of the question.

Always use headings and begin your analysis by stating who the parties are, e.g., <u>Paulie v. Poodle</u>. Follow the numerical designations given by the interrogatory in organizing your analysis. Thus, if the interrogatory is labeled "Part 1," then follow that numerical designation when writing your exam answer.

Limit the number of sentences included in each paragraph to no more than six or seven. Each paragraph should be limited to a discussion of one or two issues. Avoid the "run-on" paragraph at all costs.

You may choose to underline key words and phrases --- just be careful not to overdo it. The bar grader may be annoyed by a constant bombardment of underlined words. Underlining should focus the bar grader on key words and phrases and nothing more.

2. What to Include in Your Exam Answer

Your exam answer should contain a full discussion of the legal principles and an application of the facts to the law. In order to communicate good, sound reasoning, your analysis should include:

(1)   A STATEMENT OF THE ISSUES
(2)   A STATEMENT OF ANY APPLICABLE RULE
(3)   APPLICATION OF THE RELEVANT FACTS TO THE RULE
(4)   A CONCLUSION

In essence, your analysis should contain the basic I-R-A-C structure that stands for ISSUE, RULE, APPLICATION and CONCLUSION. These four elements are critical to any good legal analysis.

By stating the issue, you alert the bar grader to the issue you are analyzing. You must then demonstrate that you know and can recite the applicable rule of law. Next, apply the facts and your common sense to the rule and any exceptions. Finally, reach a conclusion based on the application of the law.

3.   Should You Use I-R-A-C?

Should you use strict I-R-A-C in writing your exam answer?

If you are not a prolific writer, I recommend that you use I-R-A-C. The I-R-A-C writing structure will force you to cover each and every component of a legal analysis and will help you compartmentalize your discussion of each issue. I-R-A-C will prevent you from forgetting to discuss issues that are obvious but necessary to a good exam answer.

I-R-A-C is the starting place for all good legal writing. Begin by using a strict I-R-A-C format. As you become a more proficient writer, evolve to an abbreviated form of I-R-A-C.

In the exam answers that follow, I-R-A-C is followed religiously. You will also be exposed to writing styles that are shorter and more compact versions of I-R-A-C.

Strict I-R-A-C writing is:

The issue is _____. The rule is _____. Applying the facts to the rule, _____. The conclusion is _____.

While this structure is far from exciting, it gets the job done. This basic writing structure should be adopted if you are having problems. When faced with writer's block, you may also find it helpful to use crutches to help you to write . Crutches, like glue, hold the analysis together. Phrases such as "the first issue is," or "the facts indicate" assist the writer in organizing the analysis or to jump start the writing process. Use crutches if they help you to write, but be careful not to abuse them.

4.   What is Application?

Because so many students have problems in applying the facts to the law, I will make a few comments on the term "application."

Application is the process of explaining why the facts in your case demand a certain conclusion. The operative word is "why." Application traces your thought process by explaining to the bar grader WHY the facts either support or do not support a conclusion under a particular rule of law.

Application is often the most difficult concept to grasp because we are not accustomed to explaining ourselves. Suppose a friend asks you to go to the movies. Usually, you will respond in a conclusory fashion, saying either yes or no. Most people do not demand a full, rational and logical explanation for every decision made. However, if you were required to explain your reasoning, you might say something like this:

> "The issue is whether I should go to a movie with you. The rule is that I have gone to a movie with you before, and did not enjoy myself. The reason why I did not enjoy myself is (1) you had already seen the movie and kept spoiling the suspense by telling me what was going to happen; (2) you kept talking throughout the movie; (3) you didn't share your bon-bons. Therefore I will not go to the movies with you."

Of course, unless your name is Spock, you would not ordinarily speak in this fashion. But this is what application means. You must explain your reasoning point by point, and you are to presume nothing. Pretend as if you are speaking to a child, who is demanding, "Tell me why!"

One of the most common criticisms of bar exam answers is that a particular analysis is "conclusory," meaning that the student reaches a conclusion without explaining the legal reasoning supporting the conclusion.

The key word to those who would be conclusory is the word "BECAUSE." As demonstrated in the following example, use of the word "because" forces you to explain yourself:

> *An offeree in Arnold's shoes would not consider Roxanne's words to be an offer BECAUSE Roxanne stated that she might be interested in selling her car to Arnold for the right price. The use of the word "might" indicates indecision and uncertainty. Roxanne would have used command language such as "shall" or "will" if an offer was intended, and a reasonable person hearing those words would believe his assent to it would constitute a binding legal agreement. Roxanne also used the*

word "interested," which connotes exactly that --- that Roxanne was interested but was not committed to selling her car. A reasonable person hearing the vague subject term "right" price would have no manner of determining what price was intended. Hence, no offer was intended and Roxanne's statement was simply an invitation for an offer.

A conclusory answer would be:

An offeree in Arnold's shoes would not consider Roxanne's words to be an offer. Roxanne stated that she "might be interested in selling her car for the right price." Roxanne used language which indicated her uncertainty to make an offer. Thus, there is no offer.

The first answer tells you <u>why</u> a particular result is reached while the second answer fails miserably.

The first answer explains why Roxanne's statement is too uncertain and vague to constitute an "offer." Roxanne's statement is dissected word by word, phrase by phrase; the author explains <u>why</u> each word or phrase either supports or disproves the assertion made. By contrast, the second answer reiterates Roxanne's statement, before reaching the conclusion that the statement is too uncertain, but fails to explain <u>why</u> that is so.

If you are having difficulty with writing a conclusory analysis, then employ the following method:

X's statement did not constitute an offer BECAUSE:

(1)   BECAUSE
(2)   BECAUSE
(3)   BECAUSE

This method of writing will force you to explain your reasoning, thereby avoiding conclusory statements. Your exam will be graded primarily on application, not your ability to regurgitate the facts or the law.

In applying the law to the facts, remember to discuss the various arguments that can be raised by any party. Application also means recognizing and discussing both sides of a legal argument.

Good application begets a good exam score. As you take the examinations in this book, you will be shown examples of both good application and poor application. In this way, you will learn how to avoid a conclusory analysis and improve your ability to apply the facts to the law.

5.   Summary of Writing Strategies

- USE ESSAY FORMAT TO WRITE OUT YOUR ANSWER
- USE HEADINGS AND PARAGRAPHS, AND KEEP YOUR PARAGRAPHS SIMPLE
- INCLUDE THE I-R-A-C ELEMENTS
- FOLLOW I-R-A-C IF YOU ARE NOT A PROLIFIC WRITER
- IF YOU ARE PRONE TO FORGETTING APPLICATION, USE THE WORD "BECAUSE" AND ALWAYS ASK "WHY?"

F.   REACH A CONCLUSION, SMILE AND MOVE ON!

"How many people are killed in accidents because of not wanting to let go of their umbrellas!"
---- Paul Valery (1871-1945)

In answering bar exam questions, you must reach a conclusion. Ironically, it usually does not matter what conclusion you reach. The bar grader is more interested in your application than how you actually reached the conclusion. The answer is rarely important because bar exam fact patterns often do not fit exactly within the confines of a given rule of law. Unlike mathematics, where one plus one always equals two, discussion of a close legal issue is sometimes "gray." It is your ability to distinguish arguments on both sides and raise all appropriate legal arguments that counts -- not the ultimate conclusion.

The last step also means that once the problem is over, you **smile** and **move on**. Do not agonize over a question once you have completed the problem, because to do so will interfere with your ability to complete the bar question before you.

G.   CHAPTER SUMMARY

Now that we have completed our discussion of the Six Steps of Exam Taking, let's recap each step:

(1)   READ THE QUESTION: Read the question carefully and determine which facts are relevant to solving the problem.

(2)   VISUALIZE THE FACT PATTERN: See the fact pattern come to life and commit those facts to memory.

(3)   DETERMINE WHAT QUESTIONS ARE PRESENTED AND OUTLINE THE ANSWER: Determine what particular questions or issues the problem presents and organize and plan your answer by outlining.

(4)   MAKE A SNAP DECISION ABOUT HOW MUCH TIME YOU WILL SPEND ANALYZING EACH ISSUE: Quickly divide the available time by the issues you must discuss.

(5)   APPLY THE PROBLEM-SOLVING APPROACH AND WRITE OUT YOUR ANSWER: Apply the relevant facts to the issues presented and articulate your answer. Use I-R-A-C if necessary.

(6)   REACH A CONCLUSION, SMILE AND MOVE ON! Always conclude one way or another; don't be wishy-washy!

These are the six steps you must follow religiously in solving every bar exam question. Commit these essential steps to memory until each step becomes second nature to you.

V. APPLYING THE WRITING APPROACH

Before beginning the self-study portion of this book, let's apply the *Six Steps of Exam Taking* and the *Ten Strategies of Successful Exam Writing* to an actual bar question.

The bar question that follows is a very simple one. It was selected because of its simplistic nature. View this question as the first building block in your repertoire of bar exam questions.

Bar Question #1: <u>Frank, Dennis & Conco</u>

STEP ONE: READING THE QUESTION

A. THE FIRST READ

Read the question once purely for content.

A storage shed on the suburban yard of Construction Co. (Conco) caught fire on a Sunday morning. Dennis, Conco's draftsman at its downtown office, happened to be bicycling by the yard on a personal errand. He broke into the yard office through a closed window and notified the local volunteer fire department. He next located ignition keys and moved eight pieces of heavy equipment onto an adjacent field. The heavy equipment consisted of trucks and bulldozers, which were threatened with imminent destruction, but were not damaged.

Unknown to Dennis, the adjacent field belonged to a wholesale florist, Frank. Although the field appeared to be vacant and unused, Frank had planted it with valuable tulip bulbs. Bulbs valued at $9,000 were destroyed under the weight of the heavy equipment.

After fire fighters extinguished the fire, Frank asked Dennis to come to his office to discuss the damage. Dennis agreed. As soon as Dennis entered the office, Frank told Dennis, in the presence of four of Frank's employees, that Dennis would have to remain at the office until he summoned the president of Conco and the president had arrived at the office. When the president arrived an hour later, Frank told Dennis he could leave, and Dennis left.

(1) What are Frank's rights against Dennis and against Conco? Discuss.

(2) What are Dennis' rights against Frank? Discuss.

Now you have read the question once purely for content. How did it feel? Do you remember most of what you read? Did you read the question slowly and carefully?

B. THE SECOND READ

Next, let's read the fact pattern again. Take each paragraph word by word, sentence by sentence. Allow your mind to digest each word and sentence.

A storage shed on the suburban yard of Construction Co. (Conco) caught fire on a Sunday morning. Dennis, Conco's draftsman at its downtown office, happened to be bicycling by the yard on a personal errand. He broke into the yard office through a closed window and notified the local volunteer fire department. He next located ignition keys and moved eight pieces of heavy equipment onto an adjacent field. The heavy equipment consisted of trucks and bulldozers, which were threatened with imminent destruction, but were not damaged.

Unknown to Dennis, the adjacent field belonged to a wholesale florist, Frank. Although the field appeared to be vacant and unused, Frank had planted it with valuable tulip bulbs. Bulbs valued at $9,000 were destroyed under the weight of the heavy equipment.

After fire fighters extinguished the fire, Frank asked Dennis to come to his office to discuss the damage. Dennis agreed. As soon as Dennis entered the office, Frank told Dennis, in the presence of four of Frank's employees, that Dennis would have to remain at the office until he summoned the president of Conco and the president had arrived at the office. When the president arrived an hour later, Frank told Dennis he could leave, and Dennis left.

Now what's really happening here?

The first sentence tells you that there is a storage shed in a yard. You are also introduced to a party, called "Construction Company," or "Conco" for short. You are told that Conco's shed caught fire on Sunday morning.

The second sentence introduces the second party, Dennis. You are told that Dennis works for Conco as a draftsman at its downtown office and that Dennis was riding a bicycle when he saw the shed burning. You are also told that Dennis was on a personal errand when he observed this.

In the third sentence, Dennis breaks into the yard office through a closed window and calls the fire department. In the next sentence, Dennis finds the keys to eight pieces of heavy equipment which he moves onto an adjacent field. The final sentence describes the heavy equipment as trucks and bulldozers and further states that the equipment Dennis saved would have been destroyed but for his actions.

Before moving on to the next paragraph, make sure that you have a full understanding of the first paragraph. If need be, read it again, or as many times as necessary to understand what is happening here.

C.   STEP ONE: HOW TO USE THE TECHNIQUE OF "HEADLINING"

First we reduce the entire first paragraph to a single sentence: "Dennis the draftsman, bicycling by on a personal errand, sees Conco's shed on fire and breaks into the office, calls the fire department, and moves and saves heavy equipment from imminent harm." This technique involves the creation of a "headline" summarizing the facts. By simplifying the fact pattern, it becomes easier to remember and recall. From this, we create a brief, catchy headline, **"Dennis the Draftsman saves Conco's heavy equipment from destruction."**

49

Moving on to the next paragraph, the first sentence introduces yet a third party, Frank. Frank owns the field upon which Dennis drove the heavy equipment. You are told that Dennis did not know to whom the land belonged. The field appeared to be vacant, but had been planted with tulip bulbs valued at $9,000.

Again, let's simplify this paragraph. Essentially, Dennis drove heavy equipment onto Frank's land, damaging tulip bulbs worth $9,000. The newspaper headline would read, **"Dennis Damages Frank's Tulip Bulbs to the Tune of $9,000!"**

Before moving on to the next paragraph, let us paraphrase both paragraphs in one headline: **"Dennis the Draftsman bicycling by, seeing Conco's shed on fire, breaks in office, moves heavy equipment, damaging $9,000 worth of tulip bulbs on Frank's land."**

Now, on to the final paragraph. You are told that after the fire was put out, Frank approached Dennis, and asked Dennis to come to his office to discuss the damage to the tulip field. Dennis agreed. As Dennis entered the office, Frank told Dennis, in the presence of four of Frank's employees, that he had to remain until the president of Conco arrived at the office. Next, you are told that Conco's president arrived an hour later at which time Frank told Dennis he could leave; Dennis left.

Once again, we will simplify this paragraph: "Dennis agrees to come to Frank's office but is later told by Frank, in the presence of Frank's employees, that he must remain until Conco's president arrived." The headline would read, "Dennis Remains in Frank's Office for One Hour Awaiting Conco's President!"

Now let's wrap up the entire fact pattern into one huge headline: **"DENNIS THE DRAFTSMAN BICYCLING BY, SEEING CONCO SHED ON FIRE, BREAKS INTO THE OFFICE, MOVES HEAVY EQUIPMENT, DAMAGING $9,000 WORTH OF TULIP BULBS ON FRANK'S LAND, AND REMAINS IN FRANK'S OFFICE FOR ONE HOUR AWAITING CONCO'S PRESIDENT!"**

D. STEP TWO: VISUALIZING THE FACT PATTERN

Now that you have read through the fact pattern two to three times and have thoroughly familiarized yourself with the facts, take a minute to VISUALIZE the problem.

As you are introduced to each character, visualize that character. See Dennis. Think of a relative, friend or acquaintance, or television or movie actor named Dennis and assign that character to him. See Dennis the draftsman, wearing a white shirt, a pocket full of pens and calculators, riding his bike on a bright Sunday morning. See Dennis as he looks over at Conco's suburban yard and sees Conco's shed on fire. See Dennis jump off his bike, run over to the yard office, and break the yard office window. Watch Dennis desperately search for the ignition keys and feel the urgency with which he acts as the fire continues. See Dennis as he starts up and moves the eight trucks and bulldozers to safety.

Next, meet Frank. Frank is not a happy camper. Frank is the owner of the land on which Dennis drove the equipment. See Frank's land and the poor little tulip bulbs, destroyed under the weight of the heavy equipment. See the anguish in Frank's face when he realizes that he just lost $9,000 worth of tulip bulbs.

Watch as the fire fighters put out the fire. Frank says to Dennis, "Come into my office so we can discuss the damage." See Dennis say, "Okay." Watch Dennis as he enters Frank's office, and then see Frank telling Dennis, with four of Frank's employees standing there, "You must remain here until Conco's president shows up."

See Dennis as he sits in Frank's office. The clock ticks away each minute until a full hour passes. Watch Conco's president walk through the door, and then Dennis leave.

Again, I am not suggesting that you spend twenty minutes daydreaming about the fact pattern. But as you can see, by visualizing the problem, you have a better understanding of each of the parties' positions, and the arguments likely to be raised by them.

You will find that visualization is especially important in analyzing complex fact patterns. Visualization will help you to remember the facts, and will assist you in understanding the problem before you try to solve it.

E.   STEP THREE: DETERMINING WHAT QUESTIONS ARE PRESENTED AND OUTLINING YOUR ANSWER

1. Deciding What Subject Area Is Being Tested

After reading through the facts at least twice and visualizing the fact pattern, you must now determine what subject area or areas are being tested. Remember that you will not be told which subject area is being tested or whether you are being tested on a combination of subjects, i.e., the "cross-over" type question discussed earlier.

The best indicator of the subject area being tested is found in the specific interrogatories that follow the fact pattern.

The interrogatories presented in this problem are:

(1)   What are Frank's rights against Dennis and against Conco? Discuss.

(2)   What are Dennis' rights against Frank? Discuss.

Following the order set forth in the interrogatories, the structure of your answer should be as follows:

(1A) Frank v. Dennis

(1B)   Frank v. Conco

(2)   Dennis v. Frank

The interrogatories ask you to analyze Frank's <u>rights</u> against Dennis and against Conco and Dennis' <u>rights</u> against Frank. In other words, you are being asked to evaluate the <u>personal</u> rights of the named parties. The violation of <u>personal</u> rights, of course, gives rise to tort liability. Clearly, the fact pattern evolves around property damage committed by Dennis on Frank's land, and Frank's act of confining Dennis. Personal injury and property damage are a telltale sign that a Torts problem is presented.

If you have doubts about what kind of problem this is, then use a checklist of each of the bar subjects to eliminate irrelevant areas:

REMEDIES? - NO. You are not asked to determine what remedies a party may have against another party.

CONTRACTS? - NO. There is no contract or agreement between any of the parties involved.

CIVIL PROCEDURE? - NO. No procedural questions are raised.

CRIMINAL LAW/CRIMINAL PROCEDURE? - NO. No crimes were committed, and this problem involves personal rights between parties, not a criminal action brought by the state.

REAL PROPERTY? - NO. While damage to real property occurred, no question is presented as to the ownership of any of the property interests involved.

EVIDENCE? - NO. No evidentiary issues are raised.

CONSTITUTIONAL LAW? - NO. No issues are raised under the United States Constitution.

COMMUNITY PROPERTY? - NO. This does not involve a dispute between spouses over property.

CORPORATIONS? - NO. No issues of corporate responsibility, except for Conco's vicarious liability, which falls under "Torts" general considerations.

WILLS AND TRUSTS? - NO. This problem has nothing to do with the disposition of property through a will or trust instrument.

PROFESSIONAL RESPONSIBILITY? - NO. No ethical questions are raised.

It is normally unnecessary to run through this checklist to decide what subject areas are being tested, although it might be required on a particularly tricky crossover question. Most of the time, you will be able to determine the area of law being tested. This example simply illustrates the mental process of elimination that we undergo in determining the subject area.

2. Deciding Which Facts to Use to Solve the Problem

After reading the question and the interrogatories carefully, quickly review the fact pattern to determine which facts are relevant to solving the causes of action. Decide first which causes of action in Tort law exist for each stated party. In essence, a multi-party problem is like solving "mini-problems" within one fact pattern. You must then decide which facts are relevant to solving which problems. For example, under Frank v. Dennis, the relevant facts are those that address any tortious conduct suffered by Frank, and committed by Dennis. Thus, the relevant facts are:

A storage shed on the suburban yard of Construction Co. (Conco) caught fire on a Sunday morning. Dennis, Conco's draftsman at its downtown office, happened to be bicycling by on a personal errand. He broke into the yard office through a closed window and notified the local volunteer fire department. He next located ignition keys and moved eight pieces of heavy equipment onto an adjacent field. The heavy equipment consisted of trucks and bulldozers, which were threatened with imminent destruction, but were not damaged.

Unknown to Dennis, the adjacent field belonged to a wholesale florist,

54

Frank. Although the field appeared to be vacant and unused, Frank had planted it with valuable tulip bulbs. Bulbs valued at $9,000 were destroyed under the weight of the heavy equipment.

You must cull through these facts to determine what theories of tort liability exist. As you will learn in the Torts chapter in this book, whenever you are faced with a Torts essay question, you ask the following "big picture" questions:

(1)   WHAT CAUSES OF ACTION EXIST AND ARE THE ELEMENTS MET?

(2)   DO ANY DEFENSES APPLY?

(3)   DO ANY GENERAL CONSIDERATIONS APPLY?

Begin with the intentional torts. Battery? No. Assault? No! False imprisonment? No! Intentional infliction of emotional distress? No! Trespass to land? BINGO!!!!!

Likewise, applying the second "big picture" question, you would run through the defenses to intentional torts and determine if any defenses apply. Consent? No. Defense of others? No! Defense of property? NOOOOOO! Necessity! ANOTHER BINGO!

After you have analyzed <u>Frank v. Dennis</u>, move on to the next heading, <u>Frank v. Conco</u>, and determine whether any general considerations apply. You would discuss the doctrine of vicarious liability, because Conco's liability depends on whether Dennis committed the tort within the scope of his employment. The relevant facts to solving this question are:

A storage shed on the suburban yard of Construction Co. (Conco) caught fire on a Sunday morning. Dennis, Conco's draftsman at its downtown office, happened to be bicycling by on a personal errand. He broke into the yard office through a closed window and notified the local volunteer fire department. He next located ignition keys and moved eight pieces of heavy equipment onto an adjacent field. The heavy equipment consisted of trucks and bulldozers, which were threatened with imminent destruction, but were not damaged.

After analyzing Conco's liability to Frank, you would next determine which facts were relevant to determining Frank's tort liability to Dennis:

After fire fighters extinguished the fire, Frank asked Dennis to come to his office to discuss the damage. Dennis agreed. As soon as Dennis entered the office, Frank told Dennis, in the presence of four of Frank's employees, that Dennis would have to remain at the office until he summoned the president of Conco and the president had arrived at the office. When the president arrived an hour later, Frank told Dennis he could leave, and Dennis left.

After reviewing these facts, you would find that Frank may be liable under the tort of false imprisonment. You would then go on to discuss the defense of consent.

Now that you have analyzed the question, and identified the general issues and the relevant facts, you must map out your analysis by preparing an outline.

3. Outlining the Answer and Different Outlining Techniques

As I pointed out earlier, different people outline differently.

The following are examples of different outlines of the same problem, illustrating the varying detail that can be included in an outline:

1A. <u>Frank v. Dennis</u>
    <u>Trespass to Land</u>
    <u>Defense of Necessity</u>

1B. <u>Frank v. Conco</u>
    <u>Vicarious Liability</u>

2. <u>Dennis v. Frank</u>
    <u>False Imprisonment</u>
    <u>Defense of Consent</u>

This skeletal outline contains only a list of the general issues that must be analyzed. If you are able to organize the discussion of each issue in your mind, and recall the facts necessary to solve each issue, this bare-bones outline may serve your needs.

However, if you are like most people, you will probably require more detail in your outline. Your outline would include not only a statement of the general issues, but the specific issues as well:

1A. Frank v. Dennis
    Trespass to Land
        Affirmative intentional act?
        Invading P's possessory interest?
        In land?
    Defense of Necessity
        Public or private necessity?
        Liable for damages?

1B. Frank v. Conco
    Vicarious Liability
        Doctrine of Respondeat-Superior
        Employer-employee relationship?
        Scope of employment?

2. Dennis v. Frank
    False Imprisonment
        Intentional act?
        Resulting in confinement?
        Actual awareness of confinement or injury?
    Defense of Consent
        Express consent?
        Scope of consent exceeded?

This outline only sets forth the legal issues to be analyzed. You may find it helpful to also include an analysis of the facts in your outline. Here is an example of one such outline:

1A. Frank v. Dennis

Trespass to Land

Affirmative intentional act? - D drove equipment

Invading P's possessory interest? - Frank owned land

In land?

All elements met

Defense of Necessity

Private necessity - D acted to save equipment from imminent destruction from fire.

D is liable for damages.

1B. Frank v. Conco

Vicarious Liability

Doctrine of Respondeat-Superior

Employer-employee relationship?

Scope of employment?

D employed by Conco as draftsman

Involved in personal errand

Sunday morning - not workday

D works in downtown office

Frank might argue that employee has duty to act

Conco will win.

2. Dennis v. Frank

False Imprisonment

Intentional act? - Frank's statement to Dennis.

Resulting in confinement - Dennis confined to office.

Actual awareness of confinement or injury? - Yes.

Defense of Consent

Express consent? Dennis initially agrees.

Scope of consent exceeded? Dennis not told he must wait an hour for Conco's president until he is already in the room.

Effect of presence of four employees?

This outline sets forth the facts to be argued in order.

In taking the practice examinations, experiment with each outlining style until

58

you find a comfortable method. Also, after you write an outline, make sure you use it. The purpose of an outline is to create a tool that you can use to write your analysis. It defeats the purpose of drafting an outline if you do not use it in writing your answer.

F.   STEP FOUR: MAKE A SNAP DECISION ABOUT HOW MUCH TIME YOU WILL SPEND ANALYZING EACH ISSUE

The next step is to allot the time you have to write your answer among the issues you must discuss. Do this by quickly estimating the amount of discussion required per issue.

Assuming that you used 10-15 minutes reading and visualizing the problem, and another 10 minutes outlining the problem, you would have approximately 30-35 minutes to write your answer. Here is an example of how your remaining time might be allotted among the issues in this problem:

1A. Frank v. Dennis
        Trespass to Land **(5 minutes)**
                Affirmative intentional act? - D drove equipment
                Invading P's possessory interest? - Frank owned land
                In land?
                All elements met
        Defense of Necessity **(5 minutes)**
                Private necessity - D acted to save equipment from imminent destruction from fire.
                D is liable for damages.

1B. Frank v. Conco
        Vicarious Liability **(10 minutes)**
                Doctrine of Respondeat-Superior
                Employer-employee relationship?
                Scope of employment?
                        D employed by Conco as draftsman
                        Involved in personal errand
                        Sunday morning - not workday
                        D works in downtown office

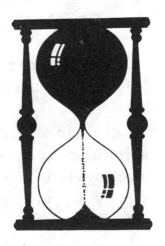

Frank might argue that employee has duty to act
Conco will win.

  2. <u>Dennis v. Frank</u>
      <u>False Imprisonment</u> **(5 minutes)**
         Intentional act? - Frank's statement to Dennis.
         Resulting in confinement - Dennis confined to office.
         Actual awareness of confinement or injury? - Yes.
      <u>Defense of Consent</u> **(10 minutes)**
         Express consent? Dennis initially agrees.
         Scope of consent exceeded? Dennis not told he must wait an
         hour for Conco's president until he is already in the room.
         Effect of presence of four employees?

The time spent discussing each issue depends on the relative importance of the issue. Because the major issues in this problem are vicarious liability and the defense of consent, ten minutes are allotted for your discussion of these issues. Trespass, necessity, and false imprisonment require only simple and straightforward discussion; only five minutes are allotted for each of these issues.

These time estimates are just that --- estimates that represent your best judgment of how long you will take to discuss all the presented issues. Spend no more than a few seconds making these estimations and stick to them. You are now ready for the next step.

G.   STEP FIVE: APPLY YOUR PROBLEM SOLVING APPROACH TO THE FACTS AND WRITE OUT THE ANSWER

At this stage you have a basic understanding of how to solve the problem. However, in Step Five, you must communicate that understanding to the grader.

There is a huge difference between knowing how to solve a problem and being able to articulate and express the reasoning process behind that solution. The challenge is to communicate your problem solving thought process to the bar grader, step by step, in a clear, concise, and grammatically correct fashion. Sound easy? It actually is!

If you are a proficient writer, then expressing yourself will not present a problem. On the other hand, if your writing is plagued by poor grammar, sentence fragments, run-on sentences, poor organization, and other no-no's, then you might consider finding a system of writing exam answers that eliminates these types of errors. That system is best known as "I-R-A-C."

I-R-A-C is the basic foundation of all legal reasoning. You will find that I-R-A-C is in each page of appellate decisions throughout the country. I-R-A-C can be found in closing arguments made before juries in both civil and criminal cases. I-R-A-C exists in legal briefs filed in every jurisdiction. And I-R-A-C will be found in passing bar exam answers.

I-R-A-C simply states the elements of a good legal analysis. It does not necessarily denote the order in which each element is listed, whether it be R-I-A-C or C-I-R-A or some other combination. Any good legal analysis will include a statement of the issue, rule, application and conclusion <u>somewhere</u> in the answer.

What I refer to as "strict I-R-A-C" contains each of the I-R-A-C elements in that specific order. Strict I-R-A-C requires rigid application of the I-R-A-C model to any and all issues.

How does strict I-R-A-C work? Let's take the defense of necessity and apply the I-R-A-C principle.

As you know, an I-R-A-C analysis includes the following components:

ISSUE: State the issue.
RULE: State the applicable rule.
APPLICATION: Apply the facts to the rule.
CONCLUSION: Reach a conclusion.

Let's translate each of these objectives into a sentence:

ISSUE: The issue is whether _____.
RULE: The rule is _____.
APPLICATION: Applying the law to the rule, _____.
CONCLUSION: The conclusion is _____.

Now fill in the blanks, using the defense of necessity as an example:

ISSUE: The issue is whether the defense of necessity bars Frank's recovery for trespass.
RULE: The rule is that where a person acts to prevent private property damage, he is liable for actual damage.
APPLICATION: Applying the law to the facts, because Dennis acted to protect Conco's property from the fire, and the heavy equipment was in imminent danger of being destroyed, his actions were justified by private necessity. However, Dennis would be liable for whatever actual damage he caused, including the $9,000 damage to the tulip bulbs.
CONCLUSION: The conclusion is that the doctrine of private necessity applies and Dennis is liable for actual damage caused.

All we have done so far is fill in the blanks with the applicable facts and rules. Now for a little magic trick. Say IRACADABRA and wave your magic pen in the air. Now let us convert it into a paragraph:

The issue is whether the defense of necessity bars Frank's recovery for trespass. The rule is that where a person acts to prevent private property damage, he is liable for actual damage. Applying the law to the facts, because Dennis acted to protect Conco's property from the fire, and the heavy equipment was in imminent danger of being destroyed, his actions were justified by private necessity. However, Dennis would be liable for whatever actual damage he caused, including the $9,000 damage to the tulip bulbs. The conclusion is that the doctrine of private necessity applies and Dennis is liable for actual damage caused.

Here we have a winning answer to the necessity issue, using strict I-R-A-C. Notice the use of "crutches" that help "jump-start" the discussion. Crutches serve an important purpose, and if you find them helpful, use them. We are all guilty of using crutches at one time or another. On the other hand, you will find that in most instances, your analysis will stand without the use of crutches:

The issue is whether the defense of necessity bars Frank's recovery for trespass. Where a person acts to prevent private property damage, she *is liable for actual damage. Because Dennis acted to protect Conco's property from the fire, and the heavy equipment was in imminent danger of being destroyed, his actions were justified by private necessity. However, Dennis would be liable for whatever actual damage he caused, including the $9,000 damage to the tulip bulbs. Thus, the doctrine of private necessity applies and Dennis is liable for actual damage caused.*

Now, focus on application. Application requires more than a mere re-statement of the facts. The application is set forth in **bold** type:

The issue is whether the defense of necessity bars Frank's recovery for trespass. Where a person acts to prevent private property damage, she is liable for actual damage. **Because Dennis acted to protect Conco's property from the fire, and the heavy equipment was in imminent danger of being destroyed, his actions were justified by private necessity. However, Dennis would be liable for whatever actual damage he caused, including the $9,000 damage to the tulip bulbs.** *Thus, the doctrine of private necessity applies and Dennis is liable for actual damage caused.*

Notice that application **EXPLAINS WHY** a particular result is warranted. Compare this answer with the following answer:

The defense of necessity applies. Dennis drove the heavy equipment from the damage, causing damage to the bulbs and thus this defense bars Frank's recovery.

This answer begins by stating the conclusion but never explains how that result is reached. As a result, this answer is CONCLUSORY.

Look at another answer, and try to guess what is wrong with it:

Dennis committed trespass against Frank by driving Conco's equipment on Frank's land, but is not liable since he acted out of a private necessity. Trespass is committed where one goes onto land of another without the owner's consent. Here, even though Dennis acted for a good

63

reason, he must still pay for whatever damage he caused. Thus, a tort was committed.

What's wrong with this answer? Are you able to tell what the author is talking about, or do you have to search for the issues discussed? It is difficult to follow the author's reasoning because the analysis is DISORGANIZED. The writer mixes the discussion of trespass to land and necessity by going back and forth between each issue.

What's wrong with the following picture?

The defense of necessity dates back to common law, where the court invoked this doctrine to permit an individual to commit a tort where there is a public or private necessity. This doctrine finds application in modern law, although it has been applied modernly to only imminent danger. A public necessity exists where the defendant acts to prevent a public danger, such as an earthquake, natural catastrophe or other act of God. A private necessity, by contrast, exists where the actor acts to prevent private property damage. Here, Dennis' conduct falls within a private necessity, since he acted to save Conco's equipment from imminent harm, and therefore this defense applies.

While the historical roots of the law of necessity may be interesting, that discussion is not called for. It is not necessary to discuss the rule of public necessity, since that issue is not raised by the facts. Because your time is limited, unnecessary words translate into a huge waste of time.

The following is an example of an I-R-A-C answer in short form:

Dennis would successfully assert the defense of necessity, since he acted for a private purpose in saving Conco's equipment from imminent destruction by fire, but would remain liable for actual damage, including the $9,000 damage to the tulip bulbs.

Study this sentence carefully and you will find:

THE ISSUE: "Dennis would . . . assert the defense of necessity . . . ."

THE RULE: "private purpose in saving . . . from imminent destruction . . . but would remain liable for actual damage . . . ."

APPLICATION: "in saving Conco's equipment from . . . destruction by fire . . . including the $9,000 damage to the tulip bulbs."

CONCLUSION: "Dennis would successfully assert . . . ."

1. Meet the Clearly Passing Answer

Frank v. Dennis

Trespass to Land

The issue is whether Frank may sue Dennis for trespass to land. Trespass to land is defined as an affirmative intentional act which invades the plaintiff's possessory interest in land. Dennis committed an intentional act by driving the heavy equipment onto Frank's land in order to avoid property damage to the equipment. The subject of the tort was land. The land was owned by Frank, and Dennis' act invaded Frank's possessory interest. Thus, all elements are met and Dennis is liable for trespass.

Defense of Necessity

Dennis will raise the defense of private necessity. Where a defendant commits a tort to avoid private property damage, the defendant is liable only for actual damage to that property. Because Dennis acted to save the heavy equipment of his employer, Conco, from fire damage, the defense of private necessity applies. Thus, Dennis will be held liable only for the amount of actual damage caused by the trespass.

Frank v. Conco

Trespass to Land - Vicarious Liability

Conco's liability for trespass will depend on whether the doctrine of respondeat superior applies. An employer is liable for all torts committed by servants within the course of employment. Dennis was employed by Conco at the time he committed the tort. However, Dennis was employed as a draftsman, not as

65

a security guard or fireman, and thus Dennis was not acting within the scope of his employment position when he committed the tort. The fire occurred on a Sunday morning when Dennis was not at work. Further, he was on a personal errand at the time the tort was committed. Frank could argue that an employee who observes damage to his employer's property would normally act to salvage such property, and therefore Conco should be liable for Dennis' acts. However, given the circumstances in this case, Frank will not likely prevail, and cannot recover from Conco.

Dennis v. Frank

False Imprisonment

The issue is whether Frank is liable to Dennis for the tort of false imprisonment. False imprisonment is defined as an act or omission with intent to confine someone resulting in actual confinement of plaintiff. Actual awareness of the confinement or injury resulting therefrom is also required. Here, Frank committed an intentional act resulting in confinement when he told Dennis he would have to remain in the office, a "bounded" area. Frank clearly intended to confine Dennis by his statement stating the same, and the presence of Frank's four employees suggests that Dennis was not free to leave the office. Dennis was subjected to "actual confinement" for one hour until Conco's president arrived. Finally, although Dennis suffered no actual injury, Dennis was no doubt aware of his confinement, as he was conscious during the confinement. Therefore, Frank is liable for false imprisonment.

Defenses of Consent

Frank may raise the defense of consent. A defendant is not liable for a tort where the plaintiff consents to the commission of the tort, either expressly or through his conduct. While Dennis initially "agreed" to entering Frank's office, such consent was vitiated because Frank did not tell Dennis he would have to remain in the office until after Dennis had entered the office. Therefore, Dennis' consent was not informed, and even if it was, the scope of consent was clearly exceeded. Thus, consent would not bar Dennis' recovery for false imprisonment.

Revisit this model answer once more, but this time note each of the strict I-R-A-C factors:

(HEADING) <u>Frank v. Dennis</u>

(THEORY OF LIABILITY) <u>Trespass to Land</u>

(ISSUE) The issue is whether Frank may sue Dennis for trespass to land. (STATE THE RULE) Trespass to land is defined as an affirmative intentional act which invades the plaintiff's possessory interest in land. (APPLY EACH ELEMENT OF THE RULE TO THE FACTS) Dennis committed an intentional act by driving the heavy equipment onto Frank's land in order to avoid property damage to the equipment. The subject of the tort was land. The land was owned by Frank, and Dennis' act invaded Frank's possessory interest. (REACH A CONCLUSION) Thus, all elements are met and Dennis is liable for trespass.

(DEFENSES?) <u>Defense of Necessity</u>

(ISSUE) Dennis will raise the defense of private necessity. (RULE) Where a defendant commits a tort to avoid private property damage, the defendant is liable only for actual damage to that property. (APPLICATION) Because Dennis acted to save the heavy equipment of his employer, Conco, from fire damage, the defense of private necessity applies. (CONCLUSION) Thus, Dennis will be held liable only for the amount of actual damage caused by the trespass.

(HEADING) <u>Frank v. Conco</u>

(GENERAL CONSIDERATION) <u>Trespass to Land - Vicarious Liability</u>

(ISSUE) Conco's liability for trespass will depend on whether the doctrine of respondeat superior applies. (RULE) An employer is liable for all torts committed by servants within the course of employment. (APPLICATION) Dennis was employed by Conco at the time he committed the tort. However, Dennis was employed as a draftsman, not a security guard or fireman, and thus Dennis was not acting within the scope of his employment position when he committed the tort. The fire occurred on a Sunday morning when Dennis was not at work. Further, Dennis was involved in a personal errand at the time the tort was committed. Frank could argue that an employee who observes damage to his employer's property would normally act to salvage such property, and therefore Conco should be liable for Dennis' acts. (CONCLUSION) However, given the circumstances in this case, Frank will not likely prevail, and cannot recover from Conco.

(HEADING) <u>Dennis v. Frank</u>

(THEORY OF LIABILITY) <u>False Imprisonment</u>

(ISSUE) The issue is whether Frank is liable to Dennis for the tort of false imprisonment. (RULE) False imprisonment is defined as an act or omission with intent to confine someone resulting in actual confinement of plaintiff. Actual awareness of the confinement or injury resulting therefrom is also required. (APPLICATION OF EACH ELEMENT) Here Frank committed an intentional act resulting in confinement when he told Dennis he would have to remain in the office, a "bounded" area. Frank clearly intended to confine Dennis by his statement stating the same, and the presence of Frank's four employees suggests that Dennis was not free to leave the office. Dennis was subjected to "actual confinement" for one hour until Conco's president arrived. Finally, although Dennis suffered no actual injury, Dennis was no doubt aware of his confinement, as he was conscious during the confinement. (CONCLUSION) Therefore, Frank is liable for false imprisonment.

(DEFENSES?) <u>Defense of Consent</u>

(ISSUE) Frank may raise the defense of consent. (RULE) A defendant is not liable for a tort where the plaintiff consents to the commission of the tort, either expressly or through his conduct. (APPLICATION) While Dennis initially "agreed" to enter Frank's office, such consent was vitiated because Frank did not tell Dennis he would have to remain in the office until after Dennis had entered the office. Therefore, Dennis' consent was not informed, and even if it was, the scope of consent was clearly exceeded. (CONCLUSION) Thus, consent would not bar Dennis' recovery for false imprisonment.

This model answer illustrates how each of the I-R-A-C components come together to form a well-organized, structured, and logical answer. Each I-R-A-C element appears exactly in that order, one after the other, like clockwork. And yes, THIS IS A PASSING PAPER of the 75 caliber. This is the <u>easiest</u> bar question I have ever seen, but it did appear on the bar exam. While most bar questions are considerably more difficult, this question will serve as the foundation for the more complicated bar questions follow.

2. Meet the Clearly Not Passing Answer

Now that you have met a "clearly passing answer" it is only proper that you see a "clearly not passing answer." Reading this exam is probably more revealing than reading the "clearly passing answer" because it illustrates some of the most common errors made by examinees.

Dennis v. Frank

Frank might recover for false imprisonment, but the facts don't say whether Dennis could have left. If Dennis could have left Frank's office, then he wasn't falsely imprisoned. False imprisonment also requires that Frank intend to confine Dennis, but the facts say that Dennis "agreed" to go into the office. If Dennis agreed, how could he now say he was imprisoned? Thus, Dennis may not recover for false imprisonment.

Another issue might be intentional infliction of emotional distress, since Dennis may have felt some distress after being in Frank's office. Frank's employees were there and might have frightened Dennis. If Dennis suffered such distress, he might recover.

Frank v. Dennis and Conco

Frank should be able to sue Dennis for trespass to his land. Frank's land was damaged by Dennis' intentional act of driving the heavy equipment on his land. Frank should also be able to sue Conco, since Dennis worked for Conco. However, Conco would say that Dennis was not working for them on Sunday and wasn't at work that day. Conco was probably closed, since we know that most businesses close on Sundays. However, if Conco was open, then Frank might win.

The author of this answer failed to follow the order of the issues dictated by the Bar Examiners. Here are some of the obvious errors inherent in this answer:

✔The issues of false imprisonment and trespass are correctly identified, but the elements of each are either not discussed or are glossed over.
✔The examinee failed to perform a comprehensive analysis of each element of false imprisonment and trespass.
✔The general consideration of vicarious liability is only remotely alluded to

69

but never identified.

✔No rules of law are stated anywhere in the analysis.

✔The discussion of the facts is disorganized and confusing, and the examinee's discussion of vicarious liability focuses too much on whether Sunday is a workday fails and to discuss other available facts.

✔The issue of necessity is completely missed.

✔The examinee also fails to discuss consent, although he mentions in passing that Dennis agreed to enter Frank's office.

✔No headings are used, so it is virtually impossible to determine what issues are being discussed in what order.

✔Note the use of contractions. Avoid contractions at all costs.

Avoid these problems in your exam answer so that you do not cause the bar grader to suffer intentional infliction of emotional distress!

Before moving on, let me squeeze one more drop of wisdom from this example. As discussed earlier, you must learn how to distinguish major issues from minor ones. How do you know when an issue is major, minor or non-existent, and how do you know how much time to devote to each issue?

In this problem, the issue of trespass is a minor issue. Here, Dennis intentionally drove tractors and bulldozers onto Frank's land. There is no question that Dennis did this. Therefore, you are not required to spend five pages of your bluebook discussing this issue. On the other hand, it is not enough to say, "Dennis committed trespass to land." No matter how obvious or simple, trespass to land is an issue that must be addressed. Some examinees made the mistake of not analyzing trespass at all and lost valuable points by failing to do so.

On the other hand, vicarious liability is an example of a major issue. It requires an in-depth discussion of whether Dennis acted in the scope of employment. While the "point-counterpoint" arguments are somewhat lop-sided, favoring Conco, many facts deserve discussion. Accordingly, more time should be spent on this issue than on trespass. Each available fact should be used and all possible arguments made in the discussion.

An example of a non-issue is whether Frank suffered intentional infliction of emotional distress, because Dennis did not act with the requisite intent to warrant a discussion of that tort. Other non-issues might be whether Dennis suffered an assault because he was afraid of Frank's four employees, or whether Conco's president is liable to Dennis for negligence in failing to arrive at Frank's office earlier. You may laugh at these non-issues, but remember that under exam pressures, it is not always a simple matter to know when you are on the right track.

In this same vein, do not reach for issues that are not there. On the bar exam, you do not need to create issues, because you will have plenty of "real" issues to solve.

3. Meet the "90" Answer

You have seen what a passing examination looks like; now take a glimpse at an 85-90 exam answer:

1A. <u>Frank v. Dennis</u>

Dennis committed trespass to land. Dennis intentionally drove the heavy equipment onto Frank's land to save Conco's equipment and purposefully invaded Frank's possessory interest in land.

However, Dennis' liability would be limited to actual damages since his actions are privileged under the doctrine of private necessity. Because Dennis acted to prevent the imminent destruction by fire of Conco's equipment, Frank's recovery is limited to $9,000 for the damaged tulip bulbs and any other consequential or incidental damages.

1B. <u>Frank v. Conco</u>

Conco's liability turns on the doctrine of respondeat-superior, since it is liable for Dennis' tortious conduct only if he acted in the scope of his employment. While Dennis was employed by Conco, he was employed as a draftsman at its downtown office, and thus Dennis had no duty arising from his employment to protect Conco's equipment at another site. Conco's argument is further buttressed by the fact that the fire occurred on a Sunday, not a workday, while Dennis was involved in a personal errand and was not working at Conco at the time the tort was committed. Frank's only argument is that Dennis had a duty as Conco's employee to save his employer's property from harm, but Conco will prevail and is not liable for Dennis' acts.

2. Dennis v. Frank

Frank committed false imprisonment. While Frank initially invited Dennis into his office, once inside the office, Frank committed an intentional act by telling Dennis he had to remain in the office, a "bounded" area. The presence of Frank's four employees supports Dennis' argument that he was subject to actual confinement, and could not have escaped by reasonable means. Dennis was also conscious during the incident, and thus need not demonstrate actual injury.

Frank would first argue that Dennis expressly consented by agreeing to enter the office. While this is true, Dennis would argue that Frank's later acts and statements exceeded the scope of his initial consent. Frank could argue that Dennis remained voluntarily after he "asked" Dennis to remain, but as a matter of semantics, the words "have to remain" indicate a command, not a request. Also, the fact that Dennis remained in the office for one hour suggests that he did so involuntarily, since a reasonable person would probably not do so unless forced.

Notice that a "85 to 90 exam answer" is not necessarily longer or more complicated. In fact, it is just the opposite: simple, clear, and concise, and SHORT. Remember you do not get credit for the number of words you write, but for the substance of your analysis. I recall one student who consistently wrote two full blue books for each bar exam question. The old saying, "Nothing exceeds like excess," applies to the bar exam as well.

VI.   HOW TO USE THIS BOOK

> *"One must learn by doing the thing; though you think you know it, you have no certainty until you try."*

> ---- Sophocles (c. 495-406 B.C.)

A final postscript before we get going.

This book is designed to help you attain your greatest exam writing potential. It is a "user-friendly" manual, and fairly self-explanatory, but here are a few hints on how to best use this book:

Read each section in chronological order. The bar questions in each chapter are arranged according to difficulty and the learning value of each problem.

The subject areas need not be covered in the order in which they appear. However, it is suggested that you begin with the Torts chapter, which emphasizes basic problem solving and writing techniques, and then move on to another subject area. In each consecutive chapter, new techniques are revealed, and these techniques are generally presented in order of difficulty.

Each chapter is organized as follows. First, you will receive a writing approach in that subject area. The writing approach always begins with the "big picture" which gives you the overall questions you must ask when confronted with a problem in that subject area. These "big picture" questions serve to narrow down the field of issues you must address. Once the "big picture" questions are applied to the hypothetical, you then answer the specific issues within that "big picture" area and in this way determine what issues are presented by the problem. For example, in Torts, the first big picture question is, "What causes of action exist and are the elements met?" To answer this "big picture" question, you must determine whether the facts give rise to an intentional tort, negligence, defamation, etc. Once you have determined what particular tort or torts must be discussed, you then analyze whether the specific elements of that tort are met.

The writing approach is not an attempt to teach you the law. The problem solving approaches you will learn in this book can be applied to all three areas of the bar. For excellent examples of problem solving approaches in all tested bar subjects, complete with color coded charts, memory mnemonics and other valuable information on how to prepare for the bar exam, check out *The Bar Exam Survival Kit*, authored by yours truly.

Each writing approach is followed by up to ten examples of recent bar questions. These questions have been carefully selected to give you the widest possible exposure to the different types of bar questions which have appeared on past examinations. You will encounter the "sucker's bar question," the "mutant" bar question, "the lying-in-wait" bar question and other mystical creations of the Bar Examiners. By learning how to identify the various ways the Bar Examiners test your ability to solve essay problems, you will develop an instinct for the way that the exam authors think. This in turn will help you solve the problems.

Finally, remember that you must practice writing answers in order to learn from this book. Reading this book a thousand times is a worthless exercise unless you take the examinations and do the exercises in each chapter. Reading the best book on skydiving is not the same as actually jumping out of a plane with a string in your hand.

Do not become overwhelmed by all of the information you have read thus far. You may be thinking, "There is no way I could do that in an hour!" If you follow the plan provided in this book, pacing yourself, and incorporating each technique one at a time, you will successfully solve problems.

The exam writing techniques are spread throughout the book in a way that makes it easy to learn and apply. When you are done with this book you will write your way to a winning bar exam score!

VII. TROUBLESHOOTING GUIDE

The purpose of this section is not to reinforce the belief that something will go wrong during the examination, i.e., Murphy's Law, but merely to give you some troubleshooting tips if something does not go exactly as planned.

A.   WHAT TO DO IF YOU BEGIN WRITING THE WRONG THING

"If you board the wrong train, it's no use running along the corridor in the other direction."

---- Dietrich Bonhoeffer (1906-1945)

If you find mid-way through your answer that you have misanalyzed the problem, stop and start again. Do not continue to answer a question incorrectly, because you will destroy whatever chances you might have had to salvage some points. If, for example, you are writing a Real Property answer and suddenly realize that the question is really a Torts problem, stop and begin solving the Torts problem.

Likewise, if you discover that you are wrong mid-way through a discussion of a particular issue, correct the error and start anew as if you had never made the earlier mistake. Do not continue to argue a clearly erroneous point of law or fact. It is better that the grader sees that you have discovered your error and attempted to correct it.

This will not happen to you if you read the exam carefully, outline your answer and follow the *Six Steps of Exam Writing*.

B. WHAT TO DO IF YOU RUN OUT OF TIME

Running out of time is like running out of money at the craps table. Do not ask for credit, because it will cost you in the end. Follow the time limits you set for yourself religiously, and if you are unable to complete your discussion of a particular issue, then move on.

Once again, if you follow the time allocation strategies in this book you will not be in this situation.

C. WHAT TO DO IF YOU FORGET THE LAW

"The advantage of a bad memory is that one enjoys several times the same good things for the first time."

---- Friedrich Nietzsche (1844-1900)

You should know the law better than you know your own name. However, if you cannot recall a particular rule, then make it up. Yes, I will repeat that again. MAKE IT UP. Think of a rule that sounds logical and write it down and apply it to the facts and reach a reasonably sounding conclusion. While you may be dead wrong, the grader will at least have the benefit of a discussion to judge as opposed to a blank page or a question mark.

While this tactic is certainly not recommended, it is preferable to writing nothing, or even worse, sitting in your chair trying to remember the law while the minutes tick away. Remember that the grader wants to see how you solve problems, and may not penalize you too severely for not knowing the right rule.

D.   WHAT TO DO IF YOU AREN'T SURE HOW TO SOLVE THE PROBLEM

"Take calculated risks. That is quite different from being rash."

---- George S. Patton (1885-1945)

If you do not know how to solve the problem, then take your best shot. Once again, if you follow the writing approaches in this book, you will not find yourself in this position.

If you are unsure whether to analyze a particular cause of action, exercise your best judgment, decide either to do it or not to do it and then move on. You do not have time to procrastinate, trying to decide whether an issue should be discussed or not. Fortunately, bar examination questions present clearcut issues.

E.   WHAT TO DO IF YOU DRAW A BLANK

"The absence of alternatives clears the mind marvelously."

---- Henry Kissinger (1923 -   )

If your mind goes completely blank, close your eyes, take a deep breath, and set on the problem before you. Realize that we are all human, and an exam black-out happens to everyone at least once during the examination.

With these pitfalls in mind, rejoice that by applying the strategies and technologies in this book, you will not find yourself among those who suffer from these exam maladies!

BARBREAKER

torts

VIII. TORTS

A.   INTRODUCTION

The law of Torts from your early days as a law student should bring back fond memories of Socratic fear, odd but interesting cases such as <u>Garratt v. Dailey</u>, i.e., the "little boy pulls the chair from under the plaintiff" case, and other miscellaneous tidbits spread throughout your ganglia. Erase all of that for a moment and consider the following.

What is the law of Torts really about? When it comes down to the bottom line, the law of Torts concerns itself with private wrongs --- one person doing something wrong to another. That is the form, as simple as it sounds, that every Torts bar question will assume. The Bar Examiners will present you with a circumstance involving a person or persons doing wrong to another. You will be required to analyze what wrongs were committed and the effect of those wrongs on each party's legal right to recover against the other.

In terms of the type of fact patterns that you will confront, you can expect to see anything and everything. Past bar questions have included auto accidents, cancer caused by nuclear testing, medical malpractice, defective elevators, and just about everything else with the exception of torts caused by UFOs. This is not to say, however, that you must understand auto mechanics, nuclear physics, human biology, medicine, or elevator repair. While the range of fact patterns in which a Torts problem may rear its head is limitless, the issues raised by a Torts problem are not. Because the number of issues available to the Bar Examiners is finite, the same issues are tested again and again.

The bar questions in this chapter represent the various types of Torts problems that regularly appear on the bar exam. By far the most popular tested area is negligence, with defamation and products liability tying for a close second. This is not to say that the Bar Examiners will not test you on more remote areas, such as the tort of malicious prosecution or the business torts. As you will see, nothing is off limits as far as the Bar Examiners are concerned, so you must be ready for anything.

B.   THE TORTS WRITING APPROACH

In our writing approach, we always begin by asking the "big picture" questions. In this way, we narrow the field of specific issues by process of elimination.

C.   THE BIG PICTURE QUESTIONS

On a Torts exam, there are three "big picture" questions. You have already learned about these questions from the Dennis, Frank, and Conco example that appeared earlier. They are:

(1) WHAT CAUSES OF ACTION EXIST AND ARE THE ELEMENTS MET?

(2) DO ANY DEFENSES APPLY?

(3) DO ANY GENERAL CONSIDERATIONS APPLY?

You should <u>always</u> ask these questions anytime you suspect that a Torts question is presented. The answer to these questions will help you decide whether you are in fact dealing with a Torts problem; if the response to each question is negative, the bar examiners are testing you in another area.

Let 's review each "big picture" question.

(1) WHAT CAUSES OF ACTION EXIST AND ARE THE ELEMENTS MET?

The cause of action refers to the specific tort action raised by the party claiming injury or seeking redress for tortious conduct by the defendant. There are seven different possible areas of tortious recovery for which you are responsible:

INTENTIONAL TORTS
NEGLIGENCE
STRICT LIABILITY
PRODUCTS LIABILITY
DEFAMATION

PRIVACY TORTS
MISCELLANEOUS TORTS

Each area of tort liability, in turn, requires the analysis of specific causes of action and/or specific elements of those causes of action. For example, to analyze an intentional torts problem, you would apply the following checklist of intentional torts:

BATTERY
ASSAULT
FALSE IMPRISONMENT
INTENTIONAL INFLICTION OF EMOTIONAL DISTRESS
TRESPASS TO LAND
TRESPASS TO CHATTELS
CONVERSION

In turn, each individual tort requires an analysis to determine whether the elements of that tort are met. For example, intentional infliction of emotional distress requires analysis of the following issues:

Did the defendant commit an extreme and outrageous act?
Did the defendant have the intent to cause severe emotional distress?
Did the defendant's act result in severe emotional distress?

By beginning with the big picture questions, you are able to narrow the field of issues to those raised by the fact pattern.

Let's take another example before moving on to defenses. Because there are different theories upon which a products liability action may be grounded, you would look to the following checklist in analyzing a products liability question:

MISREPRESENTATION (RESTATEMENT 402)
BREACH OF EXPRESS WARRANTY
STRICT PRODUCTS LIABILITY
IMPLIED WARRANTY
NEGLIGENCE

If you concluded that under the given facts, you needed to analyze Misrepresentation under Restatement of Torts section 402 you would in turn ask and answer the following questions:

Did the defendant make a misrepresentation of material fact?
Did the plaintiff rely on the representation in using the product?
Was the representation made by the defendant or fairly chargeable against him?
Was the product intended or expected to reach a class of which plaintiff is a member?
Is the defendant a commercial supplier of chattels?

Your analysis should apply each element to the fact pattern and determine whether the plaintiff may prove a prima facie case. Each element should be carefully analyzed and each available fact should be used to argue whatever point you are making. In writing out your answer, you may choose to follow the strict I-R-A-C method of writing suggested earlier in the text.

(2)   DO ANY DEFENSES APPLY?

After you have determined whether a particular cause of action has been established by the facts, you then turn to the issue of whether any defenses apply to defeat the cause of action. A defense will typically involve the defendant's conduct or asserted justification for committing the tortious act.

You should scrutinize each cause of action to determine if any defenses bar that cause of action. The same "checklist" approach of problem solving is applied to insure a comprehensive coverage of all potential defenses.

For example, the defenses to the intentional torts are:

CONSENT
DEFENSE OF PROPERTY
SELF-DEFENSE
DEFENSE OF OTHERS
NECESSITY
PRIVILEGE OF ARREST

Again, your discussion should encompass any and all defenses that may apply; do not discuss only one defense if another defense also merits discussion. As you did with your discussion of intentional torts, identify the issue, state the rule, apply each of the elements of the defense and reach a conclusion. The following questions represent the potential issues raised in a self-defense problem:

Did D reasonably believe she was in danger from P?
Was the force used reasonably necessary to prevent the harm?
Did D have a duty to retreat?
Was D the aggressor?

Any defenses should be analyzed immediately after the discussion of all torts within a particular class of torts. For example, the defenses to intentional torts should be discussed after your discussion of the intentional torts, as in the Frank, Dennis and Conco problem discussed earlier.

(3) DO ANY GENERAL CONSIDERATIONS APPLY?

After addressing all the defenses to a cause of action, the next step is to discuss whether any general considerations apply. General considerations are exactly that -- general considerations which must be addressed in every Torts problem. The list of general considerations include:

VICARIOUS LIABILITY
IMMUNITY
RECOVERY FOR INJURY TO ANOTHER
MULTIPLE DEFENDANT PROBLEMS
STATUTE OF LIMITATION PROBLEMS

The general consideration of vicarious liability, for example, involves five potential issues:

PARENT-CHILD LIABILITY
VICARIOUS LIABILITY FOR VEHICLE
EMPLOYER-EMPLOYEE LIABILITY
JOINT ENTERPRISE
DRAM SHOP ACTS

These five areas form the checklist of issues used to narrow the field of potential general considerations. Each of these areas, in turn, requires you to pose certain sub-issues to determine the applicability of the general consideration at issue. For example, vicarious liability requires a discussion of the following issues:

Is the party committing the tortious act employed by D?
Was the tort committed within the scope of such employment?

If these concepts appear unfamiliar to you, please refer to the substantive outlines for a complete statement of the law.

With that, we will quickly review the writing approach for Torts:

WRITING APPROACH FOR TORTS

I. INTENTIONAL TORTS

PRIMA FACIE CASE?

BATTERY
ASSAULT
FALSE IMPRISONMENT
INTENTIONAL INFLICTION OF EMOTIONAL DISTRESS
TRESPASS TO LAND
TRESPASS TO CHATTELS
CONVERSION

DO ANY DEFENSES APPLY?

CONSENT
DEFENSE OF PROPERTY
SELF-DEFENSE
DEFENSE OF OTHERS
NECESSITY
PRIVILEGE OF ARREST

II. NEGLIGENCE

PRIMA FACIE CASE?

DUTY
STANDARD OF CARE
BREACH OF STANDARD OF CARE
CAUSATION (actual and proximate cause)
DAMAGES

DEFENSES?

CONTRIBUTORY/COMPARATIVE NEGLIGENCE
ASSUMPTION OF THE RISK

III. STRICT LIABILITY

PRIMA FACIE CASE?

ANIMALS
ULTRAHAZARDOUS ACTIVITIES

DEFENSES?

ASSUMPTION OF THE RISK
COMPARATIVE NEGLIGENCE

IV. DEFAMATION

PRIMA FACIE CASE?

DEFAMATORY MATTER
PUBLISHED TO THIRD PARTY
SUBJECTIVELY UNDERSTOOD BY THIRD PARTY
CAUSATION
DAMAGES

DEFENSES?

    ABSOLUTE DEFENSES
    QUALIFIED DEFENSES
    EFFECT OF RETRACTION

V. PRODUCTS LIABILITY

PRIMA FACIE CASE?

    MISREPRESENTATION
    STRICT LIABILITY
    NEGLIGENCE
    EXPRESS WARRANTY
    IMPLIED WARRANTY

DEFENSES? (depends on theory)

    ASSUMPTION OF RISK
    MISUSE OF PRODUCT
    FAILURE TO FOLLOW INSTRUCTIONS
    FAILURE TO GIVE NOTICE
    STATE OF THE ART DEFENSE

VI. INVASIONS OF PRIVACY

PRIMA FACIE CASE
    INTRUSION
    MISAPPROPRIATION
    FALSE LIGHT
    PRIVATE FACTS

DEFENSES

VII. ECONOMIC TORTS

PRIMA FACIE CASE?

- DECEIT/FRAUD
- MISREPRESENTATION
- INTERFERENCE WITH PROSPECTIVE ADVANTAGE
- INTERFERENCE WITH CONTRACTUAL RELATIONS
- TRADE LIBEL

DEFENSES?

VIII. NUISANCE

PRIMA FACIE CASE?
- PUBLIC
- PRIVATE

DEFENSES?

IX. MISCELLANEOUS TORTS

- MALICIOUS PROSECUTION
- ABUSE OF PROCESS

DEFENSES?

X. GENERAL CONSIDERATIONS?

- VICARIOUS LIABILITY
- IMMUNITY
- RECOVERY FOR INJURY TO ANOTHER
- MULTIPLE DEFENDANT PROBLEMS
- STATUTE OF LIMITATIONS

This writing approach will enable you to solve any Torts problem that confronts you on the bar exam. If you have any questions concerning the substantive

86

law of Torts, please refer to the *Bar Exam Survival Kit*.

As you solve the problem, please follow the specific directions that appear in the box at the top of each page. These directions are designed to further reinforce the *Six Steps of Exam Taking* and assist you in compartmentalizing each task. Remember that it is not enough to simply read the text. If you are thinking, "Gee, I'm not ready to take examinations just yet, maybe I'll just read through the examples," stop and put down this book until you are truly serious about passing the bar exam.

D.   PROBLEM ONE: PAT v. TRANSIT AND DR. ARD

1.   The First Read

READ THROUGH THE FACT PATTERN ONCE FOR CONTENT ONLY, AND PLEASE GO ON TO THE NEXT PAGE

Transit operates buses in a city. One morning, Driver, a Transit driver, awoke with a bad cold. He consulted the yellow pages of the telephone directory and called Dr. Ard, a physician listed under the category, "Physicians & Surgeons - M.D. - Eye, Ear, Nose & Throat." Driver told Dr. Ard that he had a bad cold and was scheduled to report for work at noon that day. Dr. Ard listened to Driver describe his symptoms, said he could not give Driver an appointment, and told him to buy a bottle of "Pyrib" at a drug store and to use its contents as directed on the label. Pyrib is a cold remedy antihistamine prepared and marketed by Drugco. Driver obtained the Pyrib from a drug store, took the first dosage called for on the label, and reported for work at noon.

At 1:30 p.m. that day, while driving his bus, Driver felt drowsy. However, he continued driving and shortly thereafter, fell asleep. The bus jumped a curb and hit a pole. Pat, a paying passenger on the bus, was injured.

Pyrib is known to cause drowsiness and sleep in about 20% of the persons who take it. Dr. Ard did not warn Driver that the medication he prescribed might cause drowsiness and sleep, and the label on the bottle did not contain any such warning.

(1) What are Pat's rights against Transit? Discuss.

(2) What are Pat's rights against Dr. Ard? Discuss.

2.   The Second Read

Transit operates buses in a city. One morning, Driver, a Transit driver, awoke with a bad cold. He consulted the yellow pages of the telephone directory and called Dr. Ard, a physician listed under the category, "Physicians & Surgeons - M.D. - Eye, Ear, Nose & Throat." Driver told Dr. Ard that he had a bad cold and was scheduled to report for work at noon that day. Dr. Ard listened to Driver describe his symptoms, said he could not give Driver an appointment, and told him to buy a bottle of "Pyrib" at a drug store and to use its contents as directed on the label. Pyrib is a cold remedy antihistamine prepared and marketed by Drugco. Driver obtained the Pyrib from a drug store, took the first dosage called for on the label, and reported for work at noon.

At 1:30 p.m. that day, while driving his bus, Driver felt drowsy. However, he continued driving and shortly thereafter, fell asleep. The bus jumped a curb and hit a pole. Pat, a paying passenger on the bus, was injured.

Pyrib is known to cause drowsiness and sleep in about 20% of the persons who take it. Dr. Ard did not warn Driver that the medication prescribed might cause drowsiness and sleep, and the label on the bottle did not contain any such warning.

3.   Fact Retention Exercise

Now that you have completed the second read, please answer the following questions WITHOUT referring to the fact pattern:

1. WHO ARE THE POTENTIAL PARTIES TO ANY LEGAL ACTION?

    (1) _____

    (2) _____

    (3) _____

    (4) _____

2. WHAT TIME DID DRIVER GO TO WORK?

3. DID DRIVER ADVISE DOCTOR ARD OF THIS FACT?

4. WHAT TIME DID THE ACCIDENT OCCUR?

5. HOW DID THE ACCIDENT OCCUR?

6. WHAT DID THE BOTTLE SAY ABOUT THE MEDICATION CAUSING DROWSINESS?

If you are unable to answer any of the six questions, you are not reading the fact pattern carefully. These questions are meant only to test your ability to recall the content of what you just read. It is essential that you understand the problem before you attempt to solve it.

4.   Reading the Interrogatories

Next, study the interrogatories.

(1) What are Pat's **rights** against Transit? Discuss.

(2) What are Pat's **rights** against Dr. Ard? Discuss.

What do these interrogatories reveal? When read together with the fact pattern, they scream out for a torts analysis because you are asked to analyze one party's **rights** against another party, where personal injury is involved.

Now that you have twice read the facts carefully and determined what subject area is being tested, return to the facts. Next, use the techniques of visualization and headlining to cement those facts in your mind.

5.   Visualization Exercise

VISUALIZE THE FACTS!

VISUALIZING the facts involves the process of seeing the fact pattern come to life. Spend a few minutes reviewing the facts again, this time VISUALIZING the characters and events which unravel, word by word, sentence by sentence, paragraph by paragraph!

Transit operates buses in a city. One morning, Driver, a Transit driver, awoke with a bad cold. He consulted the yellow pages of the telephone directory and called Dr. Ard, a physician listed under the category, "Physicians & Surgeons - M.D. - Eye, Ear, Nose & Throat." Driver told Dr. Ard that he had a bad cold and was scheduled to report for work at noon that day. Dr. Ard listened to Driver describe his symptoms, said he could not give Driver an appointment, and told him to buy a bottle of "Pyrib" at a drug store and to use its contents as directed on the label. Pyrib is a cold remedy antihistamine prepared and marketed by Drugco. Driver obtained the Pyrib from a drug store, took the first dosage called for on the label, and reported for work at noon.

At 1:30 p.m. that day, while driving his bus, Driver felt drowsy. However, he continued driving and shortly thereafter, fell asleep. The bus jumped a curb and hit a pole. Pat, a paying passenger on the bus, was injured.

Pyrib is known to cause drowsiness and sleep in about 20% of the persons who take it. Dr. Ard did not warn Driver that the medication prescribed might cause drowsiness and sleep, and the label on the bottle did not contain any such warning.

6.   Headlining Exercise

Now the technique of "headlining." Pretend that you are a newspaper reporter writing a headline for tomorrow's story on Driver's accident. Now write three headlines, one for each paragraph:

HEADLINE:

Transit operates buses in a city. One morning, Driver, a Transit driver, awoke with a bad cold. He consulted the yellow pages of the telephone directory and called Dr. Ard, a physician listed under the category, "Physicians & Surgeons - M.D. - Eye, Ear, Nose & Throat." Driver told Dr. Ard that he had a bad cold and was scheduled to report for work at noon that day. Dr. Ard listened to Driver describe his symptoms, said he could not give Driver an appointment, and told him to buy a bottle of "Pyrib" at a drug store and to use its contents as directed on the label. Pyrib is a cold remedy antihistamine prepared and marketed by Drugco. Driver obtained the Pyrib from a drug store, took the first dosage called for on the label, and reported for work at noon.

HEADLINE:

  At 1:30 p.m. that day, while driving his bus, Driver felt drowsy. However, he continued driving and shortly thereafter, fell asleep. The bus jumped a curb and hit a pole. Pat, a paying passenger on the bus, was injured.

HEADLINE:

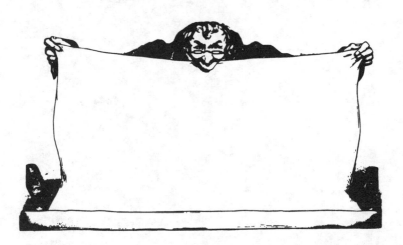

  Pyrib is known to cause drowsiness and sleep in about 20% of the persons who take it. Dr. Ard did not warn Driver that the medication prescribed might cause drowsiness and sleep, and the label on the bottle did not contain any such warning.

Now compare your "headlines" to these sample headlines listed below:

1. "DR. ARD TELLS TRANSIT DRIVER OVER PHONE TO TAKE PYRIB FOR HIS COLD!"

2. "BUS CRASHES WHEN DRIVER FALLS ASLEEP; PASSENGER INJURED!"

3. "BOTH DOCTOR AND BOTTLE LABEL FAIL TO WARN PATIENT OF KNOWN DROWSINESS CAUSED BY PYRIB!"

Again, the purpose of headlining is not to oversimplify the facts, but to summarize what occurred in order to memorize the facts for later recall. Now that you have mastered the facts, go on to solving this problem by following the third step of the *Six Steps of Exam Writing*: writing an outline.

7.   Outlining Exercise

DETERMINING WHAT QUESTIONS ARE PRESENTED AND WRITING OUT YOUR OUTLINE

Use this page to outline your answer:

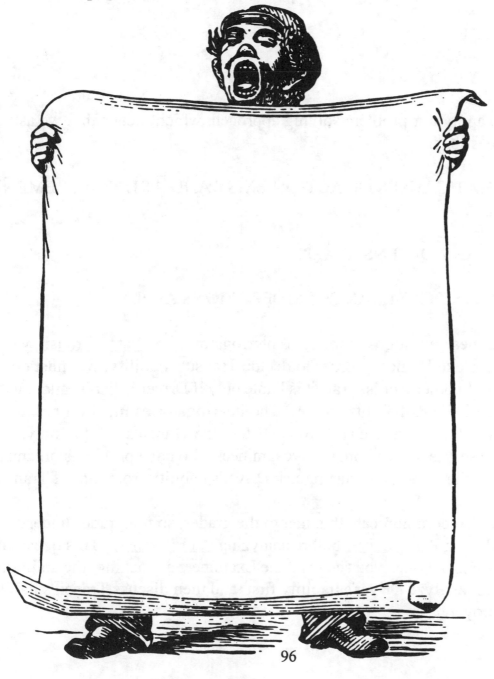

The first step of writing an outline is organizing your answer. How should this problem be organized and structured? First, we look to the interrogatories:

(1) What are Pat's rights against Transit? Discuss.

(2) What are Pat's rights against Dr. Ard? Discuss.

By following the organization and structure suggested by the question, we have:

Pat v. Transit

Pat v. Dr. Ard

Next, we apply our problem solving approach, which means that we ask the "big picture" questions:

    (1)   WHAT CAUSES OF ACTION EXIST AND ARE THE ELEMENTS MET?

    (2)   DO ANY DEFENSES APPLY?

    (3)   DO ANY GENERAL CONSIDERATIONS APPLY?

Applying these questions to the first interrogatory, i.e., Pat v. Transit, we are perhaps a bit perplexed, since in order to decide Transit's liability, we must decide Driver's liability. In other words, Transit is liable only if Driver is liable, and thus we must first decide Driver's liability to Pat. The interrogatories mention nothing of Driver's liability to Pat, but instead ask you to determine Transit's liability only. This testing technique serves to weed out those examinees who have problems organizing their answers, or otherwise fail to distinguish Driver's liability from that of Transit's.

We must also communicate this fact to the grader, so the grader understands why we are analyzing Pat v. Driver before analyzing Pat v. Transit. This question is tricky in this regard, but once you see what the Examiners are asking, the solution is simple: you must analyze Driver's liability first, and then discuss Transit's liability as Driver's employer.

Now turn to the issue of Driver's liability to Pat. The first big picture question should spell out NEGLIGENCE loud and clear. Driver did not intentionally injure Pat, and therefore intentional torts are inapplicable; the same is true of defamation and the other areas of tort liability. Here, the facts relate that Driver engaged in careless conduct, and therefore a negligence problem is raised. Once you have determined that this is a negligence problem, you then apply your negligence writing approach:

NEGLIGENCE

PRIMA FACIE CASE?

DUTY
STANDARD OF CARE
BREACH OF STANDARD OF CARE
CAUSATION (actual and proximate cause)
DAMAGES

DEFENSES?

CONTRIBUTORY/COMPARATIVE NEGLIGENCE
ASSUMPTION OF THE RISK

Once you recall the writing approach, you need only plug in the facts to complete your outline of Part One of this question:

(1) Pat v. Transit

Depends on Pat v. Driver

NEGLIGENCE: PRIMA FACIE CASE?

DUTY - Majority rule: Is Pat a foreseeable P? Zone of danger?
STANDARD OF CARE - How would a reasonable bus driver act?
BREACH OF STANDARD OF CARE - Would a reasonable person do what Driver did?
CAUSATION - Actual cause: "But for" driver's falling asleep bus

98

would not have crashed. Proximate cause: Pat's injury was directly caused by Driver's falling asleep.

DAMAGES - Pat injured.

DEFENSES?

CONTRIBUTORY/COMPARATIVE NEGLIGENCE - No evidence.
ASSUMPTION OF THE RISK - No.

GENERAL CONSIDERATIONS

VICARIOUS LIABILITY: Doctrine of respondeat-superior.
Within scope of employment? Driver driving bus at time of negligent act.

Here we have a quick outline of the issues that you should discuss in your answer. By mapping out your answer before writing, you know exactly what to discuss and the order in which to discuss each issue.

Do not forget to answer the issue addressed. Pat v. Driver is only part of the answer, for Transit's liability must be addressed. Once you establish Driver's liability for negligence, you then turn to the general consideration of vicarious liability.

Now, turn to the remaining interrogatory, Pat v. Dr. Ard, and outline this part of the answer:

(2) Pat v. Dr. Ard

NEGLIGENCE: PRIMA FACIE CASE?

DUTY - Majority rule: Pat a foreseeable P? Zone of danger?
STANDARD OF CARE - How would a reasonable doctor act?
BREACH OF STANDARD OF CARE - Would reasonable medical doctor do what Doctor Ard did?
CAUSATION - Actual cause? "But for" Dr. Ard's act of prescribing Pyrib without warning Driver of its side effects, Driver would not have fallen asleep and crashed. Proximate cause? Dr. Ard's act was an

99

indirect cause - foreseeable that P would be injured by his failure to warn Driver?
DAMAGES - Pat injured.

DEFENSES?

CONTRIBUTORY/COMPARATIVE NEGLIGENCE - No evidence.
ASSUMPTION OF THE RISK - No.

As you apply the facts to your writing approach and decide which facts are relevant to solving the issues before you, recognize that there are facts included that are not relevant to solving this problem. The Bar Examiners have included the name of the company that manufactured Pyrib, "Drugco," although neither interrogatory calls for an analysis of Drugco's liability in this case. Why? Because many people fall for the sucker punch and immediately begin discussing Drugco's liability to Pat or Driver to show off their knowledge of products liability! You can avoid this pitfall by following the problem solving steps and reading the question carefully.

Now that you have outlined your entire answer, it is time to write out your answer. Take the next thirty minutes to do exactly that. Look at the clock, put pen to paper, and return to this text when you are done. Good luck!

How was it? Now that you have completed your first bar exam answer, compare your answer to the Model Answer that follows:

8.   Model Answer

1. Pat v. Transit

The issue is whether Driver was negligent, and if so, whether Transit is vicariously liable for such negligence on a respondeat-superior theory.

Negligence is defined as the breach of a duty of due care which is the actual and proximate cause of P's injuries.

The first issue is whether Driver owed a duty to Pat. Under the Cardozo majority view, a duty is owed only to a foreseeable plaintiff or a plaintiff in the zone of danger. Pat was a foreseeable P, as Driver should have foreseen injury to a passenger on his bus due to his inability to drive the bus safely. Pat was also in the zone of danger, as she was a passenger in the bus driven by Driver. Under the Andrews minority rule, which holds that a duty is owed to all, Pat was owed a duty of due care. Finally, under the special duty owed by a common carrier to a passenger, duty will be imposed regardless of foreseeability.

The second issue is what standard of care applies. A defendant owes a duty to act as a reasonable person would have acted in the same or similar circumstances. A driver of a public transportation vehicle owes his or her passengers a duty to employ reasonable care in driving the vehicle to insure that no injury or damage occurs to the passenger, and to drive the vehicle in a safe and prudent fashion.

The third issue is whether Driver breached that standard of care. Driver was aware that he was ill, and a reasonable person should know that illness may affect a person's ability to drive safely. Driver also consumed a cold antihistamine, and again, a reasonable person should know that cold medicines may make one drowsy and unable to operate a vehicle safely. Furthermore, prior to the accident, Driver felt drowsy. At this point, he should have known that his ability to drive was impaired and that his passengers might be in danger. Hence, driver breached the applicable standard of care.

The fourth issue is that of causation. Driver's act was the cause-in-fact of Pat's injuries. But for Driver falling asleep at the wheel, Pat would not have been injured. Driver's act was also the proximate cause of Pat's injuries, as no intervening causes existed between Driver's act of falling asleep and the accident which caused Pat's injuries. Thus, both elements are met.

The final issue is that of damages. In a negligence action, plaintiff must suffer actual injuries. Here, this element is met as Pat was in fact injured.

There is no indication that the defenses of contributory or comparative negligence would bar Pat's recovery, or that she knowingly assumed the risk of Driver's negligence. Therefore, Driver would be liable to Pat on a negligence theory.

Transit's liability, once again, depends on whether Driver was acting within the scope of his employment. Driver was employed as a bus driver, and was working in the course of his employment at the time the tort was committed. Therefore, Transit is vicariously liable to Pat for Driver's negligence.

2. Pat v. Dr. Ard

The issue is whether Dr. Ard is liable to Pat for negligence, as defined in section one, <u>supra</u>.

The first issue is that of duty. Pat was a foreseeable P, because Dr. Ard was told by Driver that he was scheduled to work that day, and the Doctor should have foreseen that failing to advise a patient as to potentially dangerous side effects might result in a patient injuring another. Under the minority Andrews rule, Dr. Ard owed a duty to all persons, including Pat.

The second issue is the standard of care. Dr. Ard, as a health care professional with special training and knowledge, would be held to the same standard of care that a reasonably prudent practitioner would exercise. While a reasonable medical practitioner might instruct a patient over the phone to take cold medication to combat a common cold, a reasonable medical doctor would not fail to inform the patient as to possible side effects of the drug. Here, there was a 20% probability that Driver might be affected by drowsiness and sleep, and a reasonable practitioner would have advised Driver of the same. Thus, the third issue would be resolved against Dr. Ard, as he breached the applicable standard of care.

The fourth issue is that of causation. Dr. Ard's conduct was a cause-in-fact of Pat's injuries, because "but for" Dr. Ard's failure to advise Driver of the side effects of Pyrib, Pat would not have been injured. If advised properly, Driver would not have reported to work or alternatively, would not have taken the Pyrib before going to work. Dr. Ard may argue successfully that his conduct was not the legal or proximate cause, if he could prove that the accident was not caused by the side effects of Pyrib, and that something else was responsible for causing Driver to fall asleep. However, because no other intervening causes are cited, and because it was foreseeable that Driver would fall asleep after taking Pyrib, Dr. Ard will not prevail, and his conduct will be held to be the legal proximate cause of Pat's injuries.

Finally, as noted above, Pat suffered actual damage and therefore this requirement is met.

There is no indication that Pat was contributorily negligent or that she assumed the risk of Dr. Ard's negligence. Therefore, no defenses would bar Pat's cause of action.

As you read this answer, keep in mind that this is only one possible solution to this problem. However, while your answer might vary in presentation, the issues that you covered and the application of the facts to those issues should be identical to the Model Answer. But how do you really know whether your answer is "on the right track"? Simple. Use the *Exam Evaluator* that follows each Model Answer in this book.

9.   How to Use the Exam Evaluator

"Being entirely honest with oneself is a good exercise."

---- Sigmund Freud (1856-1939)

The *Exam Evaluator* incorporates the components of a winning exam answer by converting each issue into a numerical score, adding up to a perfect score of 100. In addition to your discussion of issues, other less tangible factors, such as neatness, organization, and "lawyer-like" writing style, are also rated. These latter factors account for 25% of the total score. While these grading criteria are designed to simulate the actual factors considered by most bar graders, these factors have been reviewed and approved by past bar graders to insure the accuracy of the evaluation process used.

While the *Exam Evaluator* is self-explanatory, it may be helpful to review each component briefly. Please refer to the next page for the *Exam Evaluator*.

The Exam Evaluator
PAT v. DRIVER, TRANSIT & DR. ARD

EXAM PRESENTATION (TOTAL POINTS AVAILABLE = 25)

	Poor										Excellent	
NEATNESS	0	1	2	3	4	5						____
ORGANIZATION	0	1	2	3	4	5	6	7	8	9	10	____
LAWYER-LIKE	0	1	2	3	4	5	6	7	8	9	10	____

DISCUSSION OF ISSUES (TOTAL POINTS AVAILABLE =75)

DRIVER'S NEGLIGENCE

30 POINTS = FULL DISCUSSION ____

15 POINTS = PARTIAL/INCOMPLETE DISCUSSION ____

TRANSIT'S LIABILITY: VICARIOUS LIABILITY

15 POINTS = FULL DISCUSSION ____

10 POINTS = PARTIAL/INCOMPLETE DISCUSSION ____

DR. ARD'S NEGLIGENCE

30 POINTS = FULL DISCUSSION ____

15 POINTS = PARTIAL/INCOMPLETE DISCUSSION ____

TOTAL SCORE . . . . ____

After reading through the *Exam Evaluator*, go through your answer and evaluate each of the following factors:

Neatness (Five points): A good paper means a legible paper, and bar graders will penalize you if your paper is unreadable. If you are not the best judge of your own handwriting, obtain another's objective opinion of how legible your writing appears. Ask that person to rate the neatness of your handwriting between 1-5 and insert that score on your *Exam Evaluator*.

Organization (Ten points): Your organization score depends on two things: whether your analyses of the various issues are structured in an organized fashion, and whether the individual sentences and paragraphs that comprise your analysis reflect a logical organization. If you organized each issue in the identical fashion as shown in the Model Answer, you have already earned five points. If each paragraph is well organized, then award yourself an additional five points.

Lawyer-like writing style (Ten points): A lawyer must write in a clear, concise, and grammatically correct fashion. Your sentences should clearly and concisely communicate the information which you seek to express. How do you know if you have accomplished this task? The best test is to read your answer aloud and ask yourself the following questions: Does each sentence really say what I intended it to say? Is each thought completed before I begin discussing the next idea or issue? Will the bar grader fully understand what it is I am trying to convey? Are my spelling, punctuation, and grammar correct? If you succeeded in each respect, award yourself ten points.

Discussion of the issues (Seventy-five points): In evaluating your discussion of each issue, look to the quality of your discussion and not merely the quantity. In other words, do not award yourself a score based solely on the number of words written. Look instead to whether your discussion of the issue is comprehensive and complete. Ask yourself the following questions: Did I discuss the same facts as in the Model Answers and make the same points? Did I correctly identify the issues and raise each possible argument? Did I miss any major or minor issues?

After you have completed each section of the *Exam Evaluator* and scored the

106

issues, add up all the points. If you received a passing grade, pat yourself on the back and go on to the next exercise. On the other hand, if your score is not passing, take the examination again. After you have completed the exercise, enter your best score on the *Master Exam Evaluator* that is included in the Appendix in the back of this book. By using the *Master Exam Evaluator*, you will be able to see how your exam writing skills improve as you go through the materials in this book.

Just a final note before moving on to the next problem. Be honest in your evaluation. An inflated exam score may inflate your ego, but will not motivate you to improve your exam writing ability.

If, after filling out your *Exam Evaluator*, you find that you have scored poorly, do not look for a bridge to jump off. Remember that you can always take the same examination again and improve your exam score by making the necessary changes in your exam strategy.

I recommend that if you do not receive a passing grade of 75 or higher, you should repeat each examination exercise until you do. Just like building a house, you must build a strong foundation, and the best way to accomplish this is to write, rewrite, and re-rewrite, if necessary, your exam answer until you obtain a passing exam score.

Repeating the same problem again and again may not be the most exciting exercise, but it will focus your efforts on the PROCESS involved in problem solving without having to become accustomed to new and different fact patterns. It will also force you to constantly critique and re-evaluate your work product.

So if your exam score does not exceed your expectations, then stop right here and take the Pat v. Driver, Transit & Dr. Ard problem again until you have written an examination that fulfills your exam writing goals.

Now that you have completed this problem, pat yourself on the back and prepare for the next challenge!

E.   PROBLEM TWO: PROF & PRIM v. SMITH, ELCO & UNIVERSITY

1.   The First and Second Read

READ THROUGH THE FACT PATTERN ONCE FOR CONTENT, AND
THEN READ THE FACT PATTERN A SECOND TIME, FOCUSING ON
IMPORTANT PARTIES, NAMES, PHRASES AND FACTS

The four-story law school building of University, a private institution open to the public, had a defective elevator which frequently stopped between floors. The elevator had an alarm button which, if pressed, would ring a bell in the hallway and thus alert persons in the building to the fact that the elevator had stopped between floors with passengers inside it. The defective condition did not create any danger that the elevator might fall or otherwise physically injure any passenger.

Elco, an elevator maintenance company, had a contract with University to inspect, service, and maintain the elevator.

One night, Prof, a law teacher, and his secretary, Prim, had been working late in Prof's office on the fourth floor of the building on an overdue manuscript. They entered the elevator to leave at about 11:20 p.m. The official closing hour for the building was 11:00 p.m., but there were exit doors from the building which could be opened from the inside. Both Prof and Prim knew that the elevator frequently stopped between floors.

The elevator stopped between the second and third floors. Prof pressed the alarm button and the bell could be heard ringing in the hallway. Smith, a law student, was the only other person still in the building. He heard the alarm bell and realized that someone was trapped in the elevator. He thought this was very funny and he deliberately did not call the campus maintenance staff.

Prof and Prim were not discovered and released until 8:00 a.m. the next day.

Prof suffered from high blood pressure. This condition and his fright at being confined in the elevator caused him to sustain a heart attack after two hours in the elevator.

Prim suffered severe emotional distress due to being confined in the elevator and her fear that Prof was dying. She was subsequently embarrassed and humiliated by remarks of students who suggested that perhaps some amorous activity in the elevator might have caused Prof's heart attack.

What rights do Prof and Prim each have against:

(a) Smith?
(b) Elco?
(c) University?

2. Headlining/Visualization Exercise

The first thing you may have noticed in comparing this problem with the two previous tort fact patterns is that this fact pattern contains more facts. However, in using the headlining technique, you will see that "more" does not mean more difficult, because this problem can be summed up in three headlines:

HEADLINE:

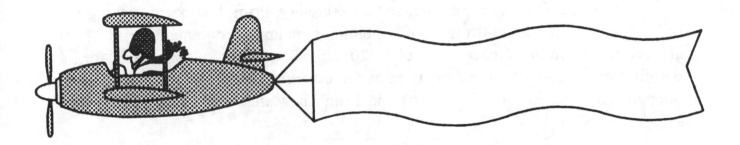

The four-story law school building of University, a private institution open to the public, had a defective elevator which frequently stopped between floors. The elevator had an alarm button which, if pressed, would ring a bell in the hallway and thus alert persons in the building to the fact that the elevator had stopped between floors with passengers inside it. The defective condition did not create any danger that the elevator might fall or otherwise physically injure any passenger.

Elco, an elevator maintenance company, had a contract with University to inspect, service, and maintain the elevator.

HEADLINE:

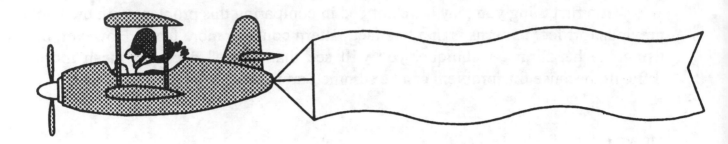

One night, Prof, a law teacher, and his secretary, Prim, had been working late in Prof's office on the fourth floor of the building on an overdue manuscript. They entered the elevator to leave at about 11:20 p.m. The official closing hour for the building was 11:00 p.m., but there were exit doors from the building which could be opened from the inside. Both Prof and Prim knew that the elevator frequently stopped between floors.

The elevator stopped between the second and third floors. Prof pressed the alarm button and the bell could be heard ringing in the hallway. Smith, a law student, was the only other person still in the building. He heard the alarm bell and realized that someone was trapped in the elevator. He thought this was very funny and he deliberately did not call the campus maintenance staff.

HEADLINE:

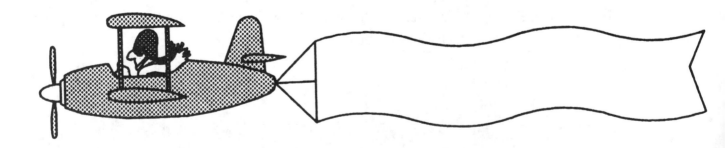

Prof and Prim were not discovered and released until 8:00 a.m. the next day.

Prof suffered from high blood pressure. This condition and his fright at being confined in the elevator caused him to sustain a heart attack after two hours in the elevator.

Prim suffered severe emotional distress due to being confined in the elevator and her fear that Prof was dying. She was subsequently embarrassed and humiliated by remarks of students who suggested that perhaps some amorous activity in the elevator might have caused Prof's heart attack.

★ ★ ★

Now look at three model "headlines":

1. UNIVERSITY CONTRACTS WITH ELCO TO INSPECT, SERVICE AND MAINTAIN ELEVATOR, WHICH IS DEFECTIVE AND STOPS BETWEEN FLOORS!

2. PROF AND SECRETARY PRIM TRAPPED IN ELEVATOR TWENTY MINUTES AFTER BUILDING CLOSED, IGNORED BY LAW STUDENT SMITH WHO DELIBERATELY DID NOT CALL CAMPUS STAFF!

3. PROF SUFFERS HEART ATTACK AND PRIM SUFFERS EMOTIONAL DISTRESS WHILE TRAPPED IN ELEVATOR; PRIM EMBARRASSED BY ALLEGATIONS OF AMOROUS DALLIANCE WITH PROF!

Armed with our headlines, we are now ready to VISUALIZE the fact pattern. Turn back to the previous page and SEE the fact pattern in your mind's eye!

3.   Outlining and Exam Writing Exercise

Now that you have mastered the facts, outline your answer to this problem. Please take the time to write out an outline.

AFTER YOU HAVE COMPLETED YOUR OUTLINE, WRITE OUT YOUR ANSWER. DO NOT TURN THE PAGE UNTIL AFTER YOU HAVE WRITTEN OUT YOUR ANSWER TO THIS PROBLEM.

Before looking at your answer, let's review your outline to this problem.

As we did with the previous problem, first examine the interrogatories to determine <u>how</u> to structure your answer:

What rights do Prof and Prim each have against:

(a) Smith?
(b) Elco?
(c) University?

What is the dilemma that faces you? How should this problem be organized? Should you begin by analyzing Prof's rights against each party or Prim's rights against each party? Think again. Look at how the Bar Examiners have phrased the problem. Why is it that they have stated the interrogatory in this fashion?

The reason is that the Examiners want you to adopt this structure:

<u>**Prof and Prim v. Smith**</u>

<u>**Prof and Prim v. Elco**</u>

<u>**Prof and Prim v. University**</u>

Thus, in solving this problem, the first thing you must determine is that Prof and Prim each have the same causes of actions against Smith, Elco, and University. There is no need to analyze Prof and Prim's rights individually from one another. Had you analyzed the problem as follows, you can see the time problems you would have encountered:

<u>Prof v. Smith</u>

<u>Prof v. Elco</u>

<u>Prof v. University</u>

<u>Prim v. Smith</u>

Prim v. Elco

Prim v. University

Believe it or not, some people who wrote this bar question did exactly this. "Why?" you might wonder. Because they did not take the time to organize the problem before solving it. That is why outlining is a must.

Now we apply our torts writing approach to this problem:

Prof and Prim v. Smith

    NEGLIGENCE?

    FALSE IMPRISONMENT?

Prof and Prim v. Elco

    NEGLIGENCE?

    PRIMA FACIE CASE?

        DUTY
        STANDARD OF CARE
        BREACH OF STANDARD OF CARE
        CAUSATION (actual and proximate cause)
        DAMAGES

    DEFENSES?

        CONTRIBUTORY/COMPARATIVE NEGLIGENCE?
        ASSUMPTION OF THE RISK?

Prof and Prim v. University

    GENERAL CONSIDERATIONS?

        VICARIOUS LIABILITY: Independent Contractor Rule

4.   Meet the "Sucker Punch" Question

Now that we have completed a skeletal outline of the answer, take a look at your outline and exam answer. Did the Examiners get you? If you completed a full negligence and/or false imprisonment analysis in Prof and Prim v. Smith, you have been victimized by the infamous "Sucker Punch" bar exam question.

A "Sucker Punch" question lures you in by giving you a non-issue that really looks like a major issue. Here, Smith is not liable to Prof or Prim for negligence because he has no duty to act. Wait, you are thinking, there's something wrong here. We cannot just let law student Smith off the hook! Why, Smith heard the alarm bell and knew Prof and Prim were in the elevator and deliberately did not call the campus maintenance staff! He must be liable!

Nope. Smith is not liable because there is no duty to act. Period.

But what about false imprisonment, you might ask? By deliberately not notifying the authorities, he acted uncouthly and in an uncivilized fashion, and that must be false imprisonment or intentional infliction of emotional distress or something!?!?

Nope. Smith is not liable for false imprisonment or any other intentional tort because he did not commit any affirmative act or omission which resulted in Prof and Prim's imprisonment. Smith was not responsible and did not cause Prof and Prim's predicament.

Why then, you might ask, did the Bar Examiners include this interrogatory? Because they wanted to know whether you could point out this fact. Remember that the Bar Examiners are not only testing your knowledge of the law, but also your ability to judge when a particular law applies and when it does not.

Not surprisingly, students who spent four or five pages discussing "negligence" or "false imprisonment" to answer the first interrogatory ran out of time. By falling for the "Sucker Punch" they were unable to complete the second and third interrogatories. A word to the wise: Duck the "Sucker Punch."

Now, plug in the facts and complete the outlining process:

Prof and Prim v. Smith

NEGLIGENCE? No duty to act!

FALSE IMPRISONMENT? No act or omission!

Prof and Prim v. Elco

NEGLIGENCE?

PRIMA FACIE CASE?

DUTY - MAJ: Prof and Prim foreseeable Ps? MIN: Duty to all!
STANDARD OF CARE - Duty to inspect, service and maintain.
BREACH OF STANDARD OF CARE - I don't know!!!!!
CAUSATION (actual and proximate cause) - I don't know!!!!!!
DAMAGES - Prof: heart attack; Prim: emotional distress.

DEFENSES?

CONTRIBUTORY/COMPARATIVE NEGLIGENCE? - Prof and
Prim knew of defect.
ASSUMPTION OF THE RISK - Voluntarily assumed risk?

Prof and Prim v. University

GENERAL CONSIDERATIONS?

VICARIOUS LIABILITY: Independent Contractor Rule
        Public policy reasons, i.e., safety, preclude delegation

5. Model Answer

Once again, compare your outline to the model outline, and then take a look at the Model Answer:

1. Prof and Prim v. Smith

False Imprisonment

(STATE THE ISSUE) *The issue is whether Prof and Prim may recover for the intentional tort of false imprisonment.* (WHAT'S THE RULE?) *False imprisonment is defined as an affirmative act or omission with the intent to confine another which results in either actual confinement or awareness thereof.* (APPLY THE RULE) *Here, there are two problems. While Smith's failure to act may have been morally reprehensible, he did not to cause Prof and Prim's confinement. No act or omission on his part created their predicament. Furthermore, Smith, as a law student, was not legally obligated to assist Prof or Prim and did not agree to do so.* (STATE THE CONCLUSION) *Thus, he cannot be held liable for false imprisonment.*

Negligence

(ISSUE) *The issue is whether Prof and Prim may recover for negligence against Smith.* (RULE) *There is no duty to aid others, unless the defendant caused plaintiff's peril. However, if a person undertakes to help another, he must use reasonable care.* (APPLY THE RULE) *Smith was not responsible for Prof and Prim's predicament, as he did not cause the elevator to malfunction. Thus, he had no obligation to notify the maintenance staff.* (CONCLUSION) *Because Smith had no duty to act, he is not liable.*

2. Prof and Prim v. Elco

Negligence

(STATE THE ISSUE) *The issue is whether Prof and Prim may recover on a negligence theory against Elco.* (RULE) *Negligence is defined as a breach of duty of due care which is the actual and proximate cause of plaintiff's injuries.*

(TAKE EACH ELEMENT ONE AT A TIME) (ISSUE) *The first element of negligence is duty.* (WHAT'S THE RULE?) *Under the majority <u>Cardoza</u> view, a duty is owed only to a foreseeable plaintiff.* (NOW APPLY IT!) *Here, both Prof and Prim are foreseeable plaintiffs, because it is foreseeable that campus personnel, including a law teacher and his secretary, would use the elevator and might be injured by a mechanical malfunction.* (DON NOT FORGET THE MINORITY VIEW) *Under the minority <u>Andrews</u> rule, a duty is owed to all members of society.* (ALWAYS CONCLUDE ONE WAY OR THE OTHER!) *Thus, under either view, the duty element is met.*

(ISSUE) *The second element of negligence is standard of care.* (RULE OF LAW!) *A defendant has a duty to act as a reasonable person would have acted in the same or similar circumstances.* (APPLY THE RULE BY ANSWERING THE ISSUE: HOW WOULD A REASONABLE PERSON ACT IN THE SHOES OF THE ELEVATOR COMPANY?) *An elevator company that contracts to inspect, service and maintain the elevator would perform these tasks as often as necessary, and would exercise due care in doing so. A competent elevator company would also immediately repair an elevator that was malfunctioning.*

(ISSUE) *The third issue is whether Elco breached this standard of care.* (RULE) *A defendant breaches the standard of care by acting in a manner which exposes others to an unreasonable risk of harm.* (APPLY THE RULE) *The terms of Elco's responsibilities under the contract are unclear. It is unknown whether Elco had begun to perform its contractual obligations, since Elco "had a contract with University." There is no indication that Elco actually inspected the elevator. If Elco had inspected the elevator and determined it to be safe when in fact it was not, then a breach would lie. On the other hand, if Elco's contractual obligations had not yet begun, or if Elco did inspect the elevator and the defective condition could not have been reasonably discovered upon a careful inspection, Elco would not be liable.* (CONCLUSION) *However, there are insufficient facts to resolve this issue.*

(ISSUE AND RULE) *The fourth issue is actual and proximate cause.* (APPLICATION) *Here it is unknown whether Elco's action or inaction was the cause-in-fact or proximate cause of the malfunction of the elevator. Again, if Elco could have determined that the elevator was defective upon reasonable inspection, and Elco did in fact inspect the elevator, then its malfeasance was both the actual and legal cause of the plaintiff's injuries, since the failure to discover the defect was an essential link in the chain of causation. If, on the other hand, Elco's duty to inspect had not yet matured, or if Elco conducted a reasonable inspection that could not have revealed the defect,* (CONCLUSION) *its conduct would not have caused the plaintiff's injuries.*

(ISSUE AND RULE) *The final issue is damages.* (APPLICATION AND CONCLUSION) *This element is met because Prof suffered a heart attack and Prim suffered emotional distress.*

(OVERALL CONCLUSION) *Based on the foregoing, if Elco was obligated to inspect or did inspect the elevator but failed to exercise due care, it would be liable to Prof and Prim on a negligence theory.*

Defenses to Negligence

(ISSUE) *The defense of contributory negligence could be raised by the defendant.* (RULE) *Contributory negligence is defined as conduct by the plaintiff that is a contributing cause to his or her injuries and that falls below the standard of care to which he is required to conform for his own protection. If met, this defense effectively bars plaintiff's recovery.* (APPLICATION) *Here, both Prof and Prim knew that the elevator frequently stopped between floors, and also presumably knew that the official closing time of the building was 11:00 PM Hence, they should have known that by getting into the defective elevator after hours that there was a risk of being trapped inside without assistance.* (CONCLUSION) *Under this doctrine, both Prof and Prim's recovery would be completely barred.*

(ISSUE AND RULE) *However, in the majority of states, the comparative negligence doctrine would be applied, requiring the court or jury to fix a certain percentage that reflects the degree of contributory negligence.* (APPLICATION) *Under a comparative negligence theory, Prof and Prim would be assessed that percentage of negligence to which their conduct contributed to their injury.* (CONCLUSION) *Therefore, the defense of contributory negligence does not bar plaintiff's recovery.*

Prof and Prim v. University

(ISSUE) *The final issue is whether University is liable for the action or inaction of Elco regarding the malfunctioning elevator.* (RULE) *In general, under the doctrine of respondeat-superior, an employer is liable for the tortious acts committed by an employee if the tortious acts occur within the scope of employment.*

(APPLICATION) *Here, the exact nature of the relationship between Elco and University is unclear. However, since Elco had a "contract" with University to inspect, service, and maintain the elevator, and Elco is in the business of elevator maintenance, Elco would be held to be an independent contractor. A principal is not liable for the tortious acts of its agent if the latter is an independent contractor. However, an exception exists when the duty is non-delegable due to public policy considerations. Here, overriding safety concerns would probably bring this case into the exception, since the University's duty to insure that the elevators are safe is non-delegable, given the extreme danger to which the public might be exposed if the duty were held to be delegable.*

(CONCLUSION) *Thus, University would be held liable despite its contract with Elco.*

(BROWNIE POINT) *A second theory of liability may be premised on negligent hiring of an independent contractor. An employer may be held liable for his or her negligence in selecting an independent contractor. However, there are no facts here indicating that University was negligent in hiring Elco. Thus, this cause of action would fail without further facts indicating that University was negligent in hiring Elco.*

This problem demonstrates that the Bar Examiners do not always test you on your ability to state a result or reach a conclusion. It is impossible to reach a conclusion to the second answer, because the Examiners do not give you enough facts to determine whether Elco breached its duty to Prof and Prim and whether the causation element was met. Instead, you need to state that there is a lack of acts to resolve these issues. The Examiners are testing to see whether or not you can recognize that there is a lack of facts necessary to solve the issue presented.

121

The Exam Evaluator
PROF & PRIM v. SMITH, ELCO & UNIVERSITY

EXAM PRESENTATION (TOTAL POINTS AVAILABLE = 25)

	Poor		Excellent	
NEATNESS	0 1 2 3 4 5			____
ORGANIZATION	0 1 2 3 4 5 6 7 8 9 10			____
LAWYER-LIKE	0 1 2 3 4 5 6 7 8 9 10			____

DISCUSSION OF ISSUES (TOTAL POINTS AVAILABLE =75)

SMITH'S LIABILITY: NEGLIGENCE

20 POINTS = FULL DISCUSSION ____

10 POINTS = PARTIAL/INCOMPLETE DISCUSSION ____

ELCO'S LIABILITY: NEGLIGENCE

30 POINTS = FULL DISCUSSION ____

15 POINTS = PARTIAL/INCOMPLETE DISCUSSION ____

UNIVERSITY'S LIABILITY: NEGLIGENCE

25 POINTS = FULL DISCUSSION ____

15 POINTS = PARTIAL/INCOMPLETE DISCUSSION ____

TOTAL SCORE . . . . ____

F.   PROBLEM THREE: CARRIE, OWNER, PLUMMER, AMY AND EMMA

1.   The First and Second Read

READ THE FACT PATTERN ONCE FOR CONTENT, AND THEN READ IT AGAIN, FOCUSING ON IMPORTANT PARTIES, NAMES, PHRASES AND FACTS. THEN PERFORM MENTAL "HEADLINING" OF THE FACTS AND VISUALIZE THE FACT PATTERN.

Owner hired Plummer, a plumbing contractor, to repair the plumbing in a store that Owner planned to lease. In performing the repair, Plummer used a connector on a hot water pipe made of a different metal than the pipe itself. As a result of the incompatibility of the two metals, the connector corroded and weakened. This condition was not obvious because the weakened connection was located within a wall. After the repair was completed, the store was leased to Amy, a swimwear retailer.

Two years after Plummer finished the repairs, the connector burst. Hot water broke through the wall and sprayed into the store, scalding Carrie, a customer who was in the store at the time. The water also ruined swimsuits on display in the store. While repairs were being made, Amy had to close her store for two months during the summer, causing significant financial loss. Emma, an employee of Amy's, lost her job because of the closure.

1.   What rights, if any, does Carrie have against Owner and against Plummer? Discuss.

2.   What rights, if any, does Amy have against Plummer? Discuss.

3.   What rights, if any, does Emma have against Owner and against Plummer? Discuss.

2.   Fact Retention Exercise

NOW THAT YOU HAVE READ AND VISUALIZED THE
PROBLEM, ARE YOU READY TO SOLVE THE PROBLEM???
LET'S TEST YOUR KNOWLEDGE OF THE FACTS BEFORE
OUTLINING YOUR ANSWER:

WHO IS PLUMMER AND WHAT DID PLUMMER DO?

WHO IS EMMA?

WHO IS OWNER?

WHO IS CARRIE?

WHAT HAPPENED TO EMMA?

WHEN DID THE CONNECTOR BURST?

WHY DID THE CONNECTOR BURST?

WHAT DAMAGE WAS CAUSED BY THE BURSTING OF THE CONNECTOR?

If you are unable to answer ANY of these questions, please go back and read the question again. Remember that a strong grasp of the facts is a prerequisite to solving the problem.

3.   Outlining and Exam Writing Exercise

NOW APPLY THE THIRD STEP OF THE *SIX STEPS OF EXAM TAKING* BY DETERMINING WHAT QUESTIONS ARE PRESENTED. OUTLINE YOUR ANSWER HERE:

4.   Meet the "Daily Double" Question

Problem Three introduces you to an exam question which I refer to as "the Daily Double." As in the game show "Jeopardy," the Daily Double exam question gives you double the credit for your answer.

Again, begin by structuring your answer according to the format set forth in the interrogatories:

CARRIE v. OWNER AND PLUMMER

AMY v. PLUMMER

EMMA v. OWNER AND PLUMMER

In solving the first issue, you must first determine whether separate discussions of Carrie v. Owner and Carrie v. Plummer are required, or whether, as in the previous example involving Prof and Prim, they may be discussed jointly. In this example, a separate discussion is called for because Owner and Plummer are not similarly situated and each may raise different and inconsistent arguments:

Carrie v. Owner

NEGLIGENCE?

PRIMA FACIE CASE?

DUTY - Was Carrie, a customer, a foreseeable P?
STANDARD OF CARE - What duty was owed by Owner to Carrie?
BREACH OF STANDARD OF CARE - Did Owner act reasonably in warning Carrie and/or hiring Plummer?
CAUSATION (actual and proximate cause) - no issue here
DAMAGES - burn injuries sufficient

DEFENSES?

> **CONTRIBUTORY/COMPARATIVE NEGLIGENCE** - No evidence
> **ASSUMPTION OF THE RISK** - No evidence

Carrie v. Plummer

NEGLIGENCE

PRIMA FACIE CASE?

> **DUTY** - Was Carrie a foreseeable P?
> **STANDARD OF CARE** - How would a reasonable plumber act?
> **BREACH OF STANDARD OF CARE** - Did Plummer act reasonably?
> **CAUSATION (actual and proximate cause)** - no issue here
> **DAMAGES** - burn injuries sufficient

DEFENSES?

> **CONTRIBUTORY/COMPARATIVE NEGLIGENCE** - No evidence
> **ASSUMPTION OF THE RISK** - No evidence

You should rule out any liability premised on intentional torts, since Plummer did not act to injure anyone intentionally. Plummer's negligence action is the issue presented under these facts. While at first glance it might appear that you could argue a products liability action, the facts do not in any way suggest that the connector itself was defective. The connector became "corroded and weakened" only "[a]s a result of the incompatibility of the two metals." Thus, a careful reading of the facts reveals that no issue of products liability exists.

After outlining both of the above causes of action, you may think that there is no way to complete this problem within your time limits. By completing the first interrogatory, you have already solved the second interrogatory.

Here is the outline of the remainder of this problem, applying the Torts writing approach:

Amy v. Plummer

NEGLIGENCE

PRIMA FACIE CASE?

DUTY - Was Amy a foreseeable P?
STANDARD OF CARE - How would a reasonable plumber act?
BREACH OF STANDARD OF CARE - Did Plummer act reasonably?
CAUSATION (actual and proximate cause) - no issue here
DAMAGES - burn injuries sufficient

DEFENSES?

CONTRIBUTORY/COMPARATIVE NEGLIGENCE - No evidence
ASSUMPTION OF THE RISK - No evidence

Now, after outlining Amy v. Plummer, you should immediately recognize that you have hit "the Daily Double." When you compare the outline of this interrogatory to your outline of Carrie v. Plummer, you find that both discussions are nearly identical. Thus, in writing out your answer, you may incorporate much of your previous discussion of Carrie v. Plummer into your answer to the second interrogatory.

You may ask yourself why the Examiners did not ask for a discussion of Plummer's liability to Carrie and Amy? The Bar Examiners are smart. They know that many examinees will fail to see that the discussion required for the second interrogatory is a virtual repeat of what has already been discussed and that examinees who rewrite the same analysis twice will run out of time.

By outlining the answer, you see where the Examiners are going before you get there. This is an example of why you should outline before writing. As emphasized in the *Ten Strategies of Successful Exam Writing*, "Know What You Are Going to Write **Before** Writing it."

Now look at the final interrogatory, the one that many examinees never reach because of poor organization:

Emma v. Owner and Plummer

NEGLIGENCE

PRIMA FACIE CASE?
NO INJURY! - purely economic damages not recoverable

As you can see, this teeny-weeny discussion, which I call the "shortcake" answer, requires very little analysis. Thus, once you have solved the first interrogatory, most of your answer is already written. The Bar Examiners have calculated the time available and determined that they can not give you an interrogatory that requires more than a few minutes discussion. The moral of the "shortcake" answer is: do not judge a book by its cover, or an exam by its appearance. While the three interrogatories appear intimidating at first glance, upon closer review, you see that the majority of your answer falls within the first interrogatory, and that the second and third interrogatories raise extremely simple problems.

5.   Model Answer

Let us review the Model Answer together:

Model Answer: Carrie, Plummer, Owner, Amy, and Emma

1A. Carrie v. Owner

The issue is whether Owner was negligent in failing to warn Carrie, a customer of Amy's, of the dangerous condition of the pipes. Negligence is defined as the breach of a duty of due care which is the actual and proximate cause of P's injuries.

The first issue is whether Owner owed a duty to Carrie. The general rule is that the lessee assumes the burden of maintaining the property to avoid injury to others. However, an exception is recognized where the lessor leases the premises knowing that the lessee intends to admit the public. Under such circumstances, the lessor is liable for unreasonably dangerous conditions existing at the time he transfers possession if he knows or should have known about such a condition.

Owner had no reason to know of the dangerous condition of the piping installed by Plummer. The defective piping connector was located inside a wall and was not visible to Owner. Also, Owner did not know that Plummer used a different metal connector, and thus had no reason to believe that a dangerous condition existed. This condition could not have been discovered by a reasonable inspection and was a latent defect in the premises. Therefore, Owner did not breach the special duty owed to third parties.

Even if it is assumed that Owner owed a duty to Carrie, he did not act unreasonably since a reasonable person could not have known of the defective condition.

Thus, Owner cannot be held liable for negligence.

1B. Carrie v. Plummer

The issue is whether Plummer is liable for negligence.

The first issue is whether Plummer owed a duty to Carrie. Under the Cardozo majority rule, a duty is owed only to a foreseeable plaintiff or a plaintiff in the zone of danger. Here Carrie was a foreseeable P, since Plummer knew that a store customer could be injured by faulty plumbing. Carrie was also in the zone of danger created by Plummer's act, since she was in the store when the pipes burst. Under the Andrews minority view, which holds that a duty is owed to all, Carrie was owed a duty as a member of the public.

The second issue is what standard of care applies. A defendant owes a duty to act as a reasonable person would have acted in the same or similar circumstances. A plumber owes a duty to employ reasonable care in repairing plumbing to avoid injury to others. Here, it must be assumed that a plumber would know that using two incompatible metals would result in a corroded and weakened connector, and that a connector in such condition would pose a substantial threat to others. Unless Plummer could show that a reasonable plumber would not know that incompatible metals caused such a reaction, he will be held to have breached the standard of care.

But for Plummer's act of using the incompatible metals to repair the plumbing, the connector would not have burst and Carrie would not have been injured. Plummer's act is therefore the actual cause of Carrie's injuries. Plummer's act also proximately caused Carrie's injury, since the use of the incorrect piping directly caused the pipe to burst, which in turn caused Carrie's injuries. No intervening causes occurred between Plummer's act and Carrie's injuries.

Carrie suffered damages as she was scalded by the hot water which came from the broken pipes and therefore this element is met.

Based on the foregoing, Plummer is liable to Carrie for negligence.

Because Carrie was not contributorily negligent and did not assume the risk of such harm, no defenses bar her action.

2. Amy v. Plummer

Amy's rights are identical to Carrie's rights.

Amy is owed a duty as a lessee of the premises that contained the plumbing. Plummer should have foreseen that faulty plumbing would cause property damage to a lessee of the premises.

The standard of care, breach and causation issues are identical to the discussion that appears in *Carrie v. Plummer*.

On the issue of damages, Amy suffered property damage to the swimsuits displayed in the store and thus sustained actual damages.

As in *Carrie v. Plummer*, no defenses bar Amy's cause of action against Plummer.

Plummer is therefore liable to Amy for negligence.

3. <u>Emma v. Owner and Plummer</u>

Emma may not recover against either Owner or Plummer for negligence because her loss of a job was not directly related to Plummer's negligent act. While she may not have lost her job had the store premises not been damaged, her claim is too remote and lacks a causal connection to Plummer's failure to fix the pipes properly.

Emma did not suffer actual damage, because unlike Carrie or Amy, she sustained no personal injury or property damage as a result of Plummer's act.

Thus, for either reason stated above, Emma may not recover against Owner or Plummer.

Before moving on to the next problem, take a few moments and study this problem, because it presents a good example of the importance of making good judgment calls. An important quality of a problem solver is knowing when to solve a problem and when not to. In order to complete this problem in an hour's time, you are required to recognize that the second interrogatory essentially calls for a repeat of an earlier performed analysis.

Remember that you need not restate rules. Notice that after the "rules" of negligence are set forth in the discussion of <u>Carrie v. Owner/Plummer</u>, they are not restated in subsequent sections of the same problem. Once you tell the bar grader that you know the rule, you need not repeat that rule ad nauseam. If it makes you feel more secure, then write "<u>See</u> above" or "<u>See</u> supra," so that you are assured that the bar grader will note your prior statement of the rule and your reason for not restating it. You may incorporate earlier discussions of identical issues in the same problem, as was done in <u>Amy v. Plummer</u>.

If you misanalyzed this problem, then repeat the exercise and chalk this up as a learning experience. In the future, beware of the Daily Double!

The Exam Evaluator
CARRIE, OWNER, PLUMMER, AMY AND EMMA

EXAM PRESENTATION (TOTAL POINTS AVAILABLE = 25)

	Poor											Excellent
NEATNESS	0	1	2	3	4	5						____
ORGANIZATION	0	1	2	3	4	5	6	7	8	9	10	____
LAWYER-LIKE	0	1	2	3	4	5	6	7	8	9	10	____

DISCUSSION OF ISSUES (TOTAL POINTS AVAILABLE =75)

CARRIE v. OWNER: NEGLIGENCE

20 POINTS = FULL DISCUSSION ____

10 POINTS = PARTIAL/INCOMPLETE DISCUSSION ____

CARRIE v. PLUMMER: NEGLIGENCE

20 POINTS = FULL DISCUSSION ____

10 POINTS = PARTIAL/INCOMPLETE DISCUSSION ____

AMY v. PLUMMER

20 POINTS = FULL DISCUSSION ____

10 POINTS = PARTIAL/INCOMPLETE DISCUSSION ____

EMMA v. PLUMMER & OWNER

       15 POINTS = FULL DISCUSSION   ____

       10 POINTS = PARTIAL/INCOMPLETE DISCUSSION   ____

TOTAL SCORE   ____

G.   PROBLEM FOUR: ED v. COURIER JOURNAL

1.   The First and Second Read, Headlining and Visualization

READ THE FACT PATTERN ONCE FOR CONTENT, AND THEN READ
IT AGAIN, FOCUSING ON IMPORTANT PARTIES, NAMES, PHRASES
AND FACTS. THEN PERFORM MENTAL "HEADLINING" OF THE
FACTS AND VISUALIZE THE FACT PATTERN.

Twenty years ago, Ed worked in the research department of Dynorad, a private armaments manufacturer doing substantial business with the government. At that time, Ed and his colleagues were testing a newly developed strain of bacteria for use in germ warfare. From tests on animals, they found the agent to be effective, and it has since been incorporated into weapons sold to the government. The strain of bacteria has never been used in combat and has never been tested on humans. However, because of inadequate safety mechanisms at Dynorad's laboratories, Ed was accidentally exposed to the bacteria.

The exposure was very brief and Ed did not suffer immediate harm, but his health has gradually deteriorated. Ed's health recently became so poor that he checked into a hospital. Doctors quickly traced his maladies to the bacteria, but cannot cure him.

Ralph, a reporter for Courier Journal, learned of Ed's condition and entered Ed's hospital room wearing a white coat and stethoscope. Ed, thinking that Ralph was a doctor, disclosed that his mental capacities were impaired, that a lung and kidney were no longer functioning, that he wore a wig because all his hair had fallen out, and that he was now impotent.

The next day Ralph published a story attacking the use of inhumane weapons by the government and the lack of safety precautions used by local arms manufacturers such as Dynorad. The story included Ed's name, an account of his accident twenty years ago, and a description of the symptoms that Ed had disclosed to Ralph. In addition, the story falsely stated that Ed's son, born a year after the accident, was mentally retarded, and that Ed experienced temporary seizures during which he became uncontrollably violent, once even beating his wife and child. Ralph had no reason to think that these false statements were true, and included them because he felt entitled to a certain poetic license as to assertions that cast no personal blame on Ed.

Discuss Ed's rights against Courier Journal.

2.   Outlining and Exam Writing Exercise

After three negligence problems, you are probably ready for a little change. After all, even in exam taking, variety is the spice of life. Even though this fact pattern tests a different area of torts, the same writing approach must be applied to achieve a successful outline. Write your outline and then write out your exam answer. When you have completed your answer, continue to the next page. Good luck!

Congratulations on making it this far in the book! It's important every once in a while to take a breather, smile, laugh, dance, or do whatever you enjoy to release the stress of preparing for the bar exam. By following the strategies and techniques you have learned thus far, you have travelled light years ahead of those who take the bar exam without this information.

Before tackling this problem head-on, take a moment to review what you have learned since Dennis, Frank and Conco:

- READ THE EXAM
    - ✓ THE FIRST AND SECOND READ
    - ✓ USE HEADLINING
- VISUALIZE THE FACTS
- DETERMINE WHAT ISSUES ARE PRESENTED AND OUTLINE YOUR ANSWER
- MAKE A SNAP DECISION ABOUT HOW MUCH TIME TO SPEND ANALYZING EACH ISSUE
- WRITE OUT YOUR ANSWER
- REACH A CONCLUSION, SMILE AND MOVE ON!

We have so far focused on the first three steps. For the remaining problems in this chapter, we will focus on the latter three steps: exam writing application, writing style, and analysis.

In this problem, we will focus particularly on application. But first, let's review the outline to this problem. Applying the writing approach, the following issues are presented:

INTENTIONAL TORTS

PRIMA FACIE CASE?

INTENTIONAL INFLICTION OF EMOTIONAL DISTRESS

DO ANY DEFENSES APPLY?

CONSENT

138

DEFAMATION

PRIMA FACIE CASE?

    DEFAMATORY MATTER
    PUBLISHED TO THIRD PARTY
    SUBJECTIVELY UNDERSTOOD BY THIRD PARTY
    CAUSATION
    DAMAGES

DEFENSES?

    ABSOLUTE DEFENSES
    QUALIFIED DEFENSES
    EFFECT OF RETRACTION

INVASIONS OF PRIVACY

PRIMA FACIE CASE?

    INTRUSION
    MISAPPROPRIATION
    FALSE LIGHT
    PRIVATE FACTS

DEFENSES?

GENERAL CONSIDERATIONS?

    VICARIOUS LIABILITY

These are the issues which should jump out at you. But the question remains as to how to organize these issues. In this problem, you are given only a general interrogatory, and are asked to discuss Ed's rights against Courier Journal. However, in order to discuss Ed's rights against Courier, you must discuss Ed's rights against Ralph, since Ralph committed the tortious acts. Thus, you should discuss the issue of vicarious liability first, similar to the analysis performed in Pat v. Driver and

Transit. Regarding the order in which you should discuss intentional infliction of emotional distress, defamation, and the privacy torts, choose whatever order you wish, since this interrogatory does not specify an order.

Let's plug in the facts to complete our outline:

Ed v. Courier Journal

GENERAL CONSIDERATIONS?

> **VICARIOUS LIABILITY - Courier's liability depends on Ralph's liability under doctrine of respondeat-superior.**

1. INTENTIONAL TORTS

PRIMA FACIE CASE?

> **INTENTIONAL INFLICTION OF EMOTIONAL DISTRESS**
> **Extreme and outrageous act**
> **Intent to cause severe emotional distress/recklessness**
> **Damages**

DO ANY DEFENSES APPLY?

> **CONSENT**
> **Consent vitiated by Ralph's impersonation of doctor?**

2. DEFAMATION

PRIMA FACIE CASE?

> **DEFAMATORY MATTER - subjects Ed to public hatred, contempt, or ridicule?**
> **PUBLISHED TO THIRD PARTY - Courier's readers**
> **SUBJECTIVELY UNDERSTOOD BY THIRD PARTY - Courier's readers**
> **CAUSATION**

DAMAGES - Slander per se?

DEFENSES

ABSOLUTE DEFENSES - Truth? Consent?
QUALIFIED DEFENSES - First amendment? Public interest?
EFFECT OF RETRACTION

3. INVASION OF PRIVACY

PRIMA FACIE CASE?

INTRUSION
Highly offensive/outrageous - symptoms/false statements
Intrusion - prying into Ed's life
Relating to private facts - unknown to public
FALSE LIGHT
Publication of objectionable facts - same as above
Placing P in false light - actions that D did not take
In the public eye - Courier readers
PRIVATE FACTS
Public disclosure of - Courier readers
Objectionable private facts - symptoms/false statements

DEFENSES?

Truth - not a defense
Consent - same as in defamation
First Amendment - In false light cases, malice required if publication is in public interest.

3.   Model Answer and Exam Analysis

As you can see, this problem requires a great deal of discussion. What is the most efficient way to write out your answer?

As I have already suggested, follow I-R-A-C if you have problems in writing a well organized and comprehensive answer:

ISSUE: Whether Courier is liable for Ralph's tortious conduct.
RULE: Under the doctrine of respondeat-superior, an employer is liable for all torts of employee committed within the scope of employment.
APPLICATION: Because Ralph obtained and published the article concerning Ed in his employment as a reporter for Courier, Ralph acted within the scope of his employment.
CONCLUSION: Courier's liability depends on Ralph's liability.

Now transform each of the I-R-A-C components into an essay answer:

The issue is whether Courier is liable for Ralph's tortious conduct. Under the doctrine of respondeat-superior, an employer is liable for all torts of the employee committed within the scope of employment. Because Ralph obtained and published the article concerning Ed in his employment as a reporter for Courier, Ralph acted within the scope of his employment. Thus, Courier's liability depends on Ralph's liability.

Notice that this paragraph contains each of the I-R-A-C components in that order, and thus comprehensively analyzes the issue. Of course, as demonstrated in earlier examples, you can say the same thing in fewer words:

Courier is liable for Ralph's tortious acts under the doctrine of respondeat superior because Ralph made and published the statements concerning Ed within the scope of his employment as a reporter by Courier.

This sentence covers the same information as its lengthier predecessor, except does so with less work. The issue of vicarious liability is not deserving of a lengthy two or three page discussion, because there is really no dispute that Ralph acted in his employment as a reporter when he published the statements about Ed.

Now use I-R-A-C for the first tort of intentional infliction of emotional distress. This issue requires a slightly more detailed discussion because you must determine whether each of the elements of that tort are met:

142

INTENTIONAL INFLICTION OF EMOTIONAL DISTRESS

ISSUE: The issue is whether Ralph is liable for intentional infliction of emotional distress.

RULE: Intentional infliction of emotional distress is an extreme and outrageous act with the intent to cause severe emotional distress resulting in severe emotional distress.

APPLICATION: Ralph's act of impersonating a doctor and thereby fraudulently obtaining private information which he later published qualifies as an extreme and outrageous act, since it goes beyond notions of common decency, and a reasonable person would be outraged by such unethical conduct. Ralph did not intend for Ed to suffer emotional distress and acted instead to sensationalize his story. However, his actions were at least reckless, because he did not consider the effect of his actions on Ed. Ralph's actions, therefore, fulfill the intent requirement. Finally, it is unknown whether Ed actually suffered emotional distress, but given the outrageous nature of the false statements, it is likely Ed suffered extreme embarrassment, humiliation, and distress.

CONCLUSION: Because all the elements are met, Ralph and Courier are liable for intentional infliction of emotional distress.

Each element of intentional infliction of emotional distress is discussed individually. It is critical that your analysis be comprehensive, and explain why each element comprising the cause of action is met.

INTENTIONAL INFLICTION OF EMOTIONAL DISTRESS

The issue is whether Ralph is liable for intentional infliction of emotional distress. Intentional infliction of emotional distress is an extreme and outrageous act with the intent to cause severe emotional distress resulting in severe emotional distress.

Ralph's act of impersonating a doctor and thereby fraudulently obtaining private information qualified as an extreme and outrageous act. It went far beyond notions of common decency, and a reasonable person would be outraged by Ralph's unethical conduct. However, Ralph did not intend for Ed to suffer emotional distress and acted instead to sensationalize his story. The purpose of Ralph's story was to attack the use of inhumane weapons, and the false statements regarding Ed's son, the seizures and beating his family were not necessary to the purpose of the story. Furthermore, Ralph's actions were at least reckless, as he did not consider the effect they would have on Ed. Thus, the intent requirement is met. Finally, it is unknown whether Ed actually suffered emotional distress, but given the outrageous nature of the false statements, it is likely Ed suffered extreme embarrassment, humiliation, and distress.

Because all the elements are met, Ralph and Courier are liable for intentional infliction of emotional distress.

This Model Answer contains 200 words. Now let's shorten it!

Ralph committed the tort of intentional infliction of emotional distress. By fraudulently impersonating a physician and obtaining and publishing private and false information, he committed an extreme and outrageous act that went beyond all common notions of decency. While Ralph could argue that he intended only to sensationalize his story and to expose the use of inhumane weapons, he acted recklessly in publishing false statements unnecessary to the purpose of his story and therefore acted with the requisite intent. Finally, although unstated, it is likely that Ed suffered extreme embarrassment, humiliation and distress because his son, family, and himself were the brunt of the damaging statements.

This answer is not only tighter and more concise, but it does the job in half as many words (105). Can you do it in less?

As the famous author Robert Browning once wrote, in *Andrea del Sarto*, (1855),

"Less is more."

144

DEFAMATION

The issue is whether Ralph is liable to Ed for defamation. Defamation is a defamatory publication to a third person, capable of being understood by third persons in a defamatory sense, causing damage to P's reputation.

First, a statement is defamatory if it exposes P to public hatred, contempt, or ridicule. Here, Ralph's article directly asserted that Ed had beaten his family during violent uncontrollable seizures and that his son was mentally retarded. Anyone depicted as a violent individual and spouse/child beater would be shunned by the community and would be subjected to public hatred. This requirement is met.

Second, the defamatory statement must be published to a third party. Here the statement was published to the Courier's readers and thus this element is met.

Third, the defamatory matter must be subjectively understood by at least one third person to be of and concerning P. Here the article named Ed and thus identified Ed to Courier's readers.

Fourth, the defamatory statement must be the actual and proximate cause of plaintiff's injuries. Here, "but for" Ralph's article, Ed's reputation would not have been impugned. Because no intervening causes occurred between the publication of the article and any resulting distress to Ed, Ralph's conduct is the proximate cause of Ed's injuries.

Last, P must suffer damage. Because the defamatory statement was in writing, general damages are presumed. Further, because Ralph's article stated that Ed engaged in criminal conduct by beating his wife and child, the defamation would qualify as slander per se. Thus, no special damages need be proven.

DEFENSES

Consent

Ralph would assert that because he obtained certain factual information from Ed, Ed consented to the interview and subsequent disclosure of information. However, because Ralph used a subterfuge to obtain Ed's consent by impersonating *a physician, Ed's consent was vitiated and invalid. Therefore, no consent defense lies.*

Truth

Truth is a complete defense to defamation, but because Ed knew the statements were not true, this defense does not lie.

First Amendment

Under the First Amendment qualified privilege, a private person must prove negligence and actual damages. Here, Ed is not a public figure since he was unknown prior to appearing in the Courier article. Because Ralph knew the statements regarding Ed's family were false and had no basis in fact, he was at least negligent in publishing those facts and no First Amendment privilege will lie.

Protection of a Public Interest

Ralph will assert that he acted to protect the public against the use of inhumane weapons by the government and out of safety concerns. He would argue that the symptoms suffered by Ed were due to the lack of safety precautions and that the same fate may befall the public. However, Ralph would have difficulty defending the false statements made regarding Ed's propensity for violence, since these statements were not necessary to protect the public. Therefore, Ralph abused the qualified privilege and it will not be accepted as a defense.

INVASION OF PRIVACY

Ed may also recover for privacy torts: intrusion, false light, and public disclosure of private facts.

INTRUSION

The privacy tort of intrusion requires a highly offensive or outrageous intrusion relating to private facts. A reasonable person would consider Ralph's acts of impersonating a doctor to obtain private, non-public information extremely offensive. Ralph utilized fraud and subterfuge to pry into the details of Ed's life and obtained information relating to Ed's symptoms which was not known to the public and was not of public record. Thus, Ed may recover on this theory.

FALSE LIGHT

The privacy tort of false light requires the publication of objectionable facts placing P in a false light in the public eye. Ralph's publication of Ed's symptoms were objectionable for the same reasons stated above. Ralph placed Ed in a false light because Ralph published false statements about actions that Ed did not take, namely, beating his son and wife. Furthermore, the statements were placed in the public eye when they were published by Courier.

PRIVATE FACTS

The privacy tort of private facts requires the public disclosure of objectionable private facts. The statements here were objectionable for the same reasons stated above. Nor were the statements in the public arena. The article served to disclose such facts to readers of the Courier. Thus, Ed may recover on this theory.

DEFENSES?

Truth

Truth is not a defense to privacy torts.

Consent

The defense of consent would be analyzed in the same manner as in the defamation analysis, above.

First Amendment

In false light cases, malice is required if publication is in the public interest. While Ralph may argue that he wrote the article to protect the public from inhumane weapons, he acted with malice in publishing false statements that had nothing to do with the asserted purpose of the article. This defense would not apply.

147

4.   Time Allocation Strategies

WHEW!?!?!?! A little overwhelming, isn't it? Do you get the sense after reading this Model Answer that this would have been a difficult exam to complete in an hour's time? Do you question anyone's ability to prepare a comprehensive answer under exam pressures? If you feel this way, go directly to the end of the line, because you are not alone. Not all bar examination problems are created equally.

One criticism of model answers is that many of them go on forever and you begin to wonder if whoever wrote the exam answer did so in an hour's time. The fact is that there are some problems that are extremely difficult to comprehensively answer in one hour. Before you get ready to raise the white flag, read the next paragraph.

REMEMBER THAT IF IT IS DIFFICULT FOR YOU, IT IS PROBABLY DIFFICULT FOR EVERYONE ELSE. Remember that exam scores are scaled in terms of difficulty. This problem was extremely difficult to outline and write under time and exam pressures. The solution is to divide the available time among the issues presented and spend your time accordingly. In other words, discipline yourself to spend only as much time as you can afford in discussing each issue. For example, if you had 35 minutes to write out this question after reading, visualizing and outlining your answer, you might divide your time as follows:

Ed v. Courier Journal

GENERAL CONSIDERATIONS? **(3 MINUTES)**

VICARIOUS LIABILITY

INTENTIONAL TORTS

PRIMA FACIE CASE? **(7 MINUTES)**

INTENTIONAL INFLICTION OF EMOTIONAL DISTRESS

148

DEFENSES?

    CONSENT

DEFAMATION? **(15 MINUTES)**

PRIMA FACIE CASE?

    DEFAMATORY MATTER
    PUBLISHED TO THIRD PARTY
    SUBJECTIVELY UNDERSTOOD BY THIRD PARTY
    CAUSATION
    DAMAGES

DEFENSES?

    ABSOLUTE DEFENSES
    QUALIFIED DEFENSES

INVASION OF PRIVACY **(10 MINUTES)**

PRIMA FACIE CASE?

    INTRUSION
    MISAPPROPRIATION
    FALSE LIGHT
    PRIVATE FACTS

DEFENSES?

After reviewing these time parameters, you may be thinking, "There is no way I could complete a full discussion of every aspect of the privacy torts in 10 minutes!" You are right, but if you took 20 minutes to discuss the privacy torts, leaving 15 minutes to discuss general considerations, intentional infliction of emotional distress, and defamation, you will never finish the examination.

You could conceivably spend an entire afternoon discussing the privacy torts, but the reality is that your time is limited.

The essence of the fourth step of exam taking is: **MAKE A SNAP JUDGMENT ABOUT HOW MUCH TIME TO SPEND ANALYZING EACH ISSUE.**

"Better bend than break."

--- Scottish proverb.

Remember that all three of the bar questions in a single session will not be of this caliber. In fact, the Bar Examiners will likely give you an easy question within the three questions to compensate for a question that they know is difficult. In my experience, the Bar Examiners strive to give a fair examination, all things considered.

You will notice that the *Exam Evaluator* contains "bonus points." While, as stated in section one, you can only receive 100 points per problem, the bonus points system accounts for the individual difficulty level of a particular problem as compared to others within the same subject area. The bonus points accurately reflect the fact that the Bar Graders will likely grade such problems more leniently than easier problems involving less complex fact patterns and issues. By aiming your goals at these bonus points, you will motivate yourself to sharpen your analysis and distinguish your analysis from all others.

Now, let's move on and meet the next challenge.

The Exam Evaluator
ED v. COURIER JOURNAL

EXAM PRESENTATION (TOTAL POINTS AVAILABLE = 25)

	Poor											Excellent
NEATNESS	0	1	2	3	4	5						_____
ORGANIZATION	0	1	2	3	4	5	6	7	8	9	10	_____
LAWYER-LIKE	0	1	2	3	4	5	6	7	8	9	10	_____

DISCUSSION OF ISSUES (TOTAL POINTS AVAILABLE =75)

GENERAL CONSIDERATIONS

10 POINTS = FULL DISCUSSION _____

5 POINTS = PARTIAL/INCOMPLETE DISCUSSION _____

INTENTIONAL INFLICTION OF EMOTIONAL DISTRESS DEFENSE OF CONSENT

15 POINTS = FULL DISCUSSION _____

10 POINTS = PARTIAL/INCOMPLETE DISCUSSION _____

DEFAMATION/DEFENSES TO DEFAMATION

25 POINTS = FULL DISCUSSION _____

15 POINTS = PARTIAL/INCOMPLETE DISCUSSION _____

PRIVACY TORTS/DEFENSES

     25 POINTS = FULL DISCUSSION   ____

     15 POINTS = PARTIAL/INCOMPLETE DISCUSSION   ____

BONUS POINTS

     5 POINTS = DISCUSSION OF DEFENSE OF PROTECTION OF
               PUBLIC INTEREST   ___

     5 POINTS = DISCUSSION OF FIRST AMENDMENT DEFENSE ___

TOTAL SCORE . . . . ____

H.   PROBLEM FIVE: ALBERT, AMY AND DORA v. DRUGCO

1.   The First and Second Read, Headlining and Visualization

> # YOU KNOW WHAT TO DO!

Bayban is an oral contraceptive manufactured by Drugco. Unlike some other birth control pills, it has no known undesirable side effects. However, it is completely ineffective with about 0.4% of all women. Bayban could not be made 100% effective without creating a risk of side effects. Bayban is advertised only through circulars mailed to doctors and is sold only on a doctor's prescription. Its label does not mention that it is ineffective with some women, although Drugco so informs the physicians to whom its promotional literature is sent.

Albert and Amy Able had three minor children. Albert's salary, their only source of income, was $28,000 a year, and was not likely to increase significantly. In June 1984, Albert and Amy concluded that three children were as many as they could hope to raise and educate adequately. They decided to have no more children. Accordingly, Amy consulted her physician, who prescribed Millpill, another contraceptive, which she took regularly until October 1984.

In October 1984, the Ables spent two weeks with their friends, the Bakers, in a nearby city. When she unpacked her bag, Amy discovered that she had forgotten her Millpills. Mrs. Baker, informed of the problem, told Amy that she would give Amy some Bayban pills which the Baker family physician had prescribed.

Although her doctor had warned her that Bayban was not 100% effective, Mrs. Baker did not mention this when she gave the package of Bayban to Amy. Amy took the Bayban pills as directed on the package during the two-week visit. In December 1984, she discovered that she was pregnant.

Since they learned of Amy's pregnancy, the Ables have suffered from severe insomnia caused by economic worries, and as a result Amy has been treated by a psychiatrist. Their 17-year-old daughter, Dora, has also been emotionally upset and under psychiatric treatment since her parents told her they now could not afford to send her to college.

Amy refused to consider an abortion even though her doctor assured her that it would present no danger to her health. Both the pregnancy and the birth were normal and uneventful. Thomas Able, a healthy baby, was born on July 10, 1985. Thomas was conceived during the time Amy was taking Bayban.

On what legal theory or theories, and for what injuries, might Albert, Amy and Dora recover from Drugco? Discuss.

2. Outlining Strategy and Exam Analysis

This problem is what I refer to as the "Bar Mutant" question. Every once in awhile, the Examiners give a problem that stands apart from the rest and tests remote areas of Tort law. These problems usually involve fact patterns that do not neatly fall within a tort theory of liability. This problem appeared in the winter of 1986 and is a prime example of a "Bar Mutant" question.

"Bar Mutant" questions are not necessarily more difficult, but require a little more creativity and flexibility. Unlike <u>Pat v. Driver and Transit</u> or <u>Prof and Prim v. Elco and University</u>, which were clearcut negligence problems, this problem requires you to stretch your imagination a little to see what causes of action exist.

The first task is to decide how to organize your discussion of each party's rights. Albert and Amy should be discussed together because as Thomas' parents, both suffered similar injuries as a result of an unwanted child. Dora, as their daughter, suffered distress due to a different cause: not being able to go to college. Since Dora's injury is obviously so remote from the tortious conduct, you should immediately realize that this problem primarily concerns the rights of Albert and Amy.

Next, let's examine the facts to determine what causes of action exist. Amy became pregnant while taking Bayban birth control pills. Her pregnancy caused Amy and her family a great deal of financial and emotional distress. The label failed to mention that the pill is ineffective in preventing pregnancy on 0.4% of all women, although Drugco informed physicians of this fact. Mrs. Baker's physician, who was informed of the ineffectiveness of the pill on a small minority of women, had informed Mrs. Baker of this fact. Mrs. Baker, however, did not pass this information on to Amy. After headlining and getting to the basics, does this problem sound so complicated?

Let's apply a little common sense. From a layperson's perspective (not a lawyer's), what would Amy be angry about? If you were Amy, you would probably say:

(1) "Those darn pills didn't work!"
(2) "Someone should have told me they didn't work!"

(3)   "My friend Mrs. Baker should have told me what her doctor told her!"

(4)   "Drugco should have had something on the bottle that told me the pills might not work!"

(5)   "I wouldn't have had this baby if it weren't for those darn pills!"

Now translate these concerns into causes of action. The first statement would suggest a products liability suit based on strict products liability and negligence. The second, third, and fourth statements might give rise to a misrepresentation action and an express or implied warranty suit. The fifth assertion raises the issue of whether one can sue for wrongful birth. With these causes of action in mind, we can next apply our writing approach:

NEGLIGENCE

      PRIMA FACIE CASE?

            DUTY
            STANDARD OF CARE
            BREACH OF STANDARD OF CARE
            CAUSATION (actual and proximate cause)
            DAMAGES

      DEFENSES?

            CONTRIBUTORY/COMPARATIVE NEGLIGENCE
            ASSUMPTION OF THE RISK

PRODUCTS LIABILITY

      PRIMA FACIE CASE?

            MISREPRESENTATION
            STRICT LIABILITY
            NEGLIGENCE
            EXPRESS WARRANTY
            IMPLIED WARRANTY

DEFENSES? (depends on theory)

ASSUMPTION OF RISK
    MISUSE OF PRODUCT
    FAILURE TO FOLLOW INSTRUCTIONS
    FAILURE TO GIVE NOTICE
    STATE OF THE ART DEFENSE

GENERAL CONSIDERATIONS?

RECOVERY FOR INJURY TO ANOTHER

Now that we have identified the potential issues for discussion, let's complete our outline by adding the facts, and reorganizing our discussion of the issues:

Albert, Amy and Dora v. Drugco

GENERAL CONSIDERATIONS?

RECOVERY FOR INJURY TO ANOTHER - wrongful birth allowed?

NEGLIGENCE (based on failure to warn)

PRIMA FACIE CASE?

DUTY - Foreseeable P?
STANDARD OF CARE - How would reasonable drug company act?
BREACH OF STANDARD OF CARE - Did Drugco act reasonably in not putting warning on Bayban bottle?
CAUSATION (actual and proximate cause) - assumed.
DAMAGES - emotional distress/economic damages sufficient.

DEFENSES?

CONTRIBUTORY/COMPARATIVE NEGLIGENCE - By using product?

ASSUMPTION OF THE RISK - Should Amy have known risk involved?

PRODUCTS LIABILITY

PRIMA FACIE CASE?

MISREPRESENTATION
Misrepresentation of material fact - pills worked!
Relied upon by P.
Made by D - but D informed physicians.
Intended to Reach P - yes, through physician.
D is a commercial supplier.

STRICT LIABILITY
D caused product to be placed on market.
Product contained an unreasonably dangerous defect - D will argue Bayban was 100% safe.
P was hurt while using product in intended and foreseeable manner.
D engaged in business of selling/supplying product.

EXPRESS WARRANTY

Same as misrepresentation but extends to anyone.

IMPLIED WARRANTY
Goods are fit for ordinary purposes for which goods are used.

DEFENSES? (depends on theory)

ASSUMPTION OF RISK - same as in negligence
MISUSE OF PRODUCT - no evidence
FAILURE TO FOLLOW INSTRUCTIONS - no evidence
STATE OF THE ART DEFENSE - may not forgive failure to warn

3. Model Answer

ALBERT, AMY AND DORA v. DRUGCO

WRONGFUL BIRTH ACTION

The first issue is whether any of the plaintiffs may recover based on Thomas' wrongful birth. Some jurisdictions allow parents to sue for wrongful birth where their child was born as a result of tortious conduct, such as a negligent sterilization operation. Thus, in such a jurisdiction, Albert and Amy may sue for their child's wrongful birth. However, no jurisdictions allow Dora to recover as Thomas' sibling, since her injury is too remote. Furthermore, in this case her distress stems from not being able to go to college, and this distress is too far removed to allow recovery. Thus, Dora may not recover.

NEGLIGENCE

The issue is whether Amy and Albert may recover for negligence because of Drugco's failure to include a warning on the bottle. Negligence is defined as a breach of a duty of due care that is the actual and proximate cause of P's injuries.

The first issue is whether Drugco owed a duty to Amy and Albert. Under the Cardozo majority rule, a duty is owed only to a foreseeable plaintiff or plaintiff in the zone of danger. Amy was a foreseeable P, because it was foreseeable that a woman seeking to avoid pregnancy would take the pill. Because privity of contract is no longer required, Amy may recover even though she received the pills from Mrs. Baker and not directly from Drugco or her physician. It is foreseeable that a woman not in privity with Drugco would take the pill as well, and a duty was therefore owed to Amy. By consuming the pill, Amy was also in the zone of danger. Under the Andrews rule, Amy is owed a duty because a duty is owed to all.

The second sub-issue is what standard of care applies. A defendant owes a duty to act as a reasonable person would have acted under the same or similar circumstances. A reasonable supplier and manufacturer of drugs would employ reasonable care in insuring that information about the effectiveness of its product is communicated to the consumer.

The third sub-issue is whether Drugco breached the above standard of care. Drugco failed to include a warning on the bottle stating the fact that their product was completely ineffective for about 0.4% women. Four out of every 1,000 women using Bayban are completely unprotected from pregnancy; this represents a significant risk to the consumers using Bayban. Thus, at a minimum, Drugco should have included a warning label on its product to inform users of this substantial risk.

Drugco would no doubt argue that its product was sold only through a doctor's prescription, insuring that the consumer would be warned by a physician. However, because Drugco would suffer little inconvenience and economic costs by including a label on the bottle, and because secondary users outside the chain of privity are likely to use the product, Drugco breached the standard of care.

The element of causation, both actual and proximate, is met since Thomas was conceived during the time Amy was taking Bayban.

Though Albert and Amy did not suffer any physical injuries, they suffered from severe insomnia, and this would likely qualify as injury. Furthermore, if a wrongful birth action is allowed, they will claim economic damages as well.

DEFENSES

Drugco may claim that Amy and Albert were contributorily negligent for using a prescription drug without consulting a doctor and therefore contributed to their predicament. If this argument is sustained, under common law, the Ables' recovery would be barred. However, under modern law the Ables' recovery would be reduced in proportion to the degree of their negligence.

Drugco may also argue that the Ables assumed the risk. However, because Bayban's potential ineffectiveness was not known to the Ables, they did not assume the risk of using a potentially ineffective product and this defense does not apply.

PRODUCTS LIABILITY

The Ables may also sue on a products liability theory, by claiming that the product itself was defective and that Drugco misrepresented Bayban's effectiveness, breaching both express and implied warranties under law.

MISREPRESENTATION

A misrepresentation action requires a misrepresentation of a material fact relied upon by P, made by D, a commercial seller. Here the Ables will claim that the label affirmatively misrepresented the 100% effectiveness of the product and that they relied on the absence of a label in assuming that the pills would prevent pregnancy. Drugco would claim that it did seek to inform the consumer through their physician, and that since the drug was not available over the counter, it could reasonably rely on the physician to warn patients of Bayban's ineffectiveness.

Here again, because Drugco could have easily and economically included a label containing the warning, the Ables will succeed on a misrepresentation theory, since they reasonably relied on the absence of a label on the Bayban package.

STRICT LIABILITY

To prevail on a strict products liability action, the Ables must show that D, a commercial supplier, caused an unreasonably dangerous product to be placed on the market and P was hurt while using the product in an intended and foreseeable manner. Here, Amy used Bayban as directed and therefore used the product as it was intended. Drugco would argue, however, that Bayban did not contain an unreasonably dangerous defect, since it is safe and has no known undesirable side effects.

Again, due to the lack of a warning label, the Ables will likely prevail because arguably Bayban was dangerous if not accompanied by a warning label.

EXPRESS WARRANTY

The express warranty analysis would be the same as in misrepresentation, above, except that liability would extend to any party who received personal injury from Amy's use of Bayban.

IMPLIED WARRANTY

There is an implied warranty that goods are merchantable and are fit for the *ordinary purposes for which such goods are used. Here again the Ables could argue that the lack of a warning label breached the implied warranty that Bayban was effective and would prevail on this theory for the same reasons argued above.*

DEFENSES

CONTRIBUTORY NEGLIGENCE

Contributory negligence, as discussed above, generally will not bar a products liability action, where the plaintiff was unaware of the product's defect.

ASSUMPTION OF RISK

Same analysis as in negligence, above.

MISUSE OF PRODUCT/FAILURE TO FOLLOW INSTRUCTIONS

Amy used the product as directed.

STATE OF THE ART DEFENSE

Drugco may assert that its product could not be made more effective without the risk of side effects and that no other drug company, using state of the art technology, could design a safer and more effective product. Again, however, this defense would be rejected because of Drugco's failure to include a label on its packaging.

Do not be discouraged if you feel that you could not discuss every issue in an hour. Remember that a difficult problem is difficult for everyone. In many ways, a difficult problem is better than an easy one; everyone does well on an easy problem, and consequently, it is harder to achieve a top score. On a difficult problem, you can easily distinguish yourself by performing a comprehensive, although not entirely complete, analysis.

If you did not know whether a parent could sue for wrongful birth and skipped over that issue, you could still receive a passing score provided that you discussed the torts of negligence and products liability. If you failed to discuss implied and express warranties, but covered the remaining issues, you could still receive a passing grade even though you missed major issues. This is because the grading curve for this particular problem is lower.

"Learning is discovering that something is possible."

---- Fritz Perls (1894 - 1970)

This is not to say that you should analyze difficult problems superficially and expect to pass. Eventually, you will be able to fully analyze a problem in less than an hour's time. To accomplish this, you must learn instead how to discipline yourself in using the available time following the time allocation principles in this book.

The Exam Evaluator
AMY, ALBERT & DORA v. DRUGCO

EXAM PRESENTATION (TOTAL POINTS AVAILABLE = 25)

	Poor											Excellent
NEATNESS	0	1	2	3	4	5						____
ORGANIZATION	0	1	2	3	4	5	6	7	8	9	10	____
LAWYER-LIKE	0	1	2	3	4	5	6	7	8	9	10	____

DISCUSSION OF ISSUES (TOTAL POINTS AVAILABLE =75)

GENERAL CONSIDERATIONS: WRONGFUL BIRTH

10 POINTS = FULL DISCUSSION ____

5 POINTS = PARTIAL/INCOMPLETE DISCUSSION ____

NEGLIGENCE

30 POINTS = FULL DISCUSSION ____

20 POINTS = PARTIAL/INCOMPLETE DISCUSSION ____

PRODUCTS LIABILITY

35 POINTS = FULL DISCUSSION ____

20 POINTS = PARTIAL/INCOMPLETE DISCUSSION ____

TOTAL . . . . ____

I.   PROBLEM SIX: DICK v. LEN

In May of 1995, Dick, who was driving a truck owned by Ace Co., his employer, failed to stop at a red light at a busy intersection. Phil was lawfully bicycling through the intersection at the time. Dick collided with Phil. The force of the collision knocked Phil to the ground. Phil's legs were broken and his bicycle destroyed. Although the cycling helmet he wore shattered when he fell, Phil escaped head injuries.

A month after the accident, Phil retained an attorney, Len. Len assured Phil that he would pursue an action against Ace Co., and Helmet Co., the manufacturer of the shattered helmet. Three years later, in June 1998, Len revealed to Phil that he had been too busy to pursue settlement or file a lawsuit in his case. Phil was furious and told Len so.

In July 1998, Len filed a complaint in state court on behalf of Phil alleging negligence against Ace Co. and Helmet Co. Len believed Phil's case was barred by his state's two-year statute of limitations for negligence actions. However, he filed the complaint to placate Phil and served the summons and complaint on Ace Co. and Helmet Co.

Ace Co. and Helmet Co. hired attorneys to defend them and filed appropriate motions to dismiss. The state court dismissed Phil's damage action against Ace Co. and Helmet Co. on the ground that it is barred by the applicable statute of limitations.

What, if any, liability does Len have to:

1. Phil? Discuss.

2. Ace Co.? Discuss.

3. Helmet Co.? Discuss.

1. Outlining Strategy and Exam Analysis

This is a pure torts problem with a slight professional responsibility twist. Applying the writing approach we come up with the following:

<u>Phil v. Len</u>

NEGLIGENCE

PRIMA FACIE CASE?

DUTY - Foreseeable P: client.
STANDARD OF CARE - How would a reasonably competent attorney act?
BREACH OF STANDARD OF CARE - Missed statute of limitations.
CAUSATION (actual and proximate cause) - Actual cause: but for Len's faulty representation, Phil may have recovered; proximate cause: Len's failure to file suit and failure to inform client so as to allow him to find alternative representation directly caused dismissal of Phil's action.
DAMAGES - Phil must show that he would have prevailed against Ace and/or Helmet Co.

DEFENSES?

CONTRIBUTORY/COMPARATIVE NEGLIGENCE - No evidence.
ASSUMPTION OF THE RISK - No evidence.

Note in order to determine Len's liability to Phil, we must necessarily determine the liability of Ace and Helmet Co. to Phil. The biggest hint that such a discussion is needed is contained in the first paragraph. Had you failed to discuss <u>Phil v. Ace and Helmet Co.</u>, you would have not included in your analysis any of the facts contained in the first paragraph of the problem. While bar questions sometimes contain irrelevant facts, as a general rule they do not. Always ask yourself, "Why did

166

the Bar Examiners include these facts?" More often than not, the facts are there so that you will use them to solve the problem.

Phil v. Ace Co.

    VICARIOUS LIABILITY - Dick driving within the course of employment.

    NEGLIGENCE

        PRIMA FACIE CASE?

        DUTY - Foreseeable P? Motorist in the zone of danger.
        STANDARD OF CARE - How would a reasonable person drive?
        BREACH OF STANDARD OF CARE - Unsafe driving: failing to stop at a red light.
        CAUSATION (actual and proximate cause) - Actual cause: but for Dick's negligent driving, Phil would not have been injured; proximate cause: Dick's negligent driving directly caused Phil's injuries.
        DAMAGES - Phil's legs broken; bike destroyed.

    DEFENSES?

        CONTRIBUTORY/COMPARATIVE NEGLIGENCE - No evidence.
        ASSUMPTION OF THE RISK - No evidence.

Phil v. Helmet Co.

    NEGLIGENCE

        PRIMA FACIE CASE?

            DUTY
            STANDARD OF CARE
            BREACH OF STANDARD OF CARE

CAUSATION (actual and proximate cause)

DAMAGES - Phil sustained no injuries other than damage to helmet itself.

PRODUCTS LIABILITY?

No evidence that helmet was defective.

<u>**Phil v. Ace Co.**</u>

MISCELLANEOUS TORTS

MALICIOUS PROSECUTION
ABUSE OF PROCESS

DEFENSES?

<u>**Phil v. Helmet Co.**</u>

SAME AS ABOVE

2.   Model Answer

The majority of this question's discussion falls within the first interrogatory. Knowing this fact <u>before</u> you begin writing your answer makes all the difference in the world, because you will know how to apportion your time between the interrogatories depending on the importance of the issues presented.

Let's indulge in another meaningful quotation before comparing your answer to the Model Answer:

"Do not use a hatchet to remove a fly from your friend's forehead."

---- Chinese proverb

1. **Phil v. Len**

NEGLIGENCE

The issue is whether Len is liable to Phil for negligence on an attorney malpractice theory.

Negligence is breach of a duty of due care that is the actual and proximate cause of P's injuries.

Len owed a duty only to a foreseeable plaintiff. Here, this element is met because Len contracted to represent Phil, his client, and therefore owed Phil a professional and ethical duty.

The standard of care required of an attorney toward his or her client is that of a reasonably competent attorney. A reasonably competent attorney would pursue his or her client's cause of action with due diligence and immediacy, and would file suit within the applicable statute of limitations. Here, Len's failure to file suit within the three-year limitations statute was unreasonable and did not measure up to what would be expected of an attorney of average competence. Indeed, a reasonable attorney would also inform his or her client if he or she was too busy to file the action and allow the client enough time to find alternative counsel. Thus, Len breached the standard of care.

But for Len's faulty representation, Phil's lawsuit would have been filed against Ace and Helmet Co. within the three-year statute of limitations. Len's failure to file suit also directly caused dismissal of Phil's action, and therefore was the proximate result of Phil's loss of his right to sue.

On the issue of damages, Phil must show that he would have prevailed against Ace and/or Helmet Co.

Phil v. Ace Co.

VICARIOUS LIABILITY

Ace Co. would be liable for the tortious conduct of its employee, Dick, under the doctrine of respondeat-superior because at the time of the accident, Dick was driving Ace's truck within the course of his employment.

NEGLIGENCE

Phil was a motorist in the zone of danger and was a foreseeable plaintiff since Dick should have known that a motorist could be injured by his unsafe driving.

The standard of care required of Dick is that of a reasonable motorist. A reasonable motorist would drive in a safe and cautious manner so as to avoid injury to others. By failing to stop at a red light at a busy intersection, Dick breached the standard of care since a reasonable driver would stop at a red light and follow all traffic and safety rules. A reasonable person would also know that failing to stop at a busy intersection would pose a substantial risk of injury to others, including pedestrians and bicyclists such as Phil. Thus, Dick breached the standard of care.

Dick's poor driving was the actual and proximate cause of Phil's injuries. But for Dick's negligent driving, Phil would not have been injured. Moreover, Dick's negligent driving directly caused Phil's injuries.

Phil has suffered actual injury since both his legs were broken and his bike was destroyed.

No defenses bar his action.

Phil v. Helmet Co.

Phil's action for negligence against Helmet Co. would fail since he sustained no head injuries and no facts indicate that Helmet Co. was negligent in designing or manufacturing the helmet.

For the same reason, unless Phil could prove the helmet was defectively designed, Phil could not recover on a products liability theory.

In conclusion, because no defenses bar Phil's action against Len, and because Phil could have recovered against Ace Co., Phil has an action in negligence against Len.

170

Ace Co. v. Len

MALICIOUS PROSECUTION

Ace may sue Len for malicious prosecution, which is the initiation of civil proceedings without probable cause and with malicious intent, terminating in defendant's favor, and which results in actual damage. No probable cause existed to file the suit because Len knew the action was barred by the statute of limitations and merely filed the suit to appease Phil. While Len may argue that he acted without malice, he acted at least recklessly because he knew that the statute of limitations had expired. Furthermore, the suit was dismissed in Ace's favor and the company presumably incurred costs to defend against the suit. Thus, Ace may recover on this basis.

Abuse of process is the misuse of the legal process for an ulterior purpose, causing actual injury. Here again, because Len actually knew the action was barred, he misused the legal proceedings for the improper purpose of placating Phil and therefore is liable for this tort as well.

Helmet Co. v. Len

Len's liability to Helmet Co. is identical to that discussed in Ace Co. v. Len.

In the earlier problem, we discussed what to do if you do not know the law. Assume that, in this problem, you could not remember the rule of "malicious prosecution." What would you do? If you did not remember the rule, you would try to think of something that sounds reasonable.

Is it reasonable that a person could be held liable for suing someone without a reason? Use your common sense to come up with a reasonable solution to Ace Co.'s plight. Now although you may not think of the tort or its elements, you can still discuss the rationale behind a tort and in the process, pick up a few points, even though you are really in the dark. Take, for instance, the following example of a possible answer:

Len is liable to Ace Company. A person may not file a lawsuit without a good reason. Here, Len filed the lawsuit against Ace knowing that it was barred by the three-year statute of limitations. Len had no reason to believe that the action would succeed since it was procedurally barred. The only reason why Len filed the lawsuit was to placate Phil; this is an improper reason. Len is thus liable to Ace on this theory.

Notice that this answer never names the tort nor any of its elements, and yet manages to express the common sense theory behind the tort. Remember that while this answer is far from complete, it is better than leaving a blank page.

Of course, you should not make a habit of creating the rules as you go along. The purpose of presenting this example is to show you that you can discuss an issue without knowing the precise rule of law. The way to avoid this predicament altogether is to know the law "inside out" so that you will not experience memory lapses on the bar exam.

The Exam Evaluator
PHIL, ACE COMPANY, HELMET COMPANY v. LEN

EXAM PRESENTATION (TOTAL POINTS AVAILABLE = 25)

	Poor											Excellent
NEATNESS	0	1	2	3	4	5						____
ORGANIZATION	0	1	2	3	4	5	6	7	8	9	10	____
LAWYER-LIKE	0	1	2	3	4	5	6	7	8	9	10	____

DISCUSSION OF ISSUES (TOTAL POINTS AVAILABLE =75)

PHIL v. LEN: NEGLIGENCE

    25 POINTS = FULL DISCUSSION   ____

    15 POINTS = PARTIAL/INCOMPLETE DISCUSSION   ____

PHIL v. ACE COMPANY: VICARIOUS LIABILITY/NEGLIGENCE

    20 POINTS = FULL DISCUSSION   ____

    10 POINTS = PARTIAL/INCOMPLETE DISCUSSION   ____

PHIL v. HELMET COMPANY: NEGLIGENCE/PRODUCTS LIABILITY

    10 POINTS = FULL DISCUSSION   ____

    5 POINTS = PARTIAL/INCOMPLETE DISCUSSION   ____

ACE COMPANY v. LEN

      10 POINTS = FULL DISCUSSION   ____

      5 POINTS = PARTIAL/INCOMPLETE DISCUSSION   ____

HELMET COMPANY v. LEN

      10 POINTS = FULL DISCUSSION   ____

      5 POINTS = PARTIAL/INCOMPLETE DISCUSSION   ____

TOTAL SCORE . . . . ____

J.   PROBLEM SEVEN: WHITE v. DAILY NEWS

White, a Marine Corps officer, was convicted of murder in 1946 in a highly publicized trial. The only evidence against him at the trial was the testimony of two former Marines that Japanese prisoners of war had been killed while in the custody of troops commanded by White during the battle for control of Guadalcanal. In 1954, one of these witnesses, who was then dying of cancer, confessed that he and the second witness had lied at the trial of White in order to avoid punishment for their own misconduct. When investigation confirmed the truth of the confession, White received a pardon, was released from prison, and entered a religious order where he lived in seclusion under vows of silence and poverty.

Late in 1984, White developed a serious illness. He reluctantly left the order and entered a hospital for treatment.

News, a daily newspaper in the city in which the hospital is located, has prepared a feature article that fully and truthfully recounts the trial, imprisonment, and the events leading to the pardon of White. The authors and editors have relied solely on information available in public records. News has notified White that it intends to publish the article. White objects to the prospect of unwelcomed publicity. White and News have been warned by White's doctors that the emotional stress White may suffer if the story is published will impede his recovery.

1.   If the story is published, on what theory or theories might White base an action for damages against News? Discuss.

2.   If White seeks an injunction to prohibit publication of the proposed story, what defense or defenses should News offer, and how should the court rule on them? Discuss.

1. Meet the Torts Cross-Over Question

"Everyone is ignorant, only on different subjects."

---- Will Rogers (1879 - 1935)

This question is a classic "cross-over" type question. A cross-over question is simply a question that simultaneously tests two or more different subject areas. In the past ten years, cross-over questions have included: Wills-Trusts, Contracts-Remedies, Torts-Remedies, Real Property-Remedies, Evidence-Real Property, Contracts-Torts, Torts-Professional Responsibility, Constitutional Law-Remedies, and Criminal Law/Procedure-Professional Responsibility. Based on this past assortment of cross-over questions, you should expect to see any conceivable combination of subject areas on future bar exams.

In solving a cross-over question, you must begin with the big picture approach. You must first determine what overall subject areas are being tested before asking the specific questions pertaining to each subject:

CONTRACTS? NO! No contractual agreement is involved.
CIVIL PROCEDURE? NO! No procedural questions are raised.
CRIMINAL LAW/CRIMINAL PROCEDURE? NO! No crimes are involved.
REAL PROPERTY? NO! No issues as to ownership of property.
EVIDENCE? NO! No evidentiary issues involved.
CONSTITUTIONAL LAW? NO. No issues arising under Constitution.
COMMUNITY PROPERTY? NO! No dispute between divorcing spouses.
WILLS AND TRUSTS? NO! No issues involving a will or trust.
PROFESSIONAL RESPONSIBILITY? NO. No ethical questions.
TORTS! YES! Possible action for violation of privacy torts.
REMEDIES? YES! The second interrogatory specifically asks you to analyze whether an injunction properly lies; thus, this question presents a remedies issue.

In most cross-over problems, the interrogatories will give you a clear indication of the areas being tested. This is because the Bar Examiners do not want to confuse the examinee as to the subject areas being tested. For this reason, Examiners are very

176

specific about the tested areas. By presenting the cross-over problem, the Bar Examiners can test your ability to identify and solve multiple bar subjects in a single problem.

You should not be intimidated by cross-over questions because they are easily identifiable. The first interrogatory asks on what theories White may base an action for damages, while the second interrogatory asks you to analyze the defenses available to News if White seeks *an injunction*. These interrogatories clearly identify this as a Torts-Remedies cross-over question.

2. Outlining Strategy

Applying our writing approach to the first interrogatory we formulate the following outline:

WHAT CAUSES OF ACTION EXIST AND ARE THE ELEMENTS MET?

DEFAMATION

>ABSOLUTE DEFENSES: No action here - article "fully and truthfully" recounts public information.

>QUALIFIED PRIVILEGE: First Amendment - D must act with malice or at least negligence. Neither is met here.

PRIVACY TORTS

INTRUSION
Highly offensive/outrageous - arguably yes.
Intrusion - no prying since matters were of public record.
Relating to private facts - facts were public record.

FALSE LIGHT
Publication of objectionable facts.
Placing P in false light - no false light since story was true.
In the public eye - published in newspaper.

PRIVATE FACTS

Public disclosure of - published in newspaper.
Objectionable private facts - while facts were objectionable to White, they were not private.

APPROPRIATION

Appropriation of P's name or likeness - name used but no photo indicated.
For D's commercial advantage - no, limited to use of P's name or likeness in connection with promotional use or advertisement of product.

INTENTIONAL INFLICTION OF EMOTIONAL DISTRESS

Extreme and outrageous act.
Intent to cause severe emotional distress/recklessness.
Damages.

3.   Model Answer

WHITE v. NEWS

DEFAMATION

Mr. White will not prevail on a defamation action for two reasons. First, truth is an absolute defense. Because the article "fully and truthfully" recounts all the events in the story, White cannot succeed. Second, White must prove that News acted with constitutional malice or at least negligence in publishing the story. Again, because the story was true, White cannot prove that News acted recklessly or with knowledge of the story's falsity.

PRIVACY TORTS

INTRUSION

The privacy tort of intrusion is a highly offensive and outrageous intrusion relating to private facts. Even if it is assumed that the story related outrageous and offensive information relating to White's past criminal history, no action exists because the facts were of public record.

FALSE LIGHT

The tort of false light requires the publication of objectionable facts placing P in false light in the public eye. While the story was published in the paper and may have related objectionable facts, the story was true and therefore did not place White in a false light.

PRIVATE FACTS

The tort of private facts is the public disclosure of objectionable private facts. Once again, because the facts were not private and were of public record, no action exists.

APPROPRIATION

Appropriation of P's name or likeness is established where D acts for commercial advantage. While it is unknown whether White's picture appeared near the article, his name was used and thus the first element is met. However, because News did not use P's name or likeness in connection with promotional use or advertisement of a product, it did not act for commercial advantage and no action exists.

INTENTIONAL INFLICTION OF EMOTIONAL DISTRESS

This tort requires an extreme and outrageous act with the intent to cause severe emotional distress or a reckless act resulting in actual and severe emotional distress. White will argue that the intent element is met because his doctors informed News that publishing the article could cause White emotional distress. White will also argue that by publishing the story with such knowledge of White's condition, News acted in reckless disregard of his health. News, however, will argue that it acted only with the intent to publish a newsworthy story and not with an intent to cause emotional distress. News will lose on this issue because it knew of the likely consequences to White's health if it published the story.

News will also argue that its conduct was not outrageous and did not transcend the bounds of decency. News will cite the fact that the story was true and mentions not only White's conviction, but also the pardon resulting from the witnesses' prior perjured testimony. News will argue that an average person of ordinary sensitivity would not be offended by a story that is true, exonerates White, and merely recounts facts already on public record. White will counterargue that even if a reasonable person would not be offended by the published story, News is still liable because it knew of White's particular sensitivity.

While it is a close issue, White would prevail if he indeed suffered severe emotional distress due to News' story.

Although you may want to dazzle the exam grader with your vast knowledge of defamation law, you have recognized this as another "Sucker Punch" question similar to <u>Prof and Prim v. Smith</u>. The examiners here bait the hook and wait for a bite. Those who bit at a defamation analysis probably spent fifteen or twenty minutes discussing each of defamation's elements. When it is clear that no liability is possible under a cause of action, just say so and move on, as you did with <u>Smith</u>.

As we move on to the privacy torts, you will see that no causes of action exist because in the case of each privacy tort, an essential element is not met. In the torts of Intrusion and Private Facts, the fact that the statements are of public record completely bars recovery. White cannot recover for false light because the statements are true. Appropriation is eliminated because News did not use White's name or likeness to promote or advertise a product. Again, the Bar Examiners are testing your ability to distinguish a good cause of action from a bad one.

Finally, intentional infliction of emotional distress presents the only major issue in this question. This is true not because it presents a difficult issue, but because it presents a close one and is deserving of more discussion than the previous torts. Here is an answer which reaches the opposite conclusion as the Model Answer:

News will prevail on an intentional infliction of emotional distress theory. That tort requires an extreme and outrageous act with the intent to cause severe emotional distress resulting in such distress. News will assert that a person of ordinary sensitivity would not suffer emotional distress due to the publication of a story which exonerated that person of criminal wrongdoing. The story recounts events which occurred in 1946 and does not portray White unfairly. White will counter because News was warned of his special sensitivity, a lower standard applies since one who acts with knowledge of a party's special disability "takes his plaintiff as he finds him." However, News will prevail since its publication of the story could not have caused White or anyone else any emotional distress.

News will successfully argue that it acted only to publish a newsworthy story which the public was entitled to know about. It merely reported the results of a public proceeding, White's trial, and collateral proceedings leading to White's pardon. These facts would not be actionable in 1946 and should not be actionable now. White's argument that News' mere knowledge of his possible reaction to the story somehow makes their act intentional will fail. News never intended to cause White any harm.

Finally, there is no evidence that White actually suffered severe emotional distress. His doctors' warnings that he might suffer such distress is insufficient to allow recovery.

4.   The Cross-Over Bridge

Now let's "cross over" into the world of Remedies. As you can see, this problem presents a very simple Remedies question, which can be answered in a few paragraphs. Let's briefly review the Remedies writing approach for injunctions:

INJUNCTION

      INADEQUATE REMEDY AT LAW
      PROPERTY RIGHT
      FEASIBILITY
      BALANCING OF THE HARDSHIPS
      DEFENSES TO INJUNCTION

As you will see in the Remedies section, the "elements" of an injunction should be analyzed in the same fashion as the elements of negligence or products liability in the examples above. Now, let's outline our answer and apply the facts to this issue:

INJUNCTION

> INADEQUATE REMEDY AT LAW - Money damages cannot protect White's reputation nor will it prevent emotional distress.
> PROPERTY RIGHT - liberally construed where a fundamental right is involved.
> FEASIBILITY - court may order News not to publish the story.
> BALANCING OF THE HARDSHIPS - hardship to D outweighs News' interest in printing a decades-old story, since it may print other stories.
> DEFENSES TO INJUNCTION - Equity will not enjoin speech.

In most cross-over questions, you will find that the issues raised tend to be fairly straightforward and simple. This is because the Bar Examiners know it will take you a few minutes to shift your course and analyze a different subject area.

INJUNCTIVE RELIEF

In order to obtain an injunction, White must prove (1) damages are an inadequate remedy at law; (2) property right; (3) feasibility of enforcement; (4) balancing of hardships weigh in his favor, and no defenses apply.

White will easily prove that damages are inadequate under the circumstances, since he is likely to suffer extreme emotional distress, and money cannot compensate him for his loss of reputation and anonymity. While traditionally, equity protected only property rights, modern law protects fundamental rights such as White's right to privacy, so this element is met. Thus the court may enjoin the paper from printing White's story. The final factor, balancing of hardships, clearly weighs in White's favor because the emotional distress he would suffer outweighs the small inconvenience suffered by News in not being able to print a decades-old story.

DEFENSES TO INJUNCTIVE RELIEF

White's injunctive relief will be denied since equity will not enjoin speech. Courts acting in equity have a strong interest in favoring free speech and against prior restraint. White will assert that the newsworthiness of a such an old story is questionable while the likelihood of danger to his health is great. Because equity will not act to limit speech, and News' story concerns matters of public record, injunctive relief will be denied.

After reading this model answer, you might be wondering if it was necessary to discuss the elements of an injunction at all. A literal reading of the interrogatory reveals that you are only asked "What defense or defenses should News offer?" This interrogatory does not ask "Please discuss White's remedies" or "What relief is White entitled to?" Instead, you are asked to address the issue of what defenses may be raised by News against an injunction obtained by White. In the model answers released by the Bar Examiners, the elements of White's injunction were addressed. However, this is not to say that the Bar Examiners expected you to discuss the elements of White's injunction. It is important to note that the answers issued by the Bar Examiners provide only examples of clearly passing answers written by bar examinees.

The interrogatory does not specifically ask you to analyze the elements of White's injunction. However, you should discuss these issues along with News' potential defenses. Bar Examiners will not penalize examinees who fail to address these issues since they only ask you to address News' defenses. Therefore, those who discuss these issues will receive bonus points. The *Exam Evaluator* reflects this probability by allowing bonus points for discussing White's injunction.

The Exam Evaluator
WHITE v. DAILY NEWS

EXAM PRESENTATION (TOTAL POINTS AVAILABLE = 25)

	Poor											Excellent
NEATNESS	0	1	2	3	4	5						_____
ORGANIZATION	0	1	2	3	4	5	6	7	8	9	10	_____
LAWYER-LIKE	0	1	2	3	4	5	6	7	8	9	10	_____

DISCUSSION OF ISSUES (TOTAL POINTS AVAILABLE =75)

DEFAMATION

10 POINTS = FULL DISCUSSION _____

5 POINTS = PARTIAL/INCOMPLETE DISCUSSION _____

INVASION OF PRIVACY

30 POINTS = FULL DISCUSSION _____

20 POINTS = PARTIAL/INCOMPLETE DISCUSSION _____

INTENTIONAL INFLICTION OF EMOTIONAL DISTRESS

15 POINTS = FULL DISCUSSION _____

10 POINTS = PARTIAL/INCOMPLETE DISCUSSION _____

2. WHITE'S REMEDIES

INJUNCTION

    10 POINTS = FULL DISCUSSION   ____

    5 POINTS = PARTIAL/INCOMPLETE DISCUSSION   ____

DEFENSES TO INJUNCTION

    10 POINTS = FULL DISCUSSION   ____

    10 POINTS = PARTIAL/INCOMPLETE DISCUSSION   ____

TOTAL SCORE   ____

Now that you have been introduced to the full gamut of Torts problems, let's move full speed ahead, and tackle three new Torts problems, using the strategies and skills we have learned thus far. Try taking each of the examinations under exam pressures, which means:

(1)   Time yourself and strive to complete the exam in one hour;

(2)   Follow the *Six Steps of Exam Taking* and the *Ten Strategies of Exam Writing Success*;

(3)   Avoid any distractions, i.e., phone calls or conversations, during the exam period;

(4)   Find an environment which best simulates the actual circumstances under which you will be taking the bar exam.

(5)   Do not view the model answer until you have completed writing out your answer.

Good luck!

K.   PROBLEM EIGHT: PETER v. JACK & DAVID

Jack, age 22, and his friend David, age 16, were riding their motorcycles around Jack's property. They decided to race each other down Jack's driveway, across a seldom used public road, and into a neighboring field.

David was ahead of Jack by about 75 feet when, without slowing down, he entered the road. David failed to see Peter's car approaching. Peter, an adult, was driving carefully but he was not a licensed driver and, he was not wearing a seatbelt required by state law.

Peter avoided hitting David by braking suddenly. This caused Peter to strike his windshield and suffer severe physical injuries.

Peter sued David and Jack in state court, alleging negligence. The parties stipulated to the facts given above. Jack moved for summary judgment on the grounds that he was not legally responsible for Peter's injuries. The motion was granted.

David moved for summary judgment on the grounds that Peter was not wearing a seat belt and was not a licensed driver. The motion was denied.

At trial, over Peter's objection, the judge instructed the jury to apply the standard of care applicable to children in assessing David's conduct.

Did the cour err in:

1.   Granting Jack's motion for summary judgment? Discuss.

2.   Denying David's motion for summary judgment? Discuss.

3.   Instructing the jury to apply the standard of care? Discuss.

1.   Outlining Strategy and Exam Analysis

What did you think of this problem? Like the earlier problem involving Len the lawyer and Phil the motorcyclist, this problem is couched in civil procedure language. Do not be fooled; this is a pure Torts problem. The examiners are simply using "civil procedure" language to ask whether Peter has a cause of action against Jack and David. Likewise, the final interrogatory simply asks for the proper standard of care where the conduct of a child is involved. If you discussed civil procedure at all, your discussion should be limited to only the standard applied in a summary judgment motion -- whether a triable issue of fact exists. No other discussion of civil procedure principles is required.

In this problem, the Bar Examiners cleverly couched the interrogatories in terms of summary judgment motions, and by doing so, created a smoke screen that confused more than one examinee. The first interrogatory, which asks whether Jack's summary judgment motion was properly granted, is really asking whether any triable issues of fact exist. When you compare this interrogatory with the typical torts interrogatory, e.g., "What relief, if any, is Peter entitled to?" it is clear that you are only required to discuss whether a prima facie case of negligence can be proven, and not whether any defenses apply. Therefore, do not discuss Jack's defenses against Peter because your inquiry is limited to whether Peter's action against David can survive a summary judgment motion.

The second interrogatory asks whether Peter's violations of the law should bar his cause of action against David, i.e., whether no triable issues exist for the trier of fact to decide. Thus, you only need to analyze David's defenses to Peter's cause of action, and not whether Peter proved a prima facie case of negligence against David, because David moved for summary judgment on the grounds that Peter was not wearing a seat belt and was not a licensed driver.

As previously stated, the third interrogatory is limited to a discussion of the proper standard of care. Although David is a minor, should he be held up to the standard of care of an adult, since he was engaged in an adult activity. Like the first and second interrogatories, you need not discuss the other elements of negligence because the interrogatory directs you to discuss only one of the five elements of negligence.

The lesson here is one you have already learned: you cannot always judge an essay problem by its appearance. In this problem, the examiners broke up a negligence problem into three parts: a prima facie case of negligence, defenses to negligence, and the standard of care. While the issues are presented in differing order, the analysis is the same.

Now apply our writing approach to this problem and view a sample outline:

1. Jack's Motion for Summary Judgment

PRIMA FACIE CASE OF NEGLIGENCE PROVEN? Summary judgment is properly granted where no triable issue of fact exists.

DUTY? Peter a foreseeable P?/In Zone of Danger?
STANDARD OF CARE? To drive safely.
BREACH? Racing down driveway, across seldom used public road.
CAUSATION? Actual cause - "but for" Jack's participation in race, accident would not have occurred; proximate cause - Was Jack's act of riding motorcycle a direct cause of Peter's injuries? Was David's act an unforeseeable intervening cause?
DAMAGES? - severe physical injuries.

2. David's Motion for Summary Judgment

DEFENSES TO NEGLIGENCE? David's motion for summary judgment claimed that Peter was contributorily negligent and therefore no triable issue of fact existed for the jury to decide.

CONTRIBUTORY NEGLIGENCE - negligence per se established by violation of statutes? Three factors: (1) Were Peter's violations unexcused? (2) Is David within class of persons intended to be protected by statute? (3) Are David's injuries of the type the statute was designed to protect against?

COMPARATIVE NEGLIGENCE - no summary judgment since P's negligence does not completely bar action.

3. Jury Instruction on Standard of Care

Child standard of care or adult standard of care? David is a 16-year-old riding a motorcycle.

As you can see, this problem neatly separates into three issues. This problem's most difficult aspects are the organizing and identifying of the issues. Once outlined this problem is no different than the typical negligence problems encountered in earlier examples. Compare your answer to the Model Answer.

2.　　Model Answer

Peter v. Jack & David

1. Jack's Summary Judgment Motion

The issue is whether the court properly granted Jack's summary judgment motion. A summary judgment motion is properly granted where no triable issue of fact exists. Thus, Jack's motion was properly granted only if Peter failed to prove a prima facie case of negligence.

NEGLIGENCE

Negligence is the breach of duty of due care that is the actual and proximate cause of P's injuries.

The first issue is whether Jack owed a duty to Peter. Under the Cardozo majority rule, a duty is owed only to a foreseeable plaintiff or a plaintiff in the zone of danger. Here Peter was a foreseeable plaintiff, since Jack knew that a car might be traveling on a public road, and should have foreseen that a motorist could be injured by the negligent driving of motorcycles. Peter was also in the zone of danger caused by Jack's act, since Jack was only 75 feet away from David and Peter's accident. Under the Andrews view, a duty is owed to all and therefore Jack owed Peter a duty of due care.

The second issue is what standard of care applies. A defendant owes a duty to act as a reasonable person would have acted in the same or similar circumstances.

190

A motorcyclist owes a duty to drive safely and prudently. Jack breached this standard of care by participating in a motorcycle race on a public road. Even though the road is seldom used, Jack still should have driven carefully because of the great risk that racing causes to other motorists. Therefore, Jack will be held to have breached the standard of care.

But for Jack's act of participating in a race with David, the accident between Peter and David would not have occurred and Peter would not have been injured. Jack is therefore the actual cause of Peter's injuries. Jack would argue that his conduct was not the direct cause of Peter's injuries, because he was 75 feet away and was not responsible for causing Peter to brake. Jack would maintain that David's failure to slow down and to see Peter's car was an unforeseeable event that broke the chain of causation. However, while Jack did not directly cause the accident, it is foreseeable that by participating in a motorcycle race on a public road, a co-participant in that race might collide with another motorist. Therefore, Jack would be an indirect but foreseeable cause of Peter's injuries and thus the proximate cause element is met.

Peter suffered severe physical injury when he struck his head on the windshield and therefore the damages element is met.

Based on the foregoing, the court improperly granted Jack's motion for summary judgment because triable issues as to Jack's negligence existed.

2. David's Motion for Summary Judgment

The issue is whether the court properly denied David's motion for summary judgment on the grounds that Peter was not wearing a seatbelt and was not a licensed driver. David's motion was properly denied if a triable issue of fact existed as to these issues.

CONTRIBUTORY NEGLIGENCE

The issue is whether Peter was contributorily negligent in causing his injuries. Contributory negligence is defined as conduct by the plaintiff that is a contributing cause to his or her injuries and that falls below the standard of care to which he is required to conform for his own protection. Because Peter was driving carefully, he did not act negligently unless Peter's violation of traffic laws establishes negligence per se.

A party's negligence may be established by violation of a criminal statute if: (1) the violations were unexcused; (2) the plaintiff (in this case the defendant) is within the class of persons intended to be protected by statute; (3) the harm caused to the plaintiff (in this case the defendant) is of the type the statute was designed to protect against.

There is no justification for Peter's non-compliance with the state seat belt law or the law requiring that all drivers be licensed. Both traffic laws were designed to protect motorists, such as David, from injury and unsafe driving by others and therefore the second element is met. As to the final element, driving without a license is a regulatory law but arguably protects the public, including David, from unsafe drivers. The seat-belt law, by contrast, is clearly intended to only protect the driver and passengers from injury, and not other motorists such as David. Thus, this element is met because Peter was an unlicensed driver.

Regardless of the violation of traffic laws, Peter's failure to wear a seat belt probably bars his recovery, since a reasonable person would follow the law and would wear seat belts to prevent injury. Because Peter may not have struck the windshield had he been wearing his seat belt, he was contributorily negligent and his recovery would be barred. Thus, the court should have granted David's motion because no issue of fact existed.

COMPARATIVE NEGLIGENCE

However, in a majority of states including California, the comparative negligence doctrine allows a jury to fix a certain percentage that reflects the degree of plaintiff's contributory negligence. In these jurisdictions, because the jury would determine the percentage of blame attributable to Peter's negligence, David's summary judgment motion was properly denied.

3. Jury Instruction on Standard of Care

The final issue is whether the court properly instructed the jury on the child standard of care. Children are held to a like standard unless they are engaged in an adult activity. Driving a motorcycle on a public street constitutes adult activity because it involves potentially dangerous activity normally engaged in by adults. Therefore, David should be held to the same standard as would an adult under the same or similar circumstances. Thus, the court erred in instructing the jury.

The Exam Evaluator
PETER v. JACK & DAVID

EXAM PRESENTATION (TOTAL POINTS AVAILABLE = 25)

	Poor	Excellent	
NEATNESS	0 1 2 3 4 5		____
ORGANIZATION	0 1 2 3 4 5 6 7 8 9 10		____
LAWYER-LIKE	0 1 2 3 4 5 6 7 8 9 10		____

DISCUSSION OF ISSUES (TOTAL POINTS AVAILABLE =75)

PETER v. JACK: NEGLIGENCE

    40 POINTS = FULL DISCUSSION   ____

    25 POINTS = PARTIAL/INCOMPLETE DISCUSSION   ____

PETER v. DAVID: CONTRIBUTORY/COMPARATIVE NEGLIGENCE

    25 POINTS = FULL DISCUSSION   ____

    10 POINTS = PARTIAL/INCOMPLETE DISCUSSION   ____

CHILD: STANDARD OF CARE JURY INSTRUCTION

    10 POINTS = FULL DISCUSSION   ____

    5 POINTS = PARTIAL/INCOMPLETE DISCUSSION

TOTAL . . . . ____

L. PROBLEM NINE: PROFESSOR JAMES & PAM v. DAN, NED & THE DAILY RECORD

Dan, a student in state university law school, posted on the law school bulletin board the following typed notice:

Professor James gave an "A" grade last semester to a woman in return for sexual favors. The facts are widely known and talked about.

The statement about sexual favors was true of a different teacher also named James (Teacher James) who had been fired from his job at a nearby college as a result. Dan knew that Teacher James had been fired but did not know why. Dan honestly believed that Professor James was the one who had given the "A" grade in return for the sexual favors. On the day after Dan posted the typed notice, Ned, editor of the Daily Record, the local newspaper, published in the Daily Record a clear picture of the posted notice, commenting only that the notice was posted on the local law school bulletin board.

Professor James had given only one "A" grade the previous semester. This was to a woman named Pam, who had never been intimate with Professor James. Her grade had appeared alongside her secret examination number on Professor James' list of grades, which had been posted on the bulletin board. Pam was never identified publicly by Professor James or the school as the recipient of the "A" grade.

1. What legal claims and defenses should be asserted in a suit by Professor James against Dan, Ned, and the Daily Record, and how should the claims and defenses by resolved? Discuss.

2. What legal claims and defenses should be asserted in a suit by Pam against Dan, Ned, and the Daily Record, and how should the claims and defenses be resolved?

1.   Outlining Strategy and Exam Analysis

This problem presents a relatively straightforward defamation problem. The interrogatories ask you to determine "what claims and defenses" should be asserted by Professor James and Pam against Dan, Ned, and the Daily Record, and "how should the claims and defenses be resolved?" Note that you are not asked to decide what remedies might be available to Professor James and Pam; you are only asked how these claims should be resolved.

As always, follow the directions of the interrogatory and determine the overall organization of the problem. Because Dan's involvement differs substantially from Ned and the Daily Record's, you should analyze Dan's liability separately from Ned and the Daily Record's liability. The same is true as to Pam.

Once again, let's apply the Torts writing approach to arrive at an outline:

PROFESSOR JAMES v. DAN

WRITING APPROACH:

INTENTIONAL INFLICTION OF EMOTIONAL DISTRESS

PRIMA FACIE CASE?
> <u>Extreme & outrageous act</u> - no, since Dan honestly believed statement was true.
> <u>Intent to cause severe emotional distress</u> - likely result of publishing statement accusing professor of exchanging grades for sexual favors.
> <u>Damages</u> - unknown whether James suffered severe emotional distress.

DEFAMATION

PRIMA FACIE CASE?
> <u>Defamatory matter</u> - Did Dan's statement subject James to public hatred, contempt or ridicule?
> <u>Published to third party</u> - Those who read bulletin board.
> <u>Subjectively understood by third party</u> - Notice named James.
> <u>Causation</u> - Dan's act was but for and direct cause of injury to James'

reputation.

Damages - Libel since Prof's employment affected.

DEFENSES?

> Absolute defenses?
>> Truth? Statement was false.
>
> Qualified defenses?
>> First Amendment.
>>> What standard applies?
>>> NY Times Standard: Public Figure - malice or reckless disregard of the truth.
>>> Gertz: Private Figure/Media Defendant - negligence and actual damages required.

PROFESSOR JAMES v. NED & DAILY RECORD

VICARIOUS LIABILITY - Ned's liability identical to liability of Daily Record.

INTENTIONAL INFLICTION OF EMOTIONAL DISTRESS

SAME ANALYSIS as above except that here not even negligence is shown.

DEFAMATION

PRIMA FACIE CASE?

> Defamatory matter - **SAME** as above.
> Published to third party - Those who read Daily Record.
> Subjectively understood by third party - **SAME** as above.
> Causation - Republisher equally liable.
> Damages - **SAME** as above.

DEFENSES?

> Absolute defenses?
> Truth? **SAME** as above.
> Qualified defenses?

FIRST AMENDMENT?
> What standard applies?
> <u>NY Times</u> Standard: **SAME** result as above.
> <u>Gertz</u>: Private Figure/Media Defendant - negligence and actual damages required.

REPORTS OF PUBLIC PROCEEDINGS
> Accurate reporting of false statements are privileged.

<u>PAM v. DAN, NED AND THE DAILY RECORD</u>

INTENTIONAL INFLICTION OF EMOTIONAL DISTRESS?

> NO, for **SAME** reasons stated above.

DEFAMATION?

> NO defamation since no one understood the statement as referring to Pam.

2.   Model Answer

PROFESSOR JAMES v. DAN

INTENTIONAL INFLICTION OF EMOTIONAL DISTRESS

This issue is whether Dan is liable to Professor James for intentional infliction of emotional distress. This tort requires an extreme and outrageous act with the intent to cause severe emotional distress resulting in severe emotional distress. Here, Dan's conduct cannot be said to be outrageous since he honestly believed that the statement was true. A reasonable person would not find that the publication of a statement believed to be true transcends normal bounds of decency.

With regard to Dan's intent, Dan acted negligently in failing to investigate the truth of the statement since he had reason to believe that "Teacher James" and not Professor James may have been the true culprit. However, because Dan believed the statement, he did not act intentionally or recklessly. Thus, Dan is not liable for this tort even if Professor James proves he suffered severe emotional distress.

198

DEFAMATION

The issue is whether Dan is liable to Professor James for defamation. Defamation is a defamatory publication to a third person, capable of being understood by third persons in a defamatory sense, causing damage to P's reputation.

First, a statement is defamatory if it exposes P to public hatred, contempt, or ridicule. The notice posted by Dan directly asserted that Professor James exchanged a grade for sexual favors. Any teacher who used his position to obtain sexual favors from a student would be subject to public hatred and likely expulsion from the teaching profession. This requirement is met.

Second, the defamatory statement must be published to a third party. Here the statement was published to those who read the notice on the bulletin board and secondarily published to the Daily Record's readers and thus this element is met.

Third, the defamatory matter must be subjectively understood by at least one person to be of and concerning P. Here, the notice explicitly named Professor James and thus this element is met.

Fourth, the defamatory statement must be the actual and proximate cause of plaintiff's injuries. Here, "but-for" Dan's notice, Professor James would not have been impugned. Because no intervening causes occurred between the posting of the notice and the resulting distress to Professor James, Dan's conduct is the proximate cause of Professor James' damages. Additionally, because it was foreseeable that the media might repeat Dan's statement, a newsworthy matter, Dan is also liable for any damages caused by the Daily Record's republication of the notice.

Last, P must suffer damage. Because the defamatory statement was in writing, general damages are presumed. Further, because Dan's statement affected Professor James' business and profession as a teacher, and would subject him to probable discipline and loss of employment, the defamation would qualify as slander per se. Thus, no special damages need be proven.

DEFENSES

Dan cannot assert truth as a defense since the statement was untrue.

Dan may argue that he has a qualified First Amendment defense. The issue is what standard of fault applies. Professor James is not a public figure, because there are no facts indicating that he was famous or notorious, or that he sought to voluntarily interject himself into public controversy. Thus, Professor James must prove that Dan acted at least negligently in publishing the statements. Because Dan had reason to know that another teacher named James had been fired, he should have at least investigated the possibility that his information was incorrect, given the seriousness of the allegations involved. His failure to do so was negligent and therefore this defense does not apply.

Thus Professor James may recover against Dan for defamation.

PROFESSOR JAMES v. NED & THE DAILY RECORD

Ned's liability, as the editor, is identical to that of the Daily Record because he acted within the scope of his employment and is thus vicariously liable.

INTENTIONAL INFLICTION OF EMOTIONAL DISTRESS

Recovery for this tort will be denied on the same grounds urged in James v. Dan.

DEFAMATION

The analysis of defamation is the same as in James v. Dan. The republisher of defamatory statements is equally as liable as the original defamer. However, under the Single Publication rule, the Daily Record's newspaper will be considered as a single publication.

DEFENSES

TRUTH

Truth is no defense as argued in <u>James v. Dan</u>.

FIRST AMENDMENT

Because Professor James is not a public figure for the same reasons as argued in <u>James v. Dan</u>, he must prove that the Daily Record acted negligently. James will argue that the Daily Record should have investigated the truth or falsity of the statement contained in the notice before printing a photograph of it. However, the court will likely find that the Daily Record had no reason to believe that the statement was false, and therefore did not act carelessly in publishing the notice. This defense bars Professor James' recovery.

REPORTS OF PUBLIC PROCEEDINGS

Under this privilege, accurate reporting of false statements is privileged. Because the Daily Record photographed the notice as it appeared, and correctly stated that it appeared on a bulletin board at a law school, its conduct is privileged and Professor James may not recover for defamation.

<u>PAM v. DAN, NED & THE DAILY RECORD</u>

INTENTIONAL INFLICTION OF EMOTIONAL DISTRESS

Pam cannot recover for this tort against any party for the same reasons stated in <u>James v. Dan</u>.

DEFAMATION

As stated above, the defamatory statement must be subjectively understood by at least one third person to be of and concerning P. Because Pam was never identified as the recipient of the "A" grade, no one understood the statement as referring to her, and therefore she cannot recover for defamation.

Yes, you have again encountered a "Daily Double," a problem in which the discussion of defamation in <u>Professor James v. Dan</u> is nearly identical to that in <u>Professor James v. Ned & The Daily Recorder</u>, with the exception of discussions of the Single Publication Rule and the defense of Public Proceedings. Therefore, you should discuss Dan's liability separately from Ned's and the Daily Recorder's liability.

"Nothing is often a good thing to do and always a good thing to say."

---- Will Durant (1885 - 1981)

The key to solving this problem is not to rehash the issues you have already discussed. Repeating yourself not only bores the reader but also wastes valuable time. The only way to recognize repetitive issues is to outline your answer <u>before</u> you begin writing.

For example, the tort of intentional infliction of emotional distress only needed to be discussed in full once. This one discussion was easily incorporated by reference in the second and third parts of this problem. Discussing this tort three times would have consumed a great deal of time. The Model Answer begins by fully analyzing intentional infliction of emotional distress in <u>James v. Dan</u>, and then simply incorporates this discussion in <u>James v. Ned & The Daily Recorder</u> and <u>Pam v. Dan, Ned & The Daily Journal</u>. Thus, you get three times the credit for one answer.

Note the answer to the second interrogatory is perhaps one of the shortest passing answers I have ever seen. The first sentence repeats the third element of defamation. The next thirty words point out that Pam has no cause of action for defamation. This goes to show that bigger does not always mean better.

Now add up your scores and see how you did!

The Exam Evaluator
PROF JAMES & PAM v. DAN, NED & DAILY RECORDER

EXAM PRESENTATION (TOTAL POINTS AVAILABLE = 25)

	Poor										Excellent	
NEATNESS	0	1	2	3	4	5						____
ORGANIZATION	0	1	2	3	4	5	6	7	8	9	10	____
LAWYER-LIKE	0	1	2	3	4	5	6	7	8	9	10	____

DISCUSSION OF ISSUES (TOTAL POINTS AVAILABLE =75)

PROFESSOR JAMES v. DAN

INTENTIONAL INFLICTION OF EMOTIONAL DISTRESS

    15 POINTS = FULL DISCUSSION   ____

    10 POINTS = PARTIAL/INCOMPLETE DISCUSSION   ____

DEFAMATION/DEFENSES TO DEFAMATION

    30 POINTS = FULL DISCUSSION   ____

    20 POINTS = PARTIAL/INCOMPLETE DISCUSSION   ____

PROFESSOR JAMES v. NED & THE DAILY RECORDER

DEFAMATION/DEFENSES TO DEFAMATION

    20 POINTS = FULL DISCUSSION   ____

10 POINTS = PARTIAL/INCOMPLETE DISCUSSION   ____

PAM v. DAN, NED & THE DAILY RECORDER

10 POINTS = FULL DISCUSSION   ____

5 POINTS = PARTIAL/INCOMPLETE DISCUSSION   ____

TOTAL SCORE   ____

M. PROBLEM TEN: PAUL v. DAN

Paul recently moved into the area to open a new restaurant. After months of searching for a personal residence, Paul offered to purchase Seller's house. With his new restaurant soon to open, Paul hired Chef to head up his kitchen staff under an agreement that allows either party to terminate the employment relationship on thirty days' notice. Paul entered into a written three-year contract with Meatco, a food supplier, for regular weekly deliveries of high quality meat.

Dan, owner of ten restaurants, learned about all of the above and resolved to do what he could to hinder the operation of Paul's new restaurant. Dan offered Chef double his current salary and told Chef that if he did not quit his job with Paul, "I can make it difficult for you to get your next job. I have many restaurant connections all over the country, you know."

Dan wrote to Meatco: "It has come to my attention that you are supplying Paul. In all candor, I must tell you that so long as you continue to do so, I will not deal with you once our contract ends in two weeks."

Dan then offered Seller a much higher price for his house than that offered by Paul, hoping that recommencing a house search would divert Paul's attention from operating his restaurant.

Chef terminated his employment with Paul and went to work for Dan. Meatco stopped deliveries to Paul. Seller accepted Dan's offer for the house.

Paul's restaurant opened but incurred significant losses. Paul's reputation in the restaurant community was adversely affected. Meanwhile, Dan's restaurants flourished.

Paul sues Dan.

What are Paul's rights and remedies, if any, against Dan? Discuss?

1.   Outlining Strategy and Exam Analysis

"The only certainty is that nothing is certain."

---- Pinny the Elder (c.23 - 79)

This Torts-Remedies question involves the remote area of economic torts, and the torts of defamation, intentional infliction of emotional distress, and of course, remedies for each cause of action. I am sure that those examinees who skipped over the area of economic torts in their studies were quite shocked to see this question.

2.   How to Guess What Areas Will Be Tested on the Bar Exam

You should always be prepared to address any issue or rule of law in all the bar subjects. Some people try, with moderate success, to guess what areas are going to be on the next bar examination. Only 6 of the 14 possible areas are tested. The chances of someone guessing correctly are roughly 50%.

The problem with trying to prepare for the exam based on predictions is that you will be in serious trouble if the predictions are wrong. Thus, you should always expect to be tested on any and all areas.

Have you noticed a pattern in the Torts problems we have analyzed? Most fact patterns tend to over-sympathize with one of the parties. In this fact pattern poor Paul is being victimized by Evil Dan. While Paul seems like an innocent, well-meaning restauranteur, Dan is his antithesis, who does everything possible to run Paul out of town. We naturally empathize with Paul just as we are disgusted by Dan's underhanded dealings. However, remember who created these facts. Why is it that the Bar Examiners create such sympathetic characters? Is it to appease our appetite for justice-seeking plaintiffs?

The Bar Examiners tend to create sympathetic characters so that emotion interferes with our ability to objectively and scientifically apply the law to the facts. While emotion and feeling has its place, it usually has little to do with legal analysis. The Bar Examiners are testing your ability to be objective. Do not fall in the trap of analyzing your answer based on emotion. Do not let the Bar Examiners manipulate you. Let's take an example of how emotion can detract from an objective analysis:

206

Paul should sue Dan for everything he's got. Dan's conduct was utterly shameless. He tried to take his home, then his business, his supplier, and even his cook. Dan profited from his evil deeds and should be punished to the full extent of the law.

This analysis sounds like a closing argument in a criminal case. While these arguments would be perfectly valid in a courtroom, they have no place in your exam answer. Objectively analyze Paul's rights and remedies and do not pass judgment on the moral correctness of Dan's acts.

Let's apply the now well-worn Torts writing approach and formulate our outline to this problem:

PAUL v. DAN

1. <u>Paul's Rights Against Dan</u>

INTENTIONAL INFLICTION OF EMOTIONAL DISTRESS

PRIMA FACIE CASE?
      Extreme and outrageous act?
      Intent to cause severe emotional distress?
      Damages - extremely likely to cause Paul extreme distress.

DEFENSES? None.

INTERFERENCE WITH CONTRACT (PAUL'S CONTRACT WITH CHEF)

PRIMA FACIE CASE?
      An act by D
      With knowledge of a contract
      For the purpose of interfering with contract right of P
      Causation
      Damages

INTERFERENCE WITH CONTRACT (PAUL'S CONTRACT WITH SELLER)

PRIMA FACIE CASE?

    An act by D

    With knowledge of a contract

    For the purpose of interfering with contract right of P - No contractual right existed since Paul had only made an offer.

    Causation

    Damages

INTERFERENCE WITH CONTRACT (PAUL'S CONTRACT WITH MEATCO)

PRIMA FACIE CASE?

    An act by D

    With knowledge of a contract

    For the purpose of interfering with contract right of P

    Causation

    Damages

INTERFERENCE WITH PROSPECTIVE ADVANTAGE

PRIMA FACIE CASE?

    An act by D

    With knowledge of P's prospective advantage

    For the purpose of interfering with P's business

    Causation

    Damages

2. <u>Paul's Remedies Against Dan</u>
   (APPLY TORTS REMEDIES WRITING APPROACH)

DAMAGES

    Compensatory Damages: for lost profits and business losses.

    Punitive Damages: available because D acted maliciously.

    Limitations on damages

RESTITUTION
Constructive trust for lost/future profits

INJUNCTION

Inadequate Remedy at Law: Damages sufficient to compensate for business losses due to interference with contract.
Property right? Land: No property right since offer never accepted.
Feasibility problems: Court cannot supervise personal service contracts.
Balancing hardships: Not appropriate where D acts willfully.
No defenses apply.

Like <u>Ed v. Courier Journal</u>, this problem gives you a general interrogatory. There is more than one way to organize this problem. You might list each cause of action factually, by the events which occurred: (1) Contract for the House; (2) Contract for Chef's Services; (3) Contract with Meatco; and so on. Then, discuss the remedies at the end of your analysis. Another example of how to organize this problem follows in the model answer.

3.   Model Answer

PAUL v. DAN

1. Paul's Rights Against Dan

INTENTIONAL INFLICTION OF EMOTIONAL DISTRESS

The issue is whether Dan is liable for intentional infliction of emotional distress. This tort requires an extreme and outrageous act committed with the intent to cause severe emotional distress resulting in severe emotional distress. Here, Dan committed outrageous acts that clearly transcended any notion of decency, by using threats and extortion to force Meatco and Chef to breach their respective contracts with Paul. Further, Dan acted with the intent to hinder the operation of Paul's new restaurant and should have known that ruining Paul's business prospects would cause Paul a great deal of emotional distress. Thus, if Paul can demonstrate that he in fact suffered severe emotional distress, he will recover for this tort.

No defenses bar Paul's action for this tort.

INTERFERENCE WITH CONTRACT (PAUL'S AGREEMENT WITH CHEF)

The issue is whether Dan is liable for wrongfully interfering with Paul's agreement with Chef. This tort requires an act by D with knowledge of a contract for the purpose of interfering with a contract right of P. The act requirement is met because Dan threatened Chef that he would ruin Chef's future employment if he did not quit his job with Paul. Further, Dan was aware of Paul's agreement with Chef, and acted with the intent to cause Chef to breach his agreement with Paul. Finally, the fact that Chef had the right to terminate his agreement upon thirty days' notice does not excuse Dan's actions nor his liability for interfering with that agreement. Thus, all the elements of this tort are met.

INTERFERENCE WITH CONTRACT (PAUL'S CONTRACT WITH SELLER)

The issue is whether Dan is liable for wrongful interference of contract for purchasing Seller's home. Here, this tort is not met because there was no contract or agreement between Paul and Seller. No contractual right existed since Paul had only made an offer to purchase Seller's home. Thus, Paul cannot recover for this tort.

INTERFERENCE WITH CONTRACT (PAUL'S CONTRACT WITH MEATCO)

The issue is whether Dan is liable for wrongfully interfering with Paul's contract with Meatco. Dan committed the required act by writing to Meatco and threatening to cancel his contract with Meatco unless it stopped supplying Paul. Dan acted with the intent to cause Meatco to breach its three-year agreement with Paul. If Paul is able to prove that he was unable to obtain meat of the same quality from another source at the same price, and that Meatco's breach caused damage to his business, he will recover for this tort.

INTERFERENCE WITH PROSPECTIVE ADVANTAGE

Paul may argue that Dan committed the tort of interference with prospective advantage. This tort requires an act by D with knowledge of P's prospective advantage for the purpose of interfering with P's business. Paul would argue that because Dan purchased a home that Paul hoped to buy, in order to adversely affect Paul's business, Dan acted to gain an unfair business advantage. Because Dan did purchase the home for this purpose, he acted with the requisite intent. However, Paul will have difficulty proving causation and damages, since he could presumably find another place to live and thereby continue his business enterprises. Thus, he may not recover for this tort.

Paul may also argue that by interfering with his agreements with Chef and Meatco, Dan interfered with his new restaurant business. Under this tort, Paul would have to prove the same elements as in an interference with contract action as argued above, except that he is not required to prove that there was an existing contract between Meatco, Chef, and himself.

2. Paul's Remedies Against Dan

The issue is what remedies Paul may recover for the torts discussed above.

DAMAGES

Paul may recover compensatory damages for lost profits and any other business losses incurred as a result of Dan's interference with his business. Paul may also recover any incidental costs incurred such as costs associated with finding a new meat supplier or chef.

Paul may also recover punitive damages, which are awarded to punish a defendant for willful and malicious conduct. Here, Dan acted willfully and wantonly with the purpose of causing Paul's business to fail, and to benefit his own business enterprises.

However, any damages recovered by Paul must have been foreseeable, unavoidable, certain, and caused by Dan's conduct. Here it was foreseeable to Dan that his acts would cause Paul's business to fail and he in fact acted with that purpose in mind. Paul would have a duty, however, to mitigate losses suffered in relation to his loss of Chef and Meatco, and to prove that the significant losses he suffered were the result of Dan's conduct. Finally, he would have to prove that any damages for lost profits were not speculative, since the restaurant business is somewhat unstable and uncertain.

RESTITUTION

Paul may seek the equitable remedy of a constructive trust, where equity creates a trust to compel D to reconvey property unjustly retained. If Paul can prove that Dan's restaurants "flourished" because of Dan's tortious conduct, he may seek to compel Paul to turn over those profits attributable to his wrongful conduct.

INJUNCTION

Paul will not be able to obtain injunctive relief.

First, there must be an inadequate remedy at law and because damages are sufficient to compensate for business losses due to interference with contract, injunctive relief will be denied as to Dan's interference with Chef's and Meatco's agreements. Furthermore, because both interferences involve personal services, an injunction would violate the prohibition against involuntary servitude.

As to Dan's interference with Paul's contract with Seller, although land is unique, Paul had no property right because Seller had not accepted his offer. Thus, injunctive relief is not an issue.

As you can see, this was not an easy problem to complete. If you did not obtain a passing score don't be discouraged. Remember that most people who answered this question found it difficult and therefore the scaled score needed to pass was substantially less. As reflected in the Exam Evaluator, a passing score was easier to obtain because this problem was more difficult.

The Exam Evaluator
PAUL V. DAN

EXAM PRESENTATION (TOTAL POINTS AVAILABLE = 25)

	Poor	Excellent	
NEATNESS	0 1 2 3 4 5		____
ORGANIZATION	0 1 2 3 4 5 6 7 8 9 10		____
LAWYER-LIKE	0 1 2 3 4 5 6 7 8 9 10		____

DISCUSSION OF ISSUES (TOTAL POINTS AVAILABLE =75)

PAUL'S RIGHTS AGAINST DAN

INTENTIONAL INFLICTION OF EMOTIONAL DISTRESS

    15 POINTS = FULL DISCUSSION   ____

    10 POINTS = PARTIAL/INCOMPLETE DISCUSSION   ____

INTERFERENCE WITH CONTRACT (PAUL'S CONTRACT WITH CHEF)

    15 POINTS = FULL DISCUSSION   ____

    10 POINTS = PARTIAL/INCOMPLETE DISCUSSION   ____

INTERFERENCE WITH CONTRACT (PAUL'S CONTRACT WITH SELLER)

15 POINTS = FULL DISCUSSION   ____

10 POINTS = PARTIAL/INCOMPLETE DISCUSSION   ____

INTERFERENCE WITH CONTRACT (PAUL'S CONTRACT WITH MEATCO)

15 POINTS = FULL DISCUSSION   ____

10 POINTS = PARTIAL/INCOMPLETE DISCUSSION   ____

INTERFERENCE WITH PROSPECTIVE ADVANTAGE

5 BONUS POINTS   ____

2. Paul's Remedies against Dan

DAMAGES

10 POINTS = FULL DISCUSSION   ____

5 POINTS = PARTIAL/INCOMPLETE DISCUSSION   ____

RESTITUTION

10 POINTS = FULL DISCUSSION   ____

5 POINTS = PARTIAL/INCOMPLETE DISCUSSION   ____

INJUNCTION

5 BONUS POINTS   ____

TOTAL SCORE   ____

N.   CHAPTER CONCLUSION

"You always pass failure on the way to success."

---- Mickey Rooney (1920 -   )

With that, your tour of duty through the land of Torts is now over. You have been exposed to the different types of Torts problems which you will encounter on the bar examination. You are, of course, free to take as many Torts examinations as you can find, and it is recommended that you do so. Remember that the more examinations you take, the better you will become at solving bar questions. Thus, let the examinations in this book be a beginning and not an end to your preparation for the Torts section of the California bar examination.

If you haven't done so, record the scores achieved on your Exam Evaluators into the Master Exam Evaluator provided at the end of this book. After having done so, look at your scores and ask yourself, are my scores improving? If not, you should re-take those examinations which reflect a score less than "75". The key to success is not succeeding the first time, but by trying as many times as necessary to succeed. Do not be shy about retaking examinations, for each examination in this book is a lesson within itself, and you should not move on to the next exercise until the one before you is sufficiently understood and mastered.

At the same time, do not be too hard on yourself. These examinations were difficult, and it is much better to learn these lessons now rather than on the actual bar examination.

BARBREAKER

community property

IX. COMMUNITY PROPERTY

A. THE COMMUNITY PROPERTY WRITING APPROACH

"There are three steps to accomplishment: Plan purposefully. Proceed positively. Pursue persistently."

---- Proverb

The law of community property finds its origin in the age old question, "Who gets what?" between a husband and wife who decide to separate or divorce. On the bar examination, it is usually this scenario which provides the backdrop to the facts of the problem you are given. Remember then, that the overall question on a community property examination is what interest each spouse has in a particular item of property.

Unlike other subject areas, you will never have any difficulty identifying a community property problem. For one, the interrogatories will always direct you to "Answer all questions according to California law." This is because community property is the only subject area that is limited to California law, and so the Bar Examiners must advise you of that fact. The inclusion of this statement in the problem is a dead give-away that a community property question is before you.

The second indicator that the Bar Examiners are testing community property is that the parties in the problem will always have names beginning with "H" and "W". Over the years, husbands have been represented by Hank, Hal, Harry, while wives have had names like Wendy, Wanda, Wilma.

You will also find that most community property problems are identical in format. The typical community property problem consists of a set of facts involving two persons who meet and marry, and after acquiring property, divorce. You are then given one to five specific interrogatories inquiring as to how certain items of property should be divided between the spouses.

Over the years, the Bar Examiners have not strayed from this basic formula, simply because the law of community property does not lend itself to many different testing formulas. Moreover, giving a problem which requires the examinee to decide the division of property upon divorce is the most practical way to test community property.

The Examiners will almost always specify which item of property they wish you to discuss. Again, this is because they do not want to give you a general interrogatory, such as "Please decide what husband and wife should receive upon divorce," because everyone would analyze the various items of property in differing order, creating a nightmare for the bar grader. As in all other subject areas, you should always follow the order indicated by the Examiners in the interrogatories.

With these strategies in mind, you should feel confident that you will never find yourself writing out a "Torts" answer to a community property question. By looking for these simple indicators, you will easily identify community property problems on the bar exam.

B.   THE BIG PICTURE QUESTIONS

There are six big picture questions you must ask yourself in solving a community property problem:

(1)   **PRELIMINARY QUESTION: DOES CALIFORNIA COMMUNITY PROPERTY LAW APPLY TO THIS ITEM OF PROPERTY?**

(2)   **WHAT IS THE SOURCE OF THE ITEM?**

(3)   **HAVE ANY ACTIONS BY THE PARTIES ALTERED THE CHARACTER OF THE PROPERTY?**

(4)   **DO ANY STATUTORY PRESUMPTIONS APPLY?**

(5)   **ARE ANY ISSUES RAISED AS TO MANAGEMENT AND CONTROL OF COMMUNITY PROPERTY DURING MARRIAGE?**

(6)   **BASED ON THE ABOVE, HOW SHOULD THE ITEM BE DIVIDED?**

Let's review each "big picture" question:

(1) PRELIMINARY QUESTION: DOES CALIFORNIA COMMUNITY PROPERTY LAW APPLY TO THIS ITEM OF PROPERTY?

Before solving the problem, you should always ask "Does California community property law APPLY?" The application of community property law depends on two things: (1) a legal marriage, and (2) a California domicile.

The first issue is a simple one: Are the parties legally married? Generally the Bar Examiners will tell you that the parties are married, for a bar question involving an invalid marriage are quite rare. However, if you are told that the marriage was invalid, then you must apply quasi-marital property principles. You should also be prepared to address any putative or meretricious spouse issues if they arise.

The second issue is whether the parties were domiciled in California. While the Bar Examiners will not test you on marital property laws of other states, it is important to determine whether the parties may have been domiciled elsewhere when the property was acquired because quasi-community property principles apply.

(2) WHAT IS THE SOURCE OF THE ITEM?

The next issue is what is the SOURCE of the item. Property takes on the character of the item used to acquire it, and so you must trace the item to its origin. It's like Darwin's theory of evolution: if it came from separate property, then it is considered separate property, and if it came from community property, it is considered as community property.

Specific rules apply to certain types of property. For example, retirement benefits are community property if "earned" during the marriage, and are usually subject to apportionment. The court may either award one-half the proceeds to the employee's spouse when and if the benefit is realized, or award the entire benefit to the employee and give employee's spouse community property of equal value.

Other specific "source" rules concern:

EARNINGS
PENSION RIGHTS
DISABILITY & WORKER'S COMPENSATION
EMPLOYEE STOCK OPTIONS
SEVERANCE PAY
GOODWILL OF A BUSINESS
FEDERAL BENEFITS
PERSONAL INJURY DAMAGES
GIFTS
REAL PROPERTY
RENTS, ISSUES & PROFITS
LIFE INSURANCE
EDUCATION & TRAINING

(3) DID ANY ACTIONS BY THE PARTY CHANGE OR ALTER THE CHARACTER OF THE PROPERTY?

After determining the source, you then look to any ACTIONS by the parties which have altered the character of the property. Generally, you will be given an item of property which comes from a separate property source but is transmuted into community property by actions of the husband or wife.

These are the ACTIONS affecting the classification of property you should watch for on bar exam questions:

AGREEMENTS BETWEEN SPOUSES AFFECTING PROPERTY
GIFTS BETWEEN THE SPOUSES
COMMINGLING OF SEPARATE PROPERTY & COMMUNITY PROPERTY
COMMUNITY SERVICES OR FUNDS ARE USED TO IMPROVE SEPARATE PROPERTY
SEPARATION

These issues are easy to spot because the Examiners must give you a factual situation that tells you which of these acts were committed by the parties. For

219

example, in order to test "commingling" principles, the Bar Examiners must necessarily give you a factual situation involving one spouse who takes separate property funds and mixes them with community property funds or vice-versa. They will have to spell out these circumstances in the fact pattern. You will see that this is true of any community property question raising these issues.

The key here is to identify the actions and then state the significance of that action on the classification and distribution of property. For example, if you are told that Hal the husband used his earnings during marriage to make principal payments on his separate property summer home, the community obtains a pro-rata interest in the separate property in proportion to amounts from separate property and community property funds. Thus, the summer home is both separate and community property. Next, you must determine what percentage of community property was used to pay off the principal owed on the summer home and then award the community a pro rata interest in the home, by multiplying the percentage of community funds used by the present market value of the home.

(4) DO ANY STATUTORY PRESUMPTIONS APPLY?

After you have determined the source of the item and the effect of any actions by the parties, you then turn to the statutory presumptions. These statutory presumptions will guide you in deciding whether the item is presumed to be separate property or community property. Think of these presumptions as "tie-breakers" in close cases where it is not quite clear whether a particular item of property is separate or community property. These presumptions should be considered in each and every case:

GENERAL PRESUMPTION

MARRIED WOMAN PRESUMPTION (APPLIES ONLY PRIOR TO 1/1/75)

WIFE AND THIRD PARTY TENANCY IN COMMON PRESUMPTION

HUSBAND AND WIFE COMMUNITY PROPERTY PRESUMPTION

JOINTLY HELD PROPERTY PRESUMPTION

For example, the "married woman" presumption holds that property acquired by a married woman prior to January 1, 1975 by an instrument in writing is presumed to be her separate property, unless a different intention is expressed in the instrument. Thus, if Wanda, the wife, takes property as "Wanda, a married woman," before January 1, 1975, that property will be presumed to be Wanda's separate property. The presumption, however, is not conclusive, and may be rebutted by contrary evidence.

(5) ARE ANY ISSUES RAISED AS TO MANAGEMENT AND CONTROL OF COMMUNITY PROPERTY DURING MARRIAGE?

The next issue, which frequently appears on bar examination questions, is whether any issues as to management and control of community property are raised. Typically this issue is being tested on bar questions when one spouse acts during the marriage to the detriment of the other spouse, by making a gift of or selling community assets without the other spouse's consent, incurring debt and so on. Testable issues in this area include:

MANAGEMENT AND CONTROL OF COMMUNITY PERSONAL AND REAL PROPERTY

MANAGEMENT AND CONTROL OF COMMUNITY PROPERTY BUSINESS

DEBTS OWED TO THIRD PARTIES AND BETWEEN HUSBAND AND WIFE

For example, if Hal, the husband, sells the family furniture to pay off a gambling debt, it should be pointed out that one spouse cannot sell or encumber the furniture of the home without the other spouse's consent. Thus, the transaction is void and can be set aside, and the furniture may be recovered.

(6) BASED ON THE ABOVE, HOW SHOULD THE ITEM BE DIVIDED?

Finally, you must tell the bar grader how the item should be divided among husband and wife and any third parties, e.g., creditors. As you will see in the questions that follow, most community property bar questions ask you to divide the community property upon the death of one or both spouses, or divorce. Upon divorce, the court must divide all community property equally, subject to certain exceptions. Upon death, each spouse may will away all of their separate property and one-half of their community property holdings.

Where possible, you must determine precisely what interest each spouse has in the item of property. The Bar Examiners usually use nice round figures in community property problems for those of us who are not mathematical geniuses. For example, if the Bar Examiners tell you that Wanda had a home worth $100,000 before she was married, but used community funds to pay off 25% of the principal owed on the home during marriage, you must tell the bar grader that 25% of the present value of the home is community property. If the home is now worth $200,000, then you must tell the grader that $50,000, or 25% of the present value of the home, is community property.

C. SPECIAL TIPS ON ANALYZING A COMMUNITY PROPERTY PROBLEM

Because community property problems tend to be similar in format, these specific strategies will help you analyze and write out your answer.

First, you should organize your answer by the items of property and these items should appear as the headings in your analysis. Let's take an example:

1. How should the following assets be classified and distributed upon dissolution:

   A. The house? Discuss.

   B. Winnie's shampoo business?

   C. Harrold's retirement benefits?

If these interrogatories are presented, your headings should be "A. The House," "B. Winnie's Shampoo Business," and "C. Harrold's Retirement Benefits." As stated in the introductory section, headings will assist you in compartmentalizing your analysis and in separating your discussion of each issue.

Secondly, it is helpful in solving most problems to state the general community property principles before you begin solving the problem. This technique avoids having to restate the general principles of community property law in the body of

222

your answer.

"Because California is a community property state, all property acquired during marriage is community property (CP), while property acquired before marriage or after permanent separation, or by gift or inheritance, is separate property (SP). The characterization of an asset as community property or separate property depends on three factors: (1) the source of the item; (2) actions of the parties which may have altered the character of the item; (3) any statutory presumptions affecting the item."

Of course, you need not state these principles before you begin analyzing the problem, and may weave them into your analysis. Also keep in mind that these suggested statements are only an example of possible introductory remarks to your exam answer. You should try and develop your own "introductory" remarks to your answer if you choose to adopt this strategy.

Do not fear that somehow everyone else taking the bar exam is writing the same thing. Bar examinations are quite different from creative writing pieces. Because everyone is applying the same set of rules to solve the problem, the bar grader expects that your answers will be similar in content.

Once you have listed the three prongs of your analysis, simply follow each step and apply the law to the facts before you. As you will see in the problems which follow, application of this writing approach will consistently solve any and all community property problems. For a more in-depth statement of the black letter law, please review the Community Property approach in the *California Bar Examination Survival Kit*.

Now let's apply the writing approach to a real life community property problem.

D.   PROBLEM ONE: HUSBAND v. WIFE

1. The First Read

Read the question once strictly for content:

The following events occurred in California.

Husband (H), a carpenter, and Wife (W), a nurse, were married in 1965. In 1966, W contracted to buy a small office building. She paid the purchase price in installments by withdrawals from a joint bank account into which H and W deposited their earnings. In 1970, W paid the last installment and received a deed conveying the building to "W, a married woman." H knew W was buying the building and made no objection. He did not know how title to the building was taken.

In 1980, H's aged uncle, Ted (T), promised H and W that if they would move into his home, maintain it in good repair, and care for him for the remainder of his life, he would will his house and furniture to H. H and W moved in with T, cared for him and maintained his home in good repair until his death in 1985. T left a valid will giving his house and furniture to H.

H and W continued to live in the house. Returning home one day, W discovered to her surprise that all the furniture had been removed. H confessed that he had sold the furniture and used the proceeds to pay gambling losses he had secretly incurred.

In a dissolution of marriage proceeding now pending, what are W's and H's rights, if any, with respect to the following:

1. The office building?
2. The house?
3. The furniture or its value?

Discuss.

Answer according to California law.

224

2. The Second Read

Now, let's read the question a second time, this time focusing on key phrases and words, indicated in bold type:

The following events occurred in California.

Husband (H), a carpenter, and Wife (W), a nurse, were **married** in 1965. In 1966, W **contracted** to buy a small office building. She paid the **purchase price** in installments by withdrawals from a **joint bank account** into which H and W deposited their earnings. In 1970, W paid the last installment and received a deed conveying the building to "**W, a married woman**." H **knew** W was buying the building and made **no objection**. He did not know how title to the building was taken.

In 1980, H's aged uncle, Ted (T), promised H and W that if they would move into his home, maintain it in good repair, and care for him for the remainder of his life, he would will his house and furniture to H. H and W moved in with T, cared for him and maintained his home in good repair until his death in 1985. T left a valid will **giving his house and furniture to H.**

H and W continued to live in the house. Returning home one day, W discovered to her surprise that all the furniture had been removed. H confessed that he had **sold the furniture** and used the proceeds to pay gambling losses he had secretly incurred.

In a **dissolution** of marriage proceeding now pending, what are W's and H's rights, if any, with respect to the following:

1. The office building?
2. The house?
3. The furniture or its value?

Discuss.

Answer according to California law.

The first thing you should recognize are the "community property" flags. This particular problem begins and ends with a flag. By stating, "The following events occurred in California," the Examiners are telling you, "THIS IS A COMMUNITY PROPERTY PROBLEM." And if there is any lingering doubt, the Examiners reiterate that you are to "[a]nswer according to California law."

As with all community property problems, the characters have names beginning with "H" and "W" and in this problem, the Examiners have blatantly named the characters Husband and Wife.

Having determined that this is a community property problem, let's move on to the facts.

You are told that Husband and Wife married in 1965. You are then told three things about their life together:

(1) Wife buys an office building in 1965, taking title as a "married woman" in 1970;

(2) Husband receives house and furniture by devise in 1985; and

(3) Husband sells furniture to pay gambling debts.

Lastly, you are told that a divorce action is now pending and asked to decide what their rights are with respect to three items of property, the office building, house and the furniture or its value.

3. Visualization Exercise

After you have carefully read the facts, the next step is to VISUALIZE the problem.

See Husband. See Wife. Visualize a face for both Husband and Wife. Since you do not know anyone named "Husband" or "Wife" it is much more difficult to see these people as real people, but you must strive to do exactly that. See Husband dressed in his carpenter's uniform and wife in her starched nurse's uniform. See Husband and Wife walk down the aisle on that blessed day in 1965.

One year later, see Wife as she signs a contract to buy a small office building. See the office building that Wife is buying. See Wife as she pays the mortgage on the office building. See her write the check from "Husband and Wife's" joint bank account, which contained both Husband's and Wife's earnings.

See Wife as she receives the deed for the building. See the words "W, a married woman" imprinted on the deed. See Wife tell husband that she was buying the building, and see Husband acknowledge that fact without objection.

Ten years later, see Husband and Wife speaking with old Uncle Ted, who says, "If you move in with me and care for me and my home for the rest of my life, I will give my house and furniture to Husband." See Husband and Wife as they move in with Ted, and care for Uncle Ted each day and maintain his home. See the will which leaves Husband Ted's home and furniture.

Now see Wife coming home one day and finding the house empty of all furniture. See Husband as he confesses, "I'm sorry! I sold the furniture because I needed the money to pay off my gambling debts. I'm sorry I didn't tell you about it!" See Wife as she walks out the door . . .

4. HEADLINING EXERCISE

By VISUALIZING the fact pattern, you are now in a position to solve the problem. However, to cement the facts even further in the recesses of your mind, let's use the technique of headlining:

HEADLINE:

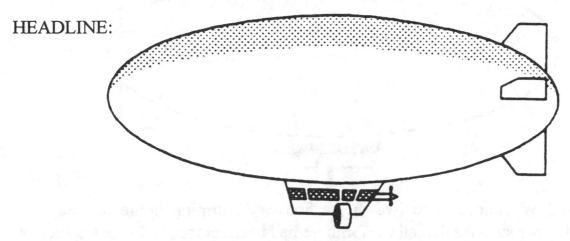

Husband (H), a carpenter, and Wife (W), a nurse, were married in 1965. In 1966, W contracted to buy a small office building. She paid the purchase price in installments by withdrawals from a joint bank account into which H and W deposited their earnings. In 1970, W paid the last installment and received a deed conveying the building to "W, a married woman." H knew W was buying the building and made no objection. He did not know how title to the building was taken.

HEADLINE:

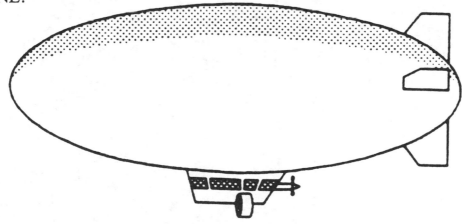

In 1980, H's aged uncle, Ted (T), promised H and W that if they would move into his home, maintain it in good repair, and care for him for the remainder of his life, he would will his house and furniture to H. H and W moved in with T, cared for

228

him and maintained his home in good repair until his death in 1985. T left a valid will giving his house and furniture to H.

HEADLINE:

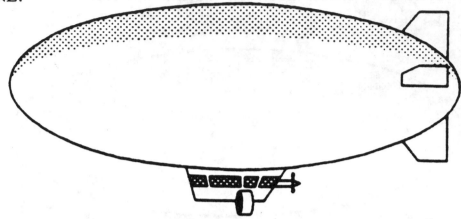

H and W continued to live in the house. Returning home one day, W discovered to her surprise that all the furniture had been removed. H confessed that he had sold the furniture and used the proceeds to pay gambling losses he had secretly incurred.

Now compare your headlines to these sample headlines:

1.   WIFE TAKES TITLE TO OFFICE BUILDING IN 1970 AS A "MARRIED WOMAN" AFTER PAYING OFF PROPERTY FROM JOINT ACCOUNT!

2.   HUSBAND GETS TED'S HOUSE AND FURNITURE AFTER CARING FOR TED FOR FIVE YEARS!

3.   WIFE DISCOVERS FURNITURE MISSING . . . HUSBAND CONFESSES THAT HE SOLD FURNITURE TO PAY OFF GAMBLING DEBTS!

While these headlines are probably beginning to sound like something out of the "National Enquirer," they serve the purpose of helping you remember the fact patterns. Even when reading a newspaper, we tend to remember not the story, but the headline which preceded it. It is the headline that catches our attention and directs us to the more detailed story which follows it.

Now that you have a firm grasp of the facts, try outlining your answer, and then turn the page.

5. Outlining Exercise

Next, let's review the outline to your answer. Remember that you must outline your answer, so you know what to write **before** you beginning writing your answer. Let's begin by studying the interrogatories:

In a dissolution of marriage proceeding now pending, what are W's and H's rights, if any, with respect to the following:

1. The office building?
2. The house?
3. The furniture or its value?

Discuss.

As you can see, there are three items of property at issue. Because you must follow the order indicated by the interrogatories, structure your answer as follows:

1. The Office Building

2. The House

3. The Furniture

Next, we apply the Community Property writing approach to determine what issues are presented. Let's begin with the office building:

(1) PRELIMINARY QUESTION: DOES CALIFORNIA COMMUNITY PROPERTY LAW APPLY TO THIS ITEM OF PROPERTY?

Yes. You are told that the events in question occurred in California and that Husband and Wife were married in 1965. Therefore, California community property principles apply to this problem.

(2) WHAT IS THE SOURCE OF THE ITEM?

You are told that Wife used funds from a joint bank account containing deposits of Husband's and Wife's earnings to buy the office building. Thus, the issue is whether the funds from the joint account are separate property or community property.

(3) HAVE ANY ACTIONS BY THE PARTIES ALTERED THE CHARACTER OF THE PROPERTY?

The proceeds of a joint bank account are presumed to be community property. There was no act by either H or W which would change the character of the proceeds. However, Wife might argue that Husband intended that his earnings in the bank account to be a gift since he knew she was buying the building.

(4) DO ANY STATUTORY PRESUMPTIONS APPLY?

Two presumptions could apply: "GENERAL PRESUMPTION" and "MARRIED WOMAN PRESUMPTION."

(5) ARE ANY ISSUES RAISED AS TO MANAGEMENT AND CONTROL OF COMMUNITY PROPERTY DURING MARRIAGE?

No, not as to the office building.

(6) BASED ON THE ABOVE, HOW SHOULD THE ITEM BE DIVIDED?

Depends on whether Husband can rebut the "Married Woman" presumption.

This six-step analysis represents the mental process anyone solving this problem would necessarily go through in deciding what issues are presented. By asking these six questions, you are able to narrow the field of issues raised by the fact pattern. Now that we have identified the issues raised by the first interrogatory, let's draw a road map of our answer:

INTRO: CA COMMUNITY PROPERTY LAW APPLIES

1. Office Building

    SOURCE: H's and W's joint account

ACTIONS: Gift? Depends on H's intent.
PRESUMPTION: Married woman's presumption vs. general presumption.
DISPOSITION: SP unless H can rebut married woman's presumption.

This is of course only one example of an outline. Your outline might contain more or less detail, depending on your individual needs. Some people need a detailed set of directions to get to where they are going, while others do not. The key is to devise an outline that works for you. Let's take another example of an outline of this same issue:

1. Office Building

> **SOURCE:** Office building was purchased with money from H's and W's joint account.
> **ACTIONS:** Wife will argue that Husband intended a gift because (1) he knew W purchased building; (2) he had control over joint account and never objected; (3) H's signature does not appear on deed. H will counter that (1) he did not know how title was held; (2) no direct evidence that gift was intended.
> **PRESUMPTIONS:** Married woman's presumption applies since title taken before 1-1-75. Property is therefore SP unless H can rebut. H will rebut by (1) direct tracing; (2) general presumption; (3) knowledge of purchase of building not the same as agreeing to form of title.
> **DISPOSITION:** SP unless H can rebut.

This outline contains more detail than the previous one. All potential arguments are set forth and the reasoning process is set forth in its entirety. However, in writing out your outline to this problem, do not concern yourself with the length of the outline --- it is the end result that counts, not the outline. You must experiment with different types of outlining to see what best works for you.

Let's outline the second and third issues:

2. The House

> **SOURCE:** Gift is H's SP. W will argue that house was compensation for work performed and that house is CP.
> **ACTIONS:** None.

PRESUMPTIONS: General presumption - all "earnings" during marriage.
DISPOSITION: CP since spousal labor expended.

3. The Furniture

SOURCE/ACTIONS/PRESUMPTION: Same analysis as above.
MANAGEMENT & CONTROL ISSUE: Furniture cannot be sold or encumbered without other spouse's consent.
DISPOSITION: Furniture or its value may be recovered.

Although initially, outlining may seem time consuming, it will prove to be a valuable investment in the long run.

Outlining the answer gives you the foresight to see that the third interrogatory requires very little discussion. You are then able to devote most of the available time to answering the first and second interrogatories. Just like anything else in life, a little planning never hurts.

6. Model Answer

Let's review the model answer to this problem. Notice that we begin by setting forth the general community property principles before attacking each of the interrogatories:

WIFE v. HUSBAND

(DOES CALIFORNIA COMMUNITY PROPERTY LAW APPLY?) *Here H and W were domiciled in California, where they were validly married and therefore California community property laws apply.*

(EXPLANATION OF COMMUNITY PROPERTY RULES) *Because California is a community property state, all property acquired during marriage is community property (CP), while property acquired before marriage or after permanent separation, or by gift or inheritance, is separate property (SP).*

The characterization of an asset as community property or separate property depends on three factors: (1) the source of the item; (2) actions of the parties which may have altered the character of the item; (3) any statutory presumptions affecting the item.

1. The Office Building

(SOURCE: COMMUNITY PROPERTY OR SEPARATE PROPERTY?) *The source of the office building was funds taken from H's and W's joint account. This account contained W's and H's earnings during marriage, which are community property. Thus, the source of the purchase price was community property.*

(ACTION: ANY ACTIONS WHICH ALTERED THE CHARACTER OF THE OFFICE BUILDING?) *W will argue that H intended to make a gift of the proceeds of the joint account. She would argue that H was fully aware that W had purchased the building and that she was using funds from their joint account. W would also claim that H had control over their joint account and never objected. W's strongest argument is that H's signature does not appear on the deed, and that H's name would have been included if the office building was community property. However, H will counter that he did not know how title was held and there is no direct evidence that a gift was intended, i.e., statements or written agreement. These arguments present a close issue.*

(PRESUMPTIONS: WHAT PRESUMPTIONS APPLY?) *W will also raise the Married Woman's presumption. Under this presumption, property acquired by a married woman prior to January 1, 1975, by an instrument in writing is presumed to be her separate property unless a different intention is expressed in the instrument. Thus, the office building is presumed to be separate property unless H can rebut this presumption. H will rebut by proving through direct tracing that the funds came from their joint account and thus the office building was purchased with community property. He will also raise the general presumption that all property acquired during marriage is presumed to be community property. Finally, H will assert that mere knowledge of W's purchase of building is not the same as agreeing to form of title.*

(DISPOSITION OF PROPERTY) *While it is a close issue, because community earnings were used to purchase the building and the court will find that it is community property, and will award H one-half the present value of the office building. If the court finds that H did not rebut the presumption, it will rule that the office building is W's separate property.*

2. The House

(SOURCE) *The source of the house is a gift from Uncle Ted to H. Gifts and devises are the separate property of the recipient regardless of when acquired. Here the house was specifically devised to H and is therefore H's separate property.*

W will argue that the house was intended as compensation for community labor. W will rely on Uncle Ted's promise to will the house to H in exchange for their agreement to move into his home and take care of him and the house. W will seek to construe this promise as a contract for services. Her argument is further supported by the fact that she is a nurse, who presumably rendered nursing services to Uncle Ted until his death, and H was a carpenter, who presumably used his skills to care for the house.

(PRESUMPTION) *W would also raise the general presumption, arguing that because all "earnings" during marriage are community property, any compensation for work performed in caring for Uncle Ted is community property.*

(DISPOSITION) *A court would tend to agree with W, since a substantial amount of spousal labor was expended over a five-year period. This labor is community labor and the court will award W a one-half interest in the home even though the house was willed to H only.*

3. The Furniture

The parties' interest in the furniture is the same as the house. Thus, the furniture is community property for the same reasons stated above.

(DISPOSITION) *Both spouses have management and control of furniture in the home. However, furniture cannot be sold or encumbered by one spouse without the other spouse's consent. Thus, H's sale of the furniture to pay gambling debts was invalid. W may set aside the transaction and recover the furniture, or recover one-half its value from H.*

Conclusion

Upon divorce, community property is equally divided among the spouses, although a court may award an asset to one spouse so long as the court makes a substantially equal distribution of the total CP assets. Thus, both H & W will receive a one-half interest in the office building and house, and H must reimburse W for one-half the value of the furnishings.

Notice that not a single cite is referred to above. It is not necessary to state code sections. The bar grader is more concerned with whether you know the rule than your ability to cite code sections. You should also be aware that the bar grader will know the correct code sections, and so if you refer to the wrong section, it will be hard for the grader not to hold it against you. The key here is to remember and cite the rules, not the numbers.

If, in reviewing your exam answer, you missed issues or misanalyzed the problem, take this problem again. Building a strong foundation works not only for houses, but for exam writing as well.

The Exam Evaluator
HUSBAND v. WIFE

EXAM PRESENTATION (TOTAL POINTS AVAILABLE = 25)

	Poor											Excellent	
NEATNESS	0	1	2	3	4	5							_____
ORGANIZATION	0	1	2	3	4	5	6	7	8	9	10		_____
LAWYER-LIKE	0	1	2	3	4	5	6	7	8	9	10		_____

DISCUSSION OF ISSUES (TOTAL POINTS AVAILABLE =75)

THE OFFICE BUILDING

35 POINTS = FULL DISCUSSION _____

20 POINTS = PARTIAL/INCOMPLETE DISCUSSION _____

THE HOUSE

30 POINTS = FULL DISCUSSION _____

20 POINTS = PARTIAL/INCOMPLETE DISCUSSION _____

THE FURNITURE

10 POINTS = FULL DISCUSSION _____

5 POINTS = PARTIAL/INCOMPLETE DISCUSSION _____

TOTAL SCORE

_____

E.   PROBLEM TWO: H v. W

   1. The First and Second Read

Read this question once for content, and then a second time, picking up on key phrases and words.

The following events occurred in California.

H, an engineer, married W, a dentist, in 1976. Before marriage they orally agreed that the earnings of W after marriage would be her separate property. Later W told friends in H's presence that she would have refused to marry H had he not agreed to this. After marriage, W deposited her earnings in her separate bank account.

Beginning in 1977, without H's knowledge, W used withdrawals from the account to buy common stocks in her name. By 1985, she had accumulated a valuable portfolio.

In 1977, H and W purchased a single family residence as their home. The deed conveyed the property to "H and W in joint tenancy with right of survivorship." H made the down payment from separate earnings accumulated before the marriage. H and W signed a note and trust deed for the balance of the purchase price. H made monthly payments of the note from his current earnings until 1983, when he was disabled in an accident caused by the negligence of X. Thereafter, W made the payments from her current earnings.

H settled his damages claim against X for $200,000, and over W's strenuous objection used the money to build a vacation cottage on land he had inherited. Due to market conditions, the value of the land and improvement is increasing rapidly.

In 1985 H died, leaving a properly executed will made a few weeks before death. The will included an accurate description of the family residence and a devise of "my one-half interest in said property" to S, an adult son from an earlier marriage. The will also provided that all other assets were left to S.

What are S's and W's rights, if any, with respect to the following properties:

1. The stock portfolio? Discuss.

2. The family residence? Discuss.

3. The vacation cottage? Discuss.

Answer according to California law.

2. Fact Retention Exercise

This problem demonstrates the importance of skills such as VISUALIZATION and HEADLINING. In Problem One, the facts supporting each interrogatory were presented separately and apart, and therefore were easy to read and comprehend. In this problem, the facts of the stock portfolio are intertwined with the family residence and the vacation cottage.

It is therefore helpful to separate the facts supporting each interrogatory:

THE STOCK PORTFOLIO

(1)   Prenuptial oral agreement that W's earnings would be her separate property;

(2)   W's marriage earnings deposited in separate account;

(3)   Stocks purchased without H's knowledge.

THE FAMILY RESIDENCE

(1)   H and W purchased home in joint tenancy with right of survivorship;

(2)   H used SP to make down payment and paid mortgage payments with CP earnings until 1983;

(3)   Wife made mortgage payments from CP earnings thereafter.

(4)   H's 1/2 interest in residence devised to S.

THE VACATION COTTAGE

(1)   House built with $200,000 personal injury settlement;

(2)   Land is inherited;

(3)   All other assets left to S.

Now that you can see this problem for what it is, it really is not as confusing as it originally appeared. Anytime you are confronted with a fact pattern that appears confusing or overly complex, simplify it by culling through the facts and reorganizing them if necessary. Next, go back and read through the fact pattern again, this time VISUALIZING THE FACTS and using the technique of headlining. When you are done, turn to the next exercise.

ANSWER ALL QUESTIONS:

1. How are W and H employed?

2. Where did W get the money to purchase the stocks?

3. What was the source of the payments put towards the family residence?

4. What did W tell her friends about her prenuptial agreement with H?

5. Who owned the land that the vacation cottage was built on?

6. What form of title was the single family residence taken in?

7. What did H devise to his son S in his will?

3. Outlining Strategy

Now that you have mastered the facts, we now apply our writing approach to determine what specific issues are presented. As in all community property problems, we begin with the interrogatories:

What are S's and W's rights, if any, with respect to the following properties:

1. The stock portfolio? Discuss.

2. The family residence? Discuss.

3. The vacation cottage? Discuss.

Our headings merely reflect the items of property stated in the interrogatories.

1. The Stock Portfolio

2. The Family Residence

3. The Vacation Cottage

Next, let's apply our approach to arrive at our road map of the issues:

INTRODUCTION: CA CP APPLIES.

1. The Stock Portfolio

> **SOURCE:** From earnings during marriage, which are CP.
> **ACTIONS:** Prenuptial agreement provided that W's earnings are SP.
> **PRESUMPTIONS:** General presumption rebutted.
> **DISPOSITION:** Valid oral prenuptial; thus stocks are W's SP.

2. The Family Residence

> **SOURCE:** Down payment from H's SP; payments from H's and W's CP.

ACTIONS: Commingling of CP and SP; title taken in joint tenancy.
PRESUMPTIONS: General presumption that home acquired during marriage is CP.
DISPOSITION: House is CP, and goes to W upon H's death because of right of survivorship; upon death, SP down payment used towards CP residence is presumed to be a gift.

3. The Vacation Cottage

SOURCE: Inherited land is H's SP; home purchased with proceeds from H's personal injury settlement.
ACTIONS: Was community share of $200,000 a gift to H's SP?
PRESUMPTIONS: General presumption that cottage acquired during marriage is CP, but land is SP.
DISPOSITION: Both CP and SP should receive a pro-rata share based on amounts contributed. Court may order property sold and pro-rata shares awarded, or may allow cottage to pass to S by devise but order reimbursement to community.

The most difficult issue presented in this problem concerns the vacation cottage, because the solution involves a number of conflicting statutes and rules, and relies mostly on common sense in arriving at a fair result. Never, ever forget to apply common sense, especially in situations which demand it. The practical concern for the court is how it will resolve the fact that the cottage itself is CP while the land is SP. Since the court cannot sever the house from the land, it must give the cottage and land to either W or S, and reimburse the non-taking party.

Also tricky was the question of whether the oral prenuptial agreement was valid. Prenuptial agreements made after January 1, 1986 must be in writing, and the agreement here clearly occurred prior to that date and therefore was valid. If you missed this issue, do not kick yourself; many of the examinees who took this exam missed it as well.

Before reviewing the model examination, let's take a look at a few "not so model" examinations. In the next exercise, you will experience first hand what it feels like to be a bar grader.

4. Bar Grading Exercise

"I can pardon everyone's mistakes but my own."

---- Cato the Elder (234-149 B.C.)

For this next exercise, you will adopt the persona of a bar grader. In order to help you slip into your new role, here again are the five characteristics of a bar grader:

(1)   **I am a human being, subject to the same human frailties which affect all human beings;**

(2)   **I have only a few minutes to grade this examination;**

(3)   **I have worked a full eight-to-twelve-hour day before sitting down to read this examination;**

(4)   **This examination is one of the thousand or so examinations I must grade;**

(5)   **I want to be fair.**

After adopting the "Top Five Characteristics of Bar Graders," get out your red marking pen and grade this examination with a vengeance:

In California, community property laws apply to people married in California. S's and W's rights depend on how California community property law applies.

S's rights depends on whether the provisions of H's will are honored. H gave S "one-half interest" in the cottage and "all other assets." H therefore gave S everything he owned. Under California law, however, a spouse can only give away 1/2 of his community property.

The vacation cottage was probably H's community property. The cottage was bought with H's money received during marriage. But the land was obtained during marriage. Therefore the land is community property as well. Thus, H could give away 1/2 of the cottage since it was community property.

The house, however, is another story. The house was bought by both H and W. H paid the down payment from his money, but W also helped out in making payments. Thus, because they commingled their money, the house is presumed to be community property. Thus, H can give away 1/2 of the house.

W gets the stocks. She gets the stock because she used her money to buy them. It was her money because she would not have married H unless he agreed to let her keep money earned from her dental practice. She even told her friends that she wouldn't have married H if he didn't agree. She also put it in a separate account.

What did you think of this answer? Should the author take a bow or consider a new profession? While it is easy to criticize another's work, it is more difficult to articulate just exactly what is wrong with it. In this next exercise, state three reasons why this answer is not deserving of a passing grade.

I GIVE THIS ANSWER A " _____ " (INSERT GRADE) BECAUSE:

I.

II.

III.

Now, let's compare your list to this laundry list of problems. Were you able to isolate each of these things?

246

I. The answer is disorganized. While the interrogatories clearly spell out the order to follow, i.e., "1. The stock portfolio, 2. The family residence, 3. The vacation cottage," the author of this exam chose to dictate a different order and instead organized this problem according to S's rights and W's rights. This violates the rule that one should always follow the order indicated in the interrogatories.

While the answer discusses each item of property individually, headings would have helped to compartmentalize the discussion of each item, and to inform the grader of which issues were being discussed.

II. The analysis is poor. The author failed to state or even identify the pertinent rules of law. In discussing the vacation cottage, the rule that property acquired through inheritance is separate property should have been stated, as well as the rules governing personal injury settlement. The author failed to mention these rules and did not apply them. The author's conclusion that the cottage is community property is conclusory, because it fails to state what rules of law and facts support it.

The same is true of the author's discussion of the residence and stocks. The issue relating to the form of title is ignored, and the issue of joint tenancy is never addressed. The wrong conclusion is reached due to a superficial analysis and a failure to spot the issues.

III. The author did not have a strong grasp of the facts before attempting to solve the problem.

This is evident from the author's failure to mention the prenuptial agreement in relation to the stock issue. This basic fact was apparently overlooked or not read. The author also misstates that the land used for the cottage home was inherited <u>before</u> marriage. In fact, the facts only say that H had inherited this land, and does not make reference as to <u>when</u> this land was inherited.

Now count to three, and you will leave the persona of the bar grader and become yourself at the count of three . . . One . . . two . . . three!

Let's review the model answer.

5. Model Answer

Here H and W were domiciled in California, where they were validly married and therefore California community property laws apply.

(EXPLANATION OF COMMUNITY PROPERTY RULES) Because California is a community property state, all property acquired during marriage is community property (CP), while property acquired before marriage or after permanent separation, or by gift or inheritance, is separate property (SP).

The characterization of an asset as community property or separate property depends on three factors: (1) the source of the item; (2) actions of the parties which may have altered the character of the item; (3) any statutory presumptions affecting the item.

Upon death, a spouse may will all of his separate property and 1/2 of his community property to anyone. W's and S's respective interests depend on the characterization of H's property as separate or community property.

1. The Stock Portfolio

The source of the funds used to purchase the stocks were W's post-marriage earnings. All earnings during marriage are community property, and therefore the source was community property.

However, an oral agreement between the spouses to change the character of property is valid if based on full disclosure. Here H orally agreed that W's post-marriage earnings were to be her separate property. Because oral agreements before 1-1-86 are valid if based on full disclosure, this agreement will be upheld. Further, W detrimentally relied on the prenuptial agreement, as she stated she would not have married H had he not made this promise. Thus, the stock is W's separate property.

The fact that W used the money to purchase stock, however, does not change the character of that property. Even though H was unaware that W was purchasing stock with her separate property earnings, his consent was not required because H has no management and control over W's separate property.

Thus S has no interest in the stock portfolio.

2. The Family Residence

The source of the family residence was both separate and community property. The down payment came from H's separate pre-marriage earnings. The mortgage payments on the balance of the purchase price came from H and W's earnings during marriage. Thus both separate property and community was used to purchase the residence.

If separate property and community property are commingled, the court may apportion the value of the item between the two. Thus, the court may award the residence to the community, but order W to reimburse H's estate for the amount of the down payment, or award a pro-rata share of the residence to both S and W.

However, here W would successfully argue that because title was taken in joint tenancy with right of survivorship, H's down payment was intended as a gift and she takes the residence. Where title to realty is taken in joint tenancy with right of survivorship, the surviving spouse takes all. Because H knowingly took title as a joint tenant with the right of survivorship, he must have intended that the survivor take all, including the down payment. Thus, W takes the residence and S takes nothing.

S would raise the general presumption that all property acquired during marriage is CP, but the fact that title was taken in joint tenancy would defeat his claim. Furthermore, upon death, a separate property down payment which is used towards a community property residence is presumed to be a gift.

3. The Vacation Cottage

Because the source of the land was H's inheritance, the land is H's separate property. The cottage, however, was paid for with H's personal injury settlement. Because the accident with X occurred during marriage, the $200,000 settlement was community property.

S would argue that the $200,000 settlement was a gift to H's SP from the community. However, given that W objected strenuously to the purchase of the summer home, S would not prevail, and a gift would not be presumed.

W would raise the general presumption that all property acquired during marriage is presumed to be community property. Because the cottage was acquired during marriage, it is presumed to be community property.

Both W and S should receive a pro-rata share based on the amounts contributed from H's separate property and H's personal injury settlement. The court may order the property sold and pro-rata shares awarded to W and S, or may allow cottage to pass to S by devise but order reimbursement to the community.

CONCLUSION

W receives the stock, the family residence, and a share of the value of the vacation cottage, and S receives by devise a share of the value of the vacation cottage.

The Exam Evaluator
II v. W

EXAM PRESENTATION (TOTAL POINTS AVAILABLE = 25)

	Poor											Excellent	
NEATNESS	0	1	2	3	4	5							____
ORGANIZATION	0	1	2	3	4	5	6	7	8	9	10		____
LAWYER-LIKE	0	1	2	3	4	5	6	7	8	9	10		____

DISCUSSION OF ISSUES (TOTAL POINTS AVAILABLE =75)

THE STOCK PORTFOLIO

25 POINTS = FULL DISCUSSION ____

15 POINTS = PARTIAL/INCOMPLETE DISCUSSION ____

THE FAMILY RESIDENCE

25 POINTS = FULL DISCUSSION ____

15 POINTS = PARTIAL/INCOMPLETE DISCUSSION ____

THE VACATION COTTAGE

25 POINTS = FULL DISCUSSION ____

15 POINTS = PARTIAL/INCOMPLETE DISCUSSION ____

TOTAL SCORE . . . . ____

F.   PROBLEM THREE: HARRY v. WENDY

1.   The First and Second Read & Visualization

Read this fact pattern twice, once for content and a second time for key words and phrases, and then visualize the fact pattern.

In 1980, Harry and Wendy, a married couple, moved to California from State X where they had resided since their marriage in 1960. Under the laws of State X, a spouse's earnings are his or her separate property.

While married and residing in State X, Harry's accumulated earnings were used to purchase stock in Harry's name only and a residence in Harry's and Wendy's names as joint tenants. The residence was sold in 1980 and the proceeds of the sale were used to buy a California condominium, free and clear of indebtedness, in Harry's and Wendy's names as joint tenants.

Upon arriving in California, Harry purchased an auto repair business, using funds he had inherited. Each month, Harry withdrew from his proceeds of his repair business an amount equal to what he had been paid in his previous employment as an auto mechanic. He deposited the money in a checking account held jointly with Wendy. This account was used to meet all their monthly living expenses.

In 1982, Wendy was injured in a car accident caused by the negligence of Harry. Wendy used the insurance settlement she received for her injury to purchase savings bonds in her name.

In April 1985, Harry executed a will with a provision declaring the auto repair business to be community property.

In January 1987, Victor obtained a judgment against Wendy for an injury he suffered when she struck him during a heated argument at a condominium association meeting the prior year. Wendy's attendance at the meeting had been over Harry's strenuous objection.

Which of the follow properties will be subject to execution in satisfaction of

Victor's judgment against Wendy, and to what extent?

1. The savings bonds? Discuss.

2. The stock portfolio? Discuss.

3. The condominium? Discuss.

4. The auto repair business? Discuss.

2. Fact Retention Exercise: How to Use the "Shopping List" Technique to Organize the Facts

You will notice in this problem that the facts relating to each item of property are interwoven. The facts are organized chronologically as a group, and not according to each item of property. This makes it difficult to comprehend and retain the facts.

The answer is to segregate the facts to re-organize them in a manner which is conducive to solving the issues presented. Have you ever made a shopping list? Imagine for a moment that you are putting together a shopping list of items to make spaghetti:

Items:

1. MEAT

    Hamburger
    Italian Sausage

2. PASTA

    Fresh spaghetti noodles

3. SAUCE

    Tomatoes and tomato sauce
    Fresh garlic & seasonings
    Onions & mushrooms

4. BEVERAGE

    circa 1933 Cabernet

In this list, you have organized by item just what you need to cook up a tasty dish of spaghetti. Because each item on your shopping list is organized by subject area, you know exactly what you need from each aisle. This will save you the trouble of running from aisle to aisle, looking for whatever it is you need.

Now, in the next exercise, let's apply this same principle to a problem involving a complicated fact pattern and make up a "shopping list" of facts relevant to solving each interrogatory. Ask yourself, "What facts are relevant to each item of property indicated in the interrogatories?" Go through the facts and list each relevant fact under each item of property listed:

1. THE SAVINGS BONDS

2. THE STOCK PORTFOLIO

3. THE CONDOMINIUM

4. THE AUTO REPAIR BUSINESS

Now turn the page and compare your statement of the relevant facts with the model.

1. THE SAVINGS BONDS

(1) Wendy is injured in a car accident caused by Harry's negligence;

(2) Wendy uses insurance settlement to purchase the savings bonds;

(3) Wendy's accident occurs in California while she is married to Harry.

2. THE STOCK PORTFOLIO

(1) Harry's earnings during marriage are used to buy stock;

(2) Stock is in Harry's name only;

(3) These events occur during marriage while Harry and Wendy are living in State X;

(4) Under State X laws, a spouse's earnings are his or her separate property.

3. THE CONDOMINIUM

(1) In State X, Harry's earnings during marriage are used to buy a residence, and title is taken in Harry's and Wendy's names as joint tenants;

(2) The residence is sold and proceeds are used to buy a California condominium free and clear, and title is taken in Harry's and Wendy's names as joint tenants.

4. THE AUTO REPAIR BUSINESS

(1) Harry purchases the auto repair business using funds he had inherited;

(2) Harry withdrew a salary from the business equal to what he had been paid in the past and put these funds in a joint checking account from which living expenses were paid;

(3) Harry executed a will with a provision declaring the auto repair business to be community property.

Please note that I am not suggesting that you re-write the problem in this fashion, because to do so would consume too much time. However, if you are unable to mentally organize the facts in this fashion, make a quick checklist of the facts to help you keep track of which facts are relevant to which items of property. A quick "shopping list" might appear as follows:

1. BONDS

   Car accident caused by H

   W's proceeds used to buy bonds

   Accident occurs in CA during marriage

2. STOCKS

   H's earnings during marriage used to buy stock

   In H's name only

   Bought in State X during marriage

   State X = Earnings are SP

3. CONDO

   Harry's earnings in State X during marriage used to buy residence in joint tenancy

   Proceeds from residence used to buy CA condo in joint tenancy

4. AUTO BUSINESS

   H uses inheritance

H's salary used to pay family expenses

H's will declares auto business is CP

If you find this technique helpful, then use it. On the other hand, if you are able to accomplish the same result by other means, then do so. The point here is that you find a way to organize and segregate the facts in a way that you are able to solve the problem before you.

You will not find it necessary to use this technique on every problem. It is best reserved for those problems involving complicated fact patterns which are difficult to understand unless the facts are segregated. For example, it would probably be unnecessary to use this technique to solve the two earlier problems, since the facts concerning each item of property were organized, for the most part, in separate paragraphs. However, throughout this book, you will see how the "shopping list" technique can help simplify complicated fact patterns.

3. Outlining Strategy

Next, apply your writing approach and outline this problem. When you are done, please turn the page.

Compared to the earlier problems, this one probably made your head spin just a little. This is a community property problem with more than a few twists. For one, did you notice that the customary, "Answer according to California law," was not included in this problem? Is that because you are instead going to be tested on the marital property laws of Alaska or the North Pole? No, but the Examiners instead gave you a problem involving quasi-marital property, by stating that some of Harry and Wendy's assets were acquired while living in State X, a separate property state.

Another twist is the inclusion of a third party, who suffers tortious conduct at the hands of Wendy. Does this mean that you should analyze Wendy's right hook to determine whether a battery was committed? No. The interrogatories never ask whether Wendy committed a tort. Instead you are told that Victor obtained a judgment against Wendy and asked whether any of the named properties may be used to satisfy Victor's judgment. So what are the Examiners really asking? They are asking you to determine which items of property are community property and which are separate property, for the purpose of deciding what property is subject to creditors' claims.

Thus, this problem is like a sheep in wolf's clothing. It follows the same basic formula which all community property problems are based upon, but it is presented in a different way.

Let's apply our writing approach and outline the answer:

VICTOR v. HARRY & WENDY

(i) PRELIMINARY ISSUE: DOES CALIFORNIA COMMUNITY PROPERTY APPLY?
(ii) PRELIMINARY ISSUE: What property is subject to V's judgment? W was acting for the benefit of the community: V can reach W's CP and then her SP, but not H's SP, so we must decide what is CP and what is SP.

1. The Savings Bonds.

SOURCE: Car accident during marriage = CP; but because inflicted by H, W's SP.

ACTIONS: W's action of purchasing bonds does not change character; W uses SP to purchase bonds, thus bonds are W's SP. Even if CP, FED LAW prohibits CP set-off for savings bonds.
PRESUMPTIONS: None.
DISPOSITION: Because bonds are W's SP, V can reach.

2. The Stock Portfolio.

SOURCE: H's earnings during marriage in State X = SP; because H & W now in CA, quasi-CP principles apply.
ACTIONS: Stock in H's name only; gift intended?
PRESUMPTIONS: General presumption that all property acquired during marriage is CP.
DISPOSITION: Q-CP and V can reach.

3. The Condominium.

SOURCE: H's earnings during marriage in State X = SP; same argument as with stocks, quasi-CP principles apply.
ACTIONS: Proceeds used to buy CA condo; title taken in tenancy = H & W both own undivided 1/2 interest in SP.
PRESUMPTIONS: General presumption defeated by form of title.
DISPOSITION: SP and V can reach only W's 1/2.

4. Auto Repair Business.

SOURCE: SP inheritance = used to buy business.
ACTIONS: (1) Family expenses withdrawn from SP business: Pereira or Van Camp accounting? (2) Statement in will that business is CP --- will not effective until H's death.
PRESUMPTIONS: General presumption of CP --- H can rebut.
DISPOSITION: Business is H's SP, but V can reach CP's interest under Van Camp formula.

You can now see this problem for what it is --- the basic community property formula replayed yet another time. Once the twists and wrinkles are straightened, you see that this problem is indeed solvable!

Write out your answer using your outline, and when you are done, let's review the Model Answer together.

4. Model Answer

VICTOR v. HARRY & WENDY

The first preliminary issue is whether California community property laws apply. All property acquired while the parties were living in California is subject to community property laws. Property acquired while the parties were living in a separate property state is considered quasi-community property and is treated as community property upon death or dissolution. Thus all property acquired by Harry & Wendy while living in State X will be treated as quasi-community property.

Because California is a community property state, all property acquired during marriage is community property (CP), while property acquired before marriage or after permanent separation, or by gift or inheritance is separate property (SP).

The characterization of an asset as community property or separate property depends on three factors: (1) the source of the item; (2) actions of the parties which may have altered the character of the item; (3) any statutory presumptions affecting the item.

The classification of property as community property, separate property or quasi-community property will determine what items Victor may reach in satisfying his judgment against Wendy. If the tortious conduct occurred while spouse was performing an activity for the benefit of the community, Wendy's liability will first be satisfied from community property and then her separate property.

Here the tort occurred while Wendy attended a condominium meeting which benefited the community because the purpose of such meetings is to improve and manage living conditions. Thus, even though Harry objected to Wendy's attendance at the meeting, the community was benefited, and Victor may reach Wendy's community property and then her separate property. However, Victor may not reach Harry's separate property in satisfaction of the judgment.

263

1. The Savings Bonds.

The source of the savings bonds was a personal injury settlement for an accident which occurred during marriage. While normally such proceeds are community property, because the injury was inflicted by Harry, it is Wendy's separate property.

Wendy's act of purchasing bonds does not change the character of the property. Because Wendy used her separate property to purchase the bonds, they will be deemed her separate property. This is further supported by the fact that Wendy took the bonds in her name only. Even if these bonds are somehow found to be community property, federal preemption law prohibits any "set off" for savings bonds.

Thus, the bonds are Wendy's separate property, and Victor can reach them to satisfy his judgment.

2. The Stock Portfolio.

The source of the stocks is Harry's earnings during marriage in State X, which was Harry's separate property under State X laws. However, because Harry and Wendy are now living in California, and Harry's earnings would have been community property under California laws, the stock would be considered quasi-community property.

The act of taking the stock in Harry's name only would probably not support the argument that the stocks were a gift from the community, since there is no other evidence that a gift was intended. However, because the source was Harry's earnings, and the stock was acquired while Harry was in California, the stock will be deemed quasi-community property.

The general presumption that all property acquired during marriage is community property will further support the finding that the stocks are quasi-community property which are subject to Victor's judgment.

3. The Condominium.

The source of the condominium was Harry's earnings during marriage and the same analysis applied to the stocks, above, would apply. Thus, quasi-community property principles would apply and the condominium would be considered to be quasi-community property.

The act of taking title in joint tenancy, however, changed the character of this property, since under joint tenancy, both Harry and Wendy own an undivided one-half interest, in separate property.

The general presumption would be rebutted by the form of title.

Thus, the condominium is each spouse's separate property, and Victor may reach only Wendy's 1/2 interest.

4. Auto Repair Business.

The source of the funds used to purchase the auto repair business was Harry's inheritance, which is Harry's separate property.

The act of withdrawing family expenses from the business may give the community an interest in the separate property business of a spouse. Under the Pereira accounting method where the increase in value of a business is the owning spouse's labor, the separate property investment is given a reasonable rate of return and the remainder is deemed community property. Under the Van Camp accounting method, where the increase in value is not due to the owner spouse's services, the community receives a fair salary less any salary already paid, including family expenses, and the remainder is separate property.

Thus if any increase in the value of the business is primarily attributed to Harry's labor, Pereira should be applied and Harry's separate property investment should receive a fair rate of return and the business deemed community property. Alternatively, if Harry's labor was not the principal reason for any growth in the value of the business, Van Camp should be applied and the community has already received compensation through Harry's salary drawn from the business and the business is Harry's separate property.

265

Here <u>Van Camp</u> probably applies since the auto repair business involves mechanical labor which would not change substantially in the event that the business grew in value.

The statement in Harry's will that the business is community property does not alter the character of the property since the will is not effective until Harry's death.

The general presumption that all property acquired during marriage is community property will be sufficiently rebutted by the facts stated above.

In conclusion, the business is Harry's separate property, and Victor cannot satisfy his judgment from it.

This is one of those problems that is deserving of a huge "Whew!?!?" after reviewing the model answer. You may feel that there is no way you could have completed this problem in the allotted time, and you might be entirely right. Once again, remember that each bar question is scaled according to its difficulty. Because not all bar questions are created the same, not all bar questions will be graded on the same scale. Because very few examinees hit each and every issue contained in this model answer, it was easier to achieve a passing score, even if you missed a few issues in your answer.

The *Exam Evaluator* reflects numerous "bonus" points for discussing issues which were not necessary to a passing score but would have resulted in extra credit according to the bar graders I consulted. One example is the issue of the effect of the statement contained in Harry's will declaring the auto repair business to be community property. Most examinees missed this issue altogether, but yet a passing score was obtainable even though this issue was not discussed. The same would be true of the Federal Preemption issue.

Critical issues to a passing score include the fact that property acquired in State X is considered quasi-community property, Victor's rights as a judgment creditor, and the order in which Wendy's community and separate property are used to satisfy Victor's claim. These issues are indeed crucial to a passing score, and it is unlikely you would have passed without addressing these issues. The foundation of this problem relies heavily on how these preliminary issues are resolved.

Once these preliminary issues are resolved, the issues as to the classification of property are fairly straightforward. The savings bonds are Wendy's separate property and the exception that one spouse's settlement for tortious conduct of the other is separate property applies. As to the stock portfolio and condominium, again you are told that Harry's post-marriage earnings are the source, and given two issues relating to form of title. As to the business, you are asked to perform a <u>Van Camp</u> and <u>Pereira</u> accounting analysis.

You will notice that we have an exception to the general rule that case names need not be cited. There are some cases, which you should know. Please do not panic because these cases are covered well in your substantive outlines. In the area of community property law, <u>Van Camp</u> and <u>Pereira</u> are two cases which you should know by name. This is not to say that you cannot answer the question without knowing the cases by name. Here is an example of part of an answer which analyzes the concepts behind these cases without making reference to the case names:

Harry's act of withdrawing family expenses from the business may give the community an interest in the separate property business of a spouse. The court may choose from two different accounting methods depending on the quality and nature of Harry's contribution to the business. Under the first accounting method, if the increase in a business' worth is attributable to the manager spouse's labor, the separate property investment receives a reasonable rate of return and the remainder goes to the community. Under the second accounting method, if the increase in value is not due to the manager spouse's services, the community receives a fair salary less any salary already paid, including family expenses, and the remainder is separate property.

This answer would receive the same credit as the model answer which mentions both case names because it fully discusses the concepts underlying those cases. It is the application that is important, not the rote task of reiterating a case name. Simply citing a case without further analysis will conversely result in an incomplete answer:

Here the court will probably use <u>Van Camp</u> accounting to determine what is separate property and what is community property. <u>Pereira</u> accounting will not be applied under the circumstances presented herein. Therefore, under <u>Van Camp</u> accounting, the business is separate property.

267

This answer completely fails to explain and apply the legal concepts behind the cases cited. It states the case title and a conclusion but does not explain what proposition the case stands for, nor how or why it is relevant to solving the problem.

Let's now turn to the *Exam Evaluator* and see how you did.

The Exam Evaluator
Victor v. Harry & Wendy

EXAM PRESENTATION (TOTAL POINTS AVAILABLE = 25)

	Poor										Excellent	
NEATNESS	0	1	2	3	4	5						____
ORGANIZATION	0	1	2	3	4	5	6	7	8	9	10	____
LAWYER-LIKE	0	1	2	3	4	5	6	7	8	9	10	____

DISCUSSION OF ISSUES (TOTAL POINTS AVAILABLE =75)

PRELIMINARY ISSUES

QUASI-COMMUNITY PROPERTY ISSUES

    5 POINTS = FULL DISCUSSION   ____

    0 POINTS = PARTIAL/INCOMPLETE DISCUSSION   ____

VICTOR'S RIGHTS AS A JUDGMENT CREDITOR

    10 POINTS = FULL DISCUSSION   ____

    5 POINTS = PARTIAL/INCOMPLETE DISCUSSION   ____

THE SAVINGS BONDS

    15 POINTS = FULL DISCUSSION   ____

10 POINTS = PARTIAL/INCOMPLETE DISCUSSION   ____

THE STOCK PORTFOLIO

15 POINTS = FULL DISCUSSION   ____

10 POINTS = PARTIAL/INCOMPLETE DISCUSSION   ____

THE CONDOMINIUM

15 POINTS = FULL DISCUSSION   ____

10 POINTS = PARTIAL/INCOMPLETE DISCUSSION   ____

THE AUTO REPAIR BUSINESS

15 POINTS = FULL DISCUSSION   ____

10 POINTS = PARTIAL/INCOMPLETE DISCUSSION   ____

BONUS POINTS

WILL PROVISION (AUTO REPAIR BUSINESS) = 5 POINTS   ____

FEDERAL PRE-EMPTION ISSUE (BONDS) = 5 POINTS   ____

TOTAL SCORE . . . . ____

"We are what we repeatedly do. Excellence, then, is not an act but a habit."

---- Proverb

Next, we will forge a new trail in community property bar problems as we approach the top of the mountain. At this point in the book, if you have experienced difficulty in the previous problems, review those sections to insure that the writing approach is implanted firmly in your mind. Retake any examinations which troubled you and brace yourself --- because the road ahead offers even greater challenges as we tackle some of the most difficult community property problems ever to appear on the bar examination.

As you learn how to master these problems, you will see that these problems are not as awe inspiring as they first appear. Just like anything else in life, appearances can be deceiving. In this regard, it is important that you have the greatest confidence in your writing approach. Remember, you must believe that your writing approach will solve the problem. A loss of faith in your approach will most certainly affect your ability to solve the problem.

Your confidence will increase as you solve more and more bar questions. It is the process of taking examinations which teaches; reviewing the law without actually applying it is like reading a book on how to swim without ever touching the water. As you solve the problems in this book, you will see again and again how the writing approaches are used to successfully solve bar questions. Giving you a system to solving bar questions is what this book is all about!

271

G. PROBLEM FOUR: HANK & WENDY

The following events took place in California.

Hank and Wendy married in 1978. Hank had a son, Sam, from a prior marriage. Hank's earnings as a computer operator were consumed by his and Wendy's expenses. Their primary expense was the mortgage payment on the house they purchased shortly after their marriage. The deed to the house provided that they took title "as joint tenants with the right of survivorship."

In 1982, Hank inherited a small office building subject to an existing mortgage. He employed a professional property manager to take care of the building and Hank spent very little time on it. Hank used most of the rental income to pay for its management and upkeep and to pay the mortgage on it. Hank deposited the balance in a savings account in his name alone.

Hank paid court-ordered child support for Sam until he reached eighteen in 1984, at which time the obligation to pay child support terminated. Hank then promised Sam that he would pay Sam's tuition at a private college. At the same time, Hank purchased a $100,000 life insurance policy on his own life naming Sam as the primary beneficiary. He paid the premiums on the policy from his earnings. At the time the policy was purchased, Wendy questioned Hank about naming Sam as beneficiary and asked what provision he had made for her in the event of his death. Hank told her not to worry because everything he owned was community property and would be hers if he died.

In May 1988, one of Hank's tenants was awarded a judgment for $300,000 against Hank for injuries he received in a fall in the office building.

Hank died in October 1988, a few weeks after Sam's graduation. Hank had kept his promise to Sam and had paid approximately $60,000 for Sam's college education, using money from his savings account. Hank's 1979 will left all his separate property to Sam and his half of the community to Wendy.

The house is worth $200,000; the office building is worth $400,000, but is subject to the mortgage with a balance of $200,000; the savings account balance is $50,000.

1. What rights, if any, does Wendy have to:

   a. The house? Discuss.
   b. The office building? Discuss.
   c. The savings account? Discuss.
   d. The life insurance policy proceeds? Discuss.

2. What rights, if any, does Wendy have as a result of Hank paying Sam's tuition, and from whom can she recover?

3. What property will be subject to satisfying the tenant's judgment against Hank? Discuss.

Answer all questions according to California law.

1. Outlining Strategy and Exam Analysis

   After reading and visualizing the problem, you should have reached at least one conclusion: that this problem would be easier to solve if the facts were re-organized. Again, by following the directions in the interrogatories, we have the following headings:

1a. The House
1b. The Office Building
1c. The Savings Account
1d. The Life Insurance Policy Proceeds

2. Sam's Tuition

3. Satisfaction of Tenant's Judgment

   Next, let's look at the facts relevant to solving each interrogatory:

1a. The House

   Purchased shortly after marriage with Hank's earnings
   Title as "joint tenants with right of survivorship"
   House now worth $200,000
   Hank's will leaves SP to Sam and CP to Wendy

1b. The Office Building

   Purchased during marriage
   Involved very little of Hank's labor
   Rental income placed in savings account
   Building now worth $400,000; subject to $200,000 mortgage
   Hank's will leaves SP to Sam and CP to Wendy

1c. The Savings Account

   Rental income from office building
   Account in Hank's name alone

Savings account contains $50,000
Hank's will leaves SP to Sam and CP to Wendy

1d. The Life Insurance Policy Proceeds

Purchased during marriage
Named Sam as primary beneficiary
Premiums paid from Hank's earnings during marriage
Hank orally agrees that $100,000 policy proceeds are CP
Hank's will leaves SP to Sam and CP to Wendy

2. Sam's Tuition

Hank agrees during marriage that he would pay Sam's college education
Hank spends $60,000

3. Satisfaction of Tenant's Judgment

Tenant receives judgment for $300,000 against Hank for injuries received in a fall.

Now that you see the facts for what they are, this problem does not appear as intimidating as it did a few minutes ago. In essence, the first interrogatory asks you to determine which items or parts of each item are separate property and what is community property. Under Hank's will, you are told that Sam receives all of Hank's separate property and Wendy receives Hank's share of community property. Thus, this is just a regular, run-of-the-mill "source-action-presumption-disposition" community property problem.

The second interrogatory is limited to a discussion of what interest Wendy has in the $60,000 Hank spent on Sam's tuition, and whether she may recover anything from Sam.

The final interrogatory asks what items of property the tenant who received the $300,000 judgment against Sam can reach. Like the previous problem, this interrogatory asks you to state the rules relating to spousal-tortfeasor liability, and to identify the order in which the property may be used to satisfy the tenant's claim.

Now that we have a firm grasp of the issues we must address, let's apply the writing approach and outline our answer:

HANK & WENDY

INTRO
Wendy's interest depends on whether items are SP or CP; under Hank's will, Wendy entitled to CP and Sam gets SP.
EFFECT OF ORAL AGREEMENT - Depends on whether oral promise occurred before or after 1-1-85.

1a. The House

SOURCE: Purchased shortly after marriage with Hank's earnings = CP.
ACTIONS: (1) Form of title taken as "joint tenants with right of survivorship." Both H & W own 1/2 undivided SP interest; (2) oral agreement that "everything he owned" was CP.
PRESUMPTIONS: General presumption rebutted by form of title.
DISPOSITION: House now worth $200,000. Upon Hank's death, house passes in entirety to Wendy as her SP because of right of survivorship.

1b. The Office Building

SOURCE: Inherited during marriage = SP.
ACTIONS: <u>Van Camp</u> or <u>Pereira</u> accounting? Because very little of Hank's labor was involved and increase in value not due to spousal services, Van Camp is proper.
PRESUMPTIONS: None.
DISPOSITION: Building now worth $400,000 subject to $200,000 mortgage and is Hank's SP. Hank's will leaves SP to Sam but Wendy is entitled to receive a reasonable salary less any family expenses paid from the business, which is CP.

1c. The Savings Account

SOURCE: Rental income from office building; rent follows the character of the source and is SP.

ACTIONS: Funds placed in account in Hank's name alone = SP
PRESUMPTIONS: General presumption rebutted by act.
DISPOSITION: Savings account contains $50,000 and is SP; under Hank's will, it goes to Sam.

1d. The Life Insurance Policy Proceeds

SOURCE: Purchased during marriage; premiums paid from Hank's earnings = CP
ACTIONS: Named Sam as primary beneficiary but Hank orally tells Wendy that "everything he owned" was CP and would be hers if he died, and thus policy proceeds were SP under agreement.
PRESUMPTIONS: General presumption that all property acquired during marriage is CP.
DISPOSITION: If oral agreement is valid, then policy proceeds are SP; if not, Hank's will is invalid as to Wendy's 1/2 CP, and Wendy takes 1/2 CP.

2. Sam's Tuition

SOURCE: Paid from Hank's savings account which contains income from his SP office building.
ACTION: Hank agrees during marriage that he would pay Sam's college education; GIFT! May be voided if made without Wendy's consent.
PRESUMPTION: None.
DISPOSITION: Wendy may recover half of the $60,000 gift.

3. Satisfaction of Tenant's Judgment

Tenant receives judgment for $300,000 against Hank for injuries received in a fall.

If tort committed while Hank engaged in activity benefiting community = CP exhausted first, then Hank's SP; if for benefit of spouse's SP = Hank's SP exhausted first.

Now that you can see the issues presented, review your outline, comparing it to the model outline. This question contained two curveballs:

277

(1) How did you deal with the issue of Hank's oral statement to Wendy that "everything he owned" was community property and would go to Wendy upon his death?

(2) How did you organize the problem? Did you organize the answer in the same way it appears in the model outline? Why or why not? Did you resolve the question of what items of property Tenant may receive, or did you forget to answer this question?

While you might feel a little foolish asking yourself these questions, understanding and resolving these basic precepts are essential to solving this problem.

The first curveball the Examiners threw at you was the issue of whether Hank's promise to Wendy that "everything he owned was community property and would be hers if he died," constituted a valid transmutation of all of Hank's separate property to community property. The rule you had to know was that before 1-1-85, oral transmutation agreements were valid, but after that date, such agreements are deemed invalid unless in writing.

Now let's review the facts to see whether we can ascertain when this promise was made:

Hank paid court-ordered child support for Sam until he reached eighteen in 1984, at which time the obligation to pay child support terminated. Hank then promised Sam that he would pay Sam's tuition at a private college. At the same time, Hank purchased a $100,000 life insurance policy on his own life naming Sam as the primary beneficiary. He paid the premiums on the policy from his earnings. At the time the policy was purchased, Wendy questioned Hank about naming Sam as beneficiary and asked what provision he had made for her in the event of his death. Hank told her not to worry because everything he owed was community property and would be hers if he died.

As you can see, you are told only that Hank paid child support until 1984, and after that date promised he would pay Sam's tuition. You are then told that "[a]t the same time," Hank purchased the policy and "[a]t the time the policy was purchased," Hank made the promise. The Bar Examiners go to great lengths not to tell you exactly when this promise was made. Because of the vague nature of the facts, it could have been made in 1984 or in 1985.

Where you are confronted with a seemingly unresolvable conflict, rather than bang your head against the wall, simply argue it both ways and move on. What needed to be said here is that if the oral transmutation was made before 1-1-85 it is valid and therefore all Hank's separate property was transmuted in community property and under Hank's will, Wendy takes all. On the other hand, if the oral promise was made after 1-1-85, the oral transmutation was invalid and Wendy takes only that property deemed community property under California law. And that is all you needed to say about this issue.

Those examinees who got stuck on this issue wasted valuable time and energy by attempting to resolve a situation which was unresolvable. You were not told the date of the promise, and therefore could not decide if the oral transmutation was effective or not.

The second curveball involved the organization of this problem. As always, follow the directions contained in the interrogatories and organize the legal issues carefully.

First, Wendy's right to each of the four listed items should be discussed. However, before these issues can be resolved, the effect of Hank's oral statement needs to be discussed either before, during or after the discussion of each item of property. It is preferable to discuss this issue early on, since the resolution of this issue could affect each item of property. Discussing this issue three times with respect to each item of property would consume too much time.

Once the first interrogatory was outlined, you could clearly see how the next two pieces of the puzzle fit in. The second interrogatory dealt only with a spouse's right to recover a gift, and again you are not told whether Wendy consented and must necessarily leave this issue unresolved. This issue required minimal discussion and was an easy issue to analyze.

The final interrogatory also involved minimal discussion, requiring only that you state the order in which the items of property should be used to satisfy Tenant's judgment against Hank. Since you already determined what items were community and separate property in the first interrogatory, you only had to decide whether Hank was acting for the benefit of the community when Tenant's injury occurred. The resolution of this issue would determine which property would be used first to satisfy Tenant's judgment.

Once you identified these two curveballs, you would have been well on your way to hitting a grandslam on this problem. Let's now review the model answer and see how to run around the bases:

2. Model Answer: Hank & Wendy

Because California is a community property state, all property acquired during marriage is community property (CP), while property acquired before marriage or after permanent separation, or by gift or inheritance, is separate property (SP).

The characterization of an asset as community property or separate property depends on three factors: (1) the source of the item; (2) actions of the parties which may have altered the character of the item; (3) any statutory presumptions affecting the item.

Here Wendy's interest depends on whether these items are separate property or community property because under Hank's will, Wendy is entitled to all of Hank's community property and Sam receives all of Hank's separate property.

Wendy will first argue that all of Hank's property is community property due to the oral promise made by Hank, telling her that "everything he owned would be community property and would be hers if he died." An oral agreement transmuting property was valid before 1-1-85, but must be in writing after 1-1-85. Here it cannot be determined when Hank made this promise, since it was made sometime between 1984 and 1988. If Wendy could prove it was made before 1-1-85, then all of Hank's property is community property and she takes everything under Hank's will. The will is effective at Hank's death and since Hank had no separate property at death, Wendy takes all and Sam receives nothing.

On the other hand, if Hank's statement occurred after 1-1-85, it was invalid for want of a writing and the items of property pass according to the following analysis.

1a. The House

The source of the house was Hank's earnings during marriage and thus is community property. However, here title was taken as "joint tenants with right of survivorship," and therefore both Hank and Wendy own a one-half undivided separate property interest in the house. The form of title would rebut the general presumption that all property acquired during marriage is community property.

Thus upon Hank's death, the title to the house would pass to Wendy as the survivor and would be her separate property.

1b. The Office Building

The source of the office building was Hank's inheritance, which is separate property. Because very little of Hank's labor was involved, <u>Van Camp</u> accounting would apply. Under this method, where the principal factor in the increase in a business' value is not the spouse's services, the community receives a salary for the managing spouse's labor and separate property receives the residual. Under this method, Wendy receives the amount equal to a reasonable salary less any family expenses paid from the business.

Under <u>Pereira</u> accounting, where the principal reason for the increase in value is the spouse's services, the managing spouse's separate property receives a reasonable return on the investment and the community receives the residual. If the court adjudged Hank's labor to be the principal reason for any increase in value in the office building, Wendy would receive the residual after Sam received a reasonable return on Hank's separate property investment.

1c. The Savings Account

The source of the rental income was the office building which was Hank's separate property. Because rent follows the character of the source, the proceeds in the account are separate property. The fact that the funds were placed in an account in Hank's name alone will rebut any argument that the funds were intended to be community property and will rebut the general presumption.

Thus, the savings account containing $50,000 is Hank's separate property and *goes to Sam, and Wendy takes nothing.*

1d. The Life Insurance Policy Proceeds

The life insurance policy was purchased during marriage and the premiums paid from Hank's earnings, which is community property. If community property is used to pay the premiums on a life insurance policy, the proceeds are community property regardless of who the beneficiary is. Thus, even though Sam is named as beneficiary, the proceeds are still community property.

Sam could argue that the proceeds are separate property if the oral transmutation is effective since in consideration of Hank's promise to transmute all his property to community property, Wendy agreed that the insurance proceeds would go to Sam. Sam would prevail if the promise is determined effective.

If the oral agreement is deemed invalid, then Hank's policy is invalid as to Wendy's one-half community interest, and Wendy takes $50,000 or one-half of the proceeds.

2. Sam's Tuition

The source of Sam's tuition was Hank's savings account containing rental income from a building he inherited, which is Hank's SP. Hank's agreement to pay Sam's college education occurred during marriage and would be deemed a gift. A gift made without one spouse's consent may be voided. Wendy may therefore recover $30,000, half of the $60,000 gift.

3. Satisfaction of Tenant's Judgment

The order in which separate and community property may be used to satisfy Tenant's $300,000 judgment against Hank depends on whether the tort was committed while Hank was engaged in an activity benefiting the community. If Hank was engaged in an activity for the benefit of his separate property, then his separate property will be exhausted first. Since Hank's office building was his separate property which received a separate property benefit from Tenant's lease of the building, and Tenant's injury occurred there, Sam's separate property inheritance will be exhausted first, and then Wendy's community property inheritance.

If the oral agreement is deemed effective as discussed above, then there is no separate property at Hank's death, and Sam takes $100,000 as the beneficiary of the policy and Wendy takes all of Hank's community property, which is then subject to Tenant's claim.

This was not an easy problem to solve. Again, remember that a difficult problem is difficult for all, and that an answer less than perfect would have passed with flying colors. Let's look at an example of an answer which missed critical issues, but nonetheless would have received a passing score because of the difficulty level of the problem.

> *"The difference between failure and success is doing a thing nearly right and doing a thing exactly right."*
>
> ---- Edward Simmons

3. Less than Model Answer: Wendy & Hank

Wendy's interest depends on whether the items are separate property or community property. According to Hank's will, Wendy receives all of Hank's community property and Sam receives all of Hank's separate property.

1a. The House

Since the house came from Hank's earnings during marriage, it would normally be community property. However, because Hank and Wendy took title in joint tenancy, each had a one-half interest in separate property. On Hank's death, the house passes to Wendy because she survived Hank.

1b. The Office Building

Because the office building came from Hank's inheritance, it is his separate property. However, where community labor is expended towards separate property, the community is entitled to an interest. Hank contributed little spousal labor to the office building and had a property manager take care of it. Since any increase in the business was due to factors other than spousal labor, most courts would award the community a reasonable salary for Hank's time, and award the rest to Hank's

283

separate property. Wendy therefore receives a reasonable salary for Hank's services.

1c. The Savings Account

The money in the joint account came from the rent from Hank's separate property office building. These funds would be separate property because the character of the rent is the same as its source. Hank also put the money in an account in his name only, and this would support a finding that the account was separate property. Thus, the funds are separate property and Wendy gets nothing.

1d. The Life Insurance Policy Proceeds

Because the premiums paid on the policy came from community earnings, the proceeds are community property even though Hank named Sam as the beneficiary. Thus, Wendy is entitled to one-half of the proceeds.

2. Sam's Tuition

Hank used community earnings to pay for Sam's education. If Wendy was unaware of this fact, she could avoid the gift and recover one-half of the cost of Sam's education.

Sam might argue that Wendy intended a gift and therefore no reimbursement is required, but he would have to prove that Wendy was aware that Hank paid for Sam's education.

3. Satisfaction of Tenant's Judgment

Tenant would be able to reach Hank's separate property first, and then any community property. Tenant was injured in Hank's separate property office building, and thus the tort occurred in a manner benefiting Hank's separate property and not the community. Thus, all of Hank's separate property, willed to Sam, will be used to satisfy Tenant's judgment before Wendy's community property is used.

While clearly inferior to the model answer, this answer hits most of the major issues, and fails only to discuss the issue of Hank's oral promise. This answer is barely passing, scoring in the 70-75 range because it presents only a thin, superficial discussion of the issues, fails to state the rules and misses a major issue.

Note that in the first paragraph, community property principles are not set forth, and the author fails to state the rules he or she is applying to the problem anywhere in the answer. In discussing the house, it is not explained why the form of title rebuts the general presumption and source rule. In analyzing the community's interest in the office building, <u>Pereira</u> is not even mentioned or considered, even though it is unclear what any increase in the business' value may have been attributed to. While <u>Van Camp</u> was the more likely accounting method to be applied, <u>Pereira</u> still should have been discussed. The analysis of the savings account, however, is sufficient and its reasoning adequately explained. The discussion about Hank's life insurance policy fails to mention the oral transmutation and the effect of this transmutation on Sam's right to the insurance proceeds.

The latter two interrogatories are answered superficially, but again the major issues are identified. Yet this answer is a passing answer.

The major issue of the oral transmutation is completely missed. Missing an issue of this caliber normally means a fatal, non-passing result. However, because of the difficulty of this problem, and the resulting lower grading curve, a passing grade could be achieved even though a major issue was missed.

This is not meant as an example of how to squeak by with a barely passing answer, but illustrates that a passing answer is easier to achieve on a difficult problem than an easy one.

The Exam Evaluator
HANK & WENDY

EXAM PRESENTATION (TOTAL POINTS AVAILABLE = 25)

	Poor											Excellent
NEATNESS	0	1	2	3	4	5						____
ORGANIZATION	0	1	2	3	4	5	6	7	8	9	10	____
LAWYER-LIKE	0	1	2	3	4	5	6	7	8	9	10	____

DISCUSSION OF ISSUES (TOTAL POINTS AVAILABLE =75)

1A. THE HOUSE

10 POINTS = FULL DISCUSSION ____

5 POINTS = PARTIAL/INCOMPLETE DISCUSSION ____

1B. THE OFFICE BUILDING

10 POINTS = FULL DISCUSSION ____

5 POINTS = PARTIAL/INCOMPLETE DISCUSSION ____

1C. THE SAVINGS ACCOUNT

10 POINTS = FULL DISCUSSION ____

5 POINTS = PARTIAL/INCOMPLETE DISCUSSION ____

1D. THE LIFE INSURANCE PROCEEDS

    10 POINTS = FULL DISCUSSION   ____

    5 POINTS = PARTIAL/INCOMPLETE DISCUSSION   ____

THE ORAL TRANSMUTATION ISSUE

    15 POINTS = FULL DISCUSSION   ____

    10 POINTS = PARTIAL/INCOMPLETE DISCUSSION   ____

2. SAM'S TUITION

    10 POINTS = FULL DISCUSSION   ____

    5 POINTS = PARTIAL/INCOMPLETE DISCUSSION   ____

3. SATISFACTION OF TENANT'S JUDGMENT

    10 POINTS = FULL DISCUSSION   ____

    5 POINTS = PARTIAL/INCOMPLETE DISCUSSION   ____

TOTAL SCORE . . . . ____

Having now climbed to the top of the mountain, you are ready to apply the problem solving techniques that you have learned thus far under exam conditions. In this section, we will tackle four new Community Property problems. Once again, take each of the examinations under exam pressures which means:

(1) Time yourself and strive to complete the exam in an hour's time;

(2) Follow the *Six Steps of Exam Taking* and the *Ten Strategies of Exam Writing Success*;

(3) Avoid any distractions, i.e. phone calls or conversations, during the exam taking period;

(4) Find an environment which best simulates the actual circumstances under which you will be taking the bar exam.

(5) Do not view the Model Answer until you have completed writing out your answer.

Good luck!

H. PROBLEM FIVE: HANK v. WENDY

Wendy started Interiors, an interior decorating business, in 1960. In 1962, she purchased a house in Woods, California, for $25,000, paying $5,000 down and giving a $200,000 note for the balance. In 1965, she married Hank. Hank moved into the Woods residence with Wendy. Wendy has made all payments on the note and taxes on the Woods residence from her income from Interiors.

Hank has been employed by Ajax since 1958. Ajax maintains a pension plan which is paid for entirely by the employer. If Hank remains employed by Ajax until 1984, he will receive $1,000 per month upon retirement. If he leaves Ajax before 1984, he has the option of taking a lump sum payment or letting his vested entitlement accumulate until normal retirement age and taking a reduced pension.

In 1968, Hank's father died and Hank received $100,000 from the estate. Hank deposited $90,000 of the money in a new bank account, in his name alone, with Bank. There have been no additional deposits to this account. He used $5,000 to purchase XYZ Corporation stock and $5,000 to pay for a new roof on the Woods residence. In 1969, Hank purchased a house in Dale, California, for $150,000 taking title in his and Wendy's name as joint tenants. A down payment of $25,000 was made with funds withdrawn from Hank's bank account. The balance of the $125,000 was paid in the form of a promissory note, signed by Hank alone, and secured by mortgage on the Dale property executed by both Hank and Wendy. All of the mortgage payments and taxes on the Dale residence have been made with funds withdrawn from Hank's bank account. Hank and Wendy moved into the Dale house and kept the Woods house as an investment.

In 1970, Hank sold his XYZ stock for $10,000 and used the proceeds to buy $10,000 worth of ABC stock.

In 1978, Hank and Wendy separated and filed for dissolution of marriage in California.

What are the interests of each of them in the following property:

1. Interiors;

2. The Woods residence, now valued at $100,000;

3. The Ajax pension plan;

4. The Dale Residence, now valued at $200,000; and

5. The ABC stock, now worth $15,000.

Discuss. Ignore any income tax considerations or consequences. Answer according to California law.

1. Outlining Strategy and Exam Analysis

As you can see, this problem presents the "garden variety" community property problem, involving the disposition of various items of property upon divorce. As with the earlier examples in this book, organizing this problem required you to segregate the facts relevant to each item of property, follow the directions of the interrogatories and apply the writing approach. Let's review the outline to this problem:

OUTLINE: HANK v. WENDY

i. INTRO

1. INTERIORS

SOURCE: Pre-marriage earnings = SP source.
ACTIONS: Community interest in SP business? Pereira or Van Camp? Pereira applies since interior decorating involves mostly labor.
PRESUMPTIONS: None.
DISPOSITION: CP receives residual value --- W's initial investment and a reasonable rate of return.

2. THE WOODS RESIDENCE

SOURCE: Acquired pre-marriage = upon divorce CP.
ACTIONS: (1) CP earnings used to make principal payments; (2) new roof paid by Hank's SP = rebuttable presumption of gift.
PRESUMPTIONS: None.
DISPOSITION: Moore case holds that the community is entitled to a pro-rata interest in SP proportionate to SP/CP; unless Hank rebuts presumption of gift, community gets nothing for roof.

3. THE AJAX PENSION PLAN

SOURCE: Ajax pension plan = CP earnings.
ACTIONS: None.
PRESUMPTIONS: General CP presumption.

DISPOSITION: Community is entitled to a pro-rata interest in H's pension plan, depending on the number of years H worked at Ajax during the marriage. Court may either award community an interest or wait until H receives pension.

4. THE DALE RESIDENCE

SOURCE: Payments on Dale residence = H's SP inheritance.
ACTIONS: None.
PRESUMPTIONS: (1) General presumption that all property acquired during marriage is presumed CP; (2) for purposes of dissolution and separation, any property jointly held is presumed to be CP absent a contrary written agreement.
DISPOSITION: Both H and W should receive a 1/2 interest in the Dale residence, and H is not entitled to reimbursement.

5. THE ABC STOCK

SOURCE: Hank's SP inheritance = XYZ stock = ABC stock.
ACTIONS: None.
PRESUMPTIONS: None.
DISPOSITION: H's SP.

2. Model Answer

"It's what you learn after you know it all that counts."

---- John Wooden

As you can see from the outline, the key to solving this problem was following a system of success, and then applying that system to each interrogatory to reach a winning exam answer. The Bar Examiners just about "gave" the last interrogatory away, as sort of an added bonus to those examinees who made it to the end of the problem.

Now let's review the model examination. You will notice almost instantly that the introductory paragraph is not present in the beginning of the problem but if you look carefully, you will see that these concepts have been woven into the analysis. This is offered only as another example of how to structure your answer. Also, in this answer, key words and phrases are underlined to emphasize the issues.

HANK v. WENDY

Because Hank (H) and Wendy (W) were legally married in California, community property laws apply.

1. INTERIORS

The issue is what interest H & W have in Interiors, W's interior decorating business.

The first issue is what <u>source</u> the "Interiors" business came from. Property takes on the character of the item used to acquire it or which produced it. W started the business prior to marriage and therefore used pre-marriage earnings and labor to acquire the business.

The next issue is what <u>actions</u> may have changed the character of the property. Here W continued to operate "Interiors" after her marriage to H in 1965. Thus, the community would be entitled to an interest, depending on whether the <u>Pereira</u> or <u>Van Camp</u> formulas are applied.

Under the <u>Pereira</u> formula, where the greater factor in creating profits is the owner/manager's services, the owner/manager receives the initial separate property investment and a reasonable rate of return, while the community receives the residual. Here, because the field of interior decorating involves primarily labor, this formula should be applied.

However, the <u>Van Camp</u> formula holds that where the owner manager's services were not the greater factor in creating profits, the community is entitled to the reasonable value of the owner/manager's services, and the owner/manager receives the residual. If W's services were determined not to be the greater factor in creating profits, <u>Van Camp</u> should be applied.

Thus, the community should receive the <u>residual value</u> of "Interiors" <u>less W's</u>

2. THE WOODS RESIDENCE

The <u>source</u> of the property is W's separate property, since she purchased and acquired the Woods residence in 1962 before she was married to H. Thus, upon divorce, the Woods residence is W's separate property.

However, <u>actions</u> during marriage may alter the character of property. Here W used her income from Interiors to make principal payments on the Woods residence. Because her income during marriage was community property, under <u>Moore</u>, the community is entitled to a pro-rata interest in the separate property in proportion to amounts from separate property and community property. Thus, because the house is now valued at $100,000, but was purchased for $25,000, the community shares a pro-rata interest in the present value of the house proportionate to the amounts paid by W from her community earnings.

A remaining issue is presented by Hank's payment of the cost of a new roof on the Woods residence. Where one spouse uses his separate property to make permanent improvements on the other's separate property, there is a <u>rebuttable presumption</u> of a gift. Thus, unless Hank could produce evidence that the $5,000 from his separate property inheritance was not a gift, the community would receive nothing based on H's contribution to the Woods residence.

3. THE AJAX PENSION PLAN

The Ajax pension plan would be considered earnings. All earnings during marriage are considered CP. Vested and non-vested pension rights are subject to division, and are community property if the right to such benefits is earned during marriage. Hence, the community is entitled to a <u>pro-rata</u> <u>interest</u> in H's pension plan, depending on the number of years H worked at Ajax during the marriage.

In awarding the community an interest, the court may either value the pension right, award it to the employee and award community assets of equal value or retain jurisdiction and order 50% of the pension plan, once H begins receiving it. Thus, if H leaves Ajax before 1984 and receives the lump sum payment, the court may either value that right and award W half, or order H to pay half when he receives the lump sum payment. On the other hand, if H chooses to remain at Ajax until his normal retirement age, the court can retain jurisdiction and order H to pay half of his sum payment. On the other hand, if H chooses to remain at Ajax until his normal retirement age, the court can retain jurisdiction and order H to pay half of his pension when he begins receiving it.

4. THE DALE RESIDENCE

The <u>source</u> of the payments on the Dale residence was Hank's separate property, since H used the proceeds from his separate property inheritance, deposited with Bank for the down payment for the house and for the mortgage payments on the property.

However, under the <u>general presumption</u>, all property acquired for consideration during marriage is presumed to be community property. Furthermore, for purposes of dissolution and separation, any <u>property jointly held</u> is presumed to be community property absent a contrary written agreement. Because the Dale residence was purchased during marriage, and the property was taken in both H and W's names as joint tenants, these presumptions apply and the Dale residence is community property.

Thus, both H and W should receive a <u>one-half interest</u> in the Dale residence, and H is not entitled to reimbursement.

5. THE ABC STOCK

The <u>source</u> of the ABC stock was Hank's separate property inheritance, which he used to purchase the XYZ stock, which he in turn used to purchase the ABC stock.

Thus, because community funds were not used to purchase the XYZ stock, the stock and its appreciated value are <u>H's separate property</u>, and the community is not entitled to an interest.

The Exam Evaluator
HANK v. WENDY

EXAM PRESENTATION (TOTAL POINTS AVAILABLE = 25)

	Poor											Excellent
NEATNESS	0	1	2	3	4	5						_____
ORGANIZATION	0	1	2	3	4	5	6	7	8	9	10	_____
LAWYER-LIKE	0	1	2	3	4	5	6	7	8	9	10	_____

DISCUSSION OF ISSUES (TOTAL POINTS AVAILABLE =75)

1. INTERIORS

15 POINTS = FULL DISCUSSION _____

10 POINTS = PARTIAL/INCOMPLETE DISCUSSION _____

2. WOODS RESIDENCE

15 POINTS = FULL DISCUSSION _____

10 POINTS = PARTIAL/INCOMPLETE DISCUSSION _____

3. THE AJAX PENSION PLAN

15 POINTS = FULL DISCUSSION _____

10 POINTS = PARTIAL/INCOMPLETE DISCUSSION _____

4. THE DALE RESIDENCE

      15 POINTS = FULL DISCUSSION   ____

      10 POINTS = PARTIAL/INCOMPLETE DISCUSSION   ____

5. THE ABC STOCK

      15 POINTS = FULL DISCUSSION   ____

      10 POINTS = PARTIAL/INCOMPLETE DISCUSSION   ____

TOTAL SCORE . . . . ____

I. PROBLEM SIX: TONY, HAP AND WANDA

Tony and Wanda were married in New York in 1959. They separated in 1963, and Wanda moved to California. In 1964, Tony represented to Wanda that he had divorced her. Believing Tony, Wanda became engaged to Hap. Shortly before their duly licensed and witnessed 1965 marriage in California, Wanda and Hap orally agreed, among other things, that any insurance proceeds either might collect during their marriage would be their community property.

Six months after their marriage, Wanda received $100,000 as the beneficiary of her deceased father's life insurance policy. She deposited the $100,000 in a stock brokerage account titled in her name alone. The account was managed by her by a financial consultant, and now has a value of $300,000.

In 1980, Hap received a $200,000 inheritance from his mother, with which he purchased a restaurant. Hap has continuously managed the restaurant. It is highly rated for its food, decor, and service. Last month Hap was offered $1,000,000 for the restaurant.

In 1988, Wanda's employer purchased for her a $500,000 life insurance policy and has continued to pay all premiums on it. Wanda's insurance beneficiary designation is: "my surviving husband."

Last week Wanda died in a work-related accident. Wanda's will, duly executed in 1980, leaves all her community property to Hap, and all her separate property to her sister, Betty.

Tony has reappeared and can prove that despite his representation to Wanda, they were never divorced.

What are Hap's rights:

    a. In the stock brokerage account? Discuss.
    b. In the restaurant? Discuss.
    c. In Wanda's life insurance proceeds? Discuss.

Answer according to California law.

1. Outlining Strategy and Exam Analysis

This problem sounds more like a soap opera than a bar question. The life and times of Hap, Wanda and Tony include a bigamous marriage, a life insurance policy left to one of two surviving husbands, and Wanda's tragic death. But under these sensational facts lies a regular old community property problem. Let's once again apply our outlining strategy to create a winning outline:

i. PRELIMINARY ISSUE: Valid marriage? Hap is putative spouse & quasi-marital property laws apply.

1. STOCK BROKERAGE ACCOUNT

    SOURCE: Stock account = life insurance proceeds = SP.
    ACTIONS: Pre-1-1-85 oral agreement = CP; account in W's name.
    PRESUMPTIONS: None.
    DISPOSITION: W's SP; under will, Hap has no interest.

2. RESTAURANT

    SOURCE: H's inheritance = SP.
    ACTIONS: Community interest in H's SP; <u>Van Camp</u> or <u>Pereira</u>?
    PRESUMPTIONS: None.
    DISPOSITION: Probably <u>Pereira</u>, since Hap's labor is the greater factor: CP = residual, Hap's SP = reasonable rate of return on investment; entire restaurant goes to Hap under will.

3. WANDA'S LIFE INSURANCE PROCEEDS

    SOURCE: Paid by employer for Wanda's employment during marriage; if premiums paid by CP, then proceeds are CP.
    ACTIONS: Beneficiary = "my surviving husband."
    PRESUMPTIONS: General presumption.
    DISPOSITION: Hap takes proceeds as beneficiary or at least 1/2 as CP under will.

The directions in the interrogatory dictate that you must analyze this problem from the standpoint of Hap's rights. Thus, throughout this problem, you are concerned only with Hap's rights to each of the items, not Tony's or Betty's. Thus, your conclusions should address what Hap will receive respecting each item of property.

The first issue that must be resolved is whether California community property laws apply to an invalid marriage. Because the resolution of this issue will determine Hap's rights, you must discuss quasi-marital property principles before addressing each item of property.

Each of the issues presented in this problem were extremely straightforward as you will see in the model answer which follows.

2. Model Answer: Hap's Rights

The issue is what rights Hap has in the stock account, restaurant, and life insurance proceeds.

Hap and Wanda were never legally married, since Tony can prove that he and Wanda were never divorced. However, both Hap and Wanda believed, based on Tony's former representation, that they were legally married, having underwent a duly licensed and witnessed wedding ceremony. Therefore, upon Wanda's death, Hap would be treated as a putative spouse.

In California, a putative spouse is treated as a legal spouse, and takes according to quasi-marital property (QMP) principles.

Under quasi-marital property laws, all property acquired during the putative marriage is quasi-marital property while property acquired before the putative marriage or after permanent separation, or by gift or inheritance, is separate property (SP).

The characterization of an asset as quasi-marital property or separate property depends on three factors: (1) the source of the item; (2) actions of the parties which may have altered the character of the item; (3) any statutory presumptions affecting the item.

300

a. Stock brokerage account

The source of the funds placed in the stock brokerage account was the proceeds of Wanda's father's insurance policy, which is separate property.

However, Hap and Wanda orally agreed _before_ marriage that any life insurance proceeds either might collect would be community property. Pre-marital agreements prior to January 1, 1985, are valid if fully executed or detrimentally relied upon. Here the agreement was not fully executed because Wanda placed the funds in an account in her name only. This act would indicate that she did not carry out her agreement to declare the policy proceeds community property. On the other hand, if Wanda or her financial accountant inadvertently excluded Hap's name from the account and Hap detrimentally relied on Wanda's promise, the agreement would be given effect.

However, unless Hap can produce such evidence, the stock brokerage account is Wanda's separate property and he has no interest.

b. Restaurant

The source of the restaurant was Hap's inheritance from his mother, which is his separate property.

However, because Hap worked in the business during marriage, the community would have an interest in the restaurant. Applying _Van Camp_ accounting, the community receives a reasonable salary for Hap's services less any family expenses already expended, and Hap's separate property receives the residual. Under _Pereira_ accounting, Hap receives a reasonable rate of return on his separate property investment, and the community receives the residual.

Pereira accounting applies here if the growth in value of the restaurant is due to Hap's services and labor. Hap continuously managed the restaurant and built its reputation based on its "food, decor and service." If its present value is due to Hap's services and labor, then Hap should receive a reasonable return on his $200,000 investment and the community should receive the residual.

If, on the other hand, the $800,000 growth in value is due to other factors not

301

involving Hap's labor, such as increase in property values, the community should receive a reasonable salary for Hap's services, and Hap's separate property should receive the residual.

However, since Hap receives all of Wanda's quasi-marital property under her will, the entire restaurant goes to Hap regardless of the formula applied.

c. Wanda's life insurance proceeds

The source of Wanda's life insurance proceeds was her employer who paid the premiums on the policy. Because Wanda earned the rights to these proceeds during marriage, it would qualify as community earnings, similar to pension plans and other employment benefits.

On the other hand, it could be argued that the employer intended a gift, and as such, these proceeds are Wanda's separate property. It is unclear from the facts whether the policy was part of Wanda's benefits and earnings or whether the employer awarded Wanda a gift.

Wanda named "my surviving husband," as her beneficiary under the policy. The court will likely construe this language as referring to Hap only, because Tony had represented to Wanda that he had divorced her, and thus Wanda believed she only had one surviving husband at the time the policy was executed. Tony might counter that had Wanda intended to name Hap, she would have said so and that because he is still technically married to Wanda, he, not Hap, is Wanda's "surviving husband."

The general presumption holds that because the policy was acquired during marriage, it is presumed to be quasi-marital property.

Because these proceeds are probably quasi-marital property as Wanda's earnings during marriage, Hap would be entitled to take at least half even if Tony's argument succeeds, which is unlikely. However, Hap should be entitled to all the proceeds as Wanda's surviving husband.

In a problem such as this, it is easy to be judgmental, and you must restrain from judging the moral correctness of the parties. Most people would naturally side

302

with Hap, since Hap is portrayed as the hardworking, innocent "good-guy" who lost his beloved Wanda in an untimely tragic accident. Most people would detest Tony, who uncouthly lied to Wanda about their marital status, only to re-appear years later in attempting to collect from Wanda's estate.

You are not called on to deliver a moral assessment of Tony's character. Here's an example of an answer which does exactly that:

Tony should not be allowed to collect a nickel from Wanda's estate. Tony should not profit from his misdeeds. By misrepresenting their marital status, Tony misled Wanda into believing that they were in fact divorced. Wanda had no reason to believe that Tony's statement was false. Wanda relied on his representation, and that's why she married Hap. Thus, Tony should not be allowed to collect on Wanda's policy.

Remember that on the bar exam, your job is not to preach from a pulpit but to objectively analyze the facts as they are presented. While indeed here Tony takes nothing, you must state legal reasoning to support your analysis, not emotional appeal.

Let's now turn to the *Exam Evaluator* and gauge your ongoing progress!

The Exam Evaluator
HAP, WANDA & TONY

EXAM PRESENTATION (TOTAL POINTS AVAILABLE = 25)

	Poor										Excellent	
NEATNESS	0 1 2 3 4 5											____
ORGANIZATION	0 1 2 3 4 5 6 7 8 9 10											____
LAWYER-LIKE	0 1 2 3 4 5 6 7 8 9 10											____

DISCUSSION OF ISSUES (TOTAL POINTS AVAILABLE =75)

CORRECT STATEMENT OF QUASI-MARITAL PROPERTY PRINCIPLES

10 POINTS = FULL DISCUSSION ____

5 POINTS = PARTIAL/INCOMPLETE DISCUSSION ____

HAP'S RIGHTS IN STOCK BROKERAGE ACCOUNT

15 POINTS = FULL DISCUSSION ____

10 POINTS = PARTIAL/INCOMPLETE DISCUSSION ____

HAP'S RIGHTS IN THE RESTAURANT

20 POINTS = FULL DISCUSSION ____

10 POINTS = PARTIAL/INCOMPLETE DISCUSSION ____

HAP'S RIGHTS IN WANDA'S LIFE INSURANCE PROCEEDS

    30 POINTS = FULL DISCUSSION   ____

    20 POINTS = PARTIAL/INCOMPLETE DISCUSSION   ____

TOTAL SCORE . . . . ____

J.   PROBLEM SEVEN: H v. W

All the following events occurred in California.

Shortly before H's marriage to W in 1970, he and his father commenced a construction business, XYZ Corporation. H invested $10,000 saved from his prior earnings, for which he was issued 200 shares of XYZ stock. His father invested $10,000 in the corporation, for which he was issued 200 shares of XYZ stock. XYZ has issued no other stock.

After his marriage, H worked full time managing the corporation and received a salary of $2,500 per month. His father did not work for XYZ and received no salary. No dividends have been paid on XYZ stock. At the present time, the assets of XYZ exceed its liabilities by $1,000,000.

Since 1969, W has worked full time as a medical technician for Hospital. She has never worked for XYZ.

In 1977, H used funds saved from his salary during marriage to purchase a house and lot. Because of his potential personal liabilities in connection with the construction business, H arranged for title to the house and lot to be taken in W's name alone. Since the purchase, H and W have occupied the house as their home, and the house and lot are now worth $100,000.

In 1978, W inherited a mountain parcel improved with a cabin. At that time, the property had a market value of $20,000 but was subject to a $4,000 mortgage and liens for unpaid taxes totalling $2,000. W used funds saved from her salary during the preceding four years to satisfy both the mortgage and the tax liens. Rentals received by W from the mountain property have been used to maintain the property and pay the taxes on it. The mountain property now has a market value of $130,000.

W has commenced an action for dissolution of the marriage.

How should the following property be distributed on dissolution?

1. XYZ Corporation stock? Discuss.

2. The house and lot? Discuss.

3. The mountain parcel and cabin? Discuss.

Answer according to California law.

1. Outlining Strategy and Exam Analysis

"Everything should be made as simple as possible, but not simpler."

---- Albert Einstein (1878-1955)

Let's begin by creating a quick "shopping list" of the facts we are to analyze:

1. XYZ Corporation stock.

- Business begun before marriage
- Both H and H's father invested $10K of prior earnings = 200 shares of XYZ stock each
- H works full-time managing XYZ, receiving $2500 per month.
- Assets = 1 million net
- W never worked for XYZ

2. The house and lot.

- Purchased with H's salary earned during marriage
- In W's name alone to avoid corporate liability
- H & W lived there
- Valued at $100,000

3. The mountain parcel and cabin.

- W's inheritance
- 1978 market value: $20,000 (subject to $4K mortgage + $2K liens)
- W's salary used to pay mortgage and tax liens
- Rental used to maintain property & pay taxes
- Present market value of $130,000

As you can see from this problem, the Examiners have neatly divided the facts between the five paragraphs. The first three paragraphs relate information on XYZ Corporation, while the fourth paragraph concerns the home and the last paragraph contains facts regarding the mountain parcel and cabin.

A few preliminary observations before we outline this problem. First, you can see that the Examiners took pains to give you numerical figures in this problem. You are told how much H and H's father invested in XYZ Corporation and how much XYZ now has in net assets. You are given the precise value of the residence, and are told the historic and present value of the mountain property as well as the exact amounts of taxes, liens and mortgages outstanding when the property was acquired.

While in most instances the Examiners do not require mathematical computations, occasionally they do. When they do expect to see a little applied mathematics, they will tell you as they have here, by providing you with the figures you are to work with. The Examiners will not give you an over-complicated mathematical problem that the average person cannot solve. You will be given nice, round numbers to apply to simple mathematic formulas. The Examiners are not overly concerned with your ability to add and subtract, but want to know instead whether you can apply the facts to a mathematical rule of law.

Next, let's outline the problem:

<u>H v. W</u>

i. INTRO

1. 200 SHARES OF XYZ CORPORATION STOCK

SOURCE: H's $10,000 used to purchase XYZ stock = SP.
ACTIONS: Community interest in XYZ Stock? <u>Van Camp</u> or <u>Pereira</u> Accounting? <u>Pereira</u> likely applies since H works full-time managing XYZ.
PRESUMPTIONS: None.
DISPOSITION: Under <u>Pereira</u>, H receives $10K SP investment + reasonable rate of return and community receives remainder.

2. THE HOUSE AND LOT

SOURCE: Purchased with H's salary earned during marriage = CP.
ACTIONS: Title taken in W's name alone to avoid corporate liability; both H and W lived there.
PRESUMPTIONS: General presumption that all property acquired is CP.

309

DISPOSITION: Valued at $100,000; each receives 1/2 CP.

3. THE MOUNTAIN PARCEL AND CABIN

SOURCE: W's Inheritance = SP
ACTIONS: W used CP to pay $4K mortgage + $2K liens; community interest?
PRESUMPTIONS: None.
DISPOSITION: Community receives pro-rata share:
- Property appreciated $110,000 during marriage.
- CP interest/purchase price = 4,000/20,000; CP has 1/5 interest in 130,000 = $26,000.
- SP interest is therefore $130,000 - $26,000 = $104,000.
- Community entitled to reimbursement for $2K tax liens.

Note that the mathematics involved here required very few computations. No calculator, slide-rule or abacus is needed. For example, taking the third interrogatory, the community pro-rata interest is determined by taking the amount that the community contributed to the value of the property when acquired, i.e., $4,000, divided into property value when acquired, i.e. $20,000. 4 divided into 20 is 1/5th or 20%. The community interest is then multiplied by the present value of the property, $130,000. 20% of $130,000 or 1/5 X $130,000 equals $26,000, the community interest in the property. To arrive at the separate property interest, you need only subtract the community interest, i.e., $26,000 from the present value, i.e., $130,000, which equals $104,000.

If you are wondering what happened to the $2,000 that was paid by the community for taxes, you may recall the rule that funds used to pay taxes do not give the community an interest in the property. However, the community is entitled to reimbursement.

If you could not reach these figures, rather than throw your hands up and quit, you should have instead at least told the bar grader how to arrive at the correct figures. Here is an example of an answer which fails to compute the exact figures, but manages to explain how to get there:

The community is entitled to an interest in the mountain parcel. The *community contributed $4,000, which represents the payment on the principal made from W's community earnings. The $2,000 expended by W on tax liens does not give the community any interest in the property since this went to pay the taxes and not the principal. Using $20,000 as the value of the property when purchased, the community would be entitled to $4,000/$20,000 interest in the property presently valued at $130,000. W's separate property would receive the remainder.*

While it is clearly more desirable to state the exact figures, this answer lets the bar grader know that you know the correct formula, but that you are no Einstein when it comes to mathematics. While the grader might penalize you slightly for not stating the exact figures, the grader will give you credit for knowing how to get the right answer.

2. Model Answer

Let's review the model answer. Note the application of Einstein's quoted principle to the mathematics in this problem:

H v. W

Because California is a community property state, all property acquired during marriage is community property (CP), while property acquired before marriage or after permanent separation, or by gift or inheritance, is separate property (SP).

The characterization of an asset as community property or separate property depends on three factors: (1) the source of the item; (2) actions of the parties which may have altered the character of the item; (3) any statutory presumptions affecting the item.

Here the distribution of property depends on whether these items are separate property or community property because upon dissolution, H and W each receive 1/2 of all CP.

1. 200 shares of XYZ Corporation stock.

The source of the 200 shares of XYZ stock is H's $10,000 saved from his pre-marriage earnings, which is H's separate property.

311

However, because H worked at XYZ during marriage, the community thereby acquired an interest in the present value of the company. Under <u>Pereira</u> accounting, if the principal reason for the increase in value is the spouse's services, the managing spouse's separate property receives a reasonable return on the investment and the community receives the residual. Here H worked full time managing a construction business, which involves primarily labor, and therefore <u>Pereira</u> applies. H's SP investment of $10,000 receives a reasonable return (10% per annum) and the community receives the remainder.

Under <u>Van Camp</u>, where the principal factor in the increase in a business' value is not the spouse's services, the community receives a salary for the managing spouse's labor and separate property receives the residual. If the court applied this method, the community receives nothing if H's $2,500 monthly salary reflects a reasonable rate of return, and H's separate property receives the XYZ stock.

However, because <u>Pereira</u> accounting applies, H and W each receive one half of the $489,000.

2. The house and lot.

The source of the home was H's community earnings during marriage, which is community property.

However, because the title in the property was taken in W's name only and it could be argued that a gift was intended. H would rebut by showing that the only reason his name was not included in the title was to avoid corporate liability. Furthermore, because both H and W lived in the residence during marriage, the court will likely find that the form of title will not rebut the general presumption that all property acquired during marriage is community property.

The "Married Woman" presumption does not apply to interests taken after January 1, 1975.

Therefore, both H & W receive a one-half interest in the residence, i.e., $50,000, which is now valued at $100,000.

3. The mountain parcel and cabin.

The source of the mountain property was W's inheritance, which is separate property.

However, the community acquired a pro-rata interest because W used community earnings to pay $4,000 of the mortgage owed on the property. The community interest would be calculated by dividing the community interest into the purchase price; here the $20,000 market value would serve in lieu of the purchase price, and thus the community would have a 4,000/20,000 or 1/5th interest in the present value of the property, $130,000. The community interest is therefore one-fifth of $130,000, or $26,000. The separate property interest is $130,000 less $26,000, or $104,000.

The community is entitled to reimbursement for the $2,000 tax lien paid from W's community earnings.

Thus, H's and W's community interest is $26,000 + 2,000 reimbursement and W's separate property interest is $102,000.

The Exam Evaluator
II & W

EXAM PRESENTATION (TOTAL POINTS AVAILABLE = 25)

	Poor										Excellent	
NEATNESS	0	1	2	3	4	5						____
ORGANIZATION	0	1	2	3	4	5	6	7	8	9	10	____
LAWYER-LIKE	0	1	2	3	4	5	6	7	8	9	10	____

DISCUSSION OF ISSUES (TOTAL POINTS AVAILABLE =75)

1. XYZ CORPORATION STOCK

25 POINTS = FULL DISCUSSION ____

15 POINTS = PARTIAL/INCOMPLETE DISCUSSION ____

2. THE HOUSE AND LOT

20 POINTS = FULL DISCUSSION ____

10 POINTS = PARTIAL/INCOMPLETE DISCUSSION ____

3. THE MOUNTAIN PARCEL AND CABIN

30 POINTS = FULL DISCUSSION ____

20 POINTS = PARTIAL/INCOMPLETE DISCUSSION ____

BONUS POINTS:

THE TAX LIEN ISSUE (INTERROGATORY THREE)

    5 POINTS = FULL DISCUSSION   ____

TOTAL SCORE . . . . ____

Having ventured thus far, you have now run the entire gamut of community property problems. As you can see, almost any area within community property is fair game. By using the writing approach in this book, you will be able to solve any problem that confronts you on the examination.

This next problem represents the ultimate community property problem. Good luck!

K.   PROBLEM EIGHT: H v. W

Husband (H) and Wife (W), California domiciliaries, were married in January 1976. They immediately opened a joint checking account, into which they deposited their salary earnings, and from which they paid their living expenses and made the expenditures set forth below.

In April 1976, H's aunt died and left him desert land in California. The property was worth $30,000 but was subject to a purchase money encumbrance with an unpaid balance of $10,000, payable at the rate of $200 per month, including principal and interest. Between 1976 and 1981, H paid off the encumbrance with 60 monthly payments. H and W never discussed ownership of the land. The land remained unimproved.

In January 1984, H without prior notice to W, purchased a sports car. The purchase price was $22,000, payable $3,000 down, the deferred balance, including interest, payable at $1,000 per month for 24 months.

In September 1984, W obtained a judgment for $25,000 general damages plus $5,000 punitive damages against a driver who had injured her in a 1982 automobile accident. The judgment was paid to W's attorney, who deducted the agreed fee of one-third and remitted the remaining $20,000 to W; she deposited the $20,000 into the joint checking account.

In December 1984, H's brother, X, who was unemployed and unable to obtain further credit, asked H for a $5,000 loan to pay existing creditors. X promised to repay the loan within six months, with interest at the maximum lawful rate. Despite W's strenuous objections, H made the loan.

In January 1985, H and W separated; H moved out and took the sports car with him; W filed for dissolution of marriage and W immediately obtained a temporary restraining order, which froze the bank account until trial. There was $20,000 in the account at the time, the lowest balance in the account since W made the $20,000 deposit.

Thereafter, X was declared bankrupt and all debts were discharged. X never

317

repaid any part of the loan.

In the dissolution proceeding, the trial judge made the following rulings:

A. The parties stipulated that the land was worth $45,000 at the time of trial. The land was confirmed to H as his separate property.

B. The parties stipulated that the sports car was worth $15,000 at the time of trial. The sports car was awarded to H. H was ordered to pay W $7,500 for her share at the rate of $2,500 per year, payable on the first day of each of the next three years. H's request that he be reimbursed for the payments he had made on the sports car after the parties separated was denied.

C. W was awarded the $20,000 in the joint account.

D. W's request that H be required to reimburse her the $5,000 lost on the loan to X was denied.

Was the court correct in each of its rulings? Discuss, applying California law.

1. Belief: The Precursor to Success

"The person who believes he or she can do something is probably right, and so is the person who believes he or she can't."

---- Proverb

This problem was difficult because it <u>appeared</u> difficult. The appearance of the facts alone, which cover an entire page, "shocked" many an examinee into fearing the worst. Such fears all too often lead to panic and other unresourceful states.

Think of how you react to seeing a monster in a horror film. When you see a particular gruesome character portrayed on film, it is shocking. However, had you looked behind the costume, in most cases, you would have found an ordinary human being. The same is true of difficult bar questions. The majority of these questions are difficult because you perceive them to be difficult. You immediately lose faith in your ability to solve the problem because you believe that you cannot solve the problem.

By adopting a negative stance, you place yourself in an unresourceful state in which you probably will not be able to solve the problem. On the other hand, if you truly believe in your ability to solve a problem and you have the right tools, you will solve that problem successfully. Let's compare two sets of beliefs an examinee might possess before attempting to solve this problem:

"There's no way I or anyone else can solve this problem in an hour's time."

"The bar exam isn't fair!"

"How can anyone expect to write fast enough to answer this question!"

"There's no way I'm going to pass this question."

"This problem looks completely different from any other community property problem I've seen before! I can't solve it!"

"My approach isn't going to work on this kind of problem!"

Now compare these negative states to the thoughts of a person utilizing positive thinking in problem solving:

"I *will* solve this problem!"

"I have complete faith in my approach to solving this problem and I *know* that my approach will successfully solve this problem!"

"I *will* stick to my approach to problem solving no matter what."

"Even though this problem looks a little different than the typical community property question, I know my approach *will* solve it!"

While these statements might sound a bit silly, do you think that the performance of a person who is thinking negative things will differ from the performance of a person in a positive state of mind? The positive thinker will solve the problem because he believes he will solve it. The positive thinker adopts the resourceful state of mind required to solve the problem. The negative thinker, on the other hand, will not solve the problem because she believes the problem is unsolvable.

How do you think a person finds themselves in certain states of mind? They put themselves there. It is not happenstance that the positive thinker thinks positively. Of course, positive thinking without preparation will result in failure, but even the most prepared student may fail without positive thinking. I cannot begin to count the number of students who have come to me after failing at their first attempt at the bar examination and exclaimed, "I don't know what happened. I knew the law. I prepared for the exam. But when I went into the exam room, I panicked."

> *"A person who believes is strong; a person who doubts is weak. Strong convictions precede great actions."*
>
> ----- J.F. Clarke

While it would be unfair and inaccurate to generalize as to what caused each person's failure to achieve passing scores on the essay section of the bar examination, the common thread throughout each of their experiences is that they really did not believe in their ability to solve the bar question, and consequently, their ability to pass the exam.

Before attempting to solve any bar problem, you should make a conscious effort to place yourself in the most resourceful state possible. This will allow you to maximize your skills as a problem solver and to place you in a winning mindset that will ensure your success. Any athlete will tell you that a positive mental state is a precursor to obtaining a desired goal.

2. Outlining Strategy and Exam Analysis

With these positive thoughts in mind, let's review the outline to this problem.

First, the Examiners cleverly couched the items of property in terms of judgments issued by the court. In other words, rather than ask you about each item of property, the Examiners instead placed you in the shoes of an appellate judge, reviewing rulings made with respect to those items of property by the trial court.

However, recognize these interrogatories as being no different than the typical community property queries you have become accustomed to. Let's identify each item of property and in this way arrive at our headings:

A. The desert land

B. The sports car

C. The joint account

D. The loan to X

Now that we have isolated the items of property at issue, this problem resembles the old run-of-the-mill community problem we have come to know intimately! Next, let's isolate the relevant facts before applying our writing approach:

A. The desert land

- Aunt died, leaving H desert land
- Property worth $30K but subject to encumbrance of $10K, payable at $200 per month (principal + interest)
- 60 payments made during marriage

B. The sports car

- H bought sports car during marriage w/o W's consent
- Paid $3K down payment, and $12K over 1 year, from joint account

C. The joint account

- W deposits $20K judgment during marriage for accident that occurred during marriage
- Account frozen upon separation: $20K in account

D. The loan to X

- H loans $5K to brother X over W's objection
- X now bankrupt

Now that we have put together our quick shopping list of facts, you now see this problem for what it really is --- a rather straightforward community property problem similar to those which you have already solved. However, this problem differs in one significant way: you are provided with the solutions arrived at by the trial court, and are essentially asked if those solutions are correct. Does this mean you must adopt a different approach to solving this problem? Does this mean that your writing approach must somehow be altered or modified?

No. This means only that you are to arrive at your answer in the same fashion you have done earlier and simply compare your answer to that reached by the trial court. As you will see in this outline, other than this small deviation concerning the disposition of property, you should analyze this problem no differently than any other community property problem:

<u>H v. W</u>

INTRO

A. The desert land

> **SOURCE:** Inheritance from aunt = SP.
> **ACTIONS:** Community interest in H's SP - pro-rata interest: (CP contribution/value times present value) $10K/$30K times $45,000 = $15K; H's separate property interest is $30K ($45K minus $15K)
> **PRESUMPTIONS:** None.
> **DISPOSITION:** W should have been awarded 1/2 community interest, or $7,500 and remainder should have gone to H. If H is allowed to keep property, he must pay W $7,500 for her CP interest.

B. The sports car

> **SOURCE:** Down payment of $3K and $12K payments from joint account = CP.
> **ACTIONS:** Purchased without W's consent.
> **PRESUMPTIONS:** General presumption.
> **DISPOSITION:** Car worth $15K, but may be subject to deferred balance owed. If car is paid off, both parties entitled to 1/2 or $7,500 and court order is correct; if balance owing, then both parties entitled to 1/2 of present value of car less amount owed on loan.
> Husband should be reimbursed for any SP payments after separation.

C. The joint account

> **SOURCE:** Community earnings = CP and personal injury settlement for accident during marriage = on divorce, all damages go to SP unless interests of justice require otherwise; in all cases, at least one-half to W.
> **ACTIONS:** Commingled? Direct or indirect tracing: $20K in account.
> **PRESUMPTION:** Presumed CP.
> **DISPOSITION:** Court may award all to W.

323

D. The loan to X

> **SOURCE:** Joint account = CP earnings.
> **ACTIONS:** Gift or loan?
> **PRESUMPTIONS:** None.
> **MANAGEMENT & CONTROL ISSUES:** Did H intend a loan?
> **DISPOSITION:** If gift, because W objected, she may recover 1/2 from H's estate; if loan, then community absorbs the loss and court ruling was correct.

Now that we have devised our map, let's review the model answer.

3. Model Answer

H v. W

Because California is a community property state, all property acquired during marriage is community property (CP), while property acquired before marriage or after permanent separation, or by gift or inheritance, is separate property (SP).

The characterization of an asset as community property or separate property depends on three factors: (1) the source of the item; (2) actions of the parties which may have altered the character of the item; (3) any statutory presumptions affecting the item.

The correctness of each of the trial court's rulings depends on the classification of each item of property as community or separate property. Upon dissolution, both H & W receive one-half of all community property. However, the court may award one asset to one spouse so long as the other spouse receives a substantially equal distribution of the total CP assets.

A. The desert land

The source of the desert land was H's inheritance from his aunt, which was separate property.

However, the community acquired an interest in H's separate property because H used community property earnings from the joint account to make payments on the principal owed on the land. The community therefore receives a pro-rata interest in the present value of the property.

The community's interest is determined by taking the amount of community contributions divided into the historic value, multiplied by the present value of the desert land. The community's interest is therefore: $10K(CP Contribution)/$30K (Historic value) times $45K (present value of property) = $15K. H's separate property value is thus $30K, which is $45,000 less the community interest of $15K.

W is thus entitled to one-half of the community interest, or $7,500, and the remainder should be given to H. Because the court awarded the entire property to H as his separate property, the court erred in not giving W her community interest in the property. If H is allowed to keep the property, the court should award $7,500 in community property assets to W.

B. The sports car

The source of the payment of the sports car, including the $3,000 down payment and $12,000 in monthly payments, was H's and W's joint checking account, which is community property. The payments made by on the car after H and W separated with no intention of re-uniting would be H's separate property.

Any argument by H that the community contributions to the sports car were intended as a gift would fail, since the car was purchased without W's consent.

The general presumption holds that all property acquired during marriage is community property. Because H acquired the car during marriage, it would be presumed to be community property.

Here it is somewhat difficult to determine precisely what portion of the present $15,000 value of the sports car is community property and separate property, because the facts do not tell us whether the deferred balance was paid in full. However, if the car is paid off, the car is a community asset and both H and W are entitled to one-half the value of the car, which is $7,500. On the other hand, if there is a balance owing, then both parties are entitled to one-half the present value of the car less the amount owed on the loan.

However, H should be reimbursed for any car payments made after separation made from his earnings or funds acquired after separation, since all earnings while the parties are separated are that spouse's separate property.

The court's ruling was correct because it awarded W one-half interest in the present value of the sports car. The court had discretion to determine the manner of payment directed. However, the court should have reimbursed H for any payments made on the car after the parties separated.

C. The joint account

The source of the funds in the joint account was H's and W's salary earnings and W's personal injury settlement for an accident which occurred during marriage. The community earnings are community property, and the personal injury damages, upon divorce, pass as W's separate property, unless interests of justice require otherwise; in all cases, the injured spouse is to receive at least one-half.

Where community funds and separate property funds have been commingled, the commingled whole is presumed to be community property. A party may rebut this presumption by directly tracing the source of the funds, or by indirectly showing that community funds were exhausted, leaving only separate property. Here, $20,000 was the lowest balance in the account. Because it is presumed that family expenses were used first, this indirectly shows that the $20,000 remaining in the account was W's separate property.

Here the court may award the entire amount to W as her separate property and therefore was correct in awarding W the proceeds of the joint account.

D. The loan to X

The source of H's loan to X was community earnings, which is community property.

The actions of H in giving X $5,000 could be construed as either a gift or a loan. However, because W objected, if H intended the loan only as a gift, she could recover one-half the loan amount, or $2,500 from H's CP. If, on the other hand, H intended to loan X the money, then the community absorbs the loss due to X's *bankruptcy.*

If the court found that H intended a loan to X which X can no longer pay, it was correct in denying W recovery for half the loan amount, $2,500.

This problem had a few interesting conflicts which were not capable of a clear analysis. One was the issue of the sports car. It was not clear from the facts whether H paid off the car in full after separating from W. This question was given in the Winter of 1986, and since the payments on the sports car continued until January of 1986, it could be assumed that at the time the bar exam was given, in February of 1986, H paid for the sports car in full. This would be true if H diligently made all payments on the car. On the other hand, if H did not make all payments on the car, then both H and W take their community interests in the sports car subject to the outstanding loan amount. You are only told that H requested that "he be reimbursed for the payments he had made on the sports car after the parties separated . . ."

Why didn't the Examiners tell you that the sports car was paid off? Because again they wanted to know whether you would pick up on the fact that you needed to know this before reaching a conclusion as to the correctness of the trial court's ruling. A good lawyer knows when to ask questions before reaching a conclusion, and the Examiners are testing your ability to do exactly that.

Rather than to go round and round ad infinitum, all you needed to do here is state that the solution to this problem is dependent on the resolution of this unknown fact. In other words, point out the thing that is unknown, and then move on.

The second ambiguity was the $5,000 loan amount, as this could have been construed as either a gift or a loan. While the fact that X made a promise to repay with interest might strongly support the argument that H intended a loan, the fact that X was H's brother indicates that a gift may have been intended. Again, rather than view this as an obstacle, just discuss both sides and move on.

Let's fill out the *Exam Evaluator* and see how you did!

The Exam Evaluator
H & W

EXAM PRESENTATION (TOTAL POINTS AVAILABLE = 25)

	Poor											Excellent	
NEATNESS	0	1	2	3	4	5							____
ORGANIZATION	0	1	2	3	4	5	6	7	8	9	10	____
LAWYER-LIKE	0	1	2	3	4	5	6	7	8	9	10	____

DISCUSSION OF ISSUES (TOTAL POINTS AVAILABLE =75)

A. DESERT LAND

20 POINTS = FULL DISCUSSION ____

15 POINTS = PARTIAL/INCOMPLETE DISCUSSION ____

B. THE SPORTS CAR

20 POINTS = FULL DISCUSSION ____

15 POINTS = PARTIAL/INCOMPLETE DISCUSSION ____

C. THE SAVINGS ACCOUNT

20 POINTS = FULL DISCUSSION ____

10 POINTS = PARTIAL/INCOMPLETE DISCUSSION ____

D. THE LOAN

       15 POINTS = FULL DISCUSSION   ____

       10 POINTS = PARTIAL/INCOMPLETE DISCUSSION   ____

TOTAL SCORE . . . . ____

L.   CHAPTER CONCLUSION

"One problem thoroughly mastered is of more value than many poorly mastered."

---- Booker T. Washington (1856-1915)

Now that you have completed the eight problems in this Chapter, enter and review your scores on the Master Exam Evaluator. As always, if you have received a less than passing score on any individual examination, take that examination again. Do not become discouraged if you did not receive a 90 score on each examination. I repeat, do <u>not</u> become discouraged. If you do not obtain a satisfactory score the first time, take the examination again until you achieve the score desired.

Even if you did well in initially solving each problem, you may find it helpful to repeat the exercises and problems in this Chapter. Each examination was specially selected to demonstrate slight differences in the various testing formats found in past community property problems. By repeating examinations already taken, you will reinforce your knowledge of the different types of community property problems which consistently appear on the bar examination, as your exam taking skills excel.

Once you have mastered each of the examinations in this Chapter, you will feel a new sense of confidence in solving community property problems. True confidence and problem solving ability comes with applying the writing approach to new and different problems. Accordingly, continue to apply your writing approach to as many new and different community property problems as you can find!

BARBREAKER

evidence

X. EVIDENCE

A. THE EVIDENCE WRITING APPROACH

"It may be a long way to a goal, but it is never far to the next step towards your goal."

---- Proverb

The law of Evidence, as tested on the California bar exam, is best viewed as a series of hurdles or hoops which the "evidence" in question must jump over or through in order to be admissible. Each of these hurdles or hoops represents a different rung in the ladder of admissibility. As you will see in the writing approach which follows, the law of Evidence falls within a clearly delineated checklist of issues.

The typical Evidence question will present you with several items of evidence, both tangible and intangible, such as documents, statements, testimony and the like. You are then asked whether these particular items of evidence were properly admitted into evidence.

Ordinarily a courtroom setting provides the backdrop to the Evidence question, as it does in real life. While the case itself may concern an innumerable number of issues, the tip-off that an Evidence question is presented is that the Bar Examiners will specifically ask you whether a particular item of evidence was properly offered and received into evidence.

B. THE BIG PICTURE QUESTIONS

In an evidence problem, the overall question is, "Is this [item of evidence] admissible?" Thus, the first step is to identify the item of evidence. Normally, you are told which items of property to analyze in the interrogatories. Ordinarily, the Bar Examiners will give you a fact pattern and then ask:

(1) Was [Item #1] properly admitted into evidence or

(2) Did the court err in admitting [Item #2] into evidence?

Another common variation of this basic testing pattern is to list several explanations of things which occurred and then ask you whether the items were properly admitted:

(1) Bullwinkle testified: "After the accident, I told Rocky that I would pay his medical expenses for the rest of his life."

(2) Rocky's lawyer asked Boris on cross-examination if he had a prior conviction for misdemeanor manslaughter.

Assume that in each instance all appropriate objections were made. Were the items of evidence properly admitted? Discuss.

Regardless of the testing format employed, remember that you must first isolate the item of evidence at issue. For example, in the first interrogatory above, the item of evidence is Bullwinkle's testimony, and in the second interrogatory, Boris' prior conviction for misdemeanor manslaughter.

After you have identified the item of evidence, the next step is to put the items of evidence through each of the following hurdles:

(1) IS THE EVIDENCE RELEVANT?
   Is the evidence LOGICALLY relevant?
   Is the evidence LEGALLY relevant?

(2) IS THE EVIDENCE RELIABLE?
   Is the evidence AUTHENTICATED or based on PERSONAL KNOWLEDGE?
   Does the BEST EVIDENCE RULE apply?

(3) IS THE EVIDENCE BARRED BY EXTRINSIC POLICIES?

(4) IS THE EVIDENCE ADMISSIBLE TO SHOW CHARACTER?

(5) IS THE EVIDENCE ADMISSIBLE TO IMPEACH?

(6) IS THE EVIDENCE BARRED BY PRIVILEGE?

(7) IS THE EVIDENCE BARRED BY THE HEARSAY RULE?

Let's quickly review each "big picture" question:

(1) IS THE EVIDENCE RELEVANT?
Is the evidence LOGICALLY relevant?
Is the evidence LEGALLY relevant?

The first and easiest issue concerns logical relevance. You should always state *why* a particular item of property is relevant to the issue or issues before the court. Even though it may appear obvious to you, remember that relevance is a foremost element of admissibility which must always be shown before a particular item of evidence is admissible. Even if the Bar Examiners present you with an evidence question involving the murder weapon in a homicide case, make sure and state why it is relevant.

Note that in addition to the general question of relevance, you may also be tested on special rules of relevance, such as whether similar contracts or transactions made with a party are admissible to prove or clarify the terms of a contract made with third parties. These special rules of relevance should be included under your "relevance" checklist as well.

Legal relevance, by contrast, addresses the question of whether as a matter of legal policy, the item of evidence should be admitted. Evidence is legally irrelevant if its probative value is substantially outweighed by unfair prejudice, confusion of the issues, the danger of misleading the jury or undue time consumption. Legal relevance should be discussed whenever an argument as to any of these factors may be made.

Legal relevance also concerns itself with the form of the evidence. For example, an item of evidence may be logically relevant but the form in which it is presented is legally objectionable. For example, a leading or compound question may inquire into a logically relevant area of law but yet be improper.

(2) IS THE EVIDENCE RELIABLE?

The issue of reliability concerns whether a particular item of evidence or testimony by a witness is reliable enough to warrant its admissibility. First, you should look to the type of evidence at issue, for the nature of the evidence will dictate what foundational elements must be met. For example, writings must be sufficiently authenticated, as must voices and physical objects. Similarly, witnesses must have personal knowledge of the events they testify about.

Note as well that specific rules determine the admissibility of laywitness and expert testimony. Finally, a related issue sometimes raised on bar questions is the doctrine of judicial notice.

The second issue under reliability involves the application of the best evidence rule, which requires that in proving the contents of a writing, the original writing must be produced or shown to be unavailable unless it refers to a collateral matter. This is a very popular issue and its inclusion in this checklist reflects the fact that this issue is a favorite of the Bar Examiners.

(3) IS THE EVIDENCE BARRED BY EXTRINSIC POLICIES?

The next issue concerns the application of extrinsic or outside policies mandating exclusion of the evidence. The most commonly tested issues include insurance liability, subsequent remedial measures and offers to settle the case or plead guilty or pay medical expenses.

(4) IS THE EVIDENCE ADMISSIBLE TO SHOW CHARACTER?

The area of character evidence concerns specific rules which govern the admissibility of such evidence. Generally, character evidence is inadmissible unless offered for a specific purpose. In addressing this issue, first determine if the evidence is evidence of character, and if so, identify the type of character evidence, e.g., reputation, opinion or specific instances of conduct, and decide whether any exceptions apply.

For example, an exception to the rule excluding character evidence is that in a criminal case, the defendant may offer reputation or opinion evidence which tends to show that he or she is a good person and not criminally disposed to commit crime. Another exception is where character is in issue, such as in a defamation action where the plaintiff's character is attacked, since truth is a complete defense.

(5) IS THE EVIDENCE ADMISSIBLE TO IMPEACH?

Impeachment evidence is that evidence used to impeach a particular witness' testimony. For example, a witness' competence may be challenged by evidence tending to show that the witness' memory about the events testified to was lacking on a prior occasion.

(6) IS THE EVIDENCE BARRED BY PRIVILEGE?

Privileges have evolved through common law and disallow particular types of testimonial evidence which, for a policy reason, are not admitted into evidence. The privileges include:

> **THE ATTORNEY-CLIENT PRIVILEGE**
> **SPOUSAL WITNESS PRIVILEGE**
> **MARITAL COMMUNICATIONS PRIVILEGE**
> **PHYSICIAN-PATIENT PRIVILEGE**
> **PSYCHOTHERAPIST-PATIENT PRIVILEGE (MINORITY VIEW)**
> **CLERGYMAN-PENITENT PRIVILEGE**
> **SELF-INCRIMINATION PRIVILEGE**

In analyzing a privilege, after identifying the issue and stating the rule, state who the holder of the privilege is, and whether the holder may exercise the privilege. You should then discuss whether the evidence in question falls within the privilege, whether any exceptions apply and lastly whether any general considerations apply. An example of a general consideration issue is whether the privilege bars a communication overheard by an inessential third person, e.g., an eavesdropper.

(7) IS THE EVIDENCE BARRED BY THE HEARSAY RULE?

By far the most popular recurring issue is that of hearsay. Because it forms one of the largest areas of evidence, it is fertile testing ground for the Bar Examiners.

Analyzing a hearsay question is actually quite simple. The first question you must answer is whether the piece of evidence is in fact hearsay. Hearsay is an out-of-court statement offered for the truth of the matter stated. If the elements of this definition are met, then you determine whether any exceptions to the hearsay rule apply.

Each hearsay exception is comprised of several elements, all of which must be met before the item of evidence is admitted despite the fact that it is hearsay. This is because when the elements of a hearsay exception are met, the statement is deemed reliable enough to overcome the general presumption that out-of-court statements are often unreliable.

For example, the dying declaration exception requires that (1) the declarant be unavailable; (2) the statement was made by a person who believed his or her death was imminent; and (3) the statement related to circumstances of his or her death. Once these requirements are met, the statement is admitted. This, of course, is the California rule, which is followed in most jurisdictions. While on the multi-state examination you are to respond to questions using only the Federal Rules of Evidence (FRE); on the Essay section of the bar exam, you must apply "legal theories and principles of general application." These general principles minimally include state law and common law and probably the FRE.

You should note that under common law, this exception applies in homicide cases where the declarant is deceased. You may, but are not required, to analyze the Federal Rule on this point. The Federal Rule is that dying declarations are admissible in all civil cases and homicide prosecutions. Certainly, the bar grader would not punish you for failing to discuss the Federal Rule since the Examiners do not specifically tell you to do so, but mentioning the Federal Rule may earn you brownie points with the bar grader. Also, since you must know the Federal Rules to solve multi-state problems, you should strive to mention the Federal Rules at least when a major distinction exists between the various rules.

While the vagaries of these instructions may seem less than crystal clear, as you begin writing out your answers to Evidence bar questions, you will find that it is not as confusing as it sounds. Remember for the time being that you do not have to learn three separate approaches for common law, state law and the federal rules. There is only one approach you must learn to solve all Evidence problems.

Your checklist of hearsay exceptions should include:

ADMISSIONS
BUSINESS RECORD EXCEPTION
DECLARATION AGAINST INTEREST
DYING DECLARATIONS
EQUIVALENCY
EXCITED UTTERANCE
EXPERT CROSS-EXAMINATION
IDENTIFICATION
OFFICIAL WRITTEN STATEMENTS
PAST RECOLLECTION RECORDED
PRESENT PHYSICAL STATE
PRIOR CONSISTENT AND INCONSISTENT STATEMENTS
PRIOR TESTIMONY
SENSE IMPRESSION
STATEMENTS OF PRESENT MENTAL STATE

For a comprehensive presentation of Evidence, refer to the *Law Charts* in the *Bar Exam Survival Kit.*

Now that we have reviewed the Evidence writing approach, there's only one thing left to do. Let's apply it to an Evidence bar question and watch problem solving in action!

C.   EVIDENCE PROBLEM ONE: PAUL v. CABCO

1. The First Read

> Apply the reading strategies in Chapter One by reading the fact pattern once for content only. Good luck!

An automobile, owned and operated by Paul, collided with a taxicab driven by Don and owned by Cabco. Paul and Don were injured. Vicky, a passenger in Paul's automobile, suffered a broken leg. While she was undergoing necessary surgery to repair the fracture, she suffered a cardiac arrest and died. Action was brought in state court by Paul against Cabco for personal injuries. The parties stipulated to the above facts.

At the trial by jury, the following occurred.

a. Paul testified: "After the accident, I went over to the cab. Don was hurting real bad, and Don said, "This wouldn't have happened if I hadn't been in such a hurry to pick up a fare."

b. Cabco's counsel asked Paul on cross-examination if he had ever had a traffic accident. Paul answered: "No." Cabco's counsel then introduced a properly authenticated copy of a three-year-old unrelated conviction of Paul for vehicular manslaughter, a felony.

c. Vicky's physician, Doc, testified as a witness for Cabco that while Vicky was being prepared for surgery, he asked her how the accident happened, and she responded: "Don't tell anybody, Doc, but Paul and I were smoking marijuana. I dropped the lighted joint, and Paul had his head down looking for it when we hit the cab."

Assume that in each instance all appropriate objections were made. Were the items of evidence properly admitted? Discuss.

338

2. The Second Read

Let's pause a moment and ask, "Why bother to read the facts again? Why not just begin solving the problem?" The purpose of the first read is not to solve the problem, but to comprehend and digest the statement of facts. In the area of evidence, attempting to write out your answer without fully understanding the problem will result in a poor exam analysis.

Of course, it is sometimes difficult to restrain yourself from attempting to solve the problem when you see issues emerging from the fact pattern. For example, after reading the first interrogatory (a), you may have immediately thought "I got it! This is an admission of a party!" While you would indeed be correct, you would have missed the other important issues, such as relevance, reliability, hearsay and other less obvious hearsay exceptions. Remember that the bar exam is not a game show; the first to press the buzzer isn't always the winner.

After reading the fact pattern once, you should have focused on the fact that there was a car accident between two parties, one of whom sued the other, and at the trial, three things happened: (1) Paul testified about what Don said; (2) Paul was asked about his prior felony conviction; (3) Doc testified as to Vicky's admission that she and Paul were smoking dope.

Notice that no analysis is going on. Rather, you are only reading through the facts for content, to find out what's going on. It's like watching TV. Most of us do not psychoanalyze a sit-com or soap opera --- we just observe it.

After we have grasped the general thrust of the problem, it is then time to read it again, taking a closer look at the facts, the relationship between the parties, who the parties are and what they did to each other.

3. The Picasso Strategy

During the second read, it is sometimes helpful to circle or underline key words and phrases as you go through the fact pattern a second time. I have even known students who drew pictures to assist them. While I don't advise you to spend thirty minutes drawing a comic book version of the facts, if you find that it assists you to remember the facts, draw a quick picture or diagram. For example, you could have drawn a picture of a box, representing a car, with "P" for Paul and "V" for Vicky, colliding with another box, with "D" for Don in it. I call this the Picasso strategy. Even though you may feel a little silly, give it a try.

If this diagram helps you remember what happened here, then by all means use the Picasso technique. Keep in mind that this technique is probably best reserved for complex factual problems involving multiple parties. On the other hand, if you entered the legal profession due to a conspicuous absence of artistic talent, then don't. Not everyone learns and remembers through visual aids, and you should use this technique only if it works for you.

4. Visualizing the Problem

"Seeing is believing!"

---- Unknown origin

Imagine if the bar exam were given visually. Imagine that instead of being given a fact pattern on a cold piece of paper, you were instead shown a video tape illustrating the hypothetical. Would the problem be easier to solve? Would you obtain a quicker understanding of the factual scenario before you?

If you're like most people, you would better understand the problem by seeing it happen before you. It's like the difference between reading a book and seeing a movie. While one does not necessarily excel over the other as a medium of communication, most of us best learn by seeing. A bar question is no different.

Unfortunately, bar questions are not available in VHS format. As you have already learned in earlier chapters, learning how to visualize the problem requires a great deal of skill and effort. It requires conscious effort to fully comprehend the facts. While you have used visualization on earlier fact patterns, let's fine tune your skills and sharpen our visualization of this problem.

First, close your eyes and VISUALIZE this fact pattern. Take a good five minutes and think about the facts in the same way that you would think about something that happened to you earlier in the day. Then open your eyes and return to this exercise.

First of all, ask yourself, what did you visualize? If you performed this task correctly, you should have VISUALIZED the same thing as anyone else reading this book. While some would visualize Paul driving a hot red Ferrari and others might envision Paul in a Geo Metro, everyone should have visualized Paul driving a car with Vicky as his passenger. You would see Paul's car collide with Cabco's taxicab, driven by Don.

Next visualize Vicky's broken leg, subsequent surgery, and later death in the context of the statement she made to Doc. See Vicky and see her broken leg. She is brought in for surgery and it is then that she talks to Doc. Visualize Doc asking Vicky, "How did the accident happen?" See Vicky saying, "Don't tell anybody, Doc, but Paul and I were smoking marijuana. I dropped a lighted joint, and Paul had his head down looking for it when we hit the cab." See Vicky in surgery, when she suffers a cardiac arrest and dies.

Let me give you an example of the importance of visualization. After applying your writing approach, you would immediately find that a hearsay issue was presented. One of the applicable exceptions would be a dying declaration. In determining the applicability of this exception, is it important that the statement be made at a time when the declarant believed that his or her death was imminent and impending? You bet! Unless you visualized the problem and saw the chronology of events as they occurred, this critical fact might have been overlooked. The Examiners do not tell you that Vicky did not believe that she was going to die when she made the statement. Rather, this is an issue for you to raise and address in your discussion.

If you saw this issue without resorting to fact visualization, then I congratulate you. On the other hand, if you find this technique helpful, then use it. Even though I have literally taken hundreds of bar questions, I always take the time to visualize the problem, because it is much too easy to miss even an obvious fact on paper.

Now let's move on and solve this question!

5. Outlining Strategy and Exam Analysis

Before reading any further, apply the writing approach and draft an outline to your answer. When you're done, continue reading.

The first step in solving an Evidence problem is to identify the items of evidence to be analyzed. In this problem, you are given three items:

a. Paul's testimony re: Don's statement

b. Paul's prior conviction

c. Vicky's statement to Doc

While the items of evidence involved in this problem are extremely straightforward, this is not always true of Evidence problems. In fact, it is not uncommon for the item of evidence to be submerged under other facts, and you may have to search for it.

For example, the first interrogatory couches Don's statement in Paul's testimony. The issue is not whether Don's testimony was properly admitted, but whether Paul's testimony about what Don said was admissible. Likewise, in the second interrogatory, the issue is not whether Paul's testimony about his prior conviction is admissible, but whether the conviction itself is admissible. The same is true of the last issue. The question presented is not whether Vicky's testimony was admissible, but whether her statement to Doc as testified to by Doc was admissible. While the distinction might seem unimportant, it is important to identify just which items of evidence you are to analyze.

As you can see, the items of evidence themselves serve as the headings. Once again, always follow the order indicated in the interrogatories. Do not analyze Vicky's statement first, and then Paul's testimony. The Bar Examiners give you that order because they want you to follow it. Enough said!

Next, let's apply the approach to the first interrogatory:

a. Paul's testimony re: Don's statement

(1) IS THE EVIDENCE RELEVANT?
    Is the evidence LOGICALLY relevant? - Yes, proves Don was in a hurry and this infers that Don was negligent.
    Is the evidence LEGALLY relevant? - Probative value exceeds other concerns.

(2) IS THE EVIDENCE RELIABLE?
    Is the evidence AUTHENTICATED or based on PERSONAL KNOWLEDGE? Paul was present when the statement was made and has personal knowledge of who made it.
    Does the BEST EVIDENCE RULE apply?
    No issue is presented.

(3) IS THE EVIDENCE BARRED BY EXTRINSIC POLICIES?
    None apply here.

(4) IS THE EVIDENCE ADMISSIBLE TO SHOW CHARACTER?
    Statement does not involve Don's character.

(5) IS THE EVIDENCE ADMISSIBLE TO IMPEACH?
    Statement is not offered to impeach Paul, the witness.

(6) IS THE EVIDENCE BARRED BY PRIVILEGE?
    No privilege relationship between Don and Paul.

(7) IS THE EVIDENCE BARRED BY THE HEARSAY RULE?
    Statement is hearsay - made out of court offered for its truth.
    Exceptions:

        ADMISSION OF A PARTY: Vicarious admission?

343

DECLARATION AGAINST INTEREST
EXCITED UTTERANCE
PRESENT SENSE IMPRESSION

Next, how do we get from this outline to a written answer? Your task now shifts dramatically. Indeed, by drafting this quick outline, you have "solved" this problem by identifying the issue. But there is a big difference between this outline and a final answer.

If you are a prolific writer, you can probably afford to skip the next section. However, if you are unsure of what to write when you put pen to paper, please read on.

But before we write out our answer, let's outline the remainder of this problem:

b. Paul's prior conviction

(1) IS THE EVIDENCE RELEVANT?
Is the evidence LOGICALLY relevant? Shows that Paul was convicted before of killing another while driving.

Is the evidence LEGALLY relevant? Very prejudicial to Paul.

(2) IS THE EVIDENCE RELIABLE?
Conviction properly authenticated.

(3) IS THE EVIDENCE BARRED BY EXTRINSIC POLICIES?
No.

(4) IS THE EVIDENCE ADMISSIBLE TO SHOW CHARACTER?
No. Specific acts not admissible.

(5) IS THE EVIDENCE ADMISSIBLE TO IMPEACH?
Felony conviction admissible to impeach Paul's credibility.

(6) IS THE EVIDENCE BARRED BY PRIVILEGE?
No privilege applies.

(7) IS THE EVIDENCE BARRED BY THE HEARSAY RULE?
No, offered only to impeach.

c. Vicky's statement to Doc

(1) IS THE EVIDENCE RELEVANT?
Is the evidence LOGICALLY relevant? Shows that Paul was under the influence of drugs while driving and this may have contributed to the accident.

Is the evidence LEGALLY relevant? Very prejudicial to Paul but extremely probative of his ability to drive safely.

(2) IS THE EVIDENCE RELIABLE?
Doc had person knowledge that Vicky made statement.

(3) IS THE EVIDENCE BARRED BY EXTRINSIC POLICIES?
No.

(4) IS THE EVIDENCE ADMISSIBLE TO SHOW CHARACTER?
No. Specific acts are not admissible.

(5) IS THE EVIDENCE ADMISSIBLE TO IMPEACH?
Not offered to impeach Paul's testimony and Paul was never given the opportunity to explain or deny.

(6) IS THE EVIDENCE BARRED BY PRIVILEGE?
Physician-patient privilege does not survive when the patient is deceased.

(7) IS THE EVIDENT BARRED BY THE HEARSAY RULE?
Yes, but the following exceptions apply:

- DECLARATION AGAINST INTEREST
- STATEMENT OF PHYSICAL CONDITION
- DYING DECLARATION

6. Writing Out Your Answer: Using the "Exam Grid" Technique

In writing out the answer to this problem, we will use "Strict I-R-A-C." While this style of writing tends to be a little verbose and lengthy, and consequently, time consuming, it is the best starting place for those who wish to improve their writing style and ability. Again, if you are a prolific writer and have no difficulty expressing your analysis, skip this section and read through the model answer, checking to see if you identified and discussed all the major issues noted above.

I am a firm believer that most of your examination should already be written before you step into that exam room. You may be thinking, "What do you mean, most of my exam written? Why, I don't know what is going to be on that examination!" While it is true that you do not know what specific issues the Examiners will selectively test you on, you do know what areas you will likely be tested on. For example, you know before even stepping into the exam room that if you are tested on Evidence, you will likely be required to discuss "relevancy" or "reliability" somewhere in your analysis. You also know that the chances that you will be tested on hearsay are probably about 99.9%. Having these probabilities in mind, you can prepare your answer in advance. Of course, your answer should mirror your approach.

The "Exam Grid" technique is simply a preordained, prepared exam format which allows you to "fill in the blanks" as the issues are presented. This technique is especially helpful to those who experience writer's block or otherwise have difficulty expressing their reasoning in the exam answer.

This "exam grid" is based on the writing approach and may be used to successfully write a winning answer to any Evidence problem:

(A) ADMISSIBILITY OF (NAME ITEM OF EVIDENCE)

The issue is whether _____ is admissible.

(ALWAYS discuss LOGICAL RELEVANCE) *The first issue is whether _____ is relevant. In order to be relevant, the evidence must tend to prove or disprove a fact in dispute. Here, the evidence is relevant because _____. Thus, the evidence is relevant/irrelevant.*

(Discuss LEGAL RELEVANCE if issue presented) *The next issue is whether the court should exercise its discretion and exclude the evidence. The court should balance the probative value of the evidence against its prejudicial effect.* **(APPLICATION: "Here the evidence is more/less probative than prejudicial because . . .")** *Thus, the evidence should be excluded/admitted.*

The second issue is whether the evidence is sufficiently reliable. **(Discuss PERSONAL KNOWLEDGE REQUIREMENT, ANY WITNESS RULES, AND/OR AUTHENTICATION PROBLEMS AND THE BEST EVIDENCE RULE)**

The next issue is whether any extrinsic policies bar admission of the evidence. **(DISCUSS ANY EXTRINSIC POLICIES WHICH APPLY)**

(IDENTIFY ANY CHARACTER EVIDENCE ISSUES) *The next issue is whether the evidence is character evidence. Evidence of a person's character or disposition is inadmissible as proof of the conduct of that person except as otherwise provided by law. Here, the evidence is character evidence because _____. Thus, unless an exception applies, the evidence is inadmissible.*

(IDENTIFY THE TYPE OF CHARACTER EVIDENCE) *There are three types of character evidence: reputation, opinion, and specific instances of conduct. Here, the evidence is _____.* **(THEN APPLY EXCEPTIONS, IF ANY APPLY:** *e.g., "Here, the evidence is character evidence offered by an accused in the form of opinion evidence. A criminal defendant may offer reputation or opinion evidence, but not specific acts which tends to prove innocence. Thus, Lisa's testimony regarding her opinion of Bart's propensity for violence is inadmissible because it is being offered by the prosecution. However, should Bart introduce evidence as to his good reputation or opinion, the prosecutor may then introduce Lisa's testimony to rebut Bart's assertion of good character.")* **(ALWAYS CONCLUDE)** *Therefore the evidence is admissible/inadmissible as character evidence.*

Next, the evidence may be admissible as impeachment evidence. **(STATE THE GROUND WHICH APPLIES) (APPLY THE RULE)** *"Here the evidence as to Bambam's alcoholism may be offered to prove that Bambam is an incompetent witness and has difficulty with his memory, perception and capacity to perceive because of his drinking problem. If it were demonstrated that Bambam had been* *drinking on the evening that he witnessed the accident, this evidence could be offered to impeach Bambam's ability to recall the events accurately."* **(ALWAYS CONCLUDE)** *Therefore the evidence is admissible/inadmissible as impeachment evidence.*

The next issue is whether any privileges apply. **(STATE RULE AND APPLY IT)** *"Here, the Clergyman-Penitent privilege applies. Under this privilege, communications between a penitent and a clergyman who is the member of a religion authorized to hear penitential communications and is under a duty to keep a secret, are confidential. Here Freddie Kruger confided his criminal acts to Father Frank, a Catholic priest, and because the Catholic religion requires Father Frank to keep Kruger's communication secret, the privilege applies. Furthermore, even though he told Father Frank while he was in custody on death row, the privilege still applies since Kruger made the statement in confidence. (DAH DAH DAH DAH - Das conclusion!)"*

The final issue is whether the hearsay rule applies. Hearsay is defined as an assertion made by an out-of-court declarant offered to prove the truth of the matter stated. Here the (evidence) is hearsay/not hearsay because _____. Therefore, (the evidence) is hearsay/non-hearsay.

The next issue is whether an exception to the hearsay rule applies. **(STATE RULE AND APPLY IT)** *"Here the dying declaration exception applies. Under this exception, a statement made by an unavailable declarant who believes death is imminent relating to circumstances or threatened death with personal knowledge is admissible. Here, Dracula made the statement within moments of his death, to the paramedic, and therefore his statement was made at a time that he believed his death to be imminent. The statement, "I know it was Buffy the Vampire Killer who done me in," concerned the identity of the person who caused his death, and therefore related to circumstances surrounding his death. The statement was also made with personal knowledge of who killed him, since Dracula stated that he knew Buffy had done him in, not that a third party had told him so.* **(CONCLUSION)** *Because all the requirements of the exception are met, _____ statement is admissible."*

This, of course, is only one possible example of an exam grid. There are at least one hundred different ways that this could have been communicated to the grader. Although every examinee's answer might be expressed differently, the

348

content of each successful answer is relatively the same. In other words, everyone answering this question should identify and answer the same issues, although the expression of each individual's reasoning would differ substantially.

Next, let's use this exam grid to solve the first interrogatory:

(A) ADMISSIBILITY OF DON'S STATEMENT TO PAUL

(STATE OVERALL ISSUE) The issue is whether Don's statement to Paul **is admissible.**

(ISSUE) The first issue is whether Don's statement **is relevant. (RULE) In order to be relevant, the evidence must tend to prove or disprove a fact in dispute. (APPLICATION) Here, the evidence is relevant because** it proves that Don was in a hurry to pick up a fare and from this it may be inferred that Don drove carelessly because he was rushing. Don also stated that the accident would not have occurred but for the fact that he was in a hurry, and therefore admitted he caused the accident. **(CONCLUSION) Thus, the evidence is relevant.**

(ISSUE) The next issue is whether the court should exercise its discretion and exclude the evidence. (RULE) The court should balance the probative value of the evidence against its prejudicial effect. (APPLICATION) Here the evidence is more probative than prejudicial because it proves that Don admitted he was careless, which is presumably the central issue in this case. **(CONCLUSION) Thus, the evidence should be admitted.**

(ISSUE AND RULE) The second issue is whether the evidence is sufficiently reliable. (APPLICATION AND CONCLUSION) Because Paul heard the statement and can identify the maker as Don, he has personal knowledge and the evidence is sufficiently reliable.

(ISSUE) The final issue is whether the hearsay rule applies. (RULE) Hearsay is defined as an assertion made by an out-of-court declarant offered to prove the truth of the matter stated. (APPLICATION) Here Don's statement is **hearsay because** it was made outside the trial and is being offered to prove the truth that Don was in fact negligent. **(CONCLUSION) Therefore, the evidence is hearsay.**

(ISSUE) **The next issue is whether an exception to the hearsay rule applies.**

(STATE THE ISSUE) Here the **vicarious admission** exception applies. (THE RULE) Under this exception, **a statement admitting culpability made by an employee during the employment relationship, concerning a matter within the scope of employment is admissible against the employer.** (APPLICATION) Paul is suing Cabco, Don's employer, and because Don's admission concerning the accident was made while Don was driving a cab for Cabco during work hours, (CONCLUSION) this exception applies and Don's **statement is admissible.**

(ISSUE) **Alternatively,** Don's **statement would qualify as an excited utterance.** (RULE) **Under this exception, a statement made about an exciting event under the stress of such exciting event is admissible.** (APPLICATION) Here Don had been in a traumatic accident and was "hurting real bad." If his statement was made immediately after the accident and under the stress caused by the accident, (CONCLUSION) **it would be admissible under this exception as well.**

(ISSUE) **Finally** Don's **statement would also be admissible under the present sense impression.** (RULE) **Under this exception, the event need not be startling but must be made contemporaneously while the declarant was perceiving an event.** (APPLICATION) Because Don's statement described why the accident occurred contemporaneously with its occurrence, (CONCLUSION) **it is admissible under this exception.**

(ISSUE) **Finally,** Don's **statement may also qualify as a declaration against interest.** (RULE) **Under this exception, a statement made by an unavailable declarant is admissible if it is against the declarant's financial or penal interest when it was made.** (APPLICATION) Here, a reasonable person would not have admitted the accident was caused by his or her acts unless it were true, and such statement is directly against both his financial and penal interests. (CONCLUSION) **Thus, if Don is unavailable, his statement is admissible under this exception.**

The **bold** type portion of this answer indicates the "exam grid." This example demonstrates the importance of knowing how to structure and write out your answer before you have even seen the exam question. You will find that an "exam grid" may

350

be designed for all subject areas and for any approach.

This is not to say that you should rotely memorize your writing approach and apply it blindly. Your approach must be flexible yet pliable. However, having an exam grid to help you get started prevents exam anxiety and writer's block, and better prepares you for writing out your answer.

Now, let's apply the "exam grid" to the second and third interrogatories:

(B) ADMISSIBILITY OF PAUL'S PRIOR CONVICTION

The issue is whether Paul's prior conviction **is admissible.**

(ALWAYS discuss LOGICAL RELEVANCE) The first issue is whether Paul's prior conviction **is relevant.** (NO NEED TO RESTATE THE RULE) **Here, the evidence is relevant because** it shows that Paul was previously convicted before of killing another while driving, and that he may have driven in an unsafe fashion, thereby contributing to the accident. Paul will argue that his prior conviction is irrelevant, because his driving on another occasion does not prove how he drove on the day of the accident involving Don. While it is a close issue, **the evidence is relevant**, since Paul's driving is in issue and his conviction tends to show his dangerous driving record.

(Discuss LEGAL RELEVANCE if issue presented.) Here evidence of the felony conviction is more prejudicial than probative. Any jury hearing evidence that a party was convicted of killing another while driving would be inclined to find against that party in a personal injury accident case. Furthermore, that incident is completely unrelated to Paul's driving patterns on the date in question. **Thus, the evidence should be excluded.**

The second issue is whether the evidence is sufficiently reliable. Here Cabco's counsel introduced a properly authenticated copy of Paul's conviction and thus the evidence is sufficiently reliable.

(IDENTIFY ANY CHARACTER EVIDENCE ISSUES) The next issue is whether the evidence is character evidence. Evidence of a person's character or disposition is inadmissible proof of the conduct of that person except as

otherwise provided by law. **Here, the evidence is character evidence because** it shows that Paul is an ex-felon and a person of dubious character. **Thus, unless an exception applies, the evidence is inadmissible.**

(IDENTIFY THE TYPE OF CHARACTER EVIDENCE) There are three types of character evidence: reputation, opinion and specific instances of conduct. Here, the evidence is a specific act, that act being convicted of a crime. In a civil case, specific acts of misconduct are inadmissible to prove a person's conduct on a given occasion. **Therefore the evidence is inadmissible as character evidence.**

Next, the evidence may be admissible as impeachment evidence. (STATE THE GROUND WHICH APPLIES) Here, under state and federal law, prior <u>felony</u> convictions are admissible to impeach a witness. Because vehicular manslaughter is a felony, it may be introduced to impeach Paul. The felony conviction is also admissible to impeach Paul's claim that he had never been involved in a traffic accident. **(CONCLUDE) Therefore the evidence is admissible as impeachment evidence.**

(C) ADMISSIBILITY OF VICKY'S STATEMENT TO DOC

The issue is whether Vicky's statement to Doc **is admissible.**

(ALWAYS discuss LOGICAL RELEVANCE) The first issue is whether Vicky's statement to Doc **is relevant.** (NO NEED TO RESTATE THE RULE) **Here, the evidence is relevant because** it shows that Paul may have been under the influence of drugs while driving and may have contributed to the accident. **Thus, the evidence is relevant.**

(Discuss LEGAL RELEVANCE if issue presented.) The next issue is whether the court should exercise its discretion and exclude the evidence. The court should balance the probative value of the evidence against its prejudicial effect. Here the evidence is more probative than prejudicial because it shows that Paul's ability to drive and his perception of the event may have been affected by his use of drugs. **Thus, the evidence should be admitted.**

The second issue is whether the evidence is sufficiently reliable. Here Doc had personal knowledge that Vicky made the statement in question and thus the evidence is sufficiently reliable.

(IDENTIFY THE TYPE OF CHARACTER EVIDENCE) There are three types of character evidence: reputation, opinion and specific instances of conduct. Here, the evidence is a specific bad act and is therefore not admissible in a civil action as character evidence.

Next, the evidence may be admissible as impeachment evidence. (STATE THE GROUND WHICH APPLIES) (APPLY THE RULE) However, before a witness may be impeached, he must be given the opportunity to explain or deny the conduct. Because Paul was not asked regarding his drug usage, evidence of Vicky's statement showing that Paul used drugs cannot be offered to impeach Paul's testimony. **Therefore the evidence is inadmissible as impeachment evidence.**

The next issue is whether any privileges apply. (STATE RULE AND APPLY IT) Here, the Physician-Patient privilege applies to Vicky's communication, since she told Doc, "Don't tell anybody," and made the statement during the course of a medical diagnosis and treatment. However, because Vicky, the holder of the privilege, is deceased, the privilege no longer exists and Doc may testify. **Therefore, the privilege does not apply and the evidence is admissible** on this basis.

The final issue is whether the hearsay rule applies. Hearsay is defined as an assertion made by an out-of-court declarant offered to prove the truth of the matter stated. Here Vicky's statement **is hearsay because** it was made outside of the court proceedings and is being offered for the truth, to show that Paul smoked marijuana before the accident. **Therefore,** Vicky's statement **is hearsay.**

The next issue is whether an exception to the hearsay rule applies.

(STATE EXCEPTION AND APPLY IT) Here the dying declaration exception applies. Under this exception, a statement made by an unavailable declarant who believes death is imminent relating to circumstances or threatened death with personal knowledge is admissible. Here, at the time Vicky made the statement, she had suffered only a broken leg and had no reason to believe that she would die of a heart attack during surgery. Thus, this exception does not apply.

(STATE EXCEPTION AND APPLY IT) However, under the FRE, Vicky's statement would qualify as a statement of her past physical condition. **Under this exception,** a statement or description of a past symptom, sensation or condition is admissible if made for the diagnosis or treatment of the declarant, and if pertinent to such diagnosis or treatment. Thus, Vicky's statement that she smoked marijuana would be admissible, but the segment of the statement about how the accident occurred would be inadmissible, since it does not concern her diagnosis or treatment.

(STATE EXCEPTION AND APPLY IT) Finally, Vicky's statement would qualify as a declaration against penal interests. **Under this exception,** a statement by an unavailable declarant against penal interest is admissible. *Here a reasonable person would not admit smoking marijuana, a criminal offense, before an accident unless it were true and thus Vicky's statement is admissible under this exception.*

As you can see from the length of this answer, "Strict I-R-A-C" necessarily involves a great deal of words and writing. However, the strength of "Strict I-R-A-C" writing is that it is comprehensive and complete. While it is by far not the most exciting writing style, it gets the job done. Once you have mastered "Strict I-R-A-C" you will learn many short cuts to writing a fuller exam answer in less time, using less words. In the next problem, this point will be amply illustrated.

The Exam Evaluator
PAUL v. DON

EXAM PRESENTATION (TOTAL POINTS AVAILABLE = 25)

	Poor											Excellent	
NEATNESS	0	1	2	3	4	5							_____
ORGANIZATION	0	1	2	3	4	5	6	7	8	9	10		_____
LAWYER-LIKE	0	1	2	3	4	5	6	7	8	9	10		_____

DISCUSSION OF ISSUES (TOTAL POINTS AVAILABLE =75)

A. PAUL'S TESTIMONY RE: DON'S STATEMENT

25 POINTS = FULL DISCUSSION   _____

15 POINTS = PARTIAL/INCOMPLETE DISCUSSION   _____

B. PAUL'S PRIOR CONVICTION

25 POINTS = FULL DISCUSSION   _____

15 POINTS = PARTIAL/INCOMPLETE DISCUSSION   _____

C. DOC'S TESTIMONY RE: VICKY'S STATEMENT

25 POINTS = FULL DISCUSSION   _____

15 POINTS = PARTIAL/INCOMPLETE DISCUSSION   _____

TOTAL SCORE . . . . _____

D. EVIDENCE PROBLEM TWO: PROSECUTION v. DICK

1. The First and Second Read, and Fact Visualization

Read the question twice and perform fact visualization. When you are done, please turn to the next page.

Dick is brought to trial on an indictment charging him with larceny of a dangerous drug, a statutory offense. The prosecution's theory of the case, as revealed by its opening statement, is that Phil saw Dick enter Phil's Pharmacy, loiter about the prescription counter, reach behind the counter, grab two bottles and flee by car. Phil called police officers who arrested Dick after a lengthy high speed chase.

At the trial before a jury, the following events occur:

(a) The prosecution offers in evidence a properly authenticated transcript of testimony by Officer Oats given during a previous trial of Dick for reckless driving based on the high-speed chase from Phil's Pharmacy. Oats' testimony was that during that chase and while Dick's car was passing over a bridge, two objects were ejected from Dick's car window and into the river below. It is stipulated that Dick was represented by counsel at the earlier trial and that Oats is now deceased.

(b) The prosecution offers the testimony of Phil that the bottles seized by Dick were labeled "DLD," that the bottles were the original labeled containers received from the supplier, and that the bottles had not been opened.

(c) The prosecution requests the court to take judicial notice that "DLD" is a derivative of opium. The statute under which Dick is prosecuted does not list "DLD" as a "dangerous drug," but does define dangerous drugs to include "any derivative of opium." In support of its request the prosecution offers for the court's inspection a standard pharmacological dictionary, which defines "DLD" as an opium derivative.

(d) The prosecution offers the testimony of Dick's divorced wife, Win, that during her marriage to Dick the latter frequently used narcotics but attempted to conceal that fact from Win.

356

Assume appropriate objections are made by Dick.

How should the court rule on each of the prosecution's offers and requests? Discuss.

2. Outlining Exercise

Next, outline your answer. In organizing your answer, include headings and apply the writing approach, repeated here for your convenience:

(1) IS THE EVIDENCE RELEVANT?
   Is the evidence LOGICALLY relevant?
   Is the evidence LEGALLY relevant?

(2) IS THE EVIDENCE RELIABLE?
   Is the evidence AUTHENTICATED or based on PERSONAL KNOWLEDGE?
   Does the BEST EVIDENCE RULE apply?

(3) IS THE EVIDENCE BARRED BY EXTRINSIC POLICIES?

(4) IS THE EVIDENCE ADMISSIBLE TO SHOW CHARACTER?

(5) IS THE EVIDENCE ADMISSIBLE TO IMPEACH?

(6) IS THE EVIDENCE BARRED BY PRIVILEGE?

(7) IS THE EVIDENCE BARRED BY THE HEARSAY RULE?

3. Outlining Strategy

This problem illustrates the chameleon nature of Evidence problems. This question involved a criminal trial, and some people actually analyzed this as a Criminal Procedure problem, discussing Fourth Amendment issues in the first interrogatory. While you might think this a bit funny, under exam pressures, stranger things have occurred.

In this problem, the tell-tale signs of an evidence question were everywhere. As in most evidence questions, you were told that the events occurred in a courtroom setting where evidence problems abound. You were also squarely asked, "How should the court rule on each of the prosecution's offers and requests?" which is a dead give-away that an evidence question was anticipated.

Once again, your first task is to identify the items of evidence to be analyzed. There are four items of property contained in the interrogatories:

(a) Officer Oats' testimony

(b) Phil's testimony re: DLD

(c) Definition of DLD

(d) Win's testimony re: Dick's narcotic use

You are told to assume that Dick objected to the admission of each item of evidence at his trial, and thus the issue is how the court should rule as to each item of property. The answer, of course, is in the application of your writing approach:

(a) Officer Oats' testimony

(1) IS THE EVIDENCE RELEVANT?
   Is the evidence LOGICALLY relevant? To prove Dick's possession of DLD and efforts to destroy evidence.
   Is the evidence LEGALLY relevant? Probative to show what happened to the drugs; prosecution has no other means to prove what happened to the drugs.

(2) IS THE EVIDENCE RELIABLE?
Transcript properly authenticated.

(7) IS THE EVIDENCE BARRED BY THE HEARSAY RULE?
Yes, but former testimony exception applies.

(b) Phil's testimony re: DLD

(1) IS THE EVIDENCE RELEVANT?
Is the evidence LOGICALLY relevant? To show what was in bottles.
Is the evidence LEGALLY relevant? Probative and necessary to show that DLD was in the bottles stolen.

(2) IS THE EVIDENCE RELIABLE?
Phil had personal knowledge of what was in bottles.

Does the BEST EVIDENCE RULE apply?
Yes, but original was destroyed.

(7) IS THE EVIDENCE BARRED BY THE HEARSAY RULE?
Phil's testimony is hearsay but exceptions apply:
BUSINESS RECORDS EXCEPTION
EQUIVALENCY EXCEPTION

(c) Definition of DLD

(1) IS THE EVIDENCE RELEVANT?
Is the evidence LOGICALLY relevant? To prove that DLD is a "dangerous drug."
Is the evidence LEGALLY relevant? Because DLD not listed in statute, prosecution must prove that it falls within the definition of an opium derivative.

(2) IS THE EVIDENCE RELIABLE?
Judicial notice: Court may recognize as true an indisputable fact that is capable of verification through sources of unquestionable accuracy.

(d) Win's testimony re: Dick's narcotic use

(1) IS THE EVIDENCE RELEVANT?
    Is the evidence LOGICALLY relevant? To prove Dick's motive.
    Is the evidence LEGALLY relevant? Highly prejudicial.

(2) IS THE EVIDENCE RELIABLE?
    Win has personal knowledge of Dick's drug use.

(4) IS THE EVIDENCE ADMISSIBLE TO SHOW CHARACTER?
    Specific bad acts inadmissible as character evidence.

(6) IS THE EVIDENCE BARRED BY PRIVILEGE?
    SPOUSAL WITNESS PRIVILEGE - terminates on divorce.
    MARITAL COMMUNICATION PRIVILEGE - but are Win's observations "communications"?

Obviously, you may choose to include more detail in your outline if you find it necessary. For example, in outlining the "prior testimony" exception in the first interrogatory, you may find it helpful to list each of the elements of the exception:

    Testimony under oath: Yes.
    Given in a former hearing: Trial.
    Party against whom it is offered had opportunity and similar incentive to examine testimony: Dick's trial for reckless driving. Did Dick's counsel have similar incentive in cross-examining Oats?
    Unavailable declarant: Oats now deceased.

4. Model Answer

As has already been emphasized, it is not your outline that counts but your answer. Let's review the model answer, once again applying "Strict I-R-A-C."

(A) ADMISSIBILITY OF OFFICER OATS' TESTIMONY

The issue is whether the transcript of Officer Oats' testimony is admissible.

The first issue is whether the Oats transcript is logically relevant. In order to be relevant, the evidence must tend to prove or disprove a fact in dispute. Here, the evidence is relevant because it establishes that Oats saw Dick discard two objects from his car. Because Dick is charged with stealing drugs, it is relevant to show that the items discarded by Dick might have been DLD, and that Dick destroyed incriminating evidence against him. Thus, the evidence is relevant.

The next issue is whether the evidence is legally relevant. The court should balance the probative value of the evidence against its prejudicial effect. Here the evidence is more probative than prejudicial because it establishes what Dick did with the two bottles of DLD. The prosecution should be allowed to present Oats' testimony to explain why there is no evidence, and why no DLD was found on Dick upon his arrest. While this testimony is no doubt prejudicial to Dick's case since it proves his guilt, because the prosecutor cannot prove his case by any other means it should not be excluded on this ground. Thus, the evidence should be admitted.

The second issue is whether the evidence is sufficiently reliable. In order to be reliable, the testimony must be based on a witness' personal knowledge. Here, Oats personally observed Dick's car during the chase, and saw the two objects being ejected from Dick's car. Thus, his prior testimony was based on Oats' personal knowledge. Furthermore, because the transcript was properly authenticated, it is reliable.

The final issue is whether the hearsay rule applies. Hearsay is defined as an assertion made by an out-of-court declarant offered to prove the truth of the matter stated. Here the Oats transcript is hearsay because it is a statement by a person made out of this court proceeding, i.e., Dick's trial. Therefore, Oats' testimony is hearsay.

The next issue is whether an exception to the hearsay rule applies. Here the prior testimony exception applies. Under this exception, a statement in the form of testimony given under oath in a former hearing or disposition is admissible provided the party against whom it is offered had the opportunity and similar incentive to examine testimony and the declarant is unavailable.

Here the statement was made at a prior trial for reckless driving between the identical parties, Dick and the State, and because Oats is dead, he is legally unavailable. The major issue is whether Dick, at the prior trial, had the opportunity and similar incentive to cross-examine Oats. There, Dick was on trial for reckless driving, a criminal offense, and therefore had both the opportunity, through counsel, to cross-examine Oats in a criminal proceeding involving the same incident, and similar incentive. The subject matter of the trial involved his guilt or innocence for reckless driving, which occurred at the same time that the objects were discarded.

Presumably the prosecution introduced Oats' testimony regarding the objects on the issue of Dick's motive to speed, and Oats was cross-examined regarding what he saw. Dick will argue that because the charge did not involve theft of DLD, he did not have a similar reason to cross-examine Oats on this issue and in fact may have avoided any reference to the two objects, since Dick was not on trial for littering or discarding items from his car. Assuming, however, that Oats' testimony regarding the objects was admitted at the prior trial and he was cross-examined on that issue, Dick will lose and the statement will be admitted under this exception.

In conclusion, Oats' prior testimony is admissible.

(B) ADMISSIBILITY OF PHIL'S TESTIMONY

The issue is whether Phil's testimony regarding the DLD labels is admissible.

The first issue is whether Phil's testimony is relevant. Here, Phil's testimony is relevant because it proves that the bottles that Dick stole were in fact DLD. Phil can only testify that the bottles read "DLD" and had not been opened leading to the inference that DLD was inside the bottle. Because Dick is charged with stealing a dangerous drug, this fact directly proves an element of the offense, that Dick stole a "dangerous drug." Thus, the evidence is relevant.

The next issue is whether the evidence is legally relevant. Here again while the evidence is prejudicial because it tends to prove Dick's guilt, the prosecution has no other means to prove the fact that Dick stole DLD and not some other substance. Therefore, the evidence should not be excluded on this basis.

The second issue is whether the evidence is sufficiently reliable. Here Phil had personal knowledge that the labels read "DLD" and that the bottles had not been tampered with, since he observed these facts himself. Thus, he has personal knowledge of the matter he is testifying about.

The next issue is whether the best evidence rule bars admission of Phil's testimony. Under this rule, in proving the contents of a writing, the original writing itself must be produced or shown to be unavailable by the proponent of the secondary evidence unless the writing refers to a collateral issue.

The first element is met because the label is a writing, and the prosecution is attempting to prove that the writing is true, i.e., that the bottle contains DLD as it was labeled. The second element is not met because the original labels were presumably destroyed or are unavailable. Here the prosecution can show through Officer Oats' testimony that Dick threw the bottles and labels into the river, or at least circumstantially prove that fact. Because the prosecution can prove this latter fact, Phil's testimony would not be barred by this rule.

The final issue is whether the hearsay rule applies. Hearsay is defined as an assertion made by an out of court declarant offered to prove the truth of the matter stated. Here the label is hearsay because it is an out-of-court writing offered to prove the truth of the matter stated, that the bottle contained DLD. Therefore, the label is hearsay.

The next issue is whether an exception to the hearsay rule applies. Here the business record exception may apply. Under this exception, a written statement made in the regular course of business near the time of receipt of information made by a declarant with personal knowledge, is admissible unless the circumstances indicate a lack of trustworthiness.

Here the label was probably made by the drug manufacturer in its business of producing DLD near the time it was delivered to Phil. There is nothing indicating that the label was inaccurate or not trustworthy. Because all the requirements of the exception are met, Phil's testimony re: the label would fall within this exception.

Therefore, Phil's testimony should be admitted.

(C) JUDICIAL NOTICE

The issue is whether the Court should admit the pharmacological dictionary definition of DLD.

First, the definition is relevant and should be admitted because it proves that DLD does fall within the statute's proscription against dangerous drugs and that DLD is in fact an opium derivative.

The next issue is whether the dictionary definition is reliable and accurate. The court may take judicial notice that DLD is a derivative of opium. Under this doctrine, the court may recognize as true an indisputable fact that is common knowledge or capable of verification through sources of unquestionable accuracy. Here if the prosecution can demonstrate that the standard pharmacological dictionary is a source of unquestionable accuracy and that it is reliable and relied upon by doctors and pharmacists, the court should admit the definition.

(D) ADMISSIBILITY OF WIN'S TESTIMONY

The issue is whether Win's testimony is admissible.

The first issue is whether Win's testimony is relevant. Here, the evidence is relevant because Win's testimony regarding Dick's drug use proves that Dick used narcotics in the past and therefore had a motive to steal DLD from Phil and commit theft. Thus, the evidence is relevant.

The next issue is whether the evidence is legally relevant. The court should balance the probative value of the evidence against its prejudicial effect. Here the evidence is extremely prejudicial, since Dick's drug use gives rise to the inference that Dick is a drug user and bad person and is disposed to commit crime. The prosecution also has other evidence such as Phil's testimony and that of Officer Oats to prove the elements of the offense. Because the jury will likely convict based on this evidence alone, the evidence should be excluded.

The second issue is whether the evidence is sufficiently reliable. Here Win must have personal knowledge that Dick used drugs. If Dick did in fact conceal this fact from Win, she would have no basis or personal knowledge upon which to base her testimony that Dick "frequently used narcotics." On the other hand, if Win did in fact observe Dick using drugs, or track marks or other indicia of narcotics use, the personal knowledge requirement would be met and her testimony would be deemed reliable.

The next issue is whether the evidence is character evidence. Evidence of a person's character or disposition is inadmissible proof of the conduct of that person except as otherwise provided by law. Here, the evidence is character evidence because Win's testimony establishes that Dick has a propensity to commit crime, i.e., use drugs. Thus, unless an exception applies, the evidence is inadmissible.

There are three types of character evidence: reputation, opinion and specific instances of conduct. Here, the evidence is relevant to a non-conduct use, evidence of motive as argued above. Therefore the evidence is admissible as character evidence.

The next issue is whether any privileges apply. Here the spousal witness and marital privileges may apply. Under the spousal witness privilege, which only applies in criminal cases, communications made during marriage are privileged. However, because this privilege terminates upon divorce, the privilege does not apply.

However the marital communications privilege applies to all confidential communications made while the parties were husband and wife. Thus unless both Win and Dick waived the privilege, Win's testimony would be barred by this privilege. However, under the majority view, this privilege does not apply to non-verbal conduct, and the prosecution could argue that Win's observations regarding Dick's drug use, if any, fall within this exception. However, if Win's testimony is based solely on statements made by Dick, i.e., admissions of drug use, then her testimony is barred by the privilege. Under the minority view, non-verbal conduct is privileged if it occurs in the home, and if her observations occurred in the home they would fall within the privilege.

Thus, Win's testimony should be excluded.

After reading through this examination, you may feel that there is no way you could have written this much in an hour's time. However, remember that this answer contains the fullest expression of I-R-A-C, and the same analysis could be accomplished in fewer words. For the time being, however, if you are missing issues or failing to fully apply the facts to the law, you are better off writing out your answer in this fashion, even if it takes you 90 minutes or even two hours to do so. Once you have mastered "Strict I-R-A-C," trimming the excess surplusage from your analysis is a piece of cake.

Let's revisit a slimmed down version of the first interrogatory, which hits the same issues and contains the same analysis as its longer predecessor, but does so quicker and more succinctly:

(A) ADMISSIBILITY OF OFFICER OATS' TESTIMONY

Officer Oats' prior testimony that he saw Dick discard two objects from his car is relevant because Dick is charged with stealing drugs, and it can be inferred from Oats' observations that the objects were the stolen DLD. The evidence is also more probative than prejudicial because it establishes what Dick did with the two bottles of DLD and why the prosecution has no evidence, and therefore is legally relevant.

The transcript is sufficiently reliable because it is properly authenticated and is based on Oats' personal observations.

Oats' transcript is hearsay because it is a statement by an out-of-court declarant, Oats, offered to prove the truth of the statement, i.e., that Dick discarded two objects after a car chase.

However, the prior testimony exception applies. The statement was made at a prior trial for reckless driving between identical parties, and Oats is deceased and therefore legally unavailable. The State would argue that Dick had the opportunity and similar incentive to cross-examine Oats because he was on trial for a criminal offense, and had the opportunity, through counsel, to cross-examine Oats regarding the same incident, and a similar incentive, since a criminal penalty was involved. Dick's argument that his incentive differed because the charges were not identical will be rejected and the statement will be admitted.

In conclusion, Oats' prior testimony is admissible.

As you can see, this answer delivers the same issues and analysis, but leaves out the crutches such as "Under this exception . . ." and other phrases which add nothing to the discussion. The rules of law are not excluded, but are intertwined in the analysis. Instead of setting forth the rule of "prior testimony," this answer mentions each element of the rule in the analysis.

The Exam Evaluator
PROSECUTION v. DICK

EXAM PRESENTATION (TOTAL POINTS AVAILABLE = 25)

	Poor										Excellent	
NEATNESS	0	1	2	3	4	5						_____
ORGANIZATION	0	1	2	3	4	5	6	7	8	9	10	_____
LAWYER-LIKE	0	1	2	3	4	5	6	7	8	9	10	_____

DISCUSSION OF ISSUES (TOTAL POINTS AVAILABLE =75)

A. THE TRANSCRIPT OF OATS' TESTIMONY

20 POINTS = FULL DISCUSSION _____

15 POINTS = PARTIAL/INCOMPLETE DISCUSSION _____

B. PHIL'S TESTIMONY RE: THE BOTTLES

20 POINTS = FULL DISCUSSION _____

15 POINTS = PARTIAL/INCOMPLETE DISCUSSION _____

C. THE DEFINITION OF DLD

15 POINTS = FULL DISCUSSION _____

10 POINTS = PARTIAL/INCOMPLETE DISCUSSION _____

D. WIN'S TESTIMONY RE: DICK'S DRUG USE

    20 POINTS = FULL DISCUSSION   ____

    15 POINTS = PARTIAL/INCOMPLETE DISCUSSION   ____

TOTAL SCORE . . . . ____

E. EVIDENCE PROBLEM THREE: PAUL v. HELICO

1. The First & Second Read and Fact Visualization

> Read the facts twice, visualize the fact pattern and then please turn the page.

Paul brought a personal injury action against Helico, a helicopter manufacturer. The injury occurred when Paul attempted to board a Model Z helicopter manufactured by Helico. As he approached the helicopter from the rear, he was struck by the rotating tail rotor.

Two days after the accident, Al, the pilot of the helicopter, told Sam, an investigator of the National Transportation Safety Board (Board), that immediately after Paul was struck by the tail rotor, Paul exclaimed, "It's not anyone's fault. I just wasn't paying attention; I goofed." Sam included that statement in a report he prepared for the Board.

Paul's complaint alleged Helico was negligent because the tail rotor was not marked so as to be conspicuous when operating under normal daylight ground conditions as required by a regulation of the Federal Aviation Administration (FAA), and that Helico was strictly liable because the helicopter was defectively designed.

At the trial by jury, the following occurred:

1. Paul testified that after his suit was brought an officer of Helico not only offered to settle the action, but also admitted during settlement negotiations that the company agreed with Paul that the helicopter was defectively designed.

2. After the jury had viewed the helicopter involved in the accident, Paul called Professor Jason, a recognized expert in the areas of engineering, navigation, and the operation of aircraft. He testified that based solely on his in-court examination of photographs of the Helico Model Z helicopter and photographs of other helicopters, in his expert opinion the tail rotors on Helico Model Z helicopters are not conspicuous when operating under normal daylight ground conditions as required by the FAA.

370

3. When called by the defense, Al testified, after repeated attempts to refresh his recollection, that he could not remember what Paul said. The court then admitted Sam's report concerning what Al stated Paul had said.

Assuming that all appropriate objections were timely made, did the court properly admit the testimony of Paul and Jason, as well as Sam's report? Discuss.

2. Outlining Exercise

Next, outline the answer applying the Evidence writing approach. When you have completed this exercise, please turn the page.

(1) IS THE EVIDENCE RELEVANT?
    Is the evidence LOGICALLY relevant?
    Is the evidence LEGALLY relevant?

(2) IS THE EVIDENCE RELIABLE?
    Is the evidence AUTHENTICATED or based on PERSONAL KNOWLEDGE?
    Does the BEST EVIDENCE RULE apply?

(3) IS THE EVIDENCE BARRED BY EXTRINSIC POLICIES?

(4) IS THE EVIDENCE ADMISSIBLE TO SHOW CHARACTER?

(5) IS THE EVIDENCE ADMISSIBLE TO IMPEACH?

(6) IS THE EVIDENCE BARRED BY PRIVILEGE?

(7) IS THE EVIDENCE BARRED BY THE HEARSAY RULE?

Next, compare your outline with the outline of issues which follow. If you missed any issues, go back and re-read the facts and make sure that you understand why you overlooked a particular issue.

1. Paul's testimony re: settlement offer and admission of Helico's officer

(1) IS THE EVIDENCE RELEVANT?
Is the evidence LOGICALLY relevant? To prove that helicopter was designed defectively.
Is the evidence LEGALLY relevant? Highly prejudicial.

(2) IS THE EVIDENCE RELIABLE?
Paul has personal knowledge of statement.

(3) IS THE EVIDENCE BARRED BY EXTRINSIC POLICIES?
Yes. Offers to settle and admissions made during the course of settlement negotiations are inadmissible.

(7) IS THE EVIDENCE BARRED BY THE HEARSAY RULE?
Yes. Statement is hearsay but ADMISSION hearsay exception would apply.

2. Professor Jason's testimony

(1) IS THE EVIDENCE RELEVANT?
Is the evidence LOGICALLY relevant? To prove that helicopter was defectively designed.
Is the evidence LEGALLY relevant? Probative on the issue.

(2) IS THE EVIDENCE RELIABLE?
Expert may testify if: matter is sufficiently beyond common experience and would assist the trier of fact. Two requirements must be met: (1) witness must qualify as an expert; (2) proper basis for his opinion.
- Here jury viewed helicopter and could tell if the tail rotor was conspicuous, and therefore Jason's opinion not beyond common experience.
- Jason is an expert in engineering, navigation and operation of aircraft, not necessarily helicopters.

- Was in-court examination of photographs a proper basis for his opinion that tail rotor was not conspicuous?

3. Sam's Report

(1) IS THE EVIDENCE RELEVANT?
Is the evidence LOGICALLY relevant? To prove that Paul was guilty of contributory negligence.
Is the evidence LEGALLY relevant? Prejudicial but probative.

(2) IS THE EVIDENCE RELIABLE?
Al had personal knowledge of what Paul said when the report was written.

(5) IS THE EVIDENCE ADMISSIBLE TO IMPEACH?
Yes, since Al's failure to remember is inconsistent with his prior statement recalling what Paul said.

(7) IS THE EVIDENCE BARRED BY THE HEARSAY RULE?
Sam's report is MULTIPLE hearsay and each must qualify for a hearsay exception:
> Paul's statement to Al: Admission of a Party Opponent; Excited Utterance; Present Sense Impression.
> Al's statement to Sam: Past Recollection Recorded; Business Record Exception; Federal Rules "Catch-all" Exception.

This problem illustrates a number of points you should consider in writing all exam answers. Many bar questions as you have now seen require you to analyze the same rule more than once in the course of solving a problem. This is particularly true of Evidence essay questions, as the issues of relevance, reliability and hearsay are often repeated in each interrogatory. Once you have stated the rule, you need not state it again in your analysis. The grader will incorporate the previous rule by reference and will not expect you to state the rule again every time a "relevance" or "hearsay" question is presented. By stating the rule only once, valuable time is saved.

Secondly, you will notice that in the first interrogatory, it is quite clear that the statement by Helico's officer is inadmissible because of the extrinsic policy excluding settlement and negotiation statements and offers. Should you go on and discuss other potential issues, such as hearsay, even though it is certain that the evidence in issue is not admissible?

The answer is yes and no. It is probably advisable to discuss the relevance and reliability, since these factors are essential to every Evidence analysis. However, it is probably not necessary to discuss hearsay since the extrinsic policy demands exclusion of the statement. On the other hand, you would likely score additional points with the grader if you discussed hearsay before concluding your analysis. The inclusion of this issue should really depend on whether you have the time to discuss this additional issue. If discussing "hearsay" means that you will never reach the last interrogatory, then it is best to conclude your analysis without discussing it and move on to the next interrogatory.

Finally, this problem illustrates the fact that not all interrogatories are created equally. The first interrogatory was sweet and simple, while the second interrogatory presented much meatier issues deserving of a more in-depth discussion. The issues as to Professor Jason's expertise required discussion of both sides of the issues, and a fuller consideration of the facts. The third interrogatory fell in the middle of the other two in terms of difficulty, requiring mostly legal analysis but little factual analysis.

Now let's review the model answer, plugging the facts into the exam grid.

3. Model Answer

PAUL v. HELICO

(1) ADMISSIBILITY OF STATEMENT BY HELICO'S OFFICER

The issue is whether Paul's testimony re: the statement made by Helico's officer that the helicopter was defectively designed is admissible.

The first issue is whether the statement is relevant. In order to be relevant, the evidence must tend to prove or disprove a fact in dispute. Here, the evidence is relevant because it proves that a representative of Helico admitted that the helicopter was defectively designed, and because Paul is suing on a strict products liability theory. This statement directly proves the essence of Paul's lawsuit. Thus, the evidence is relevant.

The next issue is whether the evidence is legally relevant. The court should balance the probative value of the evidence against its prejudicial effect. Here the evidence is less probative than prejudicial because it clearly proves that Helico is liable, but the reasons underlying the officer's opinion are unknown. Thus, on this basis, the evidence should be excluded.

The second issue is whether the evidence is sufficiently reliable. In order to be reliable, the witness must have personal knowledge regarding the matter he is testifying about. Here Paul overheard the statement made in his presence and therefore has personal knowledge that the statement was made and knows the identity of the maker. Thus, this element is met.

The next issue is whether any extrinsic policies bar admission of the evidence. Evidence of respecting an offer to compromise or settle a claim is inadmissible to prove the validity of the claim. The policy behind this rule is to encourage negotiations and out-of-court settlements. Here the statement made by Helico's officer was made in the course of settlement negotiations and therefore is inadmissible.

(YOU PROBABLY COULD STOP HERE, SINCE UNDER THIS POLICY THE EVIDENCE IS <u>CLEARLY</u> INADMISSIBLE, BUT:)

The final issue is whether the hearsay rule applies. Hearsay is defined as an assertion made by an out-of-court declarant offered to prove the truth of the matter stated. Here the statement is hearsay because it was made out of court during a settlement conference. Therefore, the statement is hearsay.

The next issue is whether an exception to the hearsay rule applies. Here the statement would qualify as an admission of a party. Under this exception, a statement admitting liability which is offered against the party who made it is admissible. Here Helico's officer admitted that the helicopter was defectively designed, and therefore his statement constitutes an admission. Because all the requirements of the exception are met, the statement is not inadmissible as hearsay.

However, because the extrinsic policy bars admission, Paul's testimony regarding the statement made by Helico's officer is inadmissible.

(2) ADMISSIBILITY OF PROFESSOR JASON'S TESTIMONY

The issue is whether Professor Jason's testimony is admissible.

The first issue is whether Professor Jason's testimony is relevant. (NO NEED TO REPEAT THE RULE, NO NEED TO REPEAT THE RULE, REPEAT). *In order to be relevant, the evidence must tend to prove or disprove a fact in dispute. Here, the evidence is relevant because Paul is claiming that Helico was negligent in failing to mark the tail rotor which struck him, and Professor Jason's testimony directly proves this fact. Furthermore, a comparison of the industry practice of marking tail rotors on other helicopters would be relevant as evidence of custom. Thus, the evidence is relevant.*

(BALANCE PROBATIVE VALUE VS. PREJUDICE) *The next issue is whether the evidence is legally relevant. The court should balance the probative value of the evidence against its prejudicial effect. Here the evidence is extremely probative because it demonstrates how other helicopter tail rotors are marked and also explains why Helico's Model Z helicopter fails to comply with FAA standards. The prejudice is low since Helico may cross-examine Professor Jason if his opinion is not well-founded.*

The second issue is whether the evidence is sufficiently reliable. A witness must have personal knowledge of the matters which he is testifying about. Here Professor Jason is being offered as an expert witness. (APPLY EXPERT WITNESS RULES) *An expert may testify if the matter is sufficiently beyond common experience and would assist the trier of fact. The witness must be qualified as an expert and there must be a proper basis for his or her opinion.*

(IS PROFESSOR JASON'S TESTIMONY SUFFICIENT BEYOND COMMON EXPERIENCE AND MIGHT IT ASSIST THE TRIER OF FACT?) *Here testimony regarding the comparison of various helicopters is beyond the jury's experience, since most people would presumably not know how the tail rotor is marked on other helicopters, and such a comparison would help the jury in understanding industry custom. However, the jury viewed the helicopter and may have been able to determine from common experience and their own observations whether the tail rotor was conspicuous or not, and if so, Jason's testimony was improper.*

(IS PROFESSOR JASON AN EXPERT AND IS THERE A PROPER BASIS FOR HIS OPINION???) Here Professor Jason is a recognized expert in the areas of engineering, navigation and aircraft operation, but nothing is said of his experience in helicopter mechanics or design. Because a helicopter is designed and operates differently from an aircraft, Professor Jason would probably not qualify as an expert in helicopter mechanics.

(IS THERE A PROPER BASIS FOR HIS OPINION?) If qualified as an expert, however, the next issue is whether there is a proper basis for his opinion. Because his testimony is based solely on his in-court examination of the photograph of the Helico Model Z and photographs of other helicopters, this comparison would appear to have a basis, presuming that this illustrates that the Model Z's tail rotor was in an inconspicuous location compared to other helicopters. Thus, the in-court identification and comparison of photographs should be admissible.

(3) ADMISSIBILITY OF SAM'S REPORT

The issue is whether Sam's report is admissible.

The first issue is whether the statement made by Paul, overheard by Al, is relevant. (AGAIN, NO NEED TO REPEAT THE RULE) *Here, the evidence is relevant because it tends to show that Paul was negligent, since Paul admitted that he goofed and that the accident was not anyone's fault. Thus, the evidence is relevant.*

The second issue is whether the evidence is sufficiently reliable. Here, Sam's report must be properly authenticated to insure that it is in fact Sam's report, by a witness with personal knowledge that the report was in fact written by Sam on a certain date. If these requirements are not met, the report should not be admitted.

Next, the evidence may be admissible as impeachment evidence. Here, Paul's statement, overheard by Al, would be admissible to impeach Al. Al cannot remember what Paul said and therefore can be impeached with the prior statement he made to Sam. Therefore the evidence is admissible as impeachment evidence.

The next issue is whether the court should exercise its discretion and exclude the evidence. The court should balance the probative value of the evidence against its prejudicial effect. Here the evidence is extremely probative because it demonstrates that Paul admitted being negligent. Since Paul may testify that the statements were either not made or had some other meaning, such evidence is not unduly prejudicial.

The final issue is whether the hearsay rule applies. Hearsay is defined as an assertion made by an out-of-court declarant offered to prove the truth of the matter stated. Here, Sam's report contains multiple hearsay, as it attests to a statement told to Sam by Al, who had heard the statement made by Paul. Therefore, each level of hearsay must qualify for a hearsay exception.

Paul's Statement to Al

Paul's statement to Al would qualify as an admission of a party. (AGAIN, NO NEED TO RESTATE THE RULE) An admission is a statement offered against a party made by the party which admits liability or culpability. Here, Paul admitted that he goofed and that it was not anyone's fault, in effect admitting that he was entirely at fault. Hence, it is admissible under this exception.

Paul's statement falls within the excited utterance exception. An excited utterance is a statement made immediately after a startling event while under the stress of the event. Paul's statement was made immediately after being struck by the tail rotor, and refers to the startling event. It is therefore admissible under this exception.

This statement is also admissible as a present sense impression. Paul's statement was made contemporaneously with the occurrence of the event he experienced and thus this exception also applies.

Al's Statement to Sam

Al's statement to Sam falls within past recollection recorded. Under this exception, a written statement is admissible where the declarant has no present recollection if the statement was made when the facts were fresh, the declarant had personal knowledge at the time the statement was made and the declarant testifies *that it accurately reflects his or her prior knowledge. Because Al has no present recollection of Paul's statement, Sam's report may be introduced if Al testifies that he accurately told Sam what Paul said, when his memory was still fresh and Sam testifies that he recorded the information accurately. Under the FRE, however, the report may be read into evidence, but cannot itself by received as an exhibit unless offered by the adverse party.*

Helico might also argue that Sam's report falls within the business records exception. Under this exception, Helico must show that Sam's report was made in the ordinary course of business by one who has the duty to record such matters. However, assuming that Sam had a duty to truthfully report what he heard, Al had no similar duty to report what he observed. As an employee of Helico, his statements may be biased, and the requirement of trustworthiness is not satisfied.

Thus, because the second level of hearsay is not satisfied, Sam's report should not have been admitted into evidence.

Once again, keep in mind that this answer could have been shorter and more concise. In the model answers that follow, notice how the use of a more efficient writing style will insure that you are able to write out your exam answer in the allotted time.

Now that you have successfully solved three Evidence questions, it is time for you to "go for it" alone in the next five problems which follow. As you will see, by applying your Evidence writing approach, even the most difficult Evidence problem is solvable.

The next question will expose you to an Evidence question which is presented in a different format than the typical Evidence question, as illustrated by the last three questions. However, as you will see, your Evidence problem solving approach will successfully solve this type of question as well.

The Exam Evaluator
PAUL v. HELICO

EXAM PRESENTATION (TOTAL POINTS AVAILABLE = 25)

	Poor										Excellent	
NEATNESS	0	1	2	3	4	5						____
ORGANIZATION	0	1	2	3	4	5	6	7	8	9	10	____
LAWYER-LIKE	0	1	2	3	4	5	6	7	8	9	10	____

DISCUSSION OF ISSUES (TOTAL POINTS AVAILABLE =75)

A. PAUL'S TESTIMONY RE: NEGOTIATION STATEMENT BY HELICO'S OFFICER

25 POINTS = FULL DISCUSSION ____

15 POINTS = PARTIAL/INCOMPLETE DISCUSSION ____

B. PROFESSOR JASON'S TESTIMONY

25 POINTS = FULL DISCUSSION ____

15 POINTS = PARTIAL/INCOMPLETE DISCUSSION ____

C. SAM'S REPORT

25 POINTS = FULL DISCUSSION ____

15 POINTS = PARTIAL/INCOMPLETE DISCUSSION ____

TOTAL SCORE . . . . ____

F.   EVIDENCE PROBLEM FOUR: PAUL v. DON

Paul has commenced an action in intentional tort against Don, alleging injuries suffered from stab wounds inflicted by Don, and seeking damages. At the trial by jury, Paul was called as the first witness and the following questions were asked and answers given:

[Direct examination of plaintiff Paul]

Q: What is your name?
A: Paul Jones.
Q: Where do you live?
A: 637 Broadway, here in town.

[1]   Q: And you've lived there for the past eight years?
A: That's right.
Q: What do you do for a living?
A: For the past four years I've been the assistant dean at the College of Law.
Q: Directing your attention to January 11th of this year at about 8:00 a.m., where were you?
A: I was standing in the reception office of the law school.
Q: Tell the jury what happened when you were standing there.

[2]   A: Well, the first thing I remember is that a student, Bonnie Brown, said, "Paul, here comes Don, and he seems to be pointing at you."
Q: Then what happened?
A: I noticed that defendant Don was rushing toward the office, screaming at me and waving his arms.

[3]   Q: O.K., what happened after he rushed toward you screaming and waving a knife?
A: Well, I just turned and ran down the hall.

[4]   Q: I see. So you didn't say anything to him and you didn't provoke him in any way?
A: Yes, definitely. I didn't know what had gotten into him.

[Paul proceeded to testify about the chase, the attack, and its aftermath.]

Q: Where were you interviewed by the police?
A: At the hospital.

Q: And did you tell them anything different from what you have told the jury today?

[5] A: No, I told the police exactly what I've said here. I have had a clear recollection of what happened ever since that day.

[Paul was then examined about his damages.]

Q: How much were your medical expenses?

A: I don't remember specifically.

[6] Q: Would it refresh your recollection if I told you it was $27,520?

A: No, but it's on the bill from the University Hospital.

Q: Showing you the bill, do you now remember the specific amount?

[7] A: (Reading from the bill) Yes, it says here $27,520.

[Cross-examination of plaintiff Paul]

[8] Q: You testified that you didn't know what had provoked Don, but the day before the incident you expelled six of his students for no reason, changed the lock on his office, and scraped the parking sticker off his car. Isn't that correct?

A: That's not right.

Q: You would agree that Don and you had your differences?

[9] A: No, we always got along well, and when he came after me that morning he had a lethal weapon.

At each of the nine indicated points, what objection or objections, if any, should have been made, and how should the court have ruled?

1. Outlining Strategy and Exam Analysis

"The mind is the limit. As long as the mind can envision the fact that you can do something, you can do it --- as long as you really believe 100 percent."

---- Arnold Schwarzenegger

Many bar examinees had particular difficulty with this problem. The shock of seeing something different caused many to abandon their writing approaches in favor of a hit and miss approach. However, those who successfully solved this problem did so by applying the same approach which applies to all Evidence problems.

This problem differs in format, not in substance. An Evidence problem is an Evidence problem, regardless of the context in which the principles of Evidence are tested. By giving you a trial transcript instead of fact pattern, the Examiners changed only the format in which the facts appear, not the actual testing mechanism. The only difference between this bar question and others you have already solved is that the Examiners are also testing your ability to recognize "form" problems in conducting direct and cross-examination during trial.

The key to solving aberrant problems is not to panic but instead faithfully apply your writing approach. While flexibility is always a necessary ingredient in problem solving, do not waver in believing in your ability to solve the problem with the writing approach. So without further ado, let's do exactly that.

As always, we begin by identifying those items of evidence at issue. In this problem, there are nine:

1. Question: Length of time Paul lived in town.
2. Bonnie's statement.
3. Question regarding Don's acts.
4. Question regarding Paul's acts.
5. Response: what Paul told police.
6. Question regarding Paul's recollection of medical expense.
7. Response: Paul's reading from bill.
8. Question regarding alleged acts committed by Paul against Don.

9. Response regarding "differences" with Don.

These are the "items" of evidence in issue. The next step is simply to apply your well-worn approach to each item of evidence.

1. Length of time Paul lived in town.
    RELEVANCE:
        Logical relevance: To show P's residence/background.
        Legal relevance: Leading.

2. Bonnie's statement.
    RELEVANCE: To show Don approached Paul in a hostile manner.
    RELIABLE: Based on Bonnie's personal knowledge?
    HEARSAY: Yes, but hearsay exceptions apply: EXCITED UTTERANCE, PRESENT SENSE IMPRESSION.

3. Question regarding Don's acts.
    RELEVANCE:
        Logical: To show that Don attacked Paul.
        Legal: Question is legally irrelevant because no evidence that Don ever waved a knife.

4. Question regarding Paul's acts.
    RELEVANCE:
        Logical: To show that Don's attack was unprovoked.
        Legal: Compound question.

5. Response about what Paul told police.
    RELEVANCE:
        Logical: To show that Paul told the police the same thing as he testified to in court.
    HEARSAY: Paul's statement is hearsay, and PRIOR CONSISTENT STATEMENT exception does not apply; therefore it is inadmissible.

6. Question regarding Paul's recollection of medical expenses.
    RELEVANCE:
        Logical: To show what Paul's expenses were.

Legal: Leading question.
HEARSAY: Yes, and improper foundation laid for PRESENT RECOLLECTION REFRESHED

7. Response: Paul's reading from bill.
   RELEVANCE:
      Logical: To show what Paul's expenses were.
   HEARSAY:
      Yes, and improper foundation laid for PRESENT RECOLLECTION REFRESHED.
   But BUSINESS RECORDS EXCEPTION applies.

8. Question regarding alleged acts committed by Paul against Don.
   RELEVANCE:
      Logical: To show Paul's bias against Don and provocation for Don's attack.
      Legal: Compound question.
   CHARACTER: Specific acts not admissible.
   IMPEACHMENT: To show bias.

9. Response regarding "differences" with Don.
   RELEVANCE:
      Logical: To show Paul's bias.
      Legal: Non-responsive answer as to second half of sentence.

After seeing this problem for what it truly is, you may be thinking, "Is that all there is???" There must be more to it than this! Other than the discussion in items [6] and [7] concerning past recollection refreshed, the issues involved here are relatively simple. The Examiners know that this testing format represents a radical departure from the standard-type evidence problem and have factored in a little "shock time" to compensate for the initial reaction which usually accompanies such deviant fact patterns.

The most important thing to remember in solving problems which fall a little outside the beaten path is to apply large portions of common sense. While the law is the machinery to be applied, common sense is the oil or lubricant that makes that machine run smoothly.

For example, it does not take a rocket scientist to figure out that interrogatory [4] is a compound question. It's like saying, "Is it really six o'clock and is strawberry really your favorite flavor of ice cream?" Anyone who watches "Perry Mason" or "L.A. Law" will likely immediately jump up and say, "Compound question!" In fact, this problem very much resembles an episode out of "Perry Mason," and anyone who saw more than a few episodes could probably solve nearly half of these issues, using Perry Mason's favorite objection, "Immaterial, irrelevant, compound, leading and incompetent!!!!"

Let's review the model answer!

2. Model Answer

1. The question regarding the length of time Paul lived in town was technically irrelevant, since it did not seek to establish any element or defense involving the lawsuit. In order to be relevant, the evidence must tend to prove or disprove a fact in dispute. But harmless questions involving background are generally allowed where no prejudice results to the opposing party.

However, the form of the question was leading. Leading questions are not permitted on direct examination. The proper form should have been, "How long have you lived there?" rather than to suggest what Paul's answer should have been.

2. Bonnie's statement as testified to by Paul is relevant to show that Don approached Paul in a hostile manner prior to the incident in issue. It is also reliable because it is based on Bonnie's personal observations.

Bonnie's statement is hearsay. Hearsay is an out-of-court statement offered for the truth of the matter stated. Bonnie's statement was made out of court and is being offered for its truth, to prove that Bonnie saw Don coming towards Paul.

However, the statement would qualify as an excited utterance. An excited utterance is a statement made about an exciting event made under the stress of such excitement. Here Bonnie saw Don approaching Paul in a threatening manner, pointing his finger at Paul. While this event was not particular "exciting," it would be stressful and because Bonnie made the statement immediately after she witnessed a stressful event, this exception would apply.

387

Under FRE, a statement describing or explaining an event made immediately after the declarant perceived the event is admissible. Here Bonnie's statement describes what she saw Don doing and thus is admissible under this exception.

3. The question regarding Don's acts was relevant to show that Don attacked Paul, which is the basis for the law suit. However, the question is legally objectionable because no evidence has been presented that Don ever waved a knife. Therefore, the question assumes a fact not in evidence.

4. The question regarding Paul's acts was logically relevant to show that Don's attack was unprovoked. However, the question is legally objectionable as a compound question, because it concurrently asks two separate questions. It is improper because the trier of fact cannot determine which question the witness is responding to. Here, Paul's affirmative response is meaningless because it is not clear which question he is responding affirmatively to. The objection on this ground should be sustained and the question should be reframed as two separate questions.

5. Paul's response about what he told police is logically relevant to show that Paul told the police the same thing as he testified to in court.

However, Paul's statement is hearsay, because it is an out-of-court statement offered to prove the truth of the matter stated, that Paul gave the same statement to the police. The prior consistent statement exception does not apply, because such a statement is admissible only to rebut a prior inconsistent statement or a claim of recent fabrication or untruth.

Therefore, an objection on hearsay grounds should be sustained.

6. The question regarding Paul's recollection of the amount of medical expenses is relevant to show what expenses were incurred by Paul as a result of the incident. However, the question was legally objectionable because it was leading by suggesting what the answer should be.

Furthermore, the question made reference to a figure taken from a document which is hearsay, because it was made out of court and is being offered for its truth, i.e., to prove the amount of damages.

The document would be admissible under the past recollection refreshed exception, but the proper foundation was not laid. It is not permissible to ask the witness whether a statement in a report refreshes that witness's recollection. The witness may then test his or her present recollection as it has been refreshed by the document. Because the proper foundation was not laid, this exception does not apply.

Thus, leading and hearsay objections should be sustained by the court.

7. *Paul's reading from the bill is relevant for the same reason stated above, but again the report is hearsay and the improper foundation was laid for the present recollection refreshed exception to the hearsay rule. Here Paul read directly from the bill, and did not use the bill to refresh his recollection and then testify from his recollection as it was refreshed.*

Thus, a hearsay objection should be sustained.

However, the document itself might be admissible under the business record exception. Under this exception, a written statement made in the regular course of business near the time the information was received is admissible if the declarant has personal knowledge and circumstances indicate the record is trustworthy. If the University Hospital bill meets these requirements, the bill is admissible.

8. *The question regarding alleged acts committed by Paul against Don is relevant to show Paul's bias against Don and the existence of provocation for Don's acts. However, it is a compound question for the same reasons argued in (4), above, and an objection on this ground should be sustained.*

However, the alleged acts committed by Paul are not admissible as character evidence because specific acts are not admissible to show conduct on a given occasion. However, it may be admissible for the non-character purpose of showing the existence of provocation for Don's act on a self-defense theory.

The alleged acts would also be admissible to impeach Paul's credibility. These acts tend to show that Paul harbored a bias against Don, because he expelled Don's students without justification, changed the lock on Don's office and scraped a parking sticker off of Don's car. If true, they demonstrate that Paul might be inclined to testify falsely against Don.

Thus, this line of questioning should be allowed, but any objection to the specific question posed should be sustained on the grounds that it is compound.

9. Paul's response regarding "differences" with Don is relevant because it shows that Paul may be biased against Don. However, the question is non-responsive, since Paul's statement that Don had a lethal weapon was not responsive to the question.

Thus, the latter portion of the answer, after the word "well," should be stricken.

The Exam Evaluator
PAUL v. DON

EXAM PRESENTATION (TOTAL POINTS AVAILABLE = 25)

	Poor											Excellent	
NEATNESS	0	1	2	3	4	5							_____
ORGANIZATION	0	1	2	3	4	5	6	7	8	9	10		_____
LAWYER-LIKE	0	1	2	3	4	5	6	7	8	9	10		_____

DISCUSSION OF ISSUES (TOTAL POINTS AVAILABLE =75)

1. Question: Length of time Paul lived in town

    5 POINTS = FULL DISCUSSION   _____

    0 POINTS = PARTIAL/INCOMPLETE DISCUSSION   _____

2. Bonnie's statement

    10 POINTS = FULL DISCUSSION   _____

    5 POINTS = PARTIAL/INCOMPLETE DISCUSSION   _____

3. Question regarding Don's acts

    10 POINTS = FULL DISCUSSION   _____

    5 POINTS = PARTIAL/INCOMPLETE DISCUSSION   _____

4. Question regarding Paul's acts.

5 POINTS = FULL DISCUSSION   ____

0 POINTS = PARTIAL/INCOMPLETE DISCUSSION   ____

5. Response about what Paul told police

10 POINTS = FULL DISCUSSION   ____

5 POINTS = PARTIAL/INCOMPLETE DISCUSSION   ____

6. Question regarding Paul's recollection medical expense

10 POINTS = FULL DISCUSSION   ____

5 POINTS = PARTIAL/INCOMPLETE DISCUSSION   ____

7. Response: Paul's reading from bill.

10 POINTS = FULL DISCUSSION   ____

5 POINTS = PARTIAL/INCOMPLETE DISCUSSION   ____

8. Question regarding alleged acts committed by Paul against Don.

10 POINTS = FULL DISCUSSION   ____

5 POINTS = PARTIAL/INCOMPLETE DISCUSSION   ____

9. Response regarding "differences" with Don.

5 POINTS = PARTIAL/INCOMPLETE DISCUSSION   ____

0 POINTS = PARTIAL/INCOMPLETE DISCUSSION   ____

TOTAL SCORE . . . .   ____

3. Self-Testing Exercise

After conquering the previous four problems, you are now ready to go it alone as we tackle four new Evidence problems. Once again, take each of the examinations under exam pressures, which means:

(1) Time yourself and strive to complete the exam in an hour's time;

(2) Follow the *Six Steps of Exam Taking* and the *Ten Strategies of Exam Writing Success*;

(3) Avoid any distractions, i.e, phone calls or conversations, during the exam taking period;

(4) Find an environment which best simulates the actual circumstances under which you will be taking the bar exam.

(5) Do not view the model answer until you have written out your answer.

Good luck!

G.   PROBLEM FIVE: PAM v. DAN'S PIZZA PARLOR

While Pam was crossing the street toward her husband, Will, she was struck by a pizza delivery truck being driven by Carl, an employee of Dan's Pizza Parlor (Dan's).

Pam sued Dan's, alleging the negligence of its driver, Carl, and seeking damages for her serious personal injuries. Dan's answer admitted that Carl was its employee and was acting within the scope of his employment at the time of the accident, but denied that Carl was negligent.

Despite a diligent search by Pam, Carl cannot be located. At trial, the following occurred:

1. Pam called as a witness Erma, head of personnel for Dan's, who testified that Carl was fired the day after the accident, and that Carl had a distinctively raspy voice.

2. On cross-examination by Dan's counsel, Erma testified: that she makes decisions at Dan's regarding firings; that whenever she fires someone because of carelessness, right then she makes an entry to that effect in that person's personnel file describing the specific careless act; and that she had read Carl's personnel file, a copy of which she had with her, and there was no such entry in the file.

3. Pam called as a witness Will, who testified: "Both I and some guy I don't know reached my wife's side in a matter of seconds. The other guy said, 'That driver just wasn't looking where he was going.'"

4. Will also testified: "Four days after the accident, a guy with a raspy voice called me at home and said he had hit my wife with his truck. I didn't recognize his voice, but he asked about her, said he was sorry he hadn't been looking where he was going, and told me that he had been fired."

Assume timely and appropriate objections were made to the foregoing.

Was the testimony in Items 1 through 4 properly admitted? Discuss.

1. Outlining Strategy and Exam Analysis

This problem is a straightforward typical Evidence question, involving the admissibility of four items of property:

1. ERMA'S TESTIMONY RE: CARL'S FIRING & RASPY VOICE

2. ERMA'S TESTIMONY RE: ENTRY IN CARL'S PERSONNEL FILE

3. WILL'S TESTIMONY RE: STATEMENT OF UNKNOWN MAN AT SCENE

4. WILL'S TESTIMONY RE: CALL FROM UNKNOWN PARTY

It is imperative that the specific items of evidence are identified. It is not enough to analyze these items of evidence by referring only to the source of the evidence, i.e., Will's testimony or Erma's testimony. Rather, always be as specific as possible in narrowing down what it is the party is seeking to introduce. For example, heading (2) specifically tells the grader that you are addressing your analysis to Erma's entry in Carl's personnel file. This degree of specificity is required since the issue is whether evidence proving the absence of such entries is admissible.

Let's apply our writing approach to achieve a successful outline of the answer to follow:

1. ERMA'S TESTIMONY RE: CARL'S FIRING & RASPY VOICE

A. CARL'S FIRING

(1) IS THE EVIDENCE RELEVANT?
Is the evidence LOGICALLY relevant? Carl's firing is logically relevant to prove that he was negligent.
Is the evidence LEGALLY relevant? Carl's firing is prejudicial.

(2) IS THE EVIDENCE RELIABLE?
As head of personnel, Erma has personal knowledge over which employees were fired.

(3) IS THE EVIDENCE BARRED BY EXTRINSIC POLICIES?

Yes, SUBSEQUENT REMEDIAL MEASURES are inadmissible.

(4) IS THE EVIDENCE ADMISSIBLE TO SHOW CHARACTER?

No, specific acts are not admissible to prove Carl's bad character.

B. CARL'S RASPY VOICE

(1) IS THE EVIDENCE RELEVANT?
Is the evidence LOGICALLY relevant? Carl's raspy voice, at this point, is irrelevant but may be relevant to the identification of the phone call to Will in interrogatory (4). Offer of proof may be required.

(2) IS THE EVIDENCE RELIABLE?

Erma must have personal knowledge of Carl's voice before her lay opinion is admitted.

2. ERMA'S TESTIMONY RE: ENTRY IN CARL'S PERSONNEL FILE

(1) IS THE EVIDENCE RELEVANT?
Is the evidence LOGICALLY relevant? Yes, to prove the existence of NEGATIVE EVIDENCE: that Erma would have made an entry if D were fired due to carelessness.
Is the evidence LEGALLY relevant? Yes, extremely probative, because Carl may have been fired for other reasons.

(2) IS THE EVIDENCE RELIABLE?
Erma has personal knowledge over personnel record keeping.
BEST EVIDENCE RULE? Original record must be produced.

(7) IS THE EVIDENCE BARRED BY THE HEARSAY RULE?
Erma's statement is hearsay.
BUSINESS RECORDS EXCEPTION APPLIES.

3. WILL'S TESTIMONY RE: STATEMENT OF UNKNOWN MAN AT SCENE

(1) IS THE EVIDENCE RELEVANT?
Is the evidence LOGICALLY relevant? To prove that Carl was careless. **Is the evidence LEGALLY relevant?** Probative because it shows that Carl wasn't looking where he was going.

(2) IS THE EVIDENCE RELIABLE?
Statement made by apparent observer of accident.

(7) IS THE EVIDENCE BARRED BY THE HEARSAY RULE?
Statement is hearsay but:
> EXCITED UTTERANCE
> PRESENT SENSE IMPRESSION

4. WILL'S TESTIMONY RE: CALL FROM UNKNOWN PARTY

(1) IS THE EVIDENCE RELEVANT?
Is the evidence LOGICALLY relevant? To prove Carl admitted negligence. **Is the evidence LEGALLY relevant?** Extremely prejudicial and not very probative, since Will does not know Carl's voice.

(2) IS THE EVIDENCE RELIABLE?
Is the evidence AUTHENTICATED or based on PERSONAL KNOWLEDGE? No; because Will is not familiar with Carl's voice, he cannot testify it was Carl who called, even if Erma's testimony is allowed.

(7) IS THE EVIDENCE BARRED BY THE HEARSAY RULE?
Yes, but VICARIOUS ADMISSION & DECLARATION AGAINST INTEREST EXCEPTIONS apply.

This problem illustrates the importance of outlining your answer before you begin writing. The issue of Carl's raspy voice was raised in both interrogatories (1) and (4). In interrogatory (1), you are told that Erma has testified that Carl has a raspy voice; in interrogatory (4), you are then told this fact may be relevant to establish the foundation for Will's testimony. You are not told when Erma testified in relation to Will, or whether her testimony was offered to prove that it was Carl who called Will on the telephone. Thus, the Examiners have left this as an open issue for you to discuss.

By mapping out your analysis beforehand, you can easily integrate arguments between the two interrogatories. On the other hand, if you did not plan your analysis, you very well could have concluded your discussion of the first interrogatory without considering the possible effect this issue might have on the resolution of the final interrogatory.

2. Model Answer

Compare your answer to the model answer, and chalk up yet another exam exercise on your *Master Exam Evaluator*! As you read this answer, note the efficient and straightforward writing style which effectively and quickly discusses and resolves each of the issues presented.

1. ERMA'S TESTIMONY RE: CARL'S FIRING & RASPY VOICE

A. CARL'S FIRING

Evidence is relevant if it tends to prove an issue in dispute. Carl's firing is logically relevant to prove that he was negligent, because it can be inferred that Dan's fired Carl because of the accident. However, because the reason behind Carl's firing is unknown, it is highly prejudicial and should be excluded as legally irrelevant.

However, if the court finds the probative nature outweighs any prejudice, Erma's testimony is sufficiently reliable, because as head of personnel, Erma has personal knowledge over which of Dan's employees were fired.

Regardless of the resolution of these issues, Erma's testimony will be excluded under the extrinsic policy which precludes introduction of subsequent remedial measures. If Dan fired Carl because of the accident in an attempt to prevent his negligent driving, then evidence as to Carl's firing is inadmissible.

Dan's firing of Carl is not admissible as character evidence to prove Carl's bad character. Specific bad acts are not admissible to prove conduct in conformity with such acts.

B. CARL'S RASPY VOICE

Carl's raspy voice, at this point, is irrelevant but may be relevant in identifying the person who called Will admitting liability, as set forth in interrogatory (4). However, an offer of proof may be required if Will has not yet testified about the phone call.

If Erma is allowed to testify, she must demonstrate that she has personal knowledge of what Carl's voice sounds like before her lay opinion is admitted.

2. ERMA'S TESTIMONY RE: ENTRY IN CARL'S PERSONNEL FILE

Erma's testimony is relevant to prove that Erma would have made an entry if Carl was fired due to carelessness, and that therefore Carl was not fired for carelessness. Negative evidence is admissible where the absence of an event or record shows the non-occurrence of an event. Here, Erma testified that she would have made an entry in the record had Carl been fired for negligence, and that the absence of such notation means that he was not fired for negligence. Thus, adequate foundation was laid.

The absence of a notation is also extremely probative, because Carl may have been fired for reasons other than carelessness.

As stated above, the evidence is reliable as Erma has personal knowledge over personnel record keeping and there is no evidence that Erma's record keeping was unreliable.

However, the best evidence rule would apply, and since Erma is testifying as to the contents of a document, the original must be produced or shown to be unavailable. Thus, the original record showing that Erma made no such entry must be produced.

Erma's statement would also be hearsay, because it is an out-of-court statement offered for its truth, to prove that Carl was not fired for carelessness. However, the record itself would qualify as a business record, if it was made in the

399

regular course of business, near or at the time of the firing, by Erma, who has personal knowledge of its accuracy and reliability.

3.   WILL'S TESTIMONY RE: STATEMENT OF UNKNOWN MAN AT SCENE

Will's testimony concerning the statement of the unknown man at the scene is logically relevant to prove that Carl was careless because the man exclaimed that Carl was not looking as he drove.

The evidence, while prejudicial, is also legally relevant to prove that Carl was negligent.

The statement was made with personal knowledge and is therefore reliable, since it was made by a person who observed the accident.

The statement is hearsay because it was made out of court, and is offered to prove its truth, that Carl was not looking when he struck Pam.

However, the statement would qualify as an excited utterance. It was made under the stress of an exciting event, a car accident, and was made within a matter of seconds of the accident by a declarant with personal knowledge of the event.

It would also qualify as a present sense impression, because it describes an event, the car accident, and was made immediately after the declarant perceived that accident.

Thus, the statement by the unknown man is admissible.

4. WILL'S TESTIMONY RE: CALL FROM UNKNOWN PARTY

Will's testimony regarding the call from the unknown party is relevant if it can be proved that Carl made the call, because the caller admitted negligence.

While this evidence is extremely prejudicial since the caller admitted complete liability, it is not very probative, since Will does not know Carl's voice and cannot testify it was Carl who called.

For this reason, the call cannot be authenticated unless it can be shown that Carl's raspy voice was distinctive enough to be identified as his voice. In this regard, Erma's testimony, as it is discussed in interrogatory (1) might be introduced to establish the foundation for the phone call.

The statement, however, is hearsay, because it was made outside the trial and is being offered for its truth, that Carl confessed he was responsible.

If it is proven that Carl is the caller, the statement falls within the vicarious admission exception, since Dan's has admitted that Carl was an employee working within the scope of his employment at the time the accident occurred.

The statement also is a declaration against financial interest, since a reasonable person would not have made the statement unless it were true. Thus, if Carl is unavailable for trial and it is shown that it was Carl who called, this exception would apply.

Thus, the statement should be admitted only if it can be proved that Carl made the call.

Note the writing style employed throughout the analysis. It is simple and straightforward, and communicates its reasoning in a crystal-clear fashion. This method of writing is the type of communication and expression you should strive to attain in finding or adopting a writing style that works for you.

The Exam Evaluator
PAM v. DAN'S PIZZA PARLOR

EXAM PRESENTATION (TOTAL POINTS AVAILABLE = 25)

	Poor											Excellent	
NEATNESS	0	1	2	3	4	5							_____
ORGANIZATION	0	1	2	3	4	5	6	7	8	9	10		_____
LAWYER-LIKE	0	1	2	3	4	5	6	7	8	9	10		_____

DISCUSSION OF ISSUES (TOTAL POINTS AVAILABLE =75)

1. ERMA'S TESTIMONY RE: CARL'S FIRING & RASPY VOICE

20 POINTS = FULL DISCUSSION _____

15 POINTS = PARTIAL/INCOMPLETE DISCUSSION _____

2. ERMA'S TESTIMONY RE: ENTRY IN CARL'S PERSONNEL FILE

20 POINTS = FULL DISCUSSION _____

15 POINTS = PARTIAL/INCOMPLETE DISCUSSION _____

3. WILL TESTIMONY RE: STATEMENT OF UNKNOWN MAN AT SCENE

20 POINTS = FULL DISCUSSION _____

15 POINTS = PARTIAL/INCOMPLETE DISCUSSION _____

4. WILL'S TESTIMONY RE: CALL FROM UNKNOWN PARTY

15 POINTS = FULL DISCUSSION _____

10 POINTS = PARTIAL/INCOMPLETE DISCUSSION _____

TOTAL SCORE . . . . _____

H.   PROBLEM SIX: PEOPLE v. DAVE

Dave, a waiter at Bill's Cafe (Cafe), is on trial by jury for the crime of arson, defined by statute as setting a building afire intentionally or with gross and reckless disregard for human life.

1.   The prosecution's witness was Sam, a cook at Cafe, who testified, over objection, that just prior to the time Cafe burst into flames, Bart, another waiter, ran into the kitchen shouting that Dave was spilling gasoline all over the lobby, and that someone should call the police because what Dave was doing would kill them all. Bart cannot be located by either party.

2.   Ellen, assistant manager of Grill Restaurant (Grill), was called as a witness by the prosecution and testified, over objection, that Dave had been a busboy at Grill before he became employed at Cafe, and that she had fired him after she found Dave showing other employees how to construct a gasoline bomb.

3.   After the prosecution rested, Dave took the witness stand and testified that he had been ordered to clean the lobby doors and ornamental brass work at Cafe, and that he was using gasoline as a cleaning solution in that work when a patron entered and flipped a lit cigarette butt on the lobby floor, igniting the gasoline. On cross-examination, over objection, the prosecution elicited the fact from Dave that, two years earlier, he had been expelled from college for cheating on a final exam.

4.   The defense next called Dr. Hix, a chemist, who testified, over objection, that based on his pretrial review of standard scientific treatises, as well as his own experimentation, it was his expert opinion that although use of gasoline as a cleaning fluid cannot be recommended, its use for that purpose in normal circumstances is reasonably safe, if the gasoline vapor is kept from contact with hot filaments or burning objects.

5.   In rebuttal, the prosecution, over objection, asked the judge to take judicial notice that gasoline vapor is so combustible that use of gasoline as a cleaning fluid in space occupied by other persons constituted gross and reckless disregard for human life, as a matter of law. The court stated it took such notice.

Assuming that all objections were properly made, should the evidence objected to in Items 1 through 5 have been admitted? Discuss.

1. Outlining Strategy and Exam Analysis

The first step is to determine what items of evidence are in issue:

<u>Prosecution v. Dave</u>

1. Sam's testimony re: Bart's statement

2. Ellen's testimony re: Dave's prior bomb building activity

3. Dave's expulsion for cheating

4. Dr. Hix's testimony re: use of gasoline as cleaning fluid

5. Judicial notice re: gasoline vapor

Note that interrogatories (3) and (5) require close scrutiny to determine exactly what item of evidence is being admitted or excluded. In interrogatory (3), it is not the admissibility of Dave's testimony at issue, but whether the prior act of cheating was admissible to impeach Dave's testimony. In interrogatory (5), the issue is whether the assertion that gasoline vapor is so combustible that its use as a cleaning fluid constitutes gross and reckless disregard for human life is a proper subject for judicial notice. After isolating the precise items of evidence at issue, you are now ready to outline your answer:

<u>Prosecution v. Dave</u>

1. Sam's testimony re: Bart's statement

(1) IS THE EVIDENCE RELEVANT?
   Is the evidence LOGICALLY relevant? To prove that Bart was spilling gasoline before the fire occurred.
   Is the evidence LEGALLY relevant? First part of statement is probative to prove identity of person who set the fire. However, second portion of statement is Bart's opinion and is not admissible.

(2) IS THE EVIDENCE RELIABLE?
Based on Sam's personal observations of what he heard.

(7) IS THE EVIDENCE BARRED BY THE HEARSAY RULE?
Yes, but EXCEPTIONS apply:

      EXCITED UTTERANCE
      PRESENT SENSE IMPRESSION

2. Ellen's testimony re: Dave's prior bomb building activity

(1) IS THE EVIDENCE RELEVANT?
Is the evidence LOGICALLY relevant? To show that Dave knew how to build gasoline bombs and had shared his knowledge with others.
Is the evidence LEGALLY relevant? Probative to show Dave's knowledge.

(2) IS THE EVIDENCE RELIABLE?
Ellen observed Dave showing others how to build bomb.

(4) IS THE EVIDENCE ADMISSIBLE TO SHOW CHARACTER?
D's bad character not admissible in criminal action unless offered for non-character purpose. But may be admissible to prove motive, knowledge, common plan or scheme.

3. Dave's expulsion for cheating

(1) IS THE EVIDENCE RELEVANT?
Is the evidence LOGICALLY relevant? To prove D has history of untruthfulness.
Is the evidence LEGALLY relevant? Highly prejudicial while probative value low.

(2) IS THE EVIDENCE RELIABLE?
Based on Dave's admission.

(4) IS THE EVIDENCE ADMISSIBLE TO SHOW CHARACTER?
Character evidence inadmissible to prove bad character unless placed in issue

by D.

(5) IS THE EVIDENCE ADMISSIBLE TO IMPEACH?

Specific bad acts demonstrating moral turpitude are admissible to impeach a witness.

4. Dr. Hix's testimony re: use of gasoline as cleaning fluid

(1) IS THE EVIDENCE RELEVANT?

Is the evidence LOGICALLY relevant? To corroborate Dave's claim that he was using the gasoline as a cleaning fluid.
Is the evidence LEGALLY relevant? Highly probative.

(2) IS THE EVIDENCE RELIABLE?

Expert opinion admissible if: (1) witness is qualified as an expert (Hix is a chemist); (2) there is a proper basis for expert's opinion (flammability of gasoline); (3) matter is sufficiently beyond common experience of jury and would assist jury. (Most jurors would believe that gasoline is extremely dangerous and flammable and should not be used as a cleaning fluid.)

5. Judicial notice re: gasoline vapor

(1) IS THE EVIDENCE RELEVANT?

Is the evidence LOGICALLY relevant? To prove that Dave acted with the requisite criminal intent.
Is the evidence LEGALLY relevant? Highly prejudicial.

(2) IS THE EVIDENCE RELIABLE?

Judicial notice is proper where facts are capable of verification through sources of unquestioned accuracy. Here we do not know the source of information; also the noticed fact involves an ultimate fact for the jury. Thus, court erred in taking judicial notice.

2. The Art of Economical Writing

Often, in law school, we are exposed to lengthy treatises and case decisions, comprised of long sentences and "big" legal words, leaving us with the belief that good legal writing must necessarily be complex in nature. On the bar exam, this is not the case. Simplicity is always the key to a good exam answer. Remember that the Examiners want to know whether you will be able to explain and apply the law in a simple, common sense manner. Your task is not to write a law review article, but a clear, concise and understandable answer.

Like a gardener trimming his or her trees and shrubs, you must learn to trim the hedges in your exam answer and the result will be an answer which is comprehensive but yet direct and concise.

Let's apply this new technique, which I refer to as "trimming," to an answer to the first interrogatory of this problem:

<u>Prosecution v. Dave</u>

1. Sam's testimony re: Bart's statement

The first issue is whether the evidence is relevant. The relevance of evidence must be established before the court can admit that item of evidence. In order to be relevant, the evidence must tend to prove or disprove some fact in dispute in the action before the court. Under these facts, Bart's statement is relevant to prove that Dave was observed spilling gasoline before the fire occurred, and therefore was probably responsible for causing the fire which is the subject of the arson charge. Since this is relevant to the actus reus of the crime, it is logically relevant to proving Dave's guilt of the crime.

The next issue is whether the evidence is legally relevant. In order to be legally relevant, evidence must be sufficiently probative to outweigh any prejudice, and must not confuse or mislead the jury or consume an undue amount of time. Legally irrelevant evidence should not be admitted by the court under any circumstances. In this case, Bart's statement is tantamount to eyewitness testimony that Dave was observed committing the actus reus necessary to the crime. Hence, at least the first part of the statement should be admitted to prove the identity of the person who spilled gasoline in the lobby. Since the prosecution cannot prove that these facts occurred through other means, it should be admitted. However, the second half of the sentence is highly prejudicial and should be excluded, because Bart's request to call the police and his opinion that Dave's acts would kill them all is only Bart's opinion of Dave's intent. In this regard, it is indeed possible that Bart's beliefs and opinions were incorrect and therefore not sufficiently probative of any fact in dispute. Hence, it should be excluded as legally inadmissible and speculative in nature.

The next issue is that of reliability. In order to be reliable, testimony must be based upon personal knowledge of the witness. Only reliable testimony is admissible in a court of law. In this situation, Sam overheard Bart's statement and therefore has personal knowledge that it was made.

The final issue is whether Bart's statement, overheard by Sam, is hearsay. Hearsay is an out-of-court statement offered for the truth of the matter stated. Hearsay is traditionally excluded as unreliable and untrustworthy. Applying the facts to the case at bar, Bart's statement was made out of the trial. It is also being offered for its truth, to prove that Bart saw Dave spilling gasoline all over the lobby. Because all the elements are met, the statement qualifies as hearsay.

The next issue is whether any exceptions apply.

The first exception that would apply is the excited utterance. Under this exception, a statement made by an unavailable declarant under a stressful or exciting event is admissible if the statement is immediately made under the stress of that event by one with personal knowledge of such events. In this particular problem, it would appear that Bart was excited when he made the statement, because he had just witnessed an exciting event, Dave's act of spilling gasoline. Because Bart believed that he was witnessing Dave committing an act which endangered his life and others, the act would qualify as stressful and exciting. Bart made the statement immediately after witnessing Dave's acts and thus spoke while under the stress of the exciting event. Bart also had personal knowledge of the first portion of the statement, where he reported seeing Dave spill the gasoline. However Bart did not have personal knowledge of Dave's intentions in committing the act he observed, and therefore the second portion of the statement would be inadmissible under this exception. Thus, Bart's statement as to seeing Dave spilling gasoline would be admitted and the remainder of the statement excluded. Therefore, the excited utterance exception applies.

The present sense impression exception would apply as well. Under this *exception, a statement made while the declarant was observing an event is admissible if offered to describe that event. Under the facts herein, Bart observed Dave spilling gasoline and made the statement to describe what he had just seen. Therefore, the first part of the statement is admissible under this exception. However, the second part of the statement is not admissible, because these statements do not describe what Bart saw. Rather, they only state Bart's opinion of what he saw and what he believed Dave's intentions to be.*

Great answer? Time for an academy award? No. It's too long. By the time you wrote out your answer, your <u>time</u> would be up. So the key to writing a winning bar answer is not only to comprehensively cover all issues presented, but to do so efficiently within the time parameters you are operating under. As we saw in the earlier "time allocation" strategies, you must apportion the available time between the issues and then stick to those time restraints. In this exercise, you will learn how to eliminate unnecessary words, phrases and sentences by "trimming" crutches and fillers and by integrating and intertwining each of the I-R-A-C components into your analysis. The trick is to do all of these things without shortchanging your analysis and without leaving out any important discussion of the facts or law.

Let's revisit our lengthy answer above, this time looking for and <u>eliminating</u> the following items:

FILLERS: Fillers are unnecessary words and phrases which serve no purpose except to take up space.

The first issue is whether the evidence is relevant. The relevance of evidence must be established before the court can admit that item of evidence. In order to be relevant, the evidence must tend to prove some fact in dispute in the action before the court. Under these facts, Bart's statement is relevant to prove that Dave was observed spilling gasoline before the fire occurred, and therefore was probably responsible for causing the fire which is the subject of the arson charge. Since this is relevant to the actus reus of the crime, it is logically relevant to proving Dave's guilt of the crime.

The second sentence is a "filler" because it adds nothing. It simply re-states the proposition already stated, that evidence must be relevant. Because it serves no purpose, eliminate it! Can you find the other fillers in this answer? Read through the answer again and circle all fillers.

CRUTCHES: Now, let's find and identify all crutches. Crutches are those little phrases we rely upon again and again to walk us through the answer, such as "the facts state" (even though facts can't talk), or "under the facts herein." Read through the answer and line through all crutches.

INTEGRATION: The technique of integration is perhaps the most significant because it teaches you how to integrate the I-R-A-C components together, by interweaving and intertwining each component with one another. The objective of this technique is to do so without losing any of the substance of your reasoning, by using fewer words to say the same thing. Here's an example of integration, again using the first paragraph:

Bart's statement is relevant to prove that Dave was seen spilling gasoline before the fire occurred and is responsible for the fire, which is a fact in dispute and the actus reus of the charged crime.

Through the process of integration, five sentences become one sentence, and 104 words become 36 words. Carefully study this sentence, and ask yourself whether each of the I-R-A-C elements are present.

Now, on a separate piece of paper, try re-writing the answer above without the use of fillers or crutches, and using the process of integration. When you are done, compare your answer with the model answer that follows.

3. Model Answer

Prosecution v. Dave

1. Sam's testimony re: Bart's statement

Bart's statement is relevant to prove that Dave was seen spilling gasoline before the fire occurred and is responsible for the fire, which is a fact in dispute and the actus reus of the charged crime. However, that portion of Bart's statement relating that Dave's act would "kill them all," should be excluded as prejudicial and irrelevant, because it merely states Bart's opinion of what Dave appeared to be doing. Bart's latter statement is also unreliable, because unlike the first part of the statement, it was not made with personal knowledge, and should be excluded on this basis as well.

Bart's statement is hearsay because it was made out of court and is being offered for its truth, to prove that Dave spilled gasoline. However, the excited utterance exception would apply, since Bart is unavailable for trial and made the statement with personal knowledge immediately after perceiving Dave spilling gasoline, a potentially dangerous and exciting event. It would also qualify as a sense impression, because Bart described what he had seen immediately after observing it.

That portion of Bart's statement describing what he saw should be admitted and the remainder excluded.

2. Ellen's testimony re: Dave's prior bomb building activity

Ellen's testimony is relevant to show that Dave knew how to build gasoline bombs and had shared his knowledge with others. This prior act is extremely probative because it shows that Dave was aware of gasoline's dangerous propensity and use as an explosive. It is also reliable because Ellen observed the prior event.

However, in a criminal action, a defendant's bad character is not admissible unless offered for a non-character purpose. Dave's knowledge of gasoline bombs may be admissible to prove motive, knowledge, or common plan or scheme.

Thus, this prior act should be admitted.

3. Dave's expulsion for cheating

Dave's expulsion was relevant to prove that Dave has a history of untruthfulness, but should be excluded on the ground that it was highly prejudicial since the jury would be inclined to disbelieve Dave's testimony based on an unrelated event which occurred two years earlier. The evidence was reliable, since Dave admitted the act during cross-examination.

The cheating incident is inadmissible as character evidence unless Dave places his character in evidence, since it is a specific act. However, it is admissible because *bad acts demonstrating moral turpitude can be used to impeach a witness.*

Thus, if not prejudicial, the statement should be admitted.

4. Dr. Hix's testimony re: use of gasoline as cleaning fluid

Dr. Hix's testimony is relevant to corroborate Dave's claim that he was using the gasoline as a cleaning fluid. It is not legally inadmissible and should be admitted if it qualifies as proper expert testimony.

Dr. Hix is a chemist who is basing his opinion on both his experiments and scientific treatises and would qualify as an expert who could properly render an opinion on the flammability of gasoline. The matter he seeks to testify about is outside the common knowledge of the jury, since most people would believe that gasoline is extremely dangerous and flammable and cannot be used as a cleaning fluid under any circumstances.

Thus, Dr. Hix's testimony should be admitted.

5. Judicial notice re: gasoline vapor

While the evidence is relevant to prove that Dave acted with the requisite criminal intent, it is highly prejudicial as it constitutes a directed verdict on the issue of intent, an issue which is properly reserved for the jury.

Judicial notice is proper where facts are capable of verification through sources of unquestioned accuracy. Here we do not know the source of the information, or even if the alleged fact is capable of verification. Thus, the evidence is inadmissible.

As you can see, a good answer is not necessarily a long one. I have seen some students write two to three bluebooks responding to one question! It's no wonder that many of these same students have complained that they could barely write their names after writing that much! As you master the skill of integration, remember that it will take time. The strict I-R-A-C format taught in this book is the beginning place for all good legal writing and analysis. If you do not feel comfortable in trying a new style, then stick to strict I-R-A-C, for you can easily obtain a passing exam score using this basic writing method. On the other hand, what do you have to lose by trying a new and different method of writing that will save you both time and energy!

The Exam Evaluator
PEOPLE v. DAVE

EXAM PRESENTATION (TOTAL POINTS AVAILABLE = 25)

	Poor											Excellent	
NEATNESS	0	1	2	3	4	5							____
ORGANIZATION	0	1	2	3	4	5	6	7	8	9	10		____
LAWYER-LIKE	0	1	2	3	4	5	6	7	8	9	10		____

DISCUSSION OF ISSUES (TOTAL POINTS AVAILABLE =75)

1. Sam's testimony re: Bart's statement

15 POINTS = FULL DISCUSSION ____

10 POINTS = PARTIAL/INCOMPLETE DISCUSSION ____

2. Ellen's testimony re: Dave's prior bomb building activity

20 POINTS = FULL DISCUSSION ____

15 POINTS = PARTIAL/INCOMPLETE DISCUSSION ____

3. Dave's expulsion for cheating

15 POINTS = FULL DISCUSSION ____

10 POINTS = PARTIAL/INCOMPLETE DISCUSSION ____

4. Dr. Hix's testimony re: use of gasoline as cleaning fluid

    15 POINTS = FULL DISCUSSION   ____

    10 POINTS = PARTIAL/INCOMPLETE DISCUSSION   ____

5. Judicial notice re: gasoline vapor

    10 POINTS = FULL DISCUSSION   ____

    5 POINTS = PARTIAL/INCOMPLETE DISCUSSION   ____

TOTAL SCORE . . . . ____

I.   PROBLEM SEVEN: PROSECUTION v. ROE

In a rape prosecution against Roe, the following events occurred at the trial by jury:

1. Adam, a neighbor of the victim, Tess, testified that within five minutes after the rape was alleged to have occurred, Tess ran to his house sobbing and said that she had just been raped by a man with a large brown blemish on his left arm.

2. Detective Cable testified that, on receiving Tess' report, he examined the file of known sex offenders, that Roe was listed as a previously convicted rapist, and that Roe was described as having a blemish on his left arm.

3. Tess testified that she saw Roe on the sidewalk, recognized the blemish on Roe's left arm, and told a police officer that Roe was the man who had raped her.

4. Roe's wife voluntarily testified for the prosecution that Roe returned home on the night in question in an agitated state with scratches on his arm.

5. Roe testified in his defense and denied the act, saying that he had never been near Tess' house. In rebuttal, the prosecution offered one of Roe's shoes, seized in an illegal search of Roe's house. The shoe was introduced together with expert testimony that a shoe print identical to the shoe print made by Roe's shoe had been located outside the window the rapist had used to enter Tess' house.

6. At the prosecution's request, the judge ordered Roe to bare his left arm for the jury's inspection. Roe refused. The judge allowed the prosecutor to argue in closing argument that Roe's refusal was an attempt to hide evidence, from which the jury might infer guilt.

Assume all proper motions and objections were timely made. Did the court err in admitting the testimony in Items 1 through 4, in admitting the shoe and testimony in Item 5, or in permitting the prosecutor's argument in item 6? Discuss.

1. Outlining Strategy and Exam Analysis

This problem presents a laundry list of events which occurred at Roe's trial for analysis. Your headings should, as always, reflect each item of evidence:

1. Adam's testimony re: Tess' statement

2. Detective Cable's testimony re: Roe's record

3. Tess' testimony re: Roe's identification

4. Roe's wife's testimony

5. Roe's shoes and expert testimony about shoe print

6. Roe's refusal to bare his arm

Next, apply the now well-worn Evidence writing approach to each interrogatory:

1. Adam's testimony re: Tess' statement

(1) IS THE EVIDENCE RELEVANT?
>   **Is the evidence LOGICALLY relevant?** To prove rapist's identity and that rape occurred.
>   **Is the evidence LEGALLY relevant?** Extremely probative; no prejudice.

(2) IS THE EVIDENCE RELIABLE?
>   Adam has personal knowledge of Tess' statements.

(7) IS THE EVIDENCE BARRED BY THE HEARSAY RULE?
>   Tess' statement is hearsay, but excited utterance and present sense impression exceptions apply.

2. Detective Cable's testimony re: Roe's record

(1) IS THE EVIDENCE RELEVANT?

Is the evidence LOGICALLY relevant? To prove that Roe is a convicted sex offender and rapist, and that he has blemish on left arm as described by Tess to Adam.

Is the evidence LEGALLY relevant? Evidence relating to Roe's background was extremely prejudicial; but evidence as to blemish extremely probative.

(2) IS THE EVIDENCE RELIABLE?

Detective Cable does not have personal knowledge of facts.

Does the BEST EVIDENCE RULE apply? Yes, and record itself must be produced.

(4) IS THE EVIDENCE ADMISSIBLE TO SHOW CHARACTER?

D's bad character cannot be proved unless D offers evidence of good character.

(7) IS THE EVIDENCE BARRED BY THE HEARSAY RULE?

Yes, because Detective Cable is reading from a record and no exception applies.

3. Tess' testimony re: Roe's identification

(1) IS THE EVIDENCE RELEVANT?

Is the evidence LOGICALLY relevant? To prove that Roe raped her.

Is the evidence LEGALLY relevant? Eyewitness testimony is extremely probative on issue of identity.

(2) IS THE EVIDENCE RELIABLE?

Tess has personal knowledge re: the identity of the rapist and his characteristics.

(7) IS THE EVIDENCE BARRED BY THE HEARSAY RULE?

Statement as to what Tess said to police falls within identification exception.

4. Roe's wife's testimony

(1) IS THE EVIDENCE RELEVANT?

Is the evidence LOGICALLY relevant? To prove that Roe has no alibi and had injuries consistent with rape.

Is the evidence LEGALLY relevant? Highly probative of Roe's guilt.

(2) IS THE EVIDENCE RELIABLE?
Roe's wife has personal knowledge of events she witnessed.

(6) IS THE EVIDENCE BARRED BY PRIVILEGE?
SPOUSAL WITNESS PRIVILEGE?
MARITAL COMMUNICATIONS PRIVILEGE?

5. Roe's shoes and expert testimony about shoe print

(1) IS THE EVIDENCE RELEVANT?
Is the evidence LOGICALLY relevant? To prove rapist's identity.
Is the evidence LEGALLY relevant? Yes, because shoe seized in illegal search may be used to impeach Roe's testimony.

(2) IS THE EVIDENCE RELIABLE?
Expert may testify if: matter is sufficiently beyond common experience and would assist the trier of fact. Two requirements must be met: (1) witness must qualify as an expert; (2) proper basis for his opinion.

6. Roe's refusal to bare his arm

(1) IS THE EVIDENCE RELEVANT?
Is the evidence LOGICALLY relevant? To prove rapist's identity.
Is the evidence LEGALLY relevant? Highly probative.

(6) IS THE EVIDENCE BARRED BY PRIVILEGE?
FIFTH AMENDMENT PRIVILEGE? Does not apply to non-testimonial evidence.

2. Model Answer

1. Adam's testimony re: Tess' statement

Adam's testimony about what Tess said is relevant to prove the rapist's identity, which is a fact in dispute. Her statement that she was raped and her description of the blemish on the rapist's left arm are extremely probative to prove that she was in fact raped. Adam has personal knowledge of Tess' statement and this evidence is therefore reliable.

Tess' statement is hearsay, since it is an out-of-court statement being offered for its truth, to prove that Tess was raped. However, it would qualify as an excited utterance and a present sense impression. Tess' statement was made within five minutes of a traumatic event, a rape, and was made while Tess was still under the stress of that experience, as she was sobbing. Tess' statement qualifies as a present sense impression because Tess described an event, the rape, which she recently experienced, and thus under either exception her statement to Adam is admissible.

2. Detective Cable's testimony re: Roe's record

Detective Cable's testimony is relevant to prove that Roe is a convicted sex offender and rapist, and that he has a blemish on his left arm as described by Tess to Adam. Although the evidence concerning the blemish was probative on the issue of identity, the evidence relating to Roe's background was extremely prejudicial and should have been excluded because the jury would tend to convict Roe because he was a bad man and not based on the evidence.

This evidence is not reliable, because Detective Cable does not have personal knowledge of facts. Furthermore, the best evidence rule bars the admission of Cable's testimony, which is based on the contents of a record. Thus, the original record itself must be produced or Detective Cable's testimony is barred.

The evidence as to Roe's background is not admissible as character evidence. D's bad character cannot be proved unless D first offers evidence of good character.

Detective Cable's testimony is hearsay, because Cable is reading from a statement prepared out of that court proceeding, and no hearsay exception applies.

Thus, Detective Cable's testimony is inadmissible.

3. Tess' testimony re: Roe's identification

Tess' eyewitness testimony was relevant to prove that Roe raped her, and was extremely probative on the issue of identity. Tess had personal knowledge regarding the identity of the rapist and his characteristics and thus her testimony is reliable.

While Tess' statement to the police is hearsay because it occurred out of court and is being offered for its truth, that she identified Roe, it falls within the prior identification exception, and is admissible as non-hearsay under the FRE.

4. Roe's wife's testimony

Roe's wife's testimony is relevant to prove that Roe has no alibi and had injuries consistent with the rape, and is highly probative of Roe's guilt. Roe's wife also has personal knowledge of events she witnessed.

Roe's wife's testimony, however, is subject to the spousal witness and marital communications privileges. Under the spousal witness privilege, Roe's wife cannot testify against him, even voluntarily, although under the FRE and minority view, the wife may waive this privilege even though the husband-spouse objects. The marital communications privilege forbids disclosure of any confidential communications but does not protect non-verbal conduct, such as Roe's wife's act of observing scratches on Roe's arm or the fact that Roe appeared agitated.

Thus, Roe's wife should not have been allowed to testify against him under the majority rule.

5. Roe's shoes and expert testimony about shoe print

Roe's shoes and the expert testimony concerning the shoes and shoe print are relevant to proving the rapist's identity. The shoes are legally relevant and admissible because evidence seized in an illegal search may be used to impeach Roe's testimony. Roe testified that he had never been near Tess' house, and therefore proof that his footprint was outside her window is admissible to impeach his testimony.

An expert may testify on a matter sufficiently beyond common experience which would assist the trier of fact, provided the witness qualifies as an expert and there exists a proper basis for his opinion. Expert shoe testimony would assist the jury in identifying the wearer of the shoe and thus this evidence was properly admitted, provided the expert was qualified to testify.

6. Roe's refusal to bare his arm

This evidence is relevant to prove the identity of the rapist and is highly probative of this fact, given the testimony of Adam, Detective Cable and Tess regarding the blemish observed on the left arm of the suspect.

Roe's argument that he had a Fifth Amendment privilege to refuse to bare his arm will be rejected, because this privilege does not apply to non-testimonial evidence. Thus, the court did not err in allowing the prosecutor to argue that Roe's refusal to bare his arm constituted consciousness of guilt.

3. Five Super Power Techniques of Exam Writing

"Quality is never an accident; it is always the result of high intention, sincere effort, intelligent direction and skillful execution; it represents the wise choice of many alternatives."

---- Willa A. Foster

Now that you have mastered the evidence writing approach, do not rest on your laurels, secure with your "clearly passing" answer. It is now time to fine tune your answer. Accomplish this by making even finer distinctions. I call these finer strategies of exam writing *super power techniques*. While this title may sound like something out of a comic book, it best describes the use of these tools in essay writing. A warning, however: these advanced writing techniques should be applied only when you have truly mastered the basic I-R-A-C style of writing.

a. Super power technique one: Integrate minor issues

This technique essentially combines discussions of minor issues into single sentences and paragraphs so that you can focus your answer on the major issues presented. Often, an answer will be stuffed full of minor issues, which makes it difficult for the more important issues to stand out. An interior decorator or artist understands the concept of "cluttering," and avoids putting too much into a particular design or painting. In the same way, you can use this technique to unclutter your analysis, by melding together minor issues in a single stroke. Here is an example of this technique from the previous model answer:

423

Adam's testimony about what Tess said is relevant to prove the rapist's identity, which is a fact in dispute. Her statement that she was raped and her description of the blemish on the rapist's left arm are extremely probative that she was in fact raped. Adam has personal knowledge of Tess' statement and this evidence is therefore reliable.

This one paragraph resolves each of the minor issues of logical and legal relevancy, and reliability. The major issue is that of hearsay, which follows. The spotlight, however, is placed where it belongs, on the discussion of hearsay. The issues of relevancy and reliability, by contrast, are like good, solid supporting actors in a movie: their presence is felt but does not steal the limelight from the "stars" of the movie.

If you read through the previous model answer again, you will find numerous examples of this writing technique throughout.

b. Super power technique two: The intertwining analysis

The next technique can be a little dangerous, because if it is misused, it can result in a confusing and misleading analysis. In applying strict I-R-A-C, separation of each element and issue is strongly advocated, because of the tendency many people have to confuse the different issues with one another. For that reason, issues are taken individually. However, it can sometimes be effective to discuss two issues at once, provided that you can communicate your reasoning in a clear and concise fashion. Let's take an example, again from the preceding exam answer:

Tess' statement is hearsay, since it is an out-of-court statement being offered for its truth, to prove that Tess was raped. However, it would qualify as an excited utterance and a present sense impression. Tess' statement was made within five minutes of a traumatic event, a rape, and was made while Tess was still under the stress of that experience, as she was sobbing. Tess' statement qualifies as a present sense impression because Tess described an event, the rape, which she recently experienced, and thus under either exception her statement to Adam is admissible.

Notice how two separate exceptions are blended together and how each analysis stands on its own and apart from the other. Each issue is fully discussed and the reader is not shortchanged by a conclusory or incomplete answer.

424

c. Super power technique three: Super application

The difference between plain, ordinary, regular, garden variety application and SUPER application is like night and day. Have you ever read something that caught your attention almost instantly, like a book you couldn't put down until you finished reading the last page. Now compare that experience to reading something that you dreaded reading, like a homework assignment or a required book for a course that you hated. What do you think accounted for the difference in your level of enjoyment? It was the level of your interest. While we all have different interests, our enthusiasm is peaked by our interest in a particular subject matter.

Thus, super application strives not only to communicate and express a well-reasoned analysis, but does so in a manner which will captivate the grader.

The answer is to write with PASSION. All too often, I read papers devoid of passion. Many exam papers read like the obituary section of the local newspaper. Legal writing need not be boring and confining, as demonstrated in this section of the previous model answer:

Roe's shoes and the expert testimony concerning the shoes and shoe print are relevant to proving the rapist's identity. The shoes are legally relevant and admissible because evidence seized in an illegal search may be used to impeach Roe's testimony. Roe testified that he had never been near Tess' house, and therefore proof that his footprint was outside her window is admissible to impeach his testimony.

This one paragraph manages to cover all the issues, but does so in a passionate and intelligent fashion. It is packed with common sense and tempered with a slight degree of wit in the last sentence concerning Roe's testimony. Now compare this answer to the following one:

The first question is to determine the relevancy of the evidence. The shoes might be relevant in proving who committed the rape. But those shoes were illegally seized by police, and cannot be used against a defendant at trial. However, if a defendant chooses to testify, illegal evidence is admissible to impeach his testimony. Therefore, the evidence is admissible to impeach Dan. This is because the defendant claimed he had never been to the victim's house.

There is nothing wrong with this answer, but it does not exactly bring to mind exciting and interesting pictures.

Writing with PASSION is not a skill that can be taught. It is a power that you can summon at any time, like a genie in a magic lamp. All you need to do is resolve to do your very best in solving the problem before you and to enjoy the process of problem solving. If you meet both of these requirements, PASSION will be communicated through your answer to the grader.

d. Super power technique four: Use super rules

While there is no way around stating the rule, have you ever thought of creative and imaginative ways to state the rule? While you are of course limited to stating the rule and its elements, remember that a bar grader reading one thousand answers will likely read the same rule stated in the same or similar way one thousand times. What if you stated the rule in a way that no one else did? Do you think that might impress the grader?

This is not to say that you should make up a new rule, since creativity has its limits. But try to state the rule in a concise and air-tight fashion, as in the following example from the previous model answer:

An expert may testify on a matter sufficiently beyond common experience which would assist the trier of fact, provided the witness qualifies as an expert and there exists a proper basis for his opinion. Expert shoe testimony would assist the jury in identifying the wearer of the shoe and thus this evidence was properly admitted, provided the expert was qualified to testify.

The expert witness rule is stated in a tight and concise manner. For a great book containing all the super rules you need to know for the bar exam, get your hands on a copy of *The Bar Exam Survival Kit*. Each rule has been specifically designed to state the rule as concisely and succinctly as possible.

e. Super technique number five: Be daring

The last technique isn't really a specific technique at all, but is more of a feeling. In writing practice examinations, be daring and adventurous. Take chances by trying the many techniques you will learn in this book, adding each to your exam writing repertoire. Now is the time to practice, because you cannot afford to be daring and adventurous on the real examination.

"If there's a way to do it better . . . find it."

---- Thomas A. Edison

The most important advice, however, is to enjoy what you are doing as you do it. While it is important to keep your goal in mind, that is, passing the examination with flying colors, it is also important to enjoy the trip.

So have fun in applying these five SUPER WRITING TECHNIQUES to the next challenge!

The Exam Evaluator
PROSECUTION V. ROE

EXAM PRESENTATION (TOTAL POINTS AVAILABLE = 25)

	Poor										Excellent	
NEATNESS	0	1	2	3	4	5						____
ORGANIZATION	0	1	2	3	4	5	6	7	8	9	10	____
LAWYER-LIKE	0	1	2	3	4	5	6	7	8	9	10	____

DISCUSSION OF ISSUES (TOTAL POINTS AVAILABLE =75)

1. **Adam's Testimony re: Tess' Statement**

   10 POINTS = FULL DISCUSSION ____

   5 POINTS = PARTIAL/INCOMPLETE DISCUSSION ____

2. **Detective Cable's Testimony**

   15 POINTS = FULL DISCUSSION ____

   10 POINTS = PARTIAL/INCOMPLETE DISCUSSION ____

3. Tess' Testimony re: Roe's Identification

    10 POINTS = FULL DISCUSSION   ____

      5 POINTS = PARTIAL/INCOMPLETE DISCUSSION   ____

4. Roe's Wife's Testimony

    10 POINTS = FULL DISCUSSION   ____

      5 POINTS = PARTIAL/INCOMPLETE DISCUSSION   ____

5. Roe's Shoes and Expert Testimony about Shoe Print

    15 POINTS = FULL DISCUSSION   ____

    10 POINTS = PARTIAL/INCOMPLETE DISCUSSION   ____

6. Roe's Refusal to Bare His Arm

    15 POINTS = FULL DISCUSSION   ____

    10 POINTS = PARTIAL/INCOMPLETE DISCUSSION   ____

TOTAL SCORE . . . . ____

J.   PROBLEM EIGHT: PROSECUTION v. DAN

Dan is charged with the murder of Vickie, who was strangled with a red scarf and left in a garbage container. At the trial by jury, the following occurred:

1. Roomi, Vickie's roommate, testified for the prosecution that Vickie told her as Vickie was leaving their apartment on the night of her death, "Dan and I are going to see *The Graduate* at First Theater."

2. At the prosecutor's request, the court took judicial notice that on the night of Vickie's death, First Theater was showing *The Graduate*.

3. Sally, who had dated Dan about a year prior to Vickie's death, testified for the prosecution that when she rebuffed Dan's sexual advances he dragged her into an alley by some garbage containers, produced a red scarf, and attempted to strangle her.

4. The prosecution introduced into evidence Dan's constitutionally obtained written statement that on the night of Vickie's murder he had gone alone to Second Theater to see *Cinderella*. The prosecution then called Manny, the manager of Second Theater, who produced a photocopy of the Second Theater's computer printout that listed the movies shown during the two-week period around Vickie's death. It reveals that at no time during that period did Second Theater show *Cinderella*. The photocopy of the computer printout was received into evidence.

5. Pro, a member of the same country club to which Sally belongs, testified for the defense that Sally has a reputation at the club for lying about her golf scores.

Assume that in each instance all appropriate objections were made.

Was each item of evidence 1 through 5 properly admitted?

Discuss.

1. Outlining Strategy and Exam Analysis

Five items of evidence are presented in this problem:

1. Roomi's testimony re: Vickie's statement

2. Judicial notice

3. Sally's testimony re: Dan's prior conduct

4. Photocopy of computer printout

5. Pro's testimony re: Sally's reputation

Next, let's apply the writing approach:

Prosecution v. Dan

1. Roomi's Testimony re: Vickie's statement

(1) IS THE EVIDENCE RELEVANT?
Is the evidence LOGICALLY relevant? To prove that Vickie was with Dan that evening.
Is the evidence LEGALLY relevant? Highly probative of Vickie's whereabouts that evening.

(2) IS THE EVIDENCE RELIABLE?
Roomi has personal knowledge that a statement was made.

(7) IS THE EVIDENCE BARRED BY THE HEARSAY RULE?
Yes, but admissible under MENTAL STATE EXCEPTION as present state of mind offered to show the subsequent acts of the declarant Vickie, or admissible as non-hearsay as circumstantial evidence of the declarant's state of mind.

2. Judicial Notice

(1) IS THE EVIDENCE RELEVANT?

431

Is the evidence LOGICALLY relevant? To corroborate Vickie's statement that she went to see *The Graduate* at First Theater that night.
Is the evidence LEGALLY relevant? Probative of Vickie's whereabouts that evening.

(2) IS THE EVIDENCE RELIABLE?

Is the evidence AUTHENTICATED or based on PERSONAL KNOWLEDGE? Judicial notice is proper where the fact is easily verifiable from sources of undisputed accuracy. Here the source of information is unknown.

3. Sally's Testimony re: Dan's Prior Conduct

(1) IS THE EVIDENCE RELEVANT?

Is the evidence LOGICALLY relevant? To prove Dan's propensity to commit sexual crimes and to identify Dan as the killer.
Is the evidence LEGALLY relevant? Extremely prejudicial.

(2) IS THE EVIDENCE RELIABLE?

Sally has personal knowledge of events testified to.

(4) IS THE EVIDENCE ADMISSIBLE TO SHOW CHARACTER?

Inadmissible as character evidence unless relevant to show modus operandi.

4. Photocopy of Computer Printout

(1) IS THE EVIDENCE RELEVANT?

Is the evidence LOGICALLY relevant? To disprove Dan's claim.
Is the evidence LEGALLY relevant? Highly probative.

(2) IS THE EVIDENCE RELIABLE?

Is the evidence AUTHENTICATED or based on PERSONAL KNOWLEDGE? No foundation laid to authenticate record as genuine.
Does the BEST EVIDENCE RULE apply?
Photocopy admitted and original not produced.

(7) IS THE EVIDENCE BARRED BY THE HEARSAY RULE?

Yes, but business record exception might apply if proper foundation was laid.

5. Pro's Testimony re: Sally's Reputation

(1) IS THE EVIDENCE RELEVANT?
Is the evidence LOGICALLY relevant? To Sally's credibility.
Is the evidence LEGALLY relevant? Minimally probative.

(2) IS THE EVIDENCE RELIABLE?
Pro had personal knowledge that Sally lied about golf scores.

(4) IS THE EVIDENCE ADMISSIBLE TO SHOW CHARACTER?
No, specific acts are not admissible to show a witness' poor character.

(5) IS THE EVIDENCE ADMISSIBLE TO IMPEACH?
Specific bad acts that show the witness is not worthy of belief are admissible to impeach a witness.

2. Model Answer

Now, without skipping a beat, let's write out our answer, following the outline:

Prosecution v. Dan

1. Roomi's Testimony re: Vickie's Statement

Roomi's testimony is relevant to prove that Vickie was with Dan that evening, and is highly probative of Vickie's whereabouts that evening, and the identity of the killer. Roomi's testimony is also reliable, because she has personal knowledge that a statement was made.

Vickie's statement is hearsay, because it was made out of court and is being offered for its truth, to prove that Vickie went to the movies with Dan. However, the present mental state exception applies, because Vickie's statement is being offered to show Vickie's subsequent acts, that she stated her intent to go to the movies with Dan. Alternatively, the statement is admissible as non-hearsay as circumstantial evidence of Vickie's state of mind, to prove Vickie's belief that she was going to the movies with

Dan.

2. Judicial Notice

The movie playing at First Theater on the night of Vickie's death is relevant to corroborate Vickie's statement that she went to see The Graduate *at First Theater that night with Dan, and is also probative of Vickie's whereabouts that evening.*

The court may take judicial notice of a fact when such fact is easily verifiable from sources of undisputed accuracy. Because the source of the information is unknown, and these facts are not common knowledge in the community, the court improperly took judicial notice of these facts.

3. Sally's Testimony re: Dan's Prior Conduct

Sally's testimony regarding Dan's prior conduct is relevant to prove Dan's propensity to commit sexual crimes and to identify Dan as the killer. While this evidence is extremely prejudicial, it is also extremely probative in proving Dan's guilt of the instant charges. The evidence is reliable because Sally has personal knowledge of the events testified to.

The evidence is inadmissible as character evidence, but may be admissible for a non-character purpose, to show Dan's modus operandi. Vicky was strangled with a red scarf and left in a garbage container, and Sally's testimony establishes that Dan attempted to commit the same act on another person, in a similar type of location, using the same instrumentality, a red scarf. This evidence is also relevant on the issue of motive, since in the prior incident, Dan committed a similar act when his sexual advances were rebuffed. Thus, Sally's testimony is admissible for this non-character purpose.

4. Photocopy of Computer Printout

This evidence is relevant to disprove Dan's claim that he saw the movie Cinderella *alone on the evening of the killing, and is highly probative to show that Dan is lying. However, the record has not been shown to be reliable, because it was not properly authenticated by Manny or any other witness, and Manny did not have personal knowledge of its genuineness. The best evidence rule would also bar* admission of the photocopy, because in proving the contents of a writing, the original must be produced or shown to be unavailable. A photocopy was produced and admitted and the original was not produced; therefore, the photocopy was improperly received into evidence.

The photocopy is also objectionable as hearsay, because it is an out-of-court statement being offered to prove the truth, that Cinderella was not playing at the Second Theater on the night of Vicky's death. However, the business record exception would apply, provided the foundation was laid. Because the facts do not indicate whether the prosecution established that the record was prepared in the normal course of business at or near the time of the event and that the records were reliable, the record is inadmissible hearsay.

5. Pro's Testimony re: Sally's Reputation

Pro's testimony is relevant to prove that Sally is untruthful but is marginally probative. A person who lies about a golf score is not necessarily inclined to lie about more important matters, when testifying in court. Pro's testimony is reliable, provided he had personal knowledge that Sally lied about golf scores.

Pro's testimony is not admissible as character evidence, because specific acts are not admissible to prove a witness' poor character. However, Prof's testimony is admissible to impeach, because specific bad acts may be introduced to show the witness is not worthy of belief. Again, because lying about scores on a golf game are not probative of one's propensity to lie under oath, Prof's testimony should be excluded.

The Exam Evaluator
PROSECUTION V. DAN

EXAM PRESENTATION (TOTAL POINTS AVAILABLE = 25)

	Poor	Excellent	
NEATNESS	0 1 2 3 4 5		____
ORGANIZATION	0 1 2 3 4 5 6 7 8 9 10		____
LAWYER-LIKE	0 1 2 3 4 5 6 7 8 9 10		____

DISCUSSION OF ISSUES (TOTAL POINTS AVAILABLE =75)

1. Roomie's testimony Re: Vickie's Statement

15 POINTS = FULL DISCUSSION ____

10 POINTS = PARTIAL/INCOMPLETE DISCUSSION ____

2. Judicial Notice

15 POINTS = FULL DISCUSSION ____

10 POINTS = PARTIAL/INCOMPLETE DISCUSSION ____

3. Sally's Testimony re: Dan's Prior Conduct

15 POINTS = FULL DISCUSSION ____

10 POINTS = PARTIAL/INCOMPLETE DISCUSSION ____

4. Photocopy of Computer Printout

    15 POINTS = FULL DISCUSSION   ____

    10 POINTS = PARTIAL/INCOMPLETE DISCUSSION   ____

5. Pro's Testimony re: Sally's Reputation

    15 POINTS = FULL DISCUSSION   ____

    10 POINTS = PARTIAL/INCOMPLETE DISCUSSION   ____

TOTAL SCORE . . . . ____

H.   CHAPTER SUMMARY

"No one ever attains very eminent success by simply doing what is required of him or her; it is the amount and excellence of what is over and above the required, that determines the greatness of ultimate distinction."

---- Charles Kendall Adams

In this chapter, you have not only learned how to master problem solving in the area of Evidence, but you have learned how to make important and critical distinctions that will bring you a score which far exceeds that ordinarily awarded to the "clearly passing" answer. These techniques will, with practice, distinguish your exam answer from the thousands which surround it, and will allow you to realize your greatest potential on the Essay section of the bar exam.

Having mastered the basic steps of problem solving, it is now time to enter a new realm of problem solving, where your analysis reaches a new level of sensitivity and your application takes on a sharper and a more defined dynamic than before. Even though you can write a "clearly passing" answer with ease, by applying the *Six Steps of Exam Taking*, the *Ten Strategies of Successful Exam Writing* and the other techniques in this book, you should remain critical of your work and strive to take your answer to the limits, and as you will learn, in the world of problem solving, there are no limits.

After writing each examination answer, take a red pen and ruthlessly evaluate your answer by asking each of the following questions. These questions will assist you to make the fine distinctions, and to apply the *Super Power Techniques* of exam writing discussed in this chapter.

(1) Is there anything in my answer that can be eliminated?

(2) Have I exhausted all possible arguments on each issue or are there other arguments which can be made?

(3) Does my answer sound passionate and interesting?

(4) Does my answer directly address the issues raised, and do I answer the

438

overall call of the question?

(5) Does my answer exude problem solving confidence?

The first criteria involves the elimination of unnecessary words and phrases, such as the reappearing crutches, which we have discussed in earlier chapters. Let's take an example:

The first issue is whether Adam's testimony about what Tess said is relevant to prove the rapist's identity. The rule of relevance is that evidence is relevant if it tends to prove a fact in dispute. Applying this rule here, Tess' statement that she was raped and her description of the blemish on the rapist's left arm are extremely probative to prove that she was in fact raped. The next requirement is that a witness have personal knowledge of matters testified to. Here Adam has personal knowledge of Tess' statement and this evidence is therefore reliable. In conclusion, the evidence is relevant and reliable.

Take a red pen and eliminate every word which you think is unnecessary. Eliminate crutches such as "the first issue" or "the rule of _____ is" or "applying this rule." Banish all unnecessary words, such as "here" which add nothing to the analysis. Destroy all repetitive phrases, such as the conclusion, which is stated twice. Now let's look at our "cleaned up" version of this answer:

Adam's testimony about what Tess said is relevant to prove the rapist's identity which is a fact in dispute. Tess' statement that she was raped and her description of the blemish on the rapist's left arm are extremely probative that she was in fact raped. Adam has personal knowledge of Tess' statement and this evidence is therefore reliable.

The same information is communicated in both, but the second version is quicker and more efficient.

In applying the second criteria, compare your answer to the model answer and determine whether you missed any arguments, or whether you can find additional arguments not included in the model answer.

The third and fifth criteria are sometimes best judged by another. Ask another person to read your answer and ask them if your answer is interesting and passionate. A good answer is like a story. The opening line is like the introduction to the book, inspiring the reader to read the book. The first page serves to capture the reader's attention and interest, the middle section or "guts" of the answer delivers the story, building up to a suspenseful crescendo, which is the conclusion of your answer. Ask the person who reads your answer to rate it for "interest" and "passion" on a scale from 1-10.

The fourth question raises a qualitative issue. Does the answer leave the reader with the feeling that the problem presented was solved? An answer which fails to do this is like watching a sporting event when the participants aren't really trying to win, or aren't doing their best. By contrast, an answer squarely addressing the issues presented tackles the problem head on.

These new techniques come with a warning. Do not use these techniques until you have mastered the basic foundation of exam writing. But once you have, apply these techniques and make new distinctions that will take your problem solving ability to new heights! Remember the sky is the limit!

BARBREAKER

criminal law

XI. CRIMINAL LAW

"Always bear in mind that your own resolution to succeed is more important than any other one thing."

---- Abraham Lincoln

For those of you who are following each chapter in this book in order, you are probably ready for a little break. Take a moment and reflect on all the new problem solving strategies and techniques you have learned. Each problem solving device represents a new addition to your arsenal.

In this chapter, you will have the opportunity to apply all that you have learned to the area of Crimes, which encompasses both Criminal Law and Criminal Procedure. These two subjects are inseparable and over the past ten years havealmost always been tested together. Thus, it is imperative that you always look for both procedural and substantive issues in a Crimes problem, and for this reason the Criminal Law and Criminal Procedure writing approaches are presented together.

Procedural issues generally concern the admissibility of evidence under the Fourth and Fifth Amendments of the United States Constitution. These areas are most popular because they present the largest areas of testable issues. The most common scenario involves the police who obtain a potentially illegal statement, detaining and searching the defendant, or seizing something from her person or home. Usually, but not always, the procedural issues are raised before the substantive issues. This is so because in real life, procedural issues such as the legality of a confession are generally resolved before the guilt or innocence of the defendant is decided.

The procedural issues are often contained in the interrogatories. As in all other areas, the Bar Examiners tend to clearly spell out that the question calls for a procedural analysis:

What objections should Dudley make to the admission of his statements to the police officer and to the admission of evidence concerning the blood found on his jacket?

How should the trial court rule on Dick's motion to suppress the cocaine and

heroin?

Did the court err in admitting Ace's statement against Chuck?

By contrast, substantive issues are raised by interrogatories similar to those below:

Is the evidence sufficient to support the conviction of Madge for first degree murder?

Would proof of the conduct described above be sufficient to sustain the convictions of:

a. Bullwinkle and Rockie for theft? Discuss.

b. Boris and Natasha for attempt to receive stolen property?

If the statements of Bart and Homer are truthful, is Bart guilty of the charged offenses? Discuss.

As you can see, these interrogatories clearly spell out that you should respond by applying substantive concepts and not procedural ones. Rarely is a procedural interrogatory mixed with a substantive one. Generally, the Examiners will give you separate interrogatories, testing either procedural or substantive issues.

Here is an example of a rare question that presents only a general interrogatory:

What arguments should be made on behalf of Fred and on behalf of Barney on each of their appeals, and how should the court rule on each argument? Discuss.

When confronted with a general interrogatory, you should assume that both procedural and substantive issues are raised and then apply both the procedural and substantive approaches.

Next, let's review our writing approach.

A. THE CRIMINAL PROCEDURE/CRIMINAL LAW WRITING APPROACH

The Criminal Procedure/Criminal Law writing approach begins with procedural issues, followed by substantive issues, and reflects the order in which the Examiners most often present the issues. However, because substantive issues are occasionally presented first, you should be flexible. Just remember the first "big picture" question: "Does this interrogatory call for a procedural or substantive analysis?" As you saw earlier, by reading the interrogatory you will easily be able to determine whether the Examiners want you to analyze a procedural problem or substantive problem.

Now, let's get down to the business of the writing approach and how you should apply it.

Taking Criminal Procedure first, remember that you should focus on the rights of the accused. Thus, in any procedural question the "big picture" issue is always: "Have the rights of the accused been violated?"

B. THE BIG PICTURE QUESTIONS

(1) Have the defendant's FOURTH AMENDMENT RIGHTS been violated?

(2) Have the defendant's FIFTH AMENDMENT RIGHTS been violated?

(3) Has the defendant's SIXTH AMENDMENT RIGHT TO COUNSEL been violated?

(4) Have other rights of the accused been violated?

This approach best organizes procedural issues on a Crimes bar question. The most popular of these concern the Fourth and Fifth Amendments to the United States Constitution, appearing on the fact pattern through a search of the accused or her residence, or a statement made by the accused to police. Sixth Amendment issues revolve around the right to counsel, which, with the addition of Professional Responsibility on the essay examination in 1989, has enjoyed recent popularity, especially in the area of conflict of interest. The final catch-all issue covers all miscellaneous rights, from the right to bail to the right to be free from double jeopardy. Since these specific issues are better covered as a group of miscellaneous rules rather than individually, they form the fourth testable area. In testing these miscellaneous rules, the Examiners have tended to ask "point-blank" interrogatories which directly test your knowledge of a particular specific rule:

(5) **Did the court err in admitting the evidence of the impact of Vito's death on his family? Discuss.**

(6) **Does the imposition of the death penalty on Luca, assuming he had no intent to kill, and on Bill, assuming he neither intended to kill nor participated in the killing, violate the Eighth Amendment prohibition of cruel and unusual punishment? Discuss.**

As you can see, the Examiners want to know if you know the applicable rule, which basically is all that is required to answer these interrogatories.

Now that we have reviewed the "big picture" questions, let's take a look at each "big picture" question individually:

1. **Have the defendant's FOURTH AMENDMENT RIGHTS been violated?**

Fourth Amendment seizures involve principally four potential issues:

ILLEGAL DETENTION
ILLEGAL ARREST
ILLEGAL SEARCH AND SEIZURE
ILLEGAL ELECTRONIC SURVEILLANCE

Taking an illegal detention as an example, the problem will tell you that the defendant was stopped by police and that something was taken from his person. The interrogatory will ask whether that item should be suppressed as evidence against the accused. Thus, the specific issues are:

(A) Was the defendant detained?
(B) Did the police have a reasonable basis for believing that defendant was engaged in or about to engage in criminal activity?

(C)   Was the stop temporary and no longer than necessary?

(D)   If the defendant was frisked, did the officer have a reasonable belief that the defendant was armed?

2.   Have the defendant's FIFTH AMENDMENT RIGHTS been violated?

Any statement by a defendant must pass through three Fifth Amendment tests:

VOLUNTARINESS
ESCOBEDO
MIRANDA

For example, under <u>Miranda</u>, a statement taken from a defendant subjected to custodial interrogation is inadmissible in the prosecution's case-in-chief if <u>Miranda</u> warnings were not given. Thus, the following potential issues may be presented when <u>Miranda</u> is raised:

(A)   Was the defendant in custody (e.g., subject to physical restraint)?

(B)   Was the defendant subject to interrogation (e.g., words or conduct that the officers should have known were likely to elicit an incriminating response)

(C)   If (A) and (B) are met, was the defendant given <u>Miranda</u> warnings or their equivalent?

(D)   If so, did the defendant knowingly and intelligently waive his or her <u>Miranda</u> rights?

(E)   Are any general considerations or exceptions presented by the facts (e.g., public safety exception)?

This is an example of a checklist approach of the issues relating to <u>Miranda</u> which must be addressed anytime the admissibility of a statement is at issue in a criminal case.

3.   Has the defendant's SIXTH AMENDMENT RIGHT TO COUNSEL been violated?

Right to counsel issues concern:

ILLEGAL LINE-UPS
WAS THE DEFENDANT DEPRIVED OF COUNSEL?
WAS THE DEFENDANT'S REPRESENTATION BY COUNSEL INEFFECTIVE OR IMPAIRED BY A CONFLICT OF INTEREST?

Recently, the most popularly tested Sixth Amendment area has been that of conflict of interest between lawyer and client. In my opinion, the Examiners have favored this area because of the natural cross-over with Professional Responsibility and the ethical duties of counsel.

4.   Have other rights of the accused been violated?

As previously mentioned, you should include all miscellaneous Criminal Procedure rules in this section, including:

RIGHT TO BAIL
RIGHT TO A SPEEDY TRIAL
RIGHT TO DISCOVERY
RIGHT TO AN INDICTMENT
RIGHT TO A PUBLIC TRIAL
RIGHT TO CONFRONTATION
RIGHT NOT TO BE SUBJECTED TO CRUEL & UNUSUAL PUNISHMENT
RIGHT TO SENTENCING HEARING
RIGHT TO A PAROLE REVOCATION HEARING
RIGHT TO BE ADVISED OF CONSTITUTIONAL RIGHTS UPON GUILTY
     PLEA
RIGHT TO BE FREE FROM DOUBLE JEOPARDY

These issues tend to be raised singularly; that is, the Examiners tend to test your knowledge of a specific issue within this group of issues. Often you will be given a specific interrogatory which tests your ability to apply one of these rules to the facts. This area of Criminal Procedure is best tested this way because each issue requires a self-contained discussion.

Now let's move on to substantive issues. Substantive Criminal Law most resembles the law of Torts and in many ways is a mirror image of the dichotomy found in Torts as between the cause of action and defenses. The writing approach simply applies a checklist of the crimes and applicable defenses:

CRIMES

(1) WHAT CRIME WAS COMMITTED? ARE THE ELEMENTS OF THE CRIME MET?

(2) DO ANY DEFENSES APPLY?

These are the two "big picture" questions. Let's examine each carefully:

(1) WHAT CRIME WAS COMMITTED? ARE THE ELEMENTS OF THE CRIME MET?

ATTEMPT
SOLICITATION
CONSPIRACY

ASSAULT
BATTERY
FALSE IMPRISONMENT
KIDNAPPING
MAYHEM
RAPE
ROBBERY
HOMICIDE

ARSON
BURGLARY
EMBEZZLEMENT
EXTORTION
FALSE PRETENSES
FORGERY
LARCENY
LARCENY BY CONVERSION

LARCENY BY TRICK
RECEIVING STOLEN PROPERTY
UTTERING

Simply run down your checklist of crimes and determine which crime(s) the defendant has committed and if each element of that crime is met. As you can see, the crimes fall into three categories: (1) inchoate or planning crimes; (2) crimes against people; and (3) crimes against property.

Each crime is made up of elements that must be proven beyond a reasonable doubt before a criminal conviction may stand. Conspiracy, for example, is an agreement for an unlawful purpose; the crime is divided into two parts. The act or actus reus required is the mere act of two or more persons joining together to achieve an unlawful goal. Many states additionally require an overt act in the furtherance of the conspiracy. The mental requirement or mens rea is the actual intent to combine and the specific intent to achieve the goal. If you determine that the elements of a conspiracy are present, you must then determine whether any general considerations apply, including: (1) withdrawal; (2) vicarious liability; (3) Wharton's rule; (4) impossibility; and (5) application of chain and wheel theories of conspiracy.

Once again, you see that a "checklist" approach is employed in order to achieve a comprehensive and complete analysis.

(2)   DO ANY DEFENSES APPLY?

The next question is which defenses, if any, apply:

      AGE
      CRIME PREVENTION
      DEFENSE OF OTHERS
      DEFENSE OF PROPERTY
      DURESS
      ENTRAPMENT
      INTOXICATION
      MISTAKE
      NECESSITY
      SELF-DEFENSE

Notice immediately that this approach is extremely similar to that of Torts. As you will see in the upcoming problems, the same writing style and method used in Torts will serve you well in this area of law.

For a comprehensive checklist and statement of all substantive rules, please refer to the *Law Charts* in the *Bar Exam Survival Kit*.

For example, voluntary intoxication is a defense only to specific intent crimes, such as burglary. On the other hand, involuntary intoxication is a defense to any crime based on force, mistake, fraud or medical prescription.

Now let's apply our approach to a real life Crimes problem.

C.   PROBLEM ONE: PEOPLE v. DOUG

1.   The First and Second Read

Read the fact pattern twice, once for content, and the second time to focus on important phrases and words. Please turn the page when you have completed the exercise.

Doug was watching television in his ground floor apartment. When outside noise made it difficult to hear the sound, he looked out and saw a party in progress on the lawn. Doug yelled at the party-goers to be quiet and threw an empty bottle at the. The bottle hit a woman in the leg. Her boyfriend, Tom, ran to Doug's apartment, broke down the door, and approached Doug shaking his fist. Doug, who had been drinking heavily, reached into a drawer, removed a pistol, and immediately shot and killed Tom.

Doug fled, but was stopped the next day at the boarding gate of a publicly operated inter-city bus terminal when the pistol, which was in his pocket, activated a metal detector. The privately owned bus company had instituted the boarding procedure because it had been the object of several bomb threats in the preceding weeks.

449

Security personnel of the bus company detained Doug. Because they had read of Tom's death, and the pistol Doug was carrying was of the same caliber as that believed to have been used in the homicide, they seized the pistol. They released Doug. Later that day, they took the pistol to the police and told the police why they had taken it from Doug.

Thereafter, Doug was arrested on a city street by police officers on a charge of carrying a concealed weapon. The arresting officers told him that ballistics tests had proved his pistol had fired the bullets which killed Tom. Doug then blurted out, "I shot Tom in self-defense."

Doug has been charged with murder.

1.   What objections based on the United States Constitution should Doug make to admission of his statement and the gun into evidence at trial? Discuss.

2.   Assuming that all of the above facts are proved by competent evidence at trial, may Doug properly be convicted of first degree murder, or of any lesser included offenses, and if so, what offenses? Discuss.

2. Fact Retention Exercise

Now, let's test your recollection of the facts:

(A)   Why did Doug throw the empty bottle at the party-goers?

(B)   How did Tom get into Doug's apartment?

(C)   Did Tom do anything to Doug before Doug shot him?

(D)   How many times did Doug shoot Tom?

(E)   Why was Doug detained by the security personnel?

(F)   Was Doug arrested by the security personnel?

(G)   What did Doug say to police upon his arrest?

(H)   What happened to the gun?

(I)   What did the police say to Doug upon his arrest?

If you cannot answer any one of these questions, please return to the fact pattern and read it again.

3. Visualization Exercise

Next, visualize the fact pattern.

See Doug as he watches television in his apartment. Hear the noise from outside Doug's apartment; see Doug as he strains to hear the sound of his television. See Doug as he yells, "Be quiet," to the party-goers and watch Doug as he picks up an empty bottle and throws it toward the party-goers. The bottle hits a woman on the leg. The woman's boyfriend, Tom, runs over towards Doug's apartment. Tom breaks down Doug's apartment door. Hear the apartment door breaking. Feel the force of Tom's actions. See Tom enter Doug's apartment. See Tom as he is shaking his fist. Then see Doug, his red face, with alcohol on his breath, as he reaches into a drawer, takes out a pistol and immediately shoots Tom.

Watch Doug as he flees, and see Doug as he is stopped by the security officers at the bus terminal. Visualize the officers in their private security guard uniforms. Read a memorandum of the new boarding procedure: "All passengers must be subjected to a metal detector before boarding due to several bomb threats." See the security officers read the newspaper article about Tom's death and the caliber of the gun used. See the officers as they take the gun and release Doug. Watch the security officers give the pistol to the police and explain why they took it from Doug.

See Doug as he is arrested by police for carrying a concealed weapon. Watch the arresting officers say to Doug, "Doug, the ballistics tests show that your pistol fired the bullets that killed Tom." Listen as he blurts out, "I shot Tom in self-defense."

Only by visualizing the problem will you get a full picture of the facts. With the facts firmly planted in mind, let's tackle the next step of exam taking and write out an outline. When you have completed your outline, please turn the page.

4. Outlining Strategy and Exam Analysis

The interrogatories direct you to analyze the procedural issues first, and then the substantive issues. In the first interrogatory, the Examiners tell you specifically which items of evidence to analyze: Doug's statement and the gun. Thus, this procedural issue is whether the admission of these items violates Doug's constitutional rights.

The second interrogatory is substantive in nature and limited to Doug's substantive liability for first degree murder.

Next, let's apply our writing approach to the first interrogatory:

(1)   ADMISSIBILITY OF DOUG'S STATEMENT

Have the defendant's FIFTH AMENDMENT RIGHTS been violated?

Apply the three FIFTH AMENDMENT hoops Doug's statement must pass through:

VOLUNTARINESS
ESCOBEDO
MIRANDA

Here, Doug had not been formally charged before making the statement and therefore Escobedo does not apply, leaving two issues:

454

VOLUNTARINESS
    Prosecution must prove by preponderance of evidence.
    Was Doug's statement voluntary under the totality of the circumstances?

MIRANDA
    Was Doug subject to custodial interrogation?
    If so, Miranda warnings must be given.

5. How to Use the Technique of Exam Modeling

Exam modeling is the technique of modeling your answer after a known successful writing style. Think of it this way. There are two ways of writing a successful exam answer. One is to learn what works through trial and error. The second method is to model your exam writing after a successful style, one that you know will result in a winning exam score. The trick is to know who to emulate. Let's do exactly that here and model a successful Fifth Amendment analysis in solving the issue of the admissibility of Doug's statement:

(STATE THE OVERALL GENERAL ISSUE TO BE RESOLVED) *The basic question is whether the defendant's statement is admissible.* **(STATE THE GENERAL RULE)** *In order to be admissible, the statement must satisfy voluntariness and Miranda v. Arizona requirements.*

(STATE THE FIRST ISSUE TO BE RESOLVED) *The first issue is whether the statement was voluntary.* **(STATE THE RULE)** *To be admissible, a confession must be a product of rational intellect and free will. The court will examine the totality of the circumstances.* **(APPLICATION) (REACH A CONCLUSION)** *Therefore, the defendant's statement was voluntary/involuntary.*

(STATE THE SECOND ISSUE TO BE RESOLVED) *The second issue is whether Miranda bars admission of the statement.* **(STATE THE RULE)** *Under Miranda, a police officer must advise a defendant of certain constitutional rights if the defendant is subject to custodial interrogation.* **(APPLY THE FIRST PRONG OF MIRANDA)** *A defendant is in custody if subjected to physical restraint or deprived of his or her freedom in any significant way.* **(APPLICATION) (APPLY SECOND PRONG OF MIRANDA)** *A defendant is subject to interrogation where he is subject to words or actions by police that the police should know are reasonably*

455

likely to elicit an incriminating response. **(APPLICATION)** *Therefore, the defendant was/was not entitled to Miranda warnings.*

In conclusion, for the reasons stated, the defendant's statement was admissible/inadmissible.

As you can see, this exam model follows basic I-R-A-C, and logically addresses each issue, one at a time. The rules of law are faithfully stated and a conclusion is reached. Now we will fill in the blanks.

<u>PEOPLE v. DOUG</u> (ALWAYS STATE THE TITLE OF THE CASE)

I.A. ADMISSION OF DOUG'S STATEMENT

(STATE THE OVERALL GENERAL ISSUE TO BE SOLVED) The issue is whether **Doug's** *statement is admissible. (STATE THE GENERAL RULE) In order to be admissible, the statement must satisfy voluntariness and <u>Miranda v. Arizona</u> requirements.*

(STATE THE FIRST ISSUE TO BE RESOLVED) *The first issue is whether Doug's statement was voluntary.* **(STATE THE RULE)** *To be admissible, a confession must be a product of rational intellect and freewill. The court will examine the totality of the circumstances.* **Here Doug's statement was made in response to an accusation that the pistol seized by the security officers was responsible for Tom's death. Doug "blurted" the statement in response to being confronted with the ballistics test. From this, it can be inferred that Doug's statement was made voluntarily and not as a result of physical or mental stress. Doug will argue that anyone accused of being in possession of a murder weapon would likely feel compelled to speak, but unless there are other facts suggesting that Doug coerced by the police, his claim will likely fail.** **(CONCLUSION)** *Therefore, the defendant's statement was voluntary.*

(STATE THE SECOND ISSUE TO BE RESOLVED) *The second issue is whether <u>Miranda</u> bars admission of the statement.* **(STATE THE RULE)** *Under <u>Miranda</u>, a police officer must advise a defendant of certain constitutional rights if the defendant is subject to custodial interrogation.* **(APPLY THE FIRST PRONG OF MIRANDA)** *A defendant is in custody if subjected to physical restraint or* *deprived of his or her freedom in any significant way.* **At the time the statement was made, Doug was under arrest for carrying a concealed weapon and thus was in custody.** **(APPLY SECOND PRONG OF MIRANDA)** *A defendant is subject to interrogation where he is subject to words or actions by police that the police should know are reasonably likely to elicit an incriminating response.* **Here the police informed Doug that ballistics tests proved his pistol had fired the bullets which killed Tom. While Doug's statement was not made in response to any question posed by police, the police should know that by confronting another with evidence that he possessed the alleged murder weapon, that person would likely feel compelled to make an incriminatory statement. Therefore, the defendant was entitled to** _Miranda_ **warnings.** **(CONCLUSION)** *Because the police failed to* _Mirandize_ *Doug, the statement is inadmissible.*

(BROWNIE POINT) *It should be noted that while the statement is inadmissible in the prosecution's case-in-chief,* **it may be offered to impeach Doug if he chooses to testify on his own behalf.**

In conclusion, based on the foregoing, the defendant's statement is inadmissible, and **Doug** *should object on* _Miranda_ *grounds.*

As indicated by the **bold** type, the application is "filled" in while the remainder of the answer is pre-written. This is not to say that you must necessarily develop a different model for each issue and then memorize verbatim each word to write. Such an approach would be impractical. Rather, you should strive to develop or adopt a writing style that can be used consistently to achieve a winning exam answer.

Next, let's look at the admissibility of the gun. Because the gun was seized from Doug by the security officers at the bus terminal, a Fourth Amendment question is presented.

ILLEGAL DETENTION?
Does Doug have standing? Yes, Doug owns gun.
Governmental conduct involved? No, private security guards.

Here you are told that the security officers are private and not public, and therefore while Doug may have standing because he owns the gun, because the security officers are not police, the Fourth Amendment does not apply to their conduct, and the gun is admissible.

Once again, let's use the same writing style used in the model discussion of Doug's statement, this time involving a Fourth Amendment analysis:

ADMISSIBILITY OF _____

      (STATE THE OVERALL ISSUE) *The issue is whether evidence concerning* _____ *is admissible.*

      (STATE SPECIFIC ISSUE YOU WILL SOLVE) ____*may argue that the evidence was obtained in violation of his/her Fourth Amendment rights.*

      (ISSUE OF STANDING) *First,____must demonstrate that he has standing to assert a Fourth Amendment violation.* **(RULE OF STANDING)** *In order to prove standing, a defendant must have a substantial ownership interest in the premises searched or a reasonable expectation of privacy in the area searched.* **(APPLICATION)** *Here* **(DOES THE D HAVE A REASONABLE EXPECTATION OF PRIVACY OR OWNERSHIP INTEREST IN THING SEIZED OR PLACE SEARCHED?) (CONCLUSION)** *Thus,___ has standing to assert a Fourth Amendment violation.*

      (ISSUE OF GOVERNMENTAL CONDUCT/POLICE ACTIVITY) *Second, because police action is/is not involved, "governmental conduct" is/is not involved and the Fourth Amendment applies/does not apply.* **(THIS ONE SENTENCE CONTAINS I-R-A-C!)**

      (ISSUE OF "SEARCH") *Thirdly, the police activity must constitute a "search" or "seizure."* **(DID A SEARCH OR SEIZURE OCCUR?)** *Hence the Fourth Amendment applies/does not apply.*

      (STATE GENERAL RULE RE: WARRANTLESS SEARCH RULE) *The observations and subsequent seizure of the ____ by the police were made without a warrant, and therefore are illegal unless supported by an exception to the warrant requirement.*

      (STATE SEARCH INCIDENT TO ARREST RULE) *The search incident* *to arrest exception allows a limited search of the defendant's person and areas within his immediate reach incident to the defendant's arrest.* **(APPLICATION: DID THE POLICE HAVE PROBABLE CAUSE TO ARREST D, AND IF SO, WAS THE SEARCH LIMITED TO AREAS WITHIN D'S IMMEDIATE REACH?)** *Thus, this exception applies/does not apply.*

(CONSENT) *The issue is whether D consented to the search. A defendant's consent to search or seizure must be voluntary under the totality of circumstances.* **(APPLICATION: DID D CONSENT AND DID THE POLICE EXCEED SCOPE OF SEARCH?)** *Therefore, this exception applies/does not apply.*

(AUTO EXCEPTION) *Under the auto exception, autos may be searched if there is probable cause to believe that the auto contains contraband.* **(APPLICATION: DID THE POLICE HAVE PROBABLE CAUSE TO BELIEVE THAT THE AUTO CONTAINS CONTRABAND AND WAS THE SCOPE OF THIS SEARCH CONSISTENT WITH THAT BELIEF?)** *Thus, the search would be valid/invalid under this exception.*

(PLAIN VIEW EXCEPTION) *The plain view exception allows the warrantless seizure of items in plain view if the officer is in a place she is entitled to be in. Here,* **(APPLICATION: WERE THE POLICE LEGITIMATELY ON THE PREMISES?).** *The search and seizure is valid/invalid on this basis.*

(EXIGENT CIRCUMSTANCES) *The issue is whether the search and seizure can be justified by exigent circumstances. A warrantless search is justified where police reasonably believe delay would endanger police and public or would allow a suspect to destroy evidence.* **(APPLICATION: WERE THE POLICE REASONABLE IN THEIR BELIEF THAT THERE WAS NO TIME TO OBTAIN A WARRANT?)** *Thus, this exception applies/does not apply.*

(STATE OVERALL CONCLUSION) *Thus, the evidence of the ____ is properly admitted/excluded.*

Now that you have read through the exam model, try writing out your analysis. Use the exam model in writing out your answer. In other words, just fill in the blanks! When you have completed your answer, compare it to the model answer that follows.

I.B. ADMISSION OF THE GUN

The issue is whether the gun is admissible at trial.

Doug *may first argue that the detention and subsequent search of his person, resulting in the seizure of the gun, violated the Fourth Amendment. The first issue is whether Doug has standing to raise a Fourth Amendment violation. A defendant must have a substantial ownership interest in the item seized or reasonable expectation of privacy in the area searched.* **A person entering a security metal detector at a public transportation terminal would not have a reasonable expectation that his person would be free from unreasonable search and seizure. A reasonable person knows that a metal detector is designed to detect weapons, and that by entering and activating a metal detector, one would expect to be searched. However, Doug has a substantial ownership interest in the gun which was seized from his person, and therefore has standing to raise a Fourth Amendment violation.** *The next issue is whether governmental conduct was involved.* **In this case, because Doug was detained by security personnel of a bus company, not police officers, no government conduct is involved and the Fourth Amendment is without application.** *Therefore, the gun may be properly admitted.*

Exam modeling makes the process of exam writing easier because it removes the anxiety of not knowing what to write. Following a winning writing style and format makes writing painless!

Next, write out an exam model for homicide. But first, let's review the law of homicide. Homicide stands apart from other crimes because in addition to common law murder, it requires a multi-leveled analysis encompassing the lesser included offenses of manslaughter and statutory degrees of murder.

As a general rule, you should begin by first deciding whether a homicide occurred, that is, an unlawful killing of a human being. Once the actus reus is determined, you then decide what mental state or mens rea is involved. Most bar questions raising homicide as an issue require you to consider: common law murder, first and second degree murder, voluntary and involuntary manslaughter, and defenses to criminal homicide. Thus, your "homicide" checklist should appear as follows:

HOMICIDE

Killing of a human being by another

COMMON LAW MURDER

Intent to kill
Intent to cause serious bodily injury
Wantonness
Felony Murder Rule

STATUTORY DEGREES OF MURDER

First degree
Second degree

MANSLAUGHTER

Voluntary
Involuntary

DEFENSES TO HOMICIDE

Consent
Defense of others
Self-defense
Insanity

From this, try to develop an exam model for homicide, and then use that exam model to solve the second interrogatory. After you have completed this exercise, turn the page and compare your answer to the model answer that follows. Good luck!

II. DOUG'S LIABILITY FOR HOMICIDE.

(STATE THE GENERAL ISSUE) The issue is what crimes Doug will be convicted of.

(STATE THE FIRST SUB-ISSUE: DID DOUG COMMIT HOMICIDE?) Criminal homicide is defined as a killing of a human being by another with criminal intent. **Doug caused the death of Tom by shooting him, and therefore committed homicide.** *Doug's intent or mens rea, however, will determine his liability for murder, manslaughter or justifiable homicide.*

Common Law Murder/Statutory Degrees of Murder

(STATE RULE) Common law murder is homicide committed with malice aforethought. Malice aforethought requires actual intent to kill, an intent to inflict grave bodily injury, wantonness or conduct falling within the felony-murder rule. (APPLY RULE) **Here, Doug's intent to shoot Tom may be inferred from his act of purposely picking up his gun and shooting Tom.** *(CONCLUSION) Therefore, Doug could be found guilty of common law murder.*

Modern law categorizes murder as first or second degree. (STATE FIRST DEGREE MURDER RULE) First degree murder requires premeditation and deliberation. (APPLY RULE: DID DOUG ACT WITH PREMEDITATION OR DELIBERATION?) **Here the evidence will probably not support a finding of either premeditation or deliberation, because Doug acted quickly and rashly in shooting Tom. Doug did not plan the killing of Tom, but shot Tom in response to Tom's act of breaking down Doug's door. Doug did not carefully weigh any alternatives to killing Tom, but acted "immediately."** *(CONCLUSION) Thus, Doug should not be convicted of first degree murder.*

(STATE SECOND DEGREE MURDER RULE) Second degree murder is an intentional killing with malice aforethought but without premeditation or deliberation. (APPLY THE RULE: DID DOUG ACT WITH INTENT OR MALICE?) **Here Doug's act was intentional, as he shot Tom in order to defend himself. Doug also acted with malice, as he shot Tom, intending at least to seriously injure him.** *(STATE CONCLUSION) Thus, in the absence of mitigating or excusing factors, Doug is guilty of second degree murder.*

Manslaughter

(STATE GENERAL ISSUE) Manslaughter is divided into two types: voluntary and involuntary.

Voluntary Manslaughter

(STATE VOLUNTARY MANSLAUGHTER RULE) Voluntary manslaughter is the intentional killing of another human being with some mitigating circumstance, such as alcohol intoxication, reasonable provocation or imperfect self-defense.

(APPLY RULE: ALCOHOL INTOXICATION?) Doug may argue that alcohol intoxication affected his ability to form malice aforethought and reduces the charge from murder to manslaughter. **Doug was "drinking heavily" at the time he shot Tom, and thus may have been unable to form malice aforethought or the specific intent to kill.**

(STATE AND APPLY RULE: HEAT OF PASSION KILLING?) Doug may also argue that he acted in the heat of passion. However, in order to reduce murder to manslaughter, the provocation must be such that a reasonable person would kill and inadequate cooling time exists. **While Doug did not have adequate time to calm down, a reasonable person would probably not kill a person who threatened non-deadly force. If Doug could raise a reasonable doubt in proving that a reasonable person would fear for his life and act in a similar fashion, he could be convicted only of manslaughter.**

Involuntary Manslaughter

(STATE INVOLUNTARY MANSLAUGHTER RULE) Involuntary manslaughter is the unintentional killing of another or a killing which occurs during the course of an inherently dangerous misdemeanor (the misdemeanor-manslaughter rule). *(APPLICATION)* **Doug's intention to kill Tom can be inferred from Doug's act of reaching into a drawer, removing a pistol and then shooting Tom; thus, he could not be properly convicted of involuntary manslaughter.** *(CONCLUSION)*

(STATE ISSUE) _Doug would claim self-defense._ (STATE RULE) _An innocent person is justified in using deadly force in response to deadly force._ **Arguably, Doug is an aggressor, as he threw a bottle at a woman party-goer, but he took no actions towards Tom and was therefore entitled to protect himself against Tom. Tom not only confronted Doug, but broke down Doug's door, and approached Doug shaking his fists. A reasonable person in Doug's position might believe that Tom would fight with Doug, but would not fear death. Thus, because Tom did not threaten the use of deadly force, Doug was not entitled to use deadly force.**

(BROWNIE POINT) _However, such a situation may reduce the crime of murder to manslaughter, if the trier of fact believed that_ **Doug had a good faith unreasonable belief in the need to defend himself.**

The **bold** type once again indicates the application portion of the answer while the remainder is the exam model. Now that you have developed your own exam model, try using it again and again, improving it with each use, and in this way you will write a winning exam answer.

The Exam Evaluator
PEOPLE v. DOUG

EXAM PRESENTATION (TOTAL POINTS AVAILABLE = 25)

	Poor											Excellent
NEATNESS	0	1	2	3	4	5						____
ORGANIZATION	0	1	2	3	4	5	6	7	8	9	10	____
LAWYER-LIKE	0	1	2	3	4	5	6	7	8	9	10	____

DISCUSSION OF ISSUES (TOTAL POINTS AVAILABLE =75)

ADMISSIBILITY OF DOUG'S STATEMENT

VOLUNTARINESS:

    5 POINTS = FULL DISCUSSION   ____

    0 POINTS = PARTIAL/INCOMPLETE DISCUSSION   ____

MIRANDA ISSUES:

    10 POINTS = FULL DISCUSSION   ____

    5 POINTS = PARTIAL/INCOMPLETE DISCUSSION   ____

ADMISSIBILITY OF THE GUN

    15 POINTS = FULL DISCUSSION   ____

    10 POINTS = PARTIAL/INCOMPLETE DISCUSSION   ____

DOUG'S GUILT OF MURDER

COMMON LAW MURDER

    5 POINTS = FULL DISCUSSION   ____

    0 POINTS = PARTIAL/INCOMPLETE DISCUSSION   ____

FIRST/SECOND DEGREE MURDER

    15 POINTS = FULL DISCUSSION   ____

    10 POINTS = PARTIAL/INCOMPLETE DISCUSSION   ____

VOLUNTARY/INVOLUNTARY MANSLAUGHTER

    15 POINTS = FULL DISCUSSION   ____

    10 POINTS = PARTIAL/INCOMPLETE DISCUSSION   ____

DEFENSES TO HOMICIDE

    SELF-DEFENSE = 5 POINTS   ____

    INTOXICATION = 5 POINTS   ____

TOTAL SCORE . . . . ____

D. PROBLEM TWO: PEOPLE v. DAVE

1. The First and Second Read, Visualization and Outlining Exercise

> READ AND VISUALIZE THE FACT PATTERN AND OUTLINE YOUR
> ANSWER. WHEN YOU HAVE COMPLETED THESE EXERCISES,
> PLEASE TURN THE PAGE.

Shortly before 3:00 a.m., Officer O'Connell discovered Thompson's body lying on the floor of Thompson's pawnshop. Later that day, in an unrelated incident, police stopped a vehicle for a moving violation. The driver, Dave, not knowing why he was stopped, volunteered: "I didn't do it. Jack West did." The officer asked Dave what he meant. Dave replied: "West and I entered Thompson's pawnshop about 10:00 p.m. We thought there was no one there. When we got in through an unlocked door, we discovered that Thompson had concealed himself and was waiting. Thompson shot West, but as he fell, West shot Thompson. West looked dead so I dragged him out and dumped his body in the river."

Without asking permission, the officer looked through the window of Dave's car and observed blood stains. He thereupon arrested Dave and impounded the car.

Police had found two pools of blood on the floor of the pawnshop: one where Thompson's body had been discovered, and another near the door. Laboratory tests confirmed that the blood found near the door was the same type as that in Dave's car.

An autopsy revealed that Thompson's death was attributable to loss of blood from a gunshot wound in the abdomen. The report noted that the wound would not have been fatal had Thompson been discovered and treated earlier.

The body of West has not been recovered.

Dave has been indicted for conspiracy to commit burglary, the murder of Thompson and the murder of West. The first item of evidence offered at the trial is Dave's statements to the police officer.

1. What objections should Dave make to the admission of his statements to the police officer and to the admission of evidence concerning the blood found in Dave's car? Discuss.

2. If Dave's statement and evidence of the other facts described above are the only evidence presented by the prosecution, will the evidence be sufficient to sustain a conviction of Dave for the charged offenses? Discuss.

2. Outlining Strategy and Exam Analysis

This problem presents both procedural and substantive issues, in that order. As always, your headings should reflect the order indicated in the interrogatories:

1.A.   Admissibility of Dave's statements

1.B.   Admission of the bloodstains in Dave's car

2.   Sufficiency of evidence

Once you have determined just exactly what it is the Examiners are asking, apply the "big picture" questions. As in the previous problem, the first interrogatory contains both Fifth and Fourth Amendment issues:

1.A.   Admissibility of Dave's statements

VOLUNTARINESS? Yes, Dave "volunteered" information during routine traffic stop.
MIRANDA?

- Was Dave in custody? No, he was being detained for a mere traffic violation.

- Was Dave subject to interrogation? No, officer only asked for clarification, what Dave meant and did not seek an incriminating response.

1.B.   Admission of bloodstains in Dave's car

STANDING? Dave's car
FOURTH AMENDMENT SEARCH OR SEIZURE? Car seized.
GOVERNMENT CONDUCT? Police.
EXCEPTIONS TO WARRANT REQUIREMENT:
- Auto Exception
- Plain View
- Search Incident to Lawful Arrest

2. Sufficiency of evidence

CONSPIRACY TO COMMIT BURGLARY

CONSPIRACY? Agreement and intent to combine: No direct evidence of prior agreement to burgle pawnshop but may be inferred from unlawful presence, although another reason could exist for their presence, other than intent to steal.

MURDER OF THOMPSON

COMMON LAW MURDER? Felony murder rule --- if killing of Thompson occurred during the commission of inherently dangerous felony (burglary), Dave is guilty of murder. Common law burglary required breaking, which is not present here.

FIRST DEGREE MURDER? Modern law does not require breaking.

MURDER OF WEST

NO BODY - CORPUS DELICTI RULE? Dave's conviction cannot be based on statements alone; blood found probably insufficient to prove corpus of crime, i.e., that West is dead.

In **REDLINE AND CO-FELON** jurisdictions, Dave is not liable.

Here, the homicide discussion involves some interesting issues. For one, the corpus delicti rule is tested as to the murder of West, under the guise of the sufficiency of evidence, and the Examiners provided facts from which an argument could be made either way, e.g., the pools of blood on the floor of the pawnshop and the type of blood found in Dave's car. Secondly, the traditional homicide analysis you saw in People v. Doug is not present here, since Dave did not kill anyone, and West and Thompson shot each other. Thus, Dave's liability is limited only as to the application of the felony-murder rule. Lastly, this problem was less than clear in stating just exactly what Dave and West were doing in Thompson's pawnshop. While it might be presumed circumstantially that they were committing a burglary, neither that fact nor their intent is ever stated. This issue is instead left open for discussion.

3. Model Answer

Before reading on, write out your answer to this problem. While it is easier and more relaxing to simply read this book, remember that without practice, theory is meaningless.

Once you have completed your answer, review the model answer and see how the twists and curves in this problem are analyzed and resolved.

1.A. ADMISSIBILITY OF DAVE'S STATEMENT

(STATE THE OVERALL GENERAL ISSUE TO BE RESOLVED) *The issue is whether Dave's statement, made to police, is admissible.* (STATE THE GENERAL RULE) *In order to be admissible, the statement must satisfy voluntariness and Miranda v. Arizona requirements.*

(STATE THE FIRST ISSUE TO BE RESOLVED) *The first issue is whether the statement was voluntary.* (STATE THE RULE) *To be admissible, a confession must be a product of rational intellect and freewill. The court will examine the totality of the circumstances. Here, Dave confessed to his involvement in the incident involving West and Thompson after being stopped for a moving violation unrelated to the incident. At the time that Dave made the initial statement, "I didn't do it. Jack West did," the police had no reason to believe that Dave was involved in any crime other than the traffic violation. Dave "volunteered" the statement, and was not compelled or coerced by police to speak. Dave was not under arrest and would likely have been released after the officer cited Dave for the traffic offense.* (REACH A CONCLUSION) *Therefore, Dave's statement was voluntary.*

(STATE THE SECOND ISSUE TO BE RESOLVED) *The second issue is whether Miranda bars admission of the statement.* (STATE THE RULE) *Under Miranda, a police officer must advise a defendant of certain constitutional rights if the defendant is subject to custodial interrogation.*

(APPLY THE FIRST PRONG OF MIRANDA) *A defendant is in custody if subjected to physical restraint or deprived of his or her freedom in any significant way. Here Dave was subject to a roadside detention, but was not in police custody nor subject to arrest. Recent decisions have held that a roadside detention does not*

472

require <u>Miranda</u> warnings because the driver is not in custody.

(APPLY SECOND PRONG OF MIRANDA) A defendant is subject to interrogation where he is subject to words or actions by police that the police should know are reasonably likely to elicit an incriminating response. Dave's first statements, "I didn't do it. Jack West did," were made voluntarily and spontaneously to an officer who had no reason to believe that Dave had been involved in criminal activity. The defense might argue, however, that once Dave made this statement, the officer's subsequent question, asking Dave what he meant, called for an incriminating response. However, the prosecution will probably succeed in arguing that any question by the officer was simply made to clarify Dave's prior statement, and not to elicit an incriminating response. Even after hearing Dave's initial statement, the officer had no reason to know that Dave was involved in a crime, and thus could not have known that his question would elicit an incriminating response. Therefore, because neither prong of <u>Miranda</u> is met, Dave was not entitled to <u>Miranda</u> warnings.

In conclusion, for the reasons stated, Dave's statement is admissible in its entirety.

1.B. ADMISSION OF THE BLOODSTAINS

(STATE THE OVERALL ISSUE) The issue is whether evidence concerning the bloodstains found in Dave's car is admissible.

(STATE SPECIFIC ISSUE YOU WILL RESOLVE) Dave may argue that the bloodstain evidence was obtained in violation of his Fourth Amendment rights.

(ISSUE OF STANDING) First, Dave must demonstrate that he has standing to assert a Fourth Amendment violation. (RULE OF STANDING) In order to prove standing, a defendant must have a substantial ownership interest in the premises searched or a reasonable expectation of privacy in the area searched. (APPLICATION) Here, Dave owned the vehicle in question, and therefore had a reasonable expectation that the contents of his vehicle would remain private, as well as an ownership interest in the vehicle. (CONCLUSION) Thus, Dave has standing to assert a Fourth Amendment violation.

(ISSUE OF GOVERNMENTAL CONDUCT/POLICE ACTIVITY) *Second, because the observations of the bloodstains were made by police, "governmental conduct" is involved and the Fourth Amendment applies.* (THIS ONE SENTENCE CONTAINS I-R-A-C!)

(ISSUE OF "SEARCH") *Thirdly, the police activity must constitute a "search" or "seizure." Because the bloodstains were in plain view, arguably no search occurred. However, the auto was seized, and hence the Fourth Amendment applies.*

(STATE GENERAL RULE RE: WARRANTLESS SEARCH RULE) *The observations and subsequent seizure of the vehicle by the police were made without a warrant, and therefore are illegal unless supported by an exception to the warrant requirement.*

(STATE SEARCH INCIDENT TO ARREST RULE) *The search incident to arrest exception allows a limited search of the defendant's person and areas within his immediate reach incident to the defendant's arrest. At the time the observations were made, the police had probable cause to believe that Dave was involved in a possible murder, based on Dave's statement. Therefore, Dave's arrest was supported by probable cause, and the police could therefore search areas within Dave's immediate reach. Because the interior of the car was presumably within Dave's reach upon his arrest, the search and seizure of the car were valid under this exception.*

(AUTO EXCEPTION) *Under the auto exception, autos may be searched if there is probable cause to believe that the auto contains contraband. Here because Dave had confessed to using the car to dispose of West's body, and had admitted his involvement in the shooting of Thompson, the officers had probable cause to believe that the car might contain indicia of crime. Thus, the search would be valid under this exception.*

(BROWNIE POINT) *Furthermore, because an impounded automobile is subject to an inventory search for officer safety and security reasons, the discovery of the bloodstains would be subject to the inevitable discovery doctrine.*

(PLAIN VIEW EXCEPTION) *The plain view exception allows the warrantless seizure of items in plain view if the officer is in a place she is entitled to be in. Here, the officer was outside of Dave's vehicle, which he had properly stopped pursuant to a traffic violation. Because the officer was entitled to be outside Dave's vehicle at the time he or she made the observations, and the bloodstains were in plain view, the search and seizure of the vehicle may be validated on this basis.*

(STATE OVERALL CONCLUSION) *Thus, the evidence of the bloodstains should be admitted.*

2. Sufficiency of evidence

Conspiracy to commit burglary

(ISSUE, RULE AND CONCLUSION COMBINED!) *The evidence is insufficient to convict Dave of conspiracy, which requires an agreement to commit the target offense of burglary, coupled with the specific intent to combine.* (APPLICATION) *There is no direct evidence of a prior agreement between Dave and West to burgle the pawnshop, although felonious intent could be inferred from their unlawful presence there at night. However, they entered through an unlocked door, and there could be another reason for their presence, other than their intent to steal. Because we do not know their precise purpose in the pawnshop, and whether West and Dave either tacitly or expressly agreed to commit a burglary, the evidence is insufficient on this charge.*

Murder of Thompson

(ISSUE & RULE) *Homicide is the unlawful killing of another human being.* (APPLICATION & CONCLUSION) *Because Dave did not commit the killing act, his liability is limited to application of the felony-murder rule. If the killing of Thompson occurred during the commission of an inherently dangerous felony such as burglary, Dave is guilty of murder. For the reasons discussed above, it is not clear from the facts whether a burglary was intended. Also, common law required a breaking and because Dave and West entered through an unlocked door, the elements of the underlying felony are not met and Dave could not be convicted of murder.*

Under modern law, however, a breaking is not required and Dave would remain guilty of first degree murder if it were proven that Dave entered the pawnshop with felonious intent.

Murder of West

(ISSUE & RULE) *Under the corpus delicti rule, Dave's statements admitting his involvement in the shooting of West are inadmissible unless the corpus of the crime is proved by independent evidence. Thus, the issue is whether there is sufficient independent evidence to prove that West was killed.* (APPLICATION) *Because his body was never recovered, the only evidence is the blood found in the pawnshop and in Dave's car. Although laboratory tests confirmed that the blood was of the same type, this evidence is insufficient to prove that West is dead.* (CONCLUSION) *Thus, in the absence of more evidence, Dave cannot be convicted of the murder of West.*

(STATE MINORITY VIEW) *Additionally, in those jurisdictions which require that the victim be an innocent party, or that the co-felon commit the killing, Dave would not be liable for the killing of West, a co-felon.*

4. The Mystery of Jack West's Disappearing Body

This problem illustrates the need to be comprehensive and creative in answering bar questions. Anyone acquainted with a few good mystery novels would know the "corpus delicti" rule, yet many students who took this problem either missed that issue completely or could not recall the rule. Even if you did not know the rule you should have discerned that the Examiners wanted you to say something about the fact that Jack West's body was never found. The somewhat tricky issue is whether the identical bloodstains found both in Dave's car and in the pawnshop are sufficient to support Dave's murder conviction. The facts only prove that someone or something bled, both in Dave's car and in the pawnshop. It does not prove that Jack West is dead.

On the other hand, you were not required to write a murder mystery novel about what may have happened to poor Jack West. Whether Mr. West is sipping margaritas on a tropical beach or is six feet under is irrelevant. What is relevant is that his body was never found and thus the applicability of the corpus delicti rule must be considered.

However, even if you did not remember the corpus delicti rule, careful consideration of the other issues would still earn a passing grade.

Now, on to the next challenge!

The Exam Evaluator
PEOPLE v. DAVE

EXAM PRESENTATION (TOTAL POINTS AVAILABLE = 25)

	Poor											Excellent	
NEATNESS	0	1	2	3	4	5							____
ORGANIZATION	0	1	2	3	4	5	6	7	8	9	10		____
LAWYER-LIKE	0	1	2	3	4	5	6	7	8	9	10		____

DISCUSSION OF ISSUES (TOTAL POINTS AVAILABLE =75)

ADMISSIBILITY OF DAVE'S STATEMENT

VOLUNTARINESS:

    5 POINTS = FULL DISCUSSION   ____

    0 POINTS = PARTIAL/INCOMPLETE DISCUSSION   ____

MIRANDA ISSUES:

    10 POINTS = FULL DISCUSSION   ____

    5 POINTS = PARTIAL/INCOMPLETE DISCUSSION   ____

ADMISSIBILITY OF THE BLOODSTAINS

    15 POINTS = FULL DISCUSSION   ____

    10 POINTS = PARTIAL/INCOMPLETE DISCUSSION   ____

CONSPIRACY TO COMMIT BURGLARY

    15 POINTS = FULL DISCUSSION   ____

    10 POINTS = PARTIAL/INCOMPLETE DISCUSSION   ____

MURDER OF THOMPSON

    15 POINTS = FULL DISCUSSION   ____

    10 POINTS = PARTIAL/INCOMPLETE DISCUSSION   ____

MURDER OF WEST

    15 POINTS = FULL DISCUSSION   ____

    10 POINTS = PARTIAL/INCOMPLETE DISCUSSION   ____

TOTAL SCORE . . . . ____

E.   PROBLEM THREE: PEOPLE v. NED AND CHARLIE

1. First and Second Read, and Fact Visualization Exercise

Read the fact pattern once solely for content, and then a second time for key words and phrases. Once you have read the fact pattern, pause and VISUALIZE the facts. When you are done, please turn the page.

Police officers, believing Charlie's apartment to be a heroin distribution center, began surveillance of the apartment. Watching with the aid of binoculars from an apartment they had rented nearby, they observed the following events one night: Bart and Ned broke into Charlie's apartment and began to search it. Ned found a small box which he placed in a briefcase he had brought with him when he entered. Charlie then entered the apartment. Ned shot Charlie, who returned the fire, killing Bart.

The watching officers apprehended Ned as he left the apartment carrying the briefcase. They seized the briefcase from Ned and forced the lock. The only object found in the briefcase was the box they had seen Ned place in the briefcase. The box contained heroin.

When Charlie later surrendered himself at the police station, he was charged with possession of heroin.

Ned was charged with four offenses: first degree murder, burglary, theft, and possession of heroin.

At the separate trials of Ned and Charlie, testimony of the foregoing events was received in evidence. The heroin found in the briefcase was received after appropriate motions to exclude it had been denied. The testimony of the police officers regarding their observations during surveillance of Charlie's apartment was also admitted over appropriate objections.

Based on the above evidence, Ned was convicted of first degree murder, burglary, theft and possession of heroin, and Charlie was convicted of possession of heroin. Each has appealed.

What arguments should be made on behalf of Ned and on behalf of Charlie on each of their appeals, and how should the court rule on each argument? Discuss.

2.　　Headlining Exercise

The technique of "headlining" discussed in earlier chapters, helps you to remember and organize the facts of a case through the process of creating a "headline" capsulizing the facts of the case. The objective of headlining is to write a succinct sentence or phrase which best highlights the information in the fact pattern. In this exercise, we will create "headlines" for each paragraph as follows:

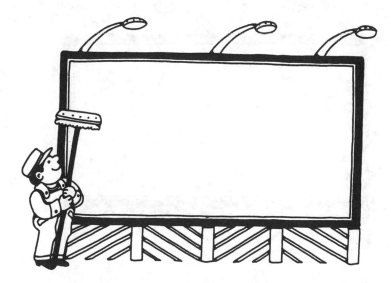

Police officers, believing Charlie's apartment to be a heroin distribution center, began surveillance of the apartment. Watching with the aid of binoculars from an apartment they had rented nearby, they observed the following events one night: Bart and Ned broke into Charlie's apartment and began to search it. Ned found a small box which he placed in a briefcase he had brought with him when he entered. Charlie then entered the apartment. Ned shot Charlie who returned the fire, killing Bart.

The watching officers apprehended Ned as he left the apartment carrying the briefcase. They seized the briefcase from Ned and forced the lock. The only object found in the briefcase was the box they had seen Ned place in the briefcase. The box contained heroin.

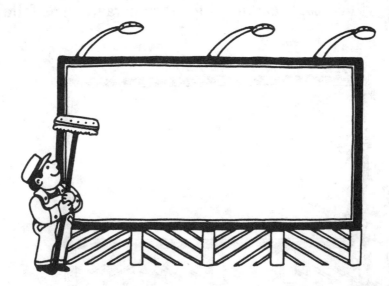

When Charlie later surrendered himself at the police station, he was charged with possession of heroin.

Ned was charged with four offenses: first degree murder, burglary, theft and possession of heroin.

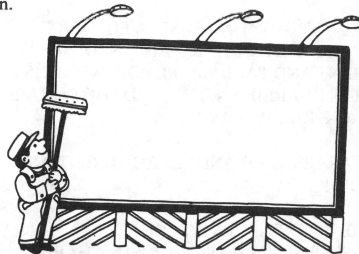

At the separate trials of Ned and Charlie, testimony of the foregoing events was received in evidence. The heroin found in the briefcase was received after appropriate motions to exclude it had been denied. The testimony of the police officers regarding their observations during surveillance of Charlie's apartment was also admitted over appropriate objections.

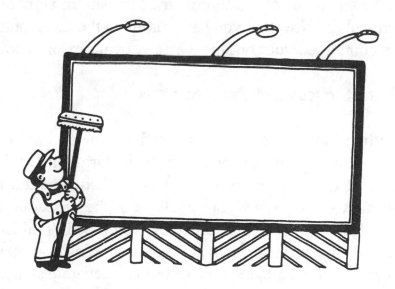

Based on the above evidence, Ned was convicted of first degree murder, burglary, theft and possession of heroin, and Charlie was convicted of possession of heroin. Each has appealed.

Now compare your headlines with these model headlines:

1. "POLICE CONDUCTING SURVEILLANCE FROM NEARBY APARTMENT WATCH BART AND NED BREAK INTO CHARLIE'S APARTMENT AND TAKE SMALL BOX, WHICH IS PUT IN BRIEFCASE, AND WHEN CHARLIE ENTERS, NED SHOT CHARLIE AND CHARLIE SHOT BACK, KILLING BART!"

2. "POLICE ARREST NED AND SEARCH BRIEFCASE CONTAINING BOX OF HEROIN!"

3. "CHARLIE SURRENDERS AT POLICE STATION AND IS CHARGED WITH HEROIN POSSESSION; NED CHARGED WITH MURDER, BURGLARY, THEFT AND HEROIN POSSESSION!"

4. "AT NED'S AND CHARLIE'S SEPARATE TRIALS, HEROIN AND POLICE SURVEILLANCE ADMITTED!"

5. "NED AND CHARLIE CONVICTED OF ALL CHARGES!"

Through the technique of headlining, the fact pattern is made more digestible and easier to remember. Now that you have mastered the facts, outline your answer. When you have completed your outline, write out your exam answer.

3. Outlining Strategy and Exam Analysis

Your outline should once again reflect the order indicated by the interrogatories. Many students experienced particular difficulty in organizing this problem because of the fact that Ned and Charlie had separate trials. However, because their trials were separate, your analysis of the procedural and substantive issues should be dealt with separately, as they would be in real life, as each would appeal separately. While reference may be made regarding arguments or discussions in each other's case, your headings should reflect two separate analyses of the liability of each:

PEOPLE v. NED

PEOPLE v. CHARLIE

Next, we apply the "big picture" questions for both the procedural and substantive issues. Because we are given only a general interrogatory, we must "start from scratch" so to speak. But as you will see, solving this problem is as easy as "A,B,C's"!

CRIMINAL PROCEDURE: WHAT RIGHTS MAY HAVE BEEN VIOLATED?

CRIMES: WHAT CRIMES HAVE BEEN COMMITTED AND WHAT DEFENSES MAY APPLY?

Now, let's answer the "big picture" questions by applying our checklist of procedural rights and crimes.

PEOPLE v. NED

PROCEDURAL QUESTIONS:
   ADMISSIBILITY OF HEROIN UNDER FOURTH AMENDMENT
   ADMISSION OF POLICE OFFICER'S OBSERVATIONS UNDER FOURTH AMENDMENT

SUBSTANTIVE QUESTIONS:
   MURDER
   BURGLARY
   THEFT
   POSSESSION OF HEROIN

PEOPLE v. CHARLIE

PROCEDURAL QUESTIONS:
   ADMISSIBILITY OF HEROIN UNDER FOURTH AMENDMENT.

SUBSTANTIVE QUESTIONS:
   POSSESSION OF HEROIN

NOW YOU KNOW EXACTLY WHAT CRIMES AND RIGHTS TO ANALYZE!!!

THIS IS YOUR ROAD MAP!

NOW, LET'S ADD EACH OF THE SPECIFIC ISSUES WHICH MUST BE ANALYZED:

PEOPLE v. NED

Criminal Procedure Questions:

ADMISSIBILITY OF HEROIN

> **Fourth Amendment analysis:**
> Does D have standing?
> Does police activity constitute a search?
> Valid search warrant obtained?
> Did the circumstances justify a warrantless search?

ADMISSIBILITY OF POLICE OFFICERS' OBSERVATIONS

> **Fourth Amendment analysis:**
> Does D have standing?
> Does police activity constitute a search?
> Valid search warrant obtained?
> Did the circumstances justify a warrantless search?
> Plain view exception?

Criminal Law Questions:

MURDER
> First degree murder: premeditated and deliberate? No.
> Felony murder rule?
> > Unintended death occur during crime?
> > FMR Felony?
> > Elements of underlying felony met?

Did the killing occur during the perpetration of felony?
Was the killing foreseeable result of felony?
Killing act performed by one of the felons?
Was the victim an innocent person?

BURGLARY: Trespassory breaking and entering into the dwelling house of another at night with the specific intent to commit a felony therein.

THEFT: Trespassory taking and carrying away of another's personal property with intent to deprive him/her of it permanently.

POSSESSION: Possession of a controlled substance.
Dominion and control exercised over heroin by Ned?

PEOPLE v. CHARLIE

ADMISSIBILITY OF HEROIN
Depends on resolution of issue above.

POSSESSION: Possession of a controlled substance.
Dominion and control exercised over heroin by Ned?

Before reviewing the model answer, compare your outline to the model outline and ask yourself these questions:

Did you identify all relevant issues?
If you did not, why did you miss issues?
Are you able to effectively use your outline as a roadmap?

The last question is particularly important, since it does not help to have a map one cannot use or read. Remember that the purpose of outlining is to simplify the process of exam writing, not to make it more complicated. A good outline does exactly that, by clearly and precisely drawing the direction which your analysis will take.

4. Model Answer

Now, on to the model answer:

I.   ADMISSION OF THE HEROIN

(STATE THE OVERALL ISSUE) *The issue is whether evidence concerning the heroin seized from Ned is admissible.*

(STATE SPECIFIC ISSUE YOU WILL RESOLVE) *Ned will argue that the heroin was seized in violation of his Fourth Amendment rights.*

(ISSUE OF STANDING) *First, Ned must demonstrate that he has standing to assert a Fourth Amendment violation.* (RULE OF STANDING) *In order to prove standing, a defendant must have a substantial ownership interest in the premises searched or a reasonable expectation of privacy in the area searched.* (APPLICATION) *Here, Ned had possession of the briefcase in question, and therefore had a reasonable expectation that the contents of the briefcase would remain private. The state would argue that Ned lacked an ownership interest in the box, which, according to the officers, he had just stolen. However, because Ned owned the briefcase that contained the box, he has a sufficient ownership interest in the contents therein, even if the contents were stolen.* (CONCLUSION) *Thus, Ned has standing to assert a Fourth Amendment violation.*

(ISSUE OF "SEARCH") *Secondly, the police activity must constitute a "search" or "seizure." Because the police seized Ned's briefcase and searched its contents, the Fourth Amendment applies.*

(STATE GENERAL RULE RE: WARRANTLESS SEARCH RULE) *The observations and subsequent seizure of the briefcase by the police were made without a warrant, and therefore are illegal unless supported by an exception to the warrant requirement.*

(STATE SEARCH INCIDENT TO ARREST RULE) *The search incident to arrest exception allows a limited search of the defendant's person and areas within his immediate reach incident to the defendant's arrest. At the time the observations were made, the police had probable cause to believe that Ned was involved in burglary and murder, based on their observations. Therefore, Ned's arrest was supported by probable cause, and the police could search areas within Ned's immediate reach. Because the briefcase was in Ned's immediate possession and within Ned's reach upon his arrest, the search and seizure of the briefcase and box were valid under this exception and the evidence properly admitted.*

II.   ADMISSION OF POLICE SURVEILLANCE/OBSERVATIONS

(STATE NEXT ISSUE TO BE RESOLVED) Ned will argue that the observations by police violated his Fourth Amendment rights and should be suppressed.

(ISSUE OF STANDING) Ned could not have a reasonable expectation that his actions in a place where he had no right to be would be outside public view. He was in the process of burglarizing Charlie's apartment and had no ownership interest in the premises. Thus, Ned has no standing and his claim will be rejected.

(ISSUE OF SEARCH) Moreover, the police surveillance did not constitute a search, since no search or seizure occurred. (ISSUE OF WARRANTLESS SEARCH AND APPLICATION OF PLAIN VIEW DOCTRINE) Even if the police activity was somehow found to be a search, the plain view doctrine would apply, as the police officers made the observations from a place they were entitled to be in, and Ned's acts were in public view. Thus, the officers' testimony as to their observations of Ned's activities was properly admitted.

III.   FIRST DEGREE MURDER

Murder is the unlawful killing of another human being with malice aforethought. First degree murder is premeditated and deliberate. Ned did not kill Bart, but may be convicted under a felony-murder rule theory. Under the felony murder rule, a co-felon may be convicted for the death of a co-felon if the killing occurs during the course of a inherently dangerous felony.

Here, Bart was killed while he and Ned committed the crime of burglary, an inherently dangerous felony. Thus, under common law, Ned is liable for Bart's death even though he did not pull the trigger. It is foreseeable that Bart could have been killed during the course of a burglary, and the killing occurred while Bart and Ned were in the apartment. However, some jurisdictions require that the killing act be performed by one of the felons or that the victim be an innocent person. In such jurisdictions, because Ned did not kill Bart, a co-felon, Ned's conviction could not stand.

In jurisdictions that apply the felony-murder rule, Ned could be guilty of first degree murder and his conviction will stand on appeal.

IV. BURGLARY

Ned was properly convicted of burglary. Burglary is the trespassory breaking and entering into the dwelling house of another at night with the specific intent to commit a felony therein. Here, Ned and Bart broke into and entered Charlie's apartment. Their intent to steal may be inferred from Ned's act of taking the small box. Because all the elements of burglary are met, Ned's conviction will stand.

V. THEFT

Theft is the trespassory taking and carrying away of another's personal property with intent to deprive him or her of it permanently. Ned's act of taking the small box and placing it into his briefcase meets all the elements of theft and thus his conviction will stand. However, because theft is a lesser included offense of burglary, Ned may only be convicted of either burglary or theft and not both.

VI. POSSESSION

Possession of a controlled substance requires that Ned exercise dominion and control over the heroin in question. Here, Ned put the box containing the heroin in his briefcase and therefore exercised control over it. Ned may defend that he did not know what was in the box and therefore did not intend to possess heroin. However, unless his explanation is accepted, his conviction will stand.

PEOPLE v. CHARLIE

I. ADMISSION OF HEROIN AGAINST CHARLIE

Charlie will object to the admissibility of the heroin on the same grounds raised by Ned. He would argue that his Fourth Amendment rights were violated by the search of Ned's briefcase. While Charlie has standing as the owner of the box, for the same reasons stated above the search will be deemed legal. Thus admission of evidence will be upheld.

II.   POSSESSION OF HEROIN

As to Charlie's conviction for possession of heroin, because the box was taken from his apartment, there is sufficient evidence for the trier of fact to conclude that Charlie exercised dominion and control over that box. This is true even though the box was possessed by Ned at the time of its seizure, since two or more persons may exercise joint control over an item.

As you can see from the *Exam Evaluator* that follows, you could have earned 20 points by correctly answering the issue pertaining to the admissibility of heroin. Since this question was posed twice, once in Charlie's trial, and once in Ned's, and because the same analysis applied to both, you could have gained points by merely incorporating the prior discussion in Ned's case to Charlie's case.

Surprisingly, one comment echoed about this problem by some examinees is that the definition of possession was unknown to them. This again demonstrates the importance of applying common sense. Possession means simply that one possess an item by exercising dominion and control over that item. Thus, the issue here is whether Charlie "possessed" the heroin, even though it was seized from Ned's immediate possession.

Let's fill in the *Exam Evaluator* and see how you did!

The Exam Evaluator
PEOPLE v. NED & CHARLIE

EXAM PRESENTATION (TOTAL POINTS AVAILABLE = 25)

	Poor										Excellent	
NEATNESS	0	1	2	3	4	5						____
ORGANIZATION	0	1	2	3	4	5	6	7	8	9	10	____
LAWYER-LIKE	0	1	2	3	4	5	6	7	8	9	10	____

DISCUSSION OF ISSUES (TOTAL POINTS AVAILABLE =75)

ADMISSIBILITY OF THE HEROIN

    15 POINTS = FULL DISCUSSION   ____

    10 POINTS = PARTIAL/INCOMPLETE DISCUSSION   ____

ADMISSIBILITY OF POLICE OBSERVATIONS

    15 POINTS = FULL DISCUSSION   ____

    10 POINTS = PARTIAL/INCOMPLETE DISCUSSION   ____

NED'S SUBSTANTIVE LIABILITY

For Murder

    15 POINTS = FULL DISCUSSION   ____

    10 POINTS = PARTIAL/INCOMPLETE DISCUSSION   ____

For Burglary, Theft & Possession

     15 POINTS = FULL DISCUSSION   ____

     10 POINTS = PARTIAL/INCOMPLETE DISCUSSION   ____

ADMISSION OF THE HEROIN AGAINST CHARLIE

     5 POINTS = FULL DISCUSSION   ____

     0 POINTS = PARTIAL/INCOMPLETE DISCUSSION   ____

CHARLIE'S SUBSTANTIVE LIABILITY

     10 POINTS = FULL DISCUSSION   ____

     5 POINTS = PARTIAL/INCOMPLETE DISCUSSION   ____

TOTAL SCORE . . . . ____

5.   Meet the Oddball Question

"You learn that, wherever you are going in life, obstacles don't matter very much. Pain or other circumstances can be there, but if you want to do a job bad enough, you'll find a way to get it done."

---- Jack Youngblood

This next question is what I call an "oddball" question. An "oddball" question, like the strange relative kept locked up in the attic, shows its face only rarely. Here is a small bit of advice on how to deal with "oddball" questions: Remember that the most important weapon in your arsenal is pure and unadulterated common sense.

In my experience, the students who have difficulty with this type of question are those who are rigid and inflexible in applying their problem-solving skills. In other words, if the shoe doesn't fit, you've got to make it fit, and those who stare at the shoe too long and are afraid to put it on are likely to fail. But don't kick yourself if this problem seems difficult. Like anything else in life, "oddball" questions take a little time to get accustomed to. Give it your best shot and remember, use COMMON SENSE.

Good luck!

F.   PROBLEM FOUR: PEOPLE v. BILL

Al and Bill decided to commit a robbery. Al showed Bill a water pistol and said he would use it to threaten a gas station attendant. Al took the attendant's cash at "gunpoint" while Bill waited outside the station in a car. Al then decided to eliminate the attendant as a witness and killed him with a knife that Bill did not know Al was carrying.

Both Al and Bill were captured as they attempted to drive from the station. They were indicted by a state grand jury on "capital murder" charges. At Bill's request he was granted a separate trial.

The state "capital murder" statute permits imposition of the death penalty on a defendant convicted of first degree murder if any one of the following special circumstances is also charged and proved: (a) the victim is a peace officer; (b) the killing is committed in the course of kidnapping, burglary, robbery, rape, or arson; or, (c) the killing is committed during an escape from a penal institution. At a separate penalty trial after a conviction of "capital murder," the jury is asked to answer the question, "Is the defendant likely to commit crimes of violence in the future?" The judge must sentence the defendant to death if the jury answers "yes." In reviewing the penalty phase of a trial, the state appellate court considers the imposition of a death penalty sentence only to determine if the evidence is sufficient to support the jury's affirmative answer to the sentencing question.

During jury selection at Bill's trial the following occurred:

1. Juror Smith was excused for cause after stating that he could not swear that the possible imposition of the death penalty would not affect his deliberations on any issue of fact presented during the guilt or penalty phase of the trial.

2. Juror Jones was excused for cause when she said she did not believe the death penalty was morally right and had doubt whether she could vote to impose it.

The jury convicted Bill of "capital murder" after finding that the homicide occurred during the course of a robbery. The jury then gave an affirmative answer to the sentencing question. The judge sentenced Bill to death.

As Bill's attorney on appeal what issues would you raise in seeking reversal of:

1. The conviction of capital murder? Discuss.

2. The imposition of the death penalty? Discuss.

1.   Exam Analysis: Tackling the "Oddball" Question

"Nothing is impossible to a willing heart."

---- John Heywood

Almost immediately, your heart may have begun palpitating as you read the first and second interrogatories concerning jury voir dire. You may be thinking, "Jury voir dire! JURY VOIR DIRE! I don't know anything about jury voir dire on a death penalty case! AAAAAAHHHHHHHH!!!!"

After recovering from the initial shock, take a second look at the problem presented:

1. Juror Smith was excused for cause after stating that he could not swear that the possible imposition of the death penalty would not affect his deliberations on any issue of fact presented during the guilt or penalty phase of the trial.

2. Juror Jones was excused for cause when she said she did not believe the death penalty was morally right and had doubt whether she could vote to impose it.

Now, what's really being asked here? While it's true that both of these interrogatories reflect issues that were argued before the United States Supreme Court, the Examiners did not expect you to cite the cases or discuss the history of jury voir dire as it pertains to the concept of "death qualified" jurors, that is, the practice of accepting jurors who state that they could impose the death penalty and excusing those who cannot. If you were not aware that this practice has been determined to be constitutional, all would not be lost.

Read through the interrogatories again. Now, return to basic principles of common sense. What is required of a juror? What does the court consider in excusing a juror for cause? Whether a juror can be fair and impartial. Let's take the discussion of this issue from this basic premise.

The issue is whether jurors Smith and Jones were properly excused for cause by the trial court. The court must excuse jurors who cannot serve fairly and impartially in deciding the defendant's guilt or innocence, or in a death penalty case, in deciding the question of penalty. Because Juror Smith stated that the possible imposition of the death penalty might affect his deliberations in both the guilt and penalty phases, he was properly excused. A juror must take an oath to be fair and impartial, and Juror Smith clearly expressed his inability to do so.

Juror Jones was also properly excused for cause. A juror should be excluded where his or her views would prevent or substantially impair the performance of the juror's duties. Because she did not believe in the death penalty and had a predisposition against the death penalty, she could not render an objective and fair verdict based on the facts. She also had "doubts" whether she could vote for death. To allow her to serve would deny the prosecution a fair trial. Therefore, she was properly excused by the trial court.

This answer would have received equal credit as the following answer, which addresses the issue in a more direct manner:

The Supreme Court has recently ruled that the impaneling of death-qualified jurors is not unconstitutional and has approved of the practice of accepting jurors who state that they could impose the death penalty and excusing those who cannot. Thus, Juror Jones was properly excused because of her expressed inability to vote for the death penalty regardless of the facts presented by the prosecution, due to her belief that the death penalty was morally wrong. A juror may only be excluded where his or her views would prevent or substantially impair the performance of the juror's duties. Juror Smith was likewise properly excused, since he was unable to swear that the possibility of capital punishment would not affect his judgment concerning issues of fact and punishment. A juror must be fair and impartial, and by his own admission, Juror Smith said he could not be.

Even an answer which completely misses the mark is better than none at all, so long as it is well-reasoned:

Juror Jones was improperly excused by the court. The fact that she possessed personal opinions about the death penalty did not require her exclusion as a juror. Rather, the issue was whether as a juror, she could put her personal opinions aside and decide questions of guilt and punishment fairly and impartially. The court also

498

erred in excusing Juror Smith. While Juror Smith expressed concerns regarding the effect the possibility of the death penalty might have on his deliberations, he did not state that he would be able to put those concerns aside. Once again, if Juror Smith stated that he could fairly and impartially decide the issues of guilt and penalty, he should have been accepted.

While this answer is certainly not desirable, as it states an incorrect principle of law and is one-sided in its focus, it is better than an empty page.

The sound of silence does not go far with bar graders, and if you write something, no matter how unsensational, at least the grader will admire your creativity and determination. Remember that there is always a dissenting voice in matters of law, so if you choose the wrong side or cite an incorrect rule, the grader will consider your arguments in support thereof to determine your ability to reason, albeit, even a legally incorrect position. While every grader I have met has told me that, as expected, they do penalize students who state the rule incorrectly, they also will consider and may even give credit for good legal reasoning, however misguided. Thus, even misadventure beats no adventure at all.

Now, let's solve the remainder of the second interrogatory. After discussing the jury selection issue, the remaining issue concerns the constitutionality of the death penalty. Again the rule here is basic but a bit remote. The rule is that the accused in a death penalty case must have the opportunity to present during the penalty phase of the trial mitigating circumstances; that is, any evidence which mitigates or lessens culpability and responsibility. This rule should be listed in your "big picture" Criminal Procedural approach under miscellaneous rights concerning the Eighth Amendment's prohibition against cruel and unusual punishment. Also, the statute must give the judge or jury discretion to impose the death penalty and guidance on how to make that decision. Clearly, all of these rules were violated by the statutory procedure employed here.

Applying these principles to the statute in question and what occurred at Bill's trial, the following issues were presented: (1) Does the statute allow for the presentation of mitigating evidence? (2) Does the jury have the discretion to impose the death penalty? (3) Was any guidance provided to the jury as to what factors to consider in rendering a death verdict?

Once again, common sense rules the day, and this problem, as you will see in this model answer:

A statute imposing the death penalty must allow the defendant to present mitigating evidence and full information regarding his background. Here the statute allowed Bill no opportunity to present any background information and instead rested solely on the jury's finding as to whether Bill would likely commit "crimes of violence" in the future. Because it provides no opportunity to present any evidence whatsoever concerning Bill's background, it must be adjudged unconstitutional.

A statute imposing the death penalty must also give the jury discretion as to whether to impose the death penalty. Here, the jury is only given the alternative of voting yes or no on a specific question, i.e., whether the defendant is likely to commit future crimes of violence. The jury is given no opportunity to vote on the death penalty, or to alternatively impose a life sentence. Thus, the statute is unconstitutional.

A law imposing the death penalty must also give the jurors guidance as to what matters they may consider in imposing the death penalty. Since this statute only specifies three categories of circumstances when the death penalty may be imposed and does not allow jurors to consider any factors concerning the defendant's history, the statute is unconstitutional.

Now that you see the arguments for what they are, you can see how simple these issues are. But, is there another issue which perhaps is not included in your trusty bar outlines but is worthy of discussion? Read the third paragraph again and ask yourself, "What's wrong with this picture???" If you still don't see it, read the second sentence. If you still don't see it, read, "Is the defendant likely to commit crimes of violence in the future?" If you still don't see it, ASK, IS IT OKAY FOR THE STATE TO KILL PEOPLE FOR THINGS THEY MIGHT DO IN THE FUTURE???

Believe it or not, many examinees flat out missed this issue. Because they were too engrossed in looking for legal issues they completely overlooked the biggest common sense issue:

The statute is also unconstitutional because the sentence of death is imposed depending on whether the jury believes the defendant will commit crimes in the future and therefore improperly punishes a defendant for the possibility of future misconduct or crimes. The appellate court's jurisdiction is limited to only considering the sufficiency of evidence on this question and therefore unconstitutionally limits the right of appeal on substantive and procedural issues. Therefore, the statute is unconstitutional.

Now, let's wrap up the rest of the problem, which presents a now familiar discussion of murder:

1.   THE CONVICTION OF CAPITAL MURDER

HOMICIDE - Unlawful killing of another

MURDER - based on Felony-Murder Rule
      Did the killing occur during an inherently dangerous felony?

CAPITAL MURDER - improper unless D played a major role in robbery

AIDING and ABETTING a robbery - Is murder a natural and probable result of robbery?

Notice that the interrogatory only asks you to analyze capital murder and not other crimes, such as robbery, conspiracy or other crimes. The Examiners have intentionally limited their request to one issue, because they know that you have plenty of other issues to deal with in the second interrogatory. Also, you can see that the discussion required is quite brief:

The issue is whether Bill is guilty of capital murder. Under the statute, a killing committed during the course of a robbery is considered capital murder. Homicide is the unlawful killing of another human being, and because Bill did not kill the station attendant, his liability must be premised on either the felony murder rule or aiding and abetting a robbery.

Under the felony-murder rule, a defendant is guilty of murder where a killing occurs during the commission of an inherently dangerous felony such as robbery. Because Bill and Al both participated in the robbery, and the killing of the attendant

501

occurred during that robbery, the felony-murder rule applies and Bill is guilty of murder. Bill may argue that because he was shown a water pistol and was told by Al that he would use it only to threaten the attendant, it was not foreseeable that a killing would occur during the robbery. However, because of the probable violence which accompanies the crime of robbery, his argument will be rejected, even though he was unaware of the specific means, i.e., the knife, by which the killing was committed.

Alternatively, Bill could be convicted for murder as an aider and abettor to a robbery. An aider and abettor incurs liability not only for the target offense, but any natural and probable consequences flowing therefrom. Because it is quite probable that a person could be killed during the course of a robbery, Bill is liable for murder as an aider and abettor.

However, Bill could not be convicted of <u>capital</u> murder on a felony murder theory where the defendant, who as an accomplice, did not take or intend to take life, or intend that lethal force be employed. The death penalty cannot be imposed in such circumstances unless the defendant participated in a major way in a felony that resulted in murder and acted with reckless indifference to human life. Bill did not know that Al would decide to kill the attendant, and in fact was told by Al that he would use a harmless, non-lethal water pistol to threaten the defendant. Also, by driving the vehicle, he did not participate in a major way in the robbery, and thus cannot be sentenced to death for murder.

By no means was this problem an easy one. The last paragraph may seem as if it came out of nowhere, but it is in fact based on two United States Supreme Court cases, <u>Enmund v. Florida</u> (1982) and <u>Tison v. Arizona</u> (1987), from which the above rules were discerned. Once again, you need not know the case names, and you may not have even known the rules behind these cases. Fortunately, even if you did not include this discussion in your answer, a passing score would still be within your reach, since the Bar Examiners have included a wealth of other issues to discuss.

If you feel that the Model Answer is one "tough cookie," even finer distinctions could be made. For example, on the jury selection issues, it could be pointed out that an improperly excluded juror is grounds for automatic reversal of a death sentence. However, as with most difficult bar questions, a passing score is easier to achieve because of the fact that a difficult problem is difficult for everyone.

502

The Exam Evaluator
PEOPLE v. BILL

EXAM PRESENTATION (TOTAL POINTS AVAILABLE = 25)

	Poor											Excellent
NEATNESS	0	1	2	3	4	5						_____
ORGANIZATION	0	1	2	3	4	5	6	7	8	9	10	_____
LAWYER-LIKE	0	1	2	3	4	5	6	7	8	9	10	_____

DISCUSSION OF ISSUES (TOTAL POINTS AVAILABLE =75)

BILL'S CONVICTION OF CAPITAL MURDER

MURDER:

    15 POINTS = FULL DISCUSSION   _____

    5 POINTS = PARTIAL/INCOMPLETE DISCUSSION   _____

MURDER BASED ON AIDING AND ABETTING A ROBBERY:
    10 POINTS = FULL DISCUSSION   _____

    5 POINTS = PARTIAL/INCOMPLETE DISCUSSION   _____

IMPOSITION OF THE DEATH PENALTY

MITIGATION EVIDENCE

    15 POINTS = FULL DISCUSSION   _____

10 POINTS = PARTIAL/INCOMPLETE DISCUSSION   ____

JUROR DISCRETION IN IMPOSING DEATH PENALTY

15 POINTS = FULL DISCUSSION   ____

10 POINTS = PARTIAL/INCOMPLETE DISCUSSION   ____

JUROR GUIDANCE/FACTORS IN IMPOSING DEATH PENALTY

10 POINTS = FULL DISCUSSION   ____

5 POINTS = PARTIAL/INCOMPLETE DISCUSSION   ____

IMPOSING DEATH BASED ON "FUTURE CRIMES"

10 POINTS = FULL DISCUSSION   ____

5 POINTS = PARTIAL/INCOMPLETE DISCUSSION   ____

BONUS POINTS:

D MUST PARTICIPATE IN "MAJOR WAY" = 10 POINTS   ____

TOTAL SCORE . . . .   ____

(THIS PAGE IS BLANK)

2. Why It Is Important to Enjoy Exam Taking

"One person has enthusiasm for 30 minutes, another for 30 days, but it is the person who has it for 30 years who makes a success of life."

---- Edward B. Butler

Now that you have conquered four real life Criminal Law bar questions, you are now ready to go it alone, blazing new trails to the ends of the universe, where no bar examinee has gone before!

Before we do that, let's take a moment to put the bar experience in its proper perspective.

Like anything else in life, the experience is what you make it. There are two ways to think of rock climbing. One way to think of it is an exciting, daring adventure, as you see yourself repelling down a cliff after making the victorious climb to the top, having courageously stood atop the towering mountain, taking in the beauty of nature below you. The other way is to view it as a scary, awful, stomach-wrenching, anxiety-causing, fearful experience, full of tortious possibilities as you edge your way up the mountainside, every moment fearing that you may lose your grip not to mention your life with one wrong move. All things considered equal, who do you think is more likely to fall?

The same philosophy applies to the bar exam. You can view your studies as the greatest challenge before you, whether this is the first time or the hundredth time you have taken the bar exam, and you will enjoy every second of it with a vengeance. If you pursue your goal with passion, you will feel confident about what you are doing. On the other hand, if you feel like the second rock climber described above, complaining every time you open your book, fearing each new bar question and hoping that a miracle will occur to save you from studying, not only will you come to hate studying, but you will also have considerable difficulty doing what you need to do to pass the examination.

The moral of the story? Enjoy the challenges before you. Look at each new bar question the way that a space traveler might view a new universe, waiting to be explored and traveled. So, as you reach your peak performance in the next four problems, HAVE FUN!

G.   PROBLEM FIVE: PEOPLE v. BOB

Acting with probable cause, but without a warrant, police forcibly entered Bob's mobile home, a licensed motorized vehicle which was parked in a motor park and connected to utilities. They seized a quantity of cocaine found in the mobile home. Although Bob lived in the mobile home, he was not present at the time the police entered. Bob has been charged with violating Section 52 of the State X Criminal Code which makes it a felony to: "knowingly possess cocaine."

Bob made a timely pretrial motion to suppress the cocaine under the Fourth Amendment. The court denied the motion.

Bob, who is indigent, made a timely pretrial motion for leave to represent himself at trial and for court-appointed "stand-by" counsel who would be available to assist if Bob desired help. The court denied Bob's motion for standby counsel. The court advised Bob that he could either proceed pro se, or have counsel appointed to conduct the entire defense. Bob competently waived the appointment of counsel. He then defended himself at trial.

At trial the cocaine was admitted in evidence over Bob's renewed objection. Bob testified that he did not realize the substance was cocaine and that he had believed it was a legally possessable cocaine-like substance which he intended to give to his friends as a joke.

The court instructed the jury: "If you find beyond a reasonable doubt that the defendant possessed cocaine, you should find him guilty unless you also find that he has proved by a preponderance of the evidence that he reasonably mistook the cocaine for a legally possessible substance."

Did the court err in:

1. Admitting the cocaine as evidence? Discuss.

2. Denying standby counsel? Discuss.

3. Giving the above jury instruction? Discuss.

1.	Outlining Strategy and Exam Analysis

You may be thinking, "Why this problem, now?" This bar question was selected because it is a rare example of a composite of the qualities found in each of the four preceding bar questions. This problem possesses three interrogatories which are quite different in their characteristics.

The first interrogatory presents an ordinary search and seizure problem which we have already seen in People v. Dave, People v. Doug and People v. Ned and Charlie. The second interrogatory contains an "oddball" issue, reminiscent of People v. Bill. The final interrogatory involves the use of our good friend and teacher, Common Sense. Let's outline our answer:

## 1.	Admission of Cocaine

Have the defendant's FOURTH AMENDMENT rights been violated?
	Does Bob have standing? Owns mobile home.
	Is governmental conduct involved? Yes, police search.
	Is there a search or seizure? Mobile home searched.
	Did the police have a warrant? No.
	If not, do any exceptions to the warrant requirement apply?
		AUTO EXCEPTION - applies to mobile homes.
	Cocaine admissible.

## 2.	Standby Counsel

Has the defendant's SIXTH AMENDMENT right to counsel been violated?

	D is guaranteed effective assistance of counsel.
	Standby counsel may be appointed but is not constitutionally required.

## 3.	Jury Instructions

	Constitution requires guilt to be proven beyond a reasonable doubt.
	Instruction shifts burden to defendant.

You may be thinking, "Gee, is that it? There must be more." But this question requires you to shift gears three times. In the first interrogatory, you coast in neutral, writing a "standard" Fourth Amendment analysis; to answer the second interrogatory, you would shift into reverse, by quickly reciting the appropriate rule and applying it; and on the final interrogatory, you then shift into drive, bringing the question home.

Next, let's compare your answer with the model answer and see how you did. As you read through this answer, observe the process of "integrating" the facts, issues, rules, application and conclusion. By interweaving these components with each other, one achieves a succinct and efficient answer.

2.   Model Answer

1.   Admission of cocaine

The issue is whether the admission of the cocaine violates the Fourth Amendment.

Bob has standing under the Fourth Amendment because he has a substantial ownership interest in the mobile home, which belongs to him, and a reasonable expectation of privacy in his own home, as any citizen would. Governmental conduct is involved and the police action constituted a "search" of Bob's home and a "seizure" of contraband, and thus the Fourth Amendment applies.

Since the police entered Bob's mobile home, the search is illegal unless supported by an exception to the warrant requirement. The only applicable exception is the auto exception, which holds that an auto may be searched if there is probable cause to believe that the auto contains contraband. Bob will argue that his mobilehome is more akin to a home not a car, as it was stationary at the time it was searched and connected to utilities. However, a recent Supreme Court decision has held that a mobile home falls within the automobile exception, because mobile homes, as motorized mobile vehicles, share the same characteristics as automobiles. Because the police had probable cause to search Bob's mobile home, their entry was legal and the cocaine admissible.

2. Denial of Standby Counsel

The Sixth Amendment right to counsel provides for effective assistance of counsel at all critical stages of a criminal proceeding. However, an accused in a criminal action also has the right to represent himself or herself provided that the right to counsel is knowingly and intelligently waived. Here, Bob competently waived his right to counsel but requested standby counsel. The court may appoint standby counsel but is not constitutionally required to do so. Thus, the court acted within its discretion in denying standby counsel to Bob.

3. Jury Instruction

The United States Constitution requires that guilt in a criminal action be proven beyond a reasonable doubt. The court's instruction to the jury shifted the burden to Bob by requiring Bob to prove that he mistook the cocaine for another substance, and therefore was improper.

You may still be thinking, "Is that it????" And the answer is yes, that is it. You may be wondering how anyone could receive an unsatisfactory score on this question. However, many did. Some people made the mistake of overanalyzing this problem. Paranoia runs deep even on the bar exam, and many a mistrusting examinee, thinking that more had to be involved here than met the eye, made up non-existent issues to discuss, like the credibility of Bob's belief that the item in question was cocaine, or the wisdom of Bob's decision to waive his right to counsel. While what constitutes an "easy" problem is a matter of opinion, do not overanalyze an easy problem out of fear.

As was said earlier, all bar questions are not created equally. Most likely, one of the six bar questions you will answer will be an "easy" question. This "easy" question, however, is usually accompanied by a few toughies. So whenever you are handed an easy question on a silver platter, enjoy it, because the Bar Examiners have included it as a breather from more difficult questions.

Speaking of difficult criminal law questions . . .

The Exam Evaluator
PROSECUTION v. BOB

EXAM PRESENTATION (TOTAL POINTS AVAILABLE = 25)

	Poor	Excellent	
NEATNESS	0 1 2 3 4 5		____
ORGANIZATION	0 1 2 3 4 5 6 7 8 9 10		____
LAWYER-LIKE	0 1 2 3 4 5 6 7 8 9 10		____

DISCUSSION OF ISSUES (TOTAL POINTS AVAILABLE =75)

ADMISSIBILITY OF COCAINE AS EVIDENCE

    40 POINTS = FULL DISCUSSION   ____

    30 POINTS = PARTIAL/INCOMPLETE DISCUSSION   ____

DENIAL OF STAND-BY COUNSEL

    20 POINTS = FULL DISCUSSION   ____

    15 POINTS = PARTIAL/INCOMPLETE DISCUSSION   ____

JURY INSTRUCTION

    15 POINTS = FULL DISCUSSION   ____

    10 POINTS = PARTIAL/INCOMPLETE DISCUSSION   ____

TOTAL . . . . ____

H.   PROBLEM SIX: PEOPLE v. BILL AND AL

Al and Bill offered Clara, whom they had just met in a bar, a ride to her home when the bar closed. She accepted, but the two men instead drove her to a remote area where first Bill, and then Al, forcibly raped her. When Clara attempted to push Al away, he subdued her by choking her. Bill watched but took no part in Al's activities. Clara died as a result of the choking.

Al and Bill were arrested. After receiving proper notice of their <u>Miranda</u> rights, which they waived, each admitted raping Clara. Al denied having intent to kill when he choked Clara, and Bill denied having either an intent that she be killed or knowledge that Al would use deadly force in raping her.

At their joint trial on charges of felony murder and rape, evidence of these events and of the defendants' statements were admitted. The court, over defendants' objections (1) excused for cause, on the prosecutor's motion, three jurors who expressed unqualified opposition to the death penalty; (2) excluded, at both the guilt and penalty phases of the trial, evidence proffered by Bill that he was mentally retarded; and (3) admitted at the penalty phase of the trial evidence offered by the prosecutor regarding the emotional impact of Clara's death on her family. The jury convicted both defendants of first degree felony murder in the commission of the rape and returned penalty verdicts of death for each defendant.

In a post-trial hearing, the defendants moved to vacate the verdicts on the basis of juror misconduct. The court refused to admit the affidavit of juror X that juror Y was intoxicated during one afternoon of the guilt phase trial. The motion to vacate the verdicts was denied and the court sentenced Al and Bill to death.

In defendants' appeals from the judgments of death, how should the court rule on arguments that:

1.   The evidence was insufficient to support the conviction of Bill for first degree felony murder? Discuss.

2.   The court erred in excusing the three jurors? Discuss.

3.   The court erred in excluding the evidence of Bill's retardation? Discuss.

4. The court erred in excluding the evidence of juror intoxication and denying the motion to vacate? Discuss.

5. The court erred in admitting the evidence of the impact of Clara's death on her family? Discuss.

6. Imposition of the death penalty on Al, assuming he had no intent to kill, and on Bill, assuming he neither intended to kill nor participated in the killing, violates the Eighth Amendment prohibition of cruel and unusual punishment? Discuss.

1.   Outlining Strategy and Exam Analysis

At first glance, these questions might seem like game show queries rather than essay questions on the bar exam. Most of the questions fall in the "you know it or you don't" category of bar questions, by testing you on specific rules of law; this is true of interrogatories (2) - (6). However, as you will see, even if you do not know the rule, you can still score points by discussing the likely arguments and facts supporting them:

1. <u>Sufficiency of Bill's murder conviction</u>

MURDER

> Homicide: Killing committed by Al.
> First Degree Murder: Felony-Murder Rule
> > Did the killing occur during an inherently dangerous felony? (rape)

AIDING AND ABETTING THEORY

> Aider and abettor liable for natural and probable consequences of act.

CONSPIRACY TO COMMIT RAPE

> Conspirator liable for all foreseeable consequences of conspiracy.

2. <u>Excusing Jurors</u>

> Can jurors be excused because they oppose the death penalty?

3. <u>Excluding Evidence of Bill's Retardation</u>

> Accused in capital case must be allowed to present mitigating evidence.

4. <u>Evidence of Juror Intoxication</u>

> MAJORITY RULE: Jurors are incompetent to impeach their own verdicts.
> MINORITY RULE: Only objective evidence of juror misconduct is

admissible.

Is intoxication during trial objective misconduct?

5. Admissibility of Victim Impact Statements

Victim impact statements are admissible at the penalty phase of a capital case.

6A. Death Sentence on Al

Death penalty may not be imposed where there is no intent to kill unless D participated in the felony in a major way that caused the death and acted with reckless indifference to human life.

6B. Death Sentence on Bill

Death penalty may not be imposed for felony-murder: unless (1) D intended to kill or intended that lethal force be employed, OR (2) D participated in the felony in a major way that caused the death and acted with reckless indifference to human life.

As you might guess, this question threw many examinees into a state of panic because they did not "know" one or more of the rules underlying each of the six interrogatories presented. Each of the interrogatories in this problem, with the exception of the first interrogatory, focused on a specific area of law and the examinee's knowledge of a particular rule of Criminal Procedure. Rather than throw a net out, the examinees put a specific lure on their fishing lines, requiring a specific "bite" before you could reel in your answer and score points. But like a fishing expedition, usually when you're not getting any bites, the person next to you isn't as well.

This is a very important point to remember. While you should certainly strive to know all testable areas of law, from time to time on an examination there will be things you do not know, especially on problems such as these. What you must keep in mind is that most people who sit for the examination will not know one or more of the specific rules of law presented on this problem either. Thus, it is not fatal to your answer if you fail to answer one of the interrogatories.

This is not to say that you should strive to understand and know only 75% or 80% of the law, but if you strive to understand and know 100% and you only really understand 80% of the tested material, you will know more than enough law to pass the examination with flying colors.

2.   Model Answer

1.   <u>Sufficiency of Bill's Murder Conviction</u>

Because Al, not Bill, actually killed Clara, Bill's liability for Clara's murder is limited to three theories: (1) felony-murder; (2) aiding and abetting; (3) conspiracy to commit rape.

FELONY-MURDER

Under the felony-murder rule, a killing which occurs during certain enumerated felonies, such as rape, is deemed first degree murder. Al choked Clara, killing her, after she pushed Al away during the rape in which Bill participated. Thus, the evidence is sufficient to sustain Bill's guilt on this theory.

AIDING AND ABETTING THEORY

The evidence is also sufficient to convict Bill as an aider and abettor. An aider and abettor is liable not only for the intended crime but also the natural and probable consequences of such act. Here, it is both natural and probable that a killing would occur during the commission of a rape, which is an inherently dangerous felony.

CONSPIRACY TO COMMIT RAPE

A conspirator is liable for all foreseeable consequences of conspiracy. By acting in concert with Bill in raping Clara, it could be inferred that the two agreed to rape Clara and did so in furtherance of that agreement. Because it is foreseeable that someone would be killed during such a violent act, Bill is liable for Clara's murder as a conspirator.

2. Excusing Jurors

A juror may be excused for cause if his or her views would substantially interfere with the juror's impartiality. Because each of the three jurors expressed "unqualified opposition" to the death penalty, each juror was properly excused because each could not perform his or her duty to decide the issue of penalty fairly.

3. Excluding Evidence of Bill's Retardation

The issue is whether the court erred in excluding evidence of Bill's retardation in the guilt and penalty phases. In the guilt phase, a defendant has the right to present a defense to the charges, and Bill's retardation may have been relevant to negate any intent to kill on his part. Further, in the penalty phase of a criminal case, an accused must be allowed to present mitigating evidence. Thus, the court erred in disallowing evidence of Bill's retardation in both phases of the trial.

4. Evidence of Juror Intoxication

At common law, jurors are incompetent to impeach their own verdicts, and thus the court's ruling excluding the juror affidavit was correct. Under the minority rule, objective evidence of juror misconduct is admissible. Because intoxication is an objective symptom, in such a jurisdiction, the affidavit was admissible and the court erred in excluding it.

5. Admissibility of Victim Impact Statements

The Supreme Court has ruled that victim impact statements are admissible in the penalty phase of a death penalty case to assist the jury in evaluating the defendant's moral culpability and blameworthiness. Thus, evidence as to the emotional impact of Clara's death on her family was properly admitted.

6A. Death Sentence on Al

The death penalty may not be imposed where there is no intent to kill unless Al participated in the felony in a major way that caused the death and acted with reckless indifference to human life. Because Al participated in the rape of Clara and acted with reckless indifference in raping and choking Clara, causing her death, Al's sentence does not violate the Eighth Amendment.

6B. <u>Death Sentence on Bill</u>

The death penalty may not be imposed on an accomplice convicted of murder on a felony-murder theory, unless D intended to kill or intended that lethal force be employed, OR D participated in the felony in a major way that caused the death and acted with reckless indifference to human life. Bill did not intend Clara's death, nor did he directly participate in her killing. However, he did participate in a major way by raping Clara and acted without regard for Clara's life in doing so. His failure to stop Al from choking Clara after he himself raped Clara shows a reckless disregard for the value of human life and he can properly receive a sentence of death.

The Exam Evaluator
PEOPLE v. BILL & AL

EXAM PRESENTATION (TOTAL POINTS AVAILABLE = 25)

	Poor										Excellent
NEATNESS	0 1 2 3 4 5										_____
ORGANIZATION	0 1 2 3 4 5 6 7 8 9 10										_____
LAWYER-LIKE	0 1 2 3 4 5 6 7 8 9 10										_____

DISCUSSION OF ISSUES (TOTAL POINTS AVAILABLE =75)

BILL'S CONVICTION FOR FIRST DEGREE MURDER

FELONY MURDER THEORY/AIDING & ABETTING/CONSPIRACY

    20 POINTS = FULL DISCUSSION   _____

    10 POINTS = PARTIAL/INCOMPLETE DISCUSSION   _____

EXCLUSION OF JURORS

    10 POINTS = FULL DISCUSSION   _____

    5 POINTS = PARTIAL/INCOMPLETE DISCUSSION   _____

EXCLUDING EVIDENCE OF BILL'S RETARDATION

    10 POINTS = FULL DISCUSSION   _____

    5 POINTS = PARTIAL/INCOMPLETE DISCUSSION   _____

EXCLUSION OF VICTIM IMPACT EVIDENCE

      10 POINTS = FULL DISCUSSION   ____

      5 POINTS = PARTIAL/INCOMPLETE DISCUSSION   ____

IMPOSITION OF THE DEATH PENALTY

AL

      15 POINTS = FULL DISCUSSION   ____

      10 POINTS = PARTIAL/INCOMPLETE DISCUSSION   ____

BILL

      10 POINTS = FULL DISCUSSION   ____

      5 POINTS = PARTIAL/INCOMPLETE DISCUSSION   ____

TOTAL SCORE . . . . ____

I.   PROBLEM SEVEN: PEOPLE v. DEFT

Deft was formally charged with a criminal offense punishable with a ninety-day maximum jail term and/or a $500 fine. As Deft was being brought by a policeman to the courtroom for arraignment, Witt, who had witnessed the charged offense and was asked by the prosecutor to be present at Deft's arraignment, said to the policeman, "Yes, that's the guy!"

At the arraignment, Deft established his indigence and requested the appointment of counsel and trial by jury. The arraignment judge denied both requests without explanation.

Representing himself in the trial court, Deft moved to exclude evidence of Witt's statement to the policeman that he recognized Deft at the arraignment, and to prevent identification of Deft by Witt at trial. The trial judge agreed to exclude evidence of Witt's statement to the policeman but refused to prevent any potential identification of Deft by Witt at trial.

After the foregoing rulings, Deft negotiated a plea bargain with the prosecutor under which Deft agreed to enter a plea of guilty without admitting that he was, in fact, guilty, and the State agreed that it would not request a jail term. The plea agreement was explained to the court. The judge then advised Deft of the maximum statutory penalty that could be imposed. The judge explained that the plea agreement did not limit the court's discretion in imposing sentence. Deft then waived his rights and agreed to go forward with the plea. After the prosecutor made a proffer of evidence to establish a factual basis for the charge, the judge accepted Deft's plea of guilty, even though Deft told the judge he was really innocent. Deft was sentenced to a fine of $500 and a thirty-day suspended jail term.

Deft has appealed. The jurisdiction permits an appeal following a plea of guilty. You may assume that each issue raised by Deft is a proper subject for appeal notwithstanding the guilty plea.

Deft argues in the appellate court that his conviction must be reversed on federal constitutional grounds because:

1.   He was denied his right to appointed counsel.

2. He was denied his right to trial by jury.
3. Any identification by Deft by Witt was inadmissible at trial.
4. His plea was not shown to be voluntary and intelligent and should not have been accepted since he had maintained that he was innocent.

How should the court rule on each of Deft's arguments? Discuss.

1. Outline Strategy and Exam Analysis

This problem is very similar to the preceding problem, but covers a different panoply of issues and was selected to illustrate yet another variation of the pure Criminal Procedure type question.

Your outline should reflect four headings of analysis:

1. Denial of right to appointed counsel

2. Denial of jury trial

3. Admissibility of Witt's identification of Deft

4. Withdrawal of plea

Each interrogatory basically tests your knowledge of a specific rule. In the first and second interrogatories, you are asked to decide whether Deft had a right to appointed counsel in a misdemeanor offense with a 90-day maximum jail term, where no actual jail sentence was imposed. In the third interrogatory, you are asked to determine whether the admissibility of Witt's identification violated the Due Process Clause and Sixth Amendment right to counsel. The final interrogatory simply asks you to determine if there are any grounds which Deft can raise to withdraw his plea of guilty.

"Genius is the ability to reduce the complicated to the simple."

---- C.W. Ceran

Sounds too easy to be true? That is exactly what many examinees thought, and to compensate for their fears that maybe they were missing something, some examinees actually "manufactured" issues that were not presented, such as whether the defendant was in fact guilty of the crime, and tangential issues, such as the availability of habeas relief. As they say, "Don't stare a gift horse in the mouth."

2.   Model Answer

As you will see in the model answer, simplicity is a goal worth fighting for:

People v. Deft

1.   Denial of right to appointed counsel

The Sixth Amendment right to counsel provides that an accused shall enjoy the right to counsel in criminal proceedings. This right has been held to apply to all felonies and any misdemeanor where actual imprisonment is imposed. Here, no imprisonment was imposed because Deft received a 30-day suspended jail term. However, if Deft is ever sentenced to jail based on this case, the right to counsel would attach.

Thus, the court did not err in not appointing counsel, unless Deft is sentenced to serve an actual jail sentence.

2.   Denial of jury trial

The Sixth Amendment right to trial by jury applies to all serious offenses, if imprisonment of more than six months is possible. Because Deft was charged with an offense carrying a maximum jail sentence of ninety days, he had no right to jury trial and his constitutional challenge will be rejected.

3.   Admissibility of Witt's identification of Deft

The Sixth Amendment right to counsel applies to post-arrest line-ups and show-ups. Deft was being brought to court when he was identified by Witt, and therefore the identification occurred after he had been arrested. The State would argue that there was no formal line-up, since Witt was simply in court when he saw Deft and identified him. Deft would counter that because the prosecutor asked Witt to be present, and presumably knew Deft would be in court, for all purposes, a show-up or one-on-one confrontation between Deft and Witt was intended and effected by the State.

If the appellate court so found, Witt's in-court identification would be excluded unless the prosecution could show that it came from an independent source. In making this determination, the court will consider the time that Witt observed Deft when the alleged crime was committed, any prior identifications or misidentifications and any other factors affecting the accuracy of his identification.

Deft could also argue that the admission of Witt's identification at trial violated the Due Process Clause. A line-up or show-up is a denial of due process if the identification is unnecessarily suggestive and there is a substantial likelihood of misidentification.

Deft would argue that since he was brought to court by a policeman and was the only individual presented to the witness, the identification process itself was unduly suggestive. Deft would argue because he was in the custody of police, it was likely that the witness presumed that the police had the right suspect and identified Deft based on that fact alone. However, it is unlikely Deft can show that there is a substantial likelihood of misidentification, since there are no facts indicating that Witt based his identification on any improper factors.

Thus, Deft's due process challenge will be rejected.

4. Withdrawal of plea

A guilty plea in a criminal case must be voluntary and intelligent. Deft was advised of his constitutional rights and the maximum penalty that could be imposed. The court also explained that the plea agreement with the prosecution did not limit the court's discretion in imposing sentence. There are no facts indicating that Deft's plea was coerced or otherwise involuntary. Therefore, Deft cannot withdraw his plea.

The fact that Deft maintained his innocence will not affect this result, because a defendant who maintains innocence may still plead guilty, providing that his choice is knowing and intelligent as discussed above.

Thus, Deft cannot withdraw his plea.

525

The Exam Evaluator
PEOPLE v. DEFT

EXAM PRESENTATION (TOTAL POINTS AVAILABLE = 25)

	Poor											Excellent	
NEATNESS	0	1	2	3	4	5							____
ORGANIZATION	0	1	2	3	4	5	6	7	8	9	10		____
LAWYER-LIKE	0	1	2	3	4	5	6	7	8	9	10		____

DISCUSSION OF ISSUES (TOTAL POINTS AVAILABLE =75)

DENIAL OF RIGHT TO JURY TRIAL

    20 POINTS = FULL DISCUSSION   ____

    10 POINTS = PARTIAL/INCOMPLETE DISCUSSION   ____

ADMISSIBILITY OF WITT'S IDENTIFICATION OF DEFT

    30 POINTS = FULL DISCUSSION   ____

    20 POINTS = PARTIAL/INCOMPLETE DISCUSSION   ____

WITHDRAWAL OF DEFT'S PLEA

    25 POINTS = FULL DISCUSSION   ____

15 POINTS = PARTIAL/INCOMPLETE DISCUSSION ____

TOTAL . . . . ___

J.   PROBLEM EIGHT: PEOPLE v. ART AND CARL

Art and Bill were involved in the transportation and distribution of illegal drugs. Bill delivered the drugs to distribution points throughout the city. Art suspected, correctly, that Bill was being followed by undercover drug enforcement officers. Unbeknownst to Bill, Art hired Carl to be Bill's bodyguard and told Carl that Bill needed protection from robbers because Bill delivered rare jewels. Carl's assignment was to follow Bill at a distance and protect him from assault.

On his third day of work as a bodyguard, Carl saw a man confront Bill, hold him, and began to search him. Bill resisted vigorously. Carl ran up and beat the man severely about the head, killing him. A police officer arrived and arrested Bill and Carl. Art was arrested soon after this when Carl told police that Art had hired him to act as a bodyguard.

The dead man was Vic, an undercover drug enforcement officer who had a valid warrant for the arrest of Bill. A briefcase Bill had been carrying contained a large amount of cocaine.

1.   On what theory or theories might Art be prosecuted for the murder of Vic?

2.   If Carl is charged with the murder of Vic, what defenses should he offer and of what degree of murder or lesser included offense, if any, should he be convicted if those defenses are accepted by the trier of fact? Discuss.

1.   Outlining Strategy and Exam Analysis

"Success is the maximum utilization of the ability that you have."

---- Zig Ziglar

If you have not outlined and written out your answer, please do so before reading on. Remember that reading this text one hundred times is less effective than actually performing the exam exercise even once. With each examination taken, you will feel your confidence growing as your exam writing skills expand dramatically.

This question presents some interesting issues involving the liability of a party who acts on behalf of another party mistakenly believing that he is justified in protecting that party. The interrogatory concerning Carl's liability is also stated in a unique fashion, as it specifically asks what defenses Carl can raise, and then asks what offenses Carl may be convicted of assuming the defenses are accepted by the trier of fact. Thus, while you must discuss both the defenses and substantive crimes, you must do so in reverse order.

Let's outline this answer:

<u>People v. Art</u>: On what theories can Art be prosecuted for murder?

SOLICITATION
     Solicit Carl to commit crime?

CONSPIRACY
     Agreement to commit crime?

FELONY-MURDER RULE
     Did killing occur during the course of an inherently dangerous felony?
     Killing committed by co-felon?

<u>People v. Carl</u>: What defenses may Carl raise?

DEFENSE OF OTHERS
D entitled to use same force as person protected.
MINORITY view protects actor's reasonable mistake.

PREVENTION OF A CRIME
D entitled to use reasonable force to prevent a robbery.

HONEST BUT UNREASONABLE BELIEF IN SELF-DEFENSE
D's liability mitigated if he had good faith belief in need to defend Bill.

HEAT OF PASSION
D's liability mitigated if he acted in heat of passion.

DEGREE OF MURDER/LESSER INCLUDEDS

First degree? No premeditation or deliberation.
Second degree? If no mitigating factors apply.
Voluntary manslaughter? If mitigation found.

2.   Model Answer

People v. Art

Carl, not Art, killed Vic, and therefore Art's liability for Vic's murder is limited to three possible theories: solicitation, conspiracy and felony murder.

SOLICITATION

Solicitation is defined as inciting another to commit any felony or misdemeanor involving breach of the peace. Because Art hired Carl to protect Bill from assault, it could be argued that he hired Carl to commit crimes to protect Bill, with the specific intent to incite Carl to commit assault. As a solicitor, Art is vicariously liable for any crimes committed by the person solicited. However, Art never directed Carl to commit murder or to kill anyone in defending Bill, and thus he will not be held liable for Vic's murder on this theory.

CONSPIRACY

Conspiracy is an agreement for an unlawful purpose. Art hired Carl for an illegal purpose, to protect Bill during his drug deliveries. However, there was no agreement between Art and Carl, because Carl was never told the true purpose of his role as a bodyguard. Thus, because Carl never believed he was acting for an illegal purpose, there was no agreement and Art cannot be held liable for Vic's murder on this theory.

FELONY-MURDER RULE

Under the felony-murder rule, a co-felon may be held liable for the killing of another, which occurs during the course of an inherently dangerous felony. Transportation and distribution of illegal drugs are not acts which are inherently dangerous, in themselves, to human life and therefore Art should not be held liable on this theory. The prosecution will argue that because drug dealing often involves killing and dangerous situations to protect and defend the sale of drugs, it should modernly be classified as an inherently dangerous felony. However, the court is likely to find against the prosecution on this issue.

The application of this rule is also forbidden in those jurisdictions which require the killing to be committed by a co-felon. Carl is not a co-felon because he was not aware of the illegal purpose for which he was hired. Because Carl is an innocent party, in such a jurisdiction, Art could not be liable on a felony-murder theory.

AIDING AND ABETTING

Alternatively, the prosecution may argue that Carl is liable on an aiding and abetting theory. Under modern law, all parties to a crime except accessories after the fact are guilty as principals. In order to be found liable, however, the accused must have assisted, counseled or encouraged the crime with the specific intent to commit the charged offense. While it could be argued that Art was encouraging Carl to commit crimes to protect Bill, Art did not intend that Carl commit murder, as Carl was only hired to protect Bill from assault. Also, it was not foreseeable that Carl would kill another while acting as Bill's bodyguard. Thus, this theory will be rejected.

People v. Carl

Carl may raise the defense of others and crime prevention defense, and may raise good faith belief in self-defense or provocation to mitigate the crime to manslaughter.

DEFENSE OF OTHERS

Under this defense, Carl is entitled to use the same force as the person protected is entitled to use. Because Bill was not privileged to use any force in resisting a lawful arrest pursuant to a valid warrant, Carl's act are not privileged. However, the minority view protects the actor's reasonable mistake, and in such a jurisdiction, Carl's act would be privileged if his use of force were deemed reasonable.

Carl's use of force would be deemed unreasonable. By beating Vic to death, he acted unreasonably, since Vic was unarmed and had merely held and searched Bill. While Carl will argue that he reasonably believed that Bill was being robbed, his use of force was not justified under these circumstances and his defense will be rejected.

PREVENTION OF A CRIME

Under this privilege, a person is entitled to use reasonable force to prevent a violent crime, such as robbery. Carl's belief that Bill was being robbed by Vic was reasonable, based on his observations and the information he had received from Art; however, Carl's use of deadly force was unreasonable, for the same reasons stated above. Therefore this defense will be rejected.

HONEST BUT UNREASONABLE BELIEF IN SELF-DEFENSE

However, Carl's liability will be mitigated to manslaughter if he had a good faith belief in the need to defend Bill from harm. Carl is guilty only of manslaughter because he honestly believed in the need to defend Bill, but used unreasonable force in doing so.

HEAT OF PASSION

Likewise, Carl's liability for murder will be mitigated to manslaughter if he acted in heat of passion. Heat of passion requires both reasonable provocation coupled with inadequate cooling time. Here Carl acted immediately upon seeing what he believed to be a robbery. If his passions were so aroused, he would be guilty of manslaughter, not murder.

DEGREE OF MURDER/LESSER INCLUDED OFFENSES

Carl would not be found guilty of first degree murder, since no premeditation or deliberation occurred prior to the beating of Vic. He acted immediately upon his belief that Bill was being robbed or assaulted. If no mitigating factors are present, then Carl would remain guilty of second degree murder. However, as explained above, if mitigation were found, then Carl would be guilty of manslaughter.

The Exam Evaluator
PEOPLE v. ART & CARL

EXAM PRESENTATION (TOTAL POINTS AVAILABLE = 25)

	Poor										Excellent
NEATNESS	0	1	2	3	4	5					____
ORGANIZATION	0	1	2	3	4	5	6	7	8	9	10 ____
LAWYER-LIKE	0	1	2	3	4	5	6	7	8	9	10 ____

DISCUSSION OF ISSUES (TOTAL POINTS AVAILABLE =75)

People v. Art: Theories of Art's liability for murder

SOLICITATION

    5 POINTS = FULL DISCUSSION   ____

    0 POINTS = PARTIAL/INCOMPLETE DISCUSSION   ____

CONSPIRACY TO COMMIT ASSAULT

    5 POINTS = FULL DISCUSSION   ____

    0 POINTS = PARTIAL/INCOMPLETE DISCUSSION   ____

FELONY MURDER RULE

    15 POINTS = FULL DISCUSSION   ____

    10 POINTS = PARTIAL/INCOMPLETE DISCUSSION   ____

CARL'S DEFENSES TO MURDER

DEFENSE OF OTHERS

     10 POINTS = FULL DISCUSSION _____

     5 POINTS = PARTIAL/INCOMPLETE DISCUSSION _____

CRIME PREVENTION

     10 POINTS = FULL DISCUSSION _____

     5 POINTS = PARTIAL/INCOMPLETE DISCUSSION _____

GOOD FAITH BELIEF IN THE NEED TO DEFEND

     10 POINTS = FULL DISCUSSION _____

     5 POINTS = PARTIAL/INCOMPLETE DISCUSSION _____

HEAT OF PASSION

     10 POINTS = FULL DISCUSSION _____

     5 POINTS = PARTIAL/INCOMPLETE DISCUSSION _____

DEGREES OF MURDER IF CARL'S DEFENSE ARE ACCEPTED

     10 POINTS = FULL DISCUSSION _____

     5 POINTS = PARTIAL/INCOMPLETE DISCUSSION _____

TOTAL SCORE . . . . _____

K.   PROBLEM NINE: PEOPLE v. DAVE

Dave suffers from a disease which sometimes causes seizures during which he is not aware of his actions and sometimes physically attacks other persons. Dave has been convicted of aggravated assault twice within the last three years.

Dave's doctor has repeatedly instructed him to avoid alcoholic beverages because of a connection between Dave's seizures and consumption of alcohol. The assaults that led to Dave's convictions occurred after Dave had consumed alcohol.

Valerie visited Dave at his apartment. Dave gave Valerie a beer and poured one for himself. In an hour, Dave consumed four bottles of beer. An argument with Valerie ensued. When Dave became irritated and his speech slurred, Valerie decided he was intoxicated and she left the apartment. Dave grabbed a fireplace poker, followed Valerie into the hall, and struck her on the head from behind. He then returned to his apartment.

Dave's first recollection after his argument with Valerie is looking out his window and seeking an emergency squad removing a motionless Valerie from the apartment building.

Dave immediately called Perry, his attorney. Perry's secretary put the call through to Perry, but pursuant to Perry's general instructions, listened to the conversation. Dave told Perry all that he could recall about the incident and that he thought Valerie was dead. Then Dave said: "The poker has blood on it. Should I get rid of it?"

Perry replied, "Leave everything as it is."

Valerie survived the attack, but could not positively identify Dave as her assailant.

Dave was charged with attempted murder. He pleaded not guilty and not guilty by reason of insanity. At trial, during the People's case-in-chief, Valerie testified that Dave had consumed four bottles of beer in a one-hour period, and that he appeared to be intoxicated when she left his apartment. Over Dave's objections, the court admitted evidence of Dave's prior assault convictions, and admitted the testimony of

Perry's secretary about the conversation between Perry and Dave.

Dave testified that he had a seizure and that he could not remember anything after his argument with Valerie. Dave's physician testified regarding the relationship of Dave's seizures to consumption of alcohol.

The trial court refused to give instructions requested by Dave on diminished capacity and insanity.

1. Did the trial court err in admitting:

(a) The evidence of prior convictions? Discuss.
(b) The testimony of Perry's secretary? Discuss.

2. Did the trial court err in refusing to instruct the jury on:

(a) Diminished capacity? Discuss.
(b) Insanity? Discuss.

1. Meet the Criminal Law Cross-Over Question

"All things are difficult before they are easy."

---- John Norley

Before reading any further, please outline and write out your answer. Merely reading this text without first completing the problem, or at least attempting to do so, is like having someone describe a great movie to you in detail before you see the movie. An exam should be experienced personally, not vicariously. So if you haven't written out an answer, STOP AND GO BACK TO THE QUESTION.

As mentioned in the introduction to this section, Criminal Law has only been tested twice with other subjects in the past ten years. Those two subjects were Professional Responsibility and Evidence. This problem was the latter of those two questions, and will prepare you for this possibility on future examinations.

For those of you who are following the chapters in this book in order, and have already worked through the Evidence writing approach, you will have no problems breezing through this question. However, if you have not yet completed the Evidence chapter, you may want to wait until you do so to complete this exercise.

The key to succeeding on cross-over questions is focus and flexibility. You must learn to react instantly and by doing so rapidly change your focus from one subject area to another. As explained in earlier chapters, in most instances, you will have little difficulty in identifying a cross-over question. The Examiners take great care to give you ample notice that you are being tested on more than one subject.

On any cross-over question, the Bar Examiners include hints as to what areas are being tested. I refer to these hints as "cross- over indicators." The Examiners include these indicators to avoid any possibility of confusion. So the key in identifying cross-over questions is to know how to find these indicators.

The first cross-over indicator will be found in the interrogatories. The interrogatory will focus you on the particular issue to be addressed, and usually contains phrases which are unique to subject area being tested. For example, Evidence and Criminal Law questions will normally ask whether a certain item of evidence is admissible. An interrogatory on a Community Property problem, by contrast, would ask how certain items of property would be divided.

The second indicator will be found in the facts. The Examiners must give you the facts necessary to solve the problem at hand. If you think that a certain area is being tested, yet no facts are provided to solve the problem, then that area is not being tested. By the time you reach the second indicator, you should have a pretty good idea of what area is being tested. However, if you still aren't certain, then the true litmus test comes with outlining your answer. If you find that you are unable to outline your answer within the scope of the interrogatories, that is, your answer does not make any sense or is not capable of being outlined, then you know that the subject you think is being tested really isn't being tested at all.

Let's apply these simple steps to this problem.

The first interrogatory asks:

1. Did the trial court err in admitting:

(a) The evidence of prior convictions? Discuss.
(b) The testimony of Perry's secretary? Discuss.

Each interrogatory concerns the question of whether the trial court properly admitted certain evidence. Recognizing this fact alone should narrow the possible subject areas to either Criminal Procedure or Evidence. Thus, by applying the first indicator, we have eliminated the field of subject areas to two possible areas.

The second indicator is found in the facts. What are you told about Dave's prior convictions and the testimony of Perry's secretary? You are told that Dave has two prior convictions for aggravated assault which were admitted against him at the attempted murder trial. You are told that Perry's secretary overheard a phone conversation where Dave made a certain admission and received advice from his attorney, Perry.

Now, assuming that you thought that a Criminal Procedure question was presented, there are no facts from which a Criminal Procedure issue would emerge. The admission of Dave's prior convictions concerns an evidentiary issue. If you were given facts indicating, for example, that Dave's prior convictions were invalid because he was denied counsel or a constitutional right, then a Criminal Procedure analysis would be in order. But you are only told that Dave has two prior convictions in the last three years. The only way to discuss Criminal Procedure issues is to manufacture facts which do not exist. Thus, application of the second indicator narrows the field to one solitary possibility: Evidence and not Criminal Procedure.

Even if you were still unsure of which subject area is being tested, by outlining the answer and applying your writing approach, no matter how the subject areas are camouflaged, their true colors will shine through. Let's apply our Criminal Procedure writing approach to this problem:

1.A.   Evidence of Dave's Prior Convictions

(1)   **Have the defendant's FOURTH AMENDMENT RIGHTS been violated?**
No search and seizure issues.

(2)   **Have the defendant's FIFTH AMENDMENT RIGHTS been violated?**
No issues as to any statements made by Dave.

(3)   **Has the defendant's SIXTH AMENDMENT RIGHT TO COUNSEL been violated?**
No right to counsel issues.

(4)   **Have other rights of the accused been violated?**
No issues as to validity of the prior convictions or any other miscellaneous rights.

You would reach the same conclusion in analyzing the testimony of Perry's secretary. Now, let's outline this answer again, applying the Evidence writing approach.

1.A.   Evidence of Dave's Prior Convictions

(1)   **IS THE EVIDENCE RELEVANT?**
Is the evidence LOGICALLY relevant? To Dave's violent history.
Is the evidence LEGALLY relevant? Prejudicial but probative since charge

is similar.

(2) IS THE EVIDENCE RELIABLE?
Is the evidence AUTHENTICATED or based on PERSONAL KNOWLEDGE? Evidence of prior convictions must be authenticated.

(3) IS THE EVIDENCE BARRED BY EXTRINSIC POLICIES?
No issues.

(4) IS THE EVIDENCE ADMISSIBLE TO SHOW CHARACTER?
Convictions not admissible as character evidence.

(5) IS THE EVIDENCE ADMISSIBLE TO IMPEACH?
Yes, <u>felony</u> convictions are.

(6) IS THE EVIDENCE BARRED BY PRIVILEGE?
No issues.

(7) IS THE EVIDENCE BARRED BY THE HEARSAY RULE?
Convictions are hearsay, but may fall within business record exceptions or official records exception.

1.B.   Testimony of Perry's Secretary

(1) IS THE EVIDENCE RELEVANT?
Is the evidence LOGICALLY relevant? To prove Dave's involvement in crime, knowledge of guilt and recall of event, and attempt to destroy evidence. **Is the evidence LEGALLY relevant?** Prejudicial but highly probative.

(2) IS THE EVIDENCE RELIABLE?
Perry's secretary has personal knowledge as she overheard phone call, but must be able to identify Dave's voice.

(3) IS THE EVIDENCE BARRED BY EXTRINSIC POLICIES?
No issues.

(4) IS THE EVIDENCE ADMISSIBLE TO SHOW CHARACTER?
No issues.

(5)   IS THE EVIDENCE ADMISSIBLE TO IMPEACH?
No issues.

(6)   IS THE EVIDENCE BARRED BY PRIVILEGE?
Attorney-client privilege?

(7)   IS THE EVIDENCE BARRED BY THE HEARSAY RULE?
Statement is hearsay, but would qualify as an admission of a party.

As you can see, only the Evidence writing approach "fits" this bar question. Let's move on to the second interrogatory and outline the criminal law portion of this answer:

2.A.   DIMINISHED CAPACITY

Voluntary intoxication?
Evidence of mental illness?

2.B.   INSANITY

Was Dave legally insane at the time the crime was committed?

M'NAGHTEN RULE
IRRESISTIBLE IMPULSE
DURHAM RULE
A.L.I. SUBSTANTIAL CAPACITY TEST

Now that we have completed our cross-over outline, let's review the model answer.

2.   Model Answer

1.A.   Evidence of Dave's Prior Convictions

Evidence must be relevant to proving a fact in dispute. Dave's prior conviction for assault is relevant to prove his propensity for violence, since Dave has been convicted of assaulting others in the past. However, this evidence is highly prejudicial, because Dave is charged with assaultive conduct in this case. Thus, the prior convictions should be excluded as legally irrelevant, given the similarity of the priors to the present offense.

The evidence of the prior convictions must also be authenticated. Here the facts are silent as to whether Dave admitted the convictions or whether they were proved through some other means, such as a certified record of conviction. Thus, this issue cannot be resolved.

While Dave's prior convictions are not admissible as character evidence, under common law and the FRE, felony convictions are admissible to impeach any witness.

Dave's prior convictions are hearsay, because they occurred outside Dave's trial and concern admissions made by Dave. If the priors were introduced through a certified record, the official record exception would apply. Also, if the conviction were offered to impeach, it would be offered on this non-hearsay theory.

1.B. Testimony of Perry's Secretary

The testimony of Perry's secretary as to Dave's admissions is relevant to prove Dave's involvement in crime, knowledge of guilt, and attempt to destroy evidence. While this evidence is highly prejudicial to Dave since it admits his knowledge of the weapon involved, it is highly probative to rebut his claim that he no longer recalls the event.

The evidence is reliable because Perry's secretary has personal knowledge of the conversation, as she overheard it, provided that she can sufficiently identify the caller's voice as belonging to Dave.

Dave will argue that the attorney-client privilege bars Perry's secretary's testimony. Under this privilege, any communication between attorney and client is privileged unless it constitutes evidence of a future crime. Here Dave asked his attorney, Perry, if he should "get rid" of a weapon involved in the charged crime, thus suggesting an attempt to destroy evidence as a prospective. However, Dave would successfully argue that his communication related to a past crime, and therefore the privilege applies. Thus, the statement should have been excluded.

It may also be argued that Perry's secretary was a non-essential eavesdropper and that the communications she overheard were unnecessary to transmit information from Perry to Dave. However, because Dave was unaware that Perry's secretary was on the phone, he did not waive the privilege, and can prevent Perry's secretary from revealing the conversation she overheard.

Dave's statement, as testified to by Perry's secretary, would also be hearsay, because it is an out of court statement offered for its truth. However, it would qualify as a party admission, because it tends to show his involvement in Valerie's death and that he admitted possession a weapon used to assault Valerie. Because it tends to show that Dave admitted consciousness of his involvement in the incident, it is admissible under this exception.

2.A. DIMINISHED CAPACITY

Voluntary intoxication may be a partial defense to attempted murder, if, due to alcohol consumption, an individual is unable to form the specific intent to kill. According to Valerie, Dave consumed four bottles of beer in one hour and was intoxicated when the crime occurred. Dave's physician also testified that there was a relationship between Dave's use of alcohol and the seizure he claimed to have suffered, which may mitigate Dave's liability to attempted manslaughter. Thus, the court erred in refusing to so instruct the jury.

Involuntary intoxication is not a defense on these facts. Dave voluntarily consumed alcohol after having been warned repeatedly that alcohol use, when combined with his illness, caused him to suffer seizures resulting in memory loss and acts of violence.

Likewise, evidence of Dave's mental illness falling short of an insanity defense could mitigate his liability to attempted manslaughter, if his illness precluded him from forming the intent to kill. Because evidence existed that Dave suffered from seizures and therefore could not recall what happened, the court erred in refusing to so instruct the jury.

2.B. INSANITY

There are four possible theories of insanity.

Under the M'Naghten Rule, if D lacks the ability at the time of his actions to know the wrongfulness of his actions and nature and quality of his acts, he is not guilty by reason of insanity. Here, there was evidence from which the trier of fact could find that Dave was unconscious due to a seizure and did not know what he did when the crime occurred. Thus, under this test, the instruction to the jury was warranted.

Under the Irresistible Impulse Test, conviction is barred where a mental disease makes D incapable of controlling his conduct. Again, because evidence existed that D suffered from uncontrollable seizures, this instruction should have been given in a jurisdiction following this rule. The prosecution could counter, however, that Dave could control his conduct by not drinking alcohol which in turn caused his seizures.

Under the Durham Test, if the crime is the product of a mental disease or defect and it would not have occurred but for the disease, the defendant is not guilty. Applying this test, the court erred because Dave presented evidence that he acted criminally only because he experienced a seizure, and that the crime would not have occurred but for the seizure.

The A.L.I. Substantial Capacity Test holds that a D must be acquitted by reason of insanity if he lacks the substantial capacity to appreciate the criminality of his conduct or conform his conduct to the requirements of law. In such a jurisdiction, an instruction should have been given because Dave presented evidence that he could not conform his conduct or appreciate the nature of it because he was in a seizure state when the offense occurred.

Thus, under any of the four rules, the court erred in failing to instruct the jury.

The Exam Evaluator
PEOPLE v. DAVE

EXAM PRESENTATION (TOTAL POINTS AVAILABLE = 25)

	Poor											Excellent
NEATNESS	0	1	2	3	4	5						_____
ORGANIZATION	0	1	2	3	4	5	6	7	8	9	10	_____
LAWYER-LIKE	0	1	2	3	4	5	6	7	8	9	10	_____

DISCUSSION OF ISSUES (TOTAL POINTS AVAILABLE =75)

1A. ADMISSION OF DAVE'S PRIOR CONVICTIONS

    20 POINTS = FULL DISCUSSION   _____

    15 POINTS = PARTIAL/INCOMPLETE DISCUSSION   _____

1B. ADMISSION OF TESTIMONY OF PERRY'S SECRETARY

    20 POINTS = FULL DISCUSSION   _____

    15 POINTS = PARTIAL/INCOMPLETE DISCUSSION   _____

2A. DIMINISHED CAPACITY

    15 POINTS = FULL DISCUSSION   _____

    10 POINTS = PARTIAL/INCOMPLETE DISCUSSION   _____

2B. INSANITY

M'NAGHTEN/IRRESISTIBLE IMPULSE RULES

20 POINTS = FULL DISCUSSION _____

15 POINTS = PARTIAL/INCOMPLETE DISCUSSION _____

BONUS POINTS

DURHAM RULE

5 POINTS = FULL DISCUSSION _____

A.L.I. SUBSTANTIAL CAPACITY TEST

5 POINTS = FULL DISCUSSION _____

TOTAL SCORE . . . . _____

L.   CHAPTER SUMMARY

"Success is a journey, not a destination."

---- Ben Sweetland

Congratulations on completing yet another chapter in your journey towards excellence in exam writing. With the ultimate system of successful exam writing, your essay answer will reflect a level of expertise and mastery that most people cannot even imagine.

So pat yourself on the back and treat yourself to something fun, like a triple chocolate sundae or an afternoon of bungee cord jumping or whatever it is you enjoy doing. I look forward to continuing our journey of success in Volume II.

BARBREAKER

master exam evaluators

Torts Master Exam Evaluator

Problem	Score	50-55	60-65	70	75	80	85	90	95	100
One										
Two										
Three										
Four										
Five										
Six										
Seven										
Eight										
Nine										
Ten										

**Community Property
Master Exam Evaluator**

Problem	Score	50-55	60-65	70	75	80	85	90	95	100
One										
Two										
Three										
Four										
Five										
Six										
Seven										
Eight										

Evidence Master Exam Evaluator

Problem	Score	50-55	60-65	70	75	80	85	90	95	100
One										
Two										
Three										
Four										
Five										
Six										
Seven										
Eight										

Criminal Law and Procedure Master Exam Evaluator

Problem	Score	50-55	60-65	70	75	80	85	90	95	100
One										
Two										
Three										
Four										
Five										
Six										
Seven										
Eight										
Nine										

GLOSSARY OF ABBREVIATED TERMS

The following abbreviations are commonly used in law school and in the legal profession.

Amd - amendment

BFP - bona fide purchaser

C/L - common law

Corp - corporation

Ct - court

D - defendant

FED - federal

FMR - felony murder rule

GC - general considerations

hrg - hearing

govt - government

juris - jurisdiction

K - contract

L - landlord

L/E - life estate

MAJ - majority view

MIN - minority view

M/L - modern law

N/A - not applicable

Obj - objective

π - plaintiff

PJ - personal jurisdiction

RaP - Rule Against Perpetuities

Restmt - restatement of law

SMJ - subject matter jurisdiction

SoF - Statute of Frauds

SoL - Statute of Limitations

st - state

T - tenant/testator

Trad - traditional

UCC - Uniform Commercial Code

V - victim

Now Used in Some Bar/Bri Essay Advantage Bar Review Courses

Bar Exam Survival Kit

The definitive guide on how to successfully pass the bar examination in your state. This book contains detailed attack strategies for commonly tested bar subjects, expert test taking tips and practical advice not taught in bar review courses.

by Jeff Adachi, Esq.

www.survival-series.com

Gives you the tools to succeed on the most important examination of your career...

The Bar Exam Survival Kit is a necessary supplement to any bar review course!

- ◆ 15 Law Charts
- ◆ Detailed attack strategies for all subjects
- ◆ Seven analyzed examples of bar exam essays
- ◆ Six steps of exam taking
- ◆ Memory mnemonics
- ◆ How the three D's can raise your confidence
- ◆ How to allot your study time
- ◆ Winning techniques you won't learn in traditional bar review courses

"The *Bar Exam Survival Kit* is the best bar exam preparation material because it is complete and at the same time, concise enough to memorize." - Janet de Mattei

"While commercial outlines contain a conceptual review of the black letter law, the *Bar Exam Survival Kit* provides the next critical step in bar preparation - that of organizing, applying and memorizing the law." - Dean Peter Keane, Golden Gate Univ. School of Law

ISBN 1-882278-01-1

The Ultimate Guide for Success on the Bar Examination

MBE Survival Kit

How to prepare and pass the national Multi-State Bar Exam

by Jeff Adachi, Esq. & Solomon Wollack, Esq.

Survival Series Publishing Company

Reading this book will give you the tools needed to succeed on the most important examination of your legal career.

The multi-state bar examination (MBE) is one of the most difficult challenges you will ever face. Consisting of 200 questions administered over a six-hour time period, you will have less than 1.8 minutes to complete each question. Whether you are preparing for the Bar Exam or the "baby" bar, this book gives you the tools you need to succeed:

♦ Written by a Bar/Bri author & professor!

♦ Over 300 simulated practice questions and explanations

♦ Includes contracts, constitutional law, criminal law & procedure, evidence, torts and real property

♦ The 4 Step MBE Attack Plan

♦ Multi-State Bar Exam Diagnostic Test

♦ 10 Rules of the MBE

THE NEWEST BOOK IN THE SERIES!

ISBN 1-882278-08-9

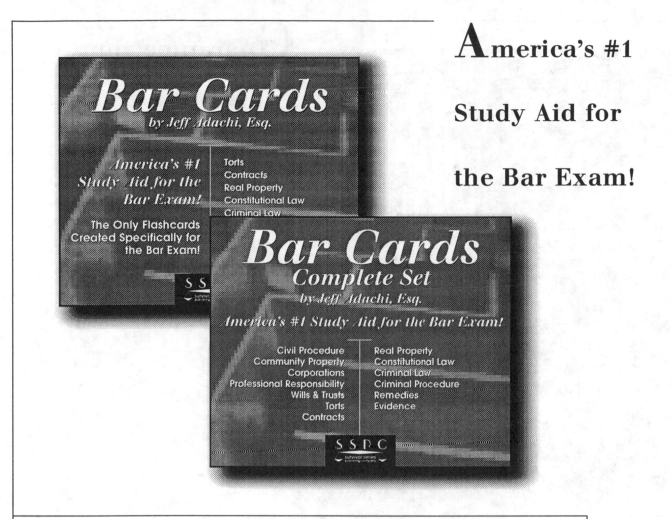

America's #1 Study Aid for the Bar Exam!

The Only Flashcards Created Specifically for the Bar Exam!

- ♦ *Bar Cards* contain only the essentials of what you need to know – no hypos, no jokes, just the law!

- ♦ When you're studying for the Bar, you don't need thousands of flash cards cluttered with insignificant details!

- ♦ Bar Cards: 460 Cards Total

- ♦ Bar Cards Complete Set: 960 Cards Total

- ♦ Approximately 50 Cards per Subject

- ♦ Written by a Bar/Bri Professor and Author!

- ♦ Includes Mnemonics & Bonus Guide to Top Memorization Techniques!

- ♦ Fully Illustrated & Color Coded to Make Memorization Easy!

PRAISE FOR THE BAR CARDS

"Far superior than any other flashcards on the market." -Carole Marasovic

"Indispensable preparation for bar doers!" -Greg McCormick

"Excellent. I recommend it to all bar candidates." -David Royston

"BAR CARDS helped me digest the enormous amount of information involved in Bar preparation." -D. Ichelson

Bar Cards Complete Set	Bar Cards
ISBN 1-882278-07-0	ISBN 1-882278-03-8

Guarantee your success in Law School and your career!

The most comprehensive book on how to succeed in Law School ever written. This book contains:

- ◆ Over 50 examples of first year essays

- ◆ How to read and brief cases

- ◆ How to create a winning outline

- ◆ Law Charts for Torts, Contracts,Civil Procedure, Crimes and Real Property

- ◆ Memory mnemonics and illustrations

- ◆ How to write superior exam answers

PRAISE FOR THE BAR EXAM SURVIVAL KIT

ISBN 1-882278-02-X

ABOUT THE SURVIVAL SERIES PUBLISHING COMPANY

Survival Series is authored by *Bar/Bri* professor and author, **Jeff Adachi, Esq**. Adachi is a former bar exam grader, bar exam question writer, and a certified criminal law specialist. He was recently elected San Francisco Public Defender. *Survival Series* is a complete series of law and bar exam books that has earned the praise of leading law schools professors and students nationwide!

For more information, visit **www.survival-series.com**!

Law School Survival Kit (233 pp.): A comprehensive guide to law school designed to give students practical advice and problem solving skills necessary to succeed in any state. This book includes Law Charts, memory mnemonics and illustrations, comprehensive strategies for case reading, briefing and exam preparation and over 50 model essays.

Bar Exam Survival Kit (217 pp): The complete bar preparation book, containing attack strategies and Law Charts for all multi-state subjects and other common bar subjects. Learn how to prepare for the bar exam in any state and how to analyze and write essay questions. Now used by some *Bar/Bri Essay Advantage* bar review courses!

Bar Breaker (2 vol., 1100 pp.): Contains over 100 past bar exam questions and model answers with analyses. Hailed as the "Bible of the California Essay Exam," this book is used by some *Bar/Bri Essay Advantage* bar review courses!

MBE Survival Kit (450 pp.): Contains over 300 multi-state, multiple choice questions and analyses for the bar exam in any state. Includes a diagnostic test, the four step MBE attack plan, and the ten rules of the MBE.

Bar Cards (460 cards): The only flashcards designed specifically for the Bar Exam! Each color coded card contains a humorous illustration, comprehensive coverage of black letter law and memory mnemonics. Bar Cards includes: torts, contracts, contracts remedies, evidence, real property, constitutional law, criminal law and criminal procedure.

Complete Bar Cards (960 pp.): Contains the multi-state subjects and also includes: community property, ethics, civil procedure, wills, corporations, and trusts.

Legal Limericks (100 pp.): Forty clever and humorous limericks about some of the most controversial and fascinating legal cases and law suits recorded in American jurisprudence.

ORDER FORM

TITLE	QUANTITY	PRICE	(QTY) x (PRICE) = TOTAL
Law School Survival Kit		$29.95	
Bar Exam Survival Kit**		$29.95	
Bar Breaker, Vol. I & II**		$99.95	
MBE Survival Kit		$29.95	
Bar Cards		$29.95	
Complete Bar Cards		$49.95	
Legal Limericks		$7.95	
Add shipping & handling $5.00 per book • $10.00 per Bar Breaker, Bar Cards & Bar Cards Complete			
(CA Residents please add 8.5% **sales tax** to total)			
Please allow two weeks for delivery Overnight service available by telephone	**TOTAL:**		

** Now used in some Bar/Bri Essay Advantage bar review courses!
(Prices are subject to change without notice)

Name: _____

Mailing Address:_____

City:_____ State:_____ Zip: _____

Telephone:_____ Email: _____ Fax:_____

Law School: _____ Year in School: _____

Method of Payment: cash ( )   check ( )   money order ( )   credit card ( )

Credit Card (circle one):   Discover   Visa   Mastercard

Card Number:_____

Signature: _____Expiration Date: _____

Please mail or FAX this form back to us and allow 2 weeks for delivery. Thank you!
The Survival Series Publishing Co., PO Box 77313, San Francisco, CA 94107
(415) 979-6785 tel., (415) 506-8870 fax.
www.survival-series.com

SURVIVAL SERIES
NOW AVAILABLE AT THESE UNIVERSITIES

Harvard Law School, MA
Yale Law School, CT
Stanford University School of Law, CA
University of California at Los Angeles, CA
New York University School of Law, NY
Boston University School of Law, MA
St. John's University, NY
Campbell University School of Law, AL
University of California at Hastings, CA
University of North Carolina, NC
Golden Gate University School of Law, CA
University of Notre Dame, IN
Howard University, DC
John F Kennedy Univ. School of Law, CA
Univ. of Wisconsin-Madison Law School, WI
Washbourne University School of Law, KS
University of Washington, WA
University of Pittsburgh, PA
McGeorge School of Law, CA
University of Kentucky, KY
Tulane University School of Law, LA
John Marshall Law School, IL
Texas Wesleyan School of Law, TX
Thomas M Cooley School of Law, MT
Lewis and Clark College School of Law, OR
Birmingham School of Law in Alabama, AL
Temple University School of Law, PA
Gonzaga University, WA
University of Maryland, MD
Suffolk University, MA
Monterey Institute of Law, CA
Texas Wesleyan, TX
University of North Carolina, NC
George Mason Bookstore, VA
Arizona State University, AZ
Georgetown University, DC
University of San Francisco, CA
Boston College, MA

Columbia University School of Law, NY
UC Berkeley Boalt School of Law, CA
Baylor University, TX
Texas Tech University, TX
University of Pennsylvania, PA
Univ. of Southern Calif. Law Center, CA
Loyola Marymount University, CA
Marquette University Law School, WI
University of California at Davis, CA
Lincoln Law School of Sacramento, CA
Regent University School of Law, VA
Cleveland University, OH
University of Texas, TX
University of South Dakota, SD
Samford Univ. School of Law, AL
Univ. of Arkansas School of Law, AR
University of Idaho College of Law, ID
Washington & Lee Univ. Law School, VA
Univ. of La Verne College of Law, CA
Widener University School of Law, DE
Seton Hall University, NJ
Univ. of North Dakota School of Law, ND
Univ. of Puget Sound School of Law, WA
Yeshiva University School of Law, NY
Univ. of Tennessee College of Law, TN
Creighton University School of Law, NE
George Washington University, DC
Wayne State Univ. School of Law, MI
South Texas College of Law, TX
Santa Clara University, CA
University of South Carolina, SC
Southwestern School of Law, CA
University of Mississippi, MS
University of Toledo, OH
University of Utah, UT
Southern Methodist University, TX
South Texas College of Law, TX
Lewis and Clark College, OR

**ALSO AVAILABLE AT
LEGAL BOOKSTORES NATIONWIDE!
VISIT WWW.SURVIVAL-SERIES.COM
FOR A RETAILER NEAR YOU!**

ORDER FORM

TITLE	QUANTITY	PRICE	(QTY) x (PRICE) = TOTAL
Law School Survival Kit		$29.95	
Bar Exam Survival Kit**		$29.95	
Bar Breaker, Vol. I & II**		$99.95	
MBE Survival Kit		$29.95	
Bar Cards		$29.95	
Complete Bar Cards		$49.95	
Legal Limericks		$7.95	
Add shipping & handling $5.00 per book • $10.00 per Bar Breaker, Bar Cards & Bar Cards Complete			
(CA Residents please add 8.5% **sales tax** to total)			
Please allow two weeks for delivery Overnight service available by telephone	**TOTAL:**		

** Now used in some Bar/Bri Essay Advantage bar review courses!
(Prices are subject to change without notice)

Name: _____

Mailing Address:_____

City:_____ State:_____ Zip: _____

Telephone:_____ Email: _____ Fax:_____

Law School: _____ Year in School: _____

Method of Payment: cash ( )   check ( )   money order ( )   credit card ( )

Credit Card (circle one):   Discover   Visa   Mastercard

Card Number:_____

Signature: _____ Expiration Date: _____

Please mail or FAX this form back to us and allow 2 weeks for delivery. Thank you!
The Survival Series Publishing Co., PO Box 77313, San Francisco, CA 94107
(415) 979-6785 tel., (415) 586 8870 fax.
www.survival-series.com

FEEDBACK FORM

We care what you think!

Did the book(s) help you with your studies?

Did you pass the bar exam?

Please fax, mail, or e-mail comments to: SSPC P.O. Box 77313 San Francisco, CA 94107. Fax 415.586.8870. E-mail "sspc@survival-series.com"

(Print clearly or type)

Book Title: _____

Name of store purchased from: _____

How did you hear about us? _____

Comments (please be specific):

May we use your name and comments in future SSPC advertising?

If so, please sign and date here:

Name: _____

School: _____

Signature: _____ Date: _____